10/10/13 DAS

Get **more** out of libraries

Please return or renew this item by the last date shown.

You can renew online at www.hants.gov.uk/library

Or by phoning **0845 603 5631**

Hampshire
County Council

THE HERETICS

Also by Will Storr

Fiction

The Hunger and the Howling of Killian Lone
(2013)

Non-Fiction

Will Storr versus the Supernatural
(2006)

WILL STORR

THE HERETICS

Adventures with the Enemies of Science

PICADOR

First published 2013 by Picador
an imprint of Pan Macmillan, a division of Macmillan Publishers Limited
Pan Macmillan, 20 New Wharf Road, London N1 9RR
Basingstoke and Oxford
Associated companies throughout the world
www.panmacmillan.com

ISBN 978-1-4472-3168-4

1 3 5 7 9 8 6 4 2

A CIP catalogue record for this book is available from the British Library.

Typeset by Ellipsis Digital Limited, Glasgow
Printed and bound by CPI Group (UK) Ltd, Croydon, CR0 4YY

For Farrah
for ending the madness

Contents

Contents

'And then he said to me – this is honestly true – he said to me, "Well you can prove anything with facts, can't you?"'

Stewart Lee
How I Escaped My Certain Fate (2010)

'A self is probably the most impressive work of art we ever produce.'

Jerome Bruner
Making Stories: Law, Literature, Life (2002)

1

'It's like treason'

It is Friday night in a town called Devil and the community hall is full. Over two hundred people are gathered here in shuffling, expectant silence. There are elderly couples and clean young families, their prams parked squarely at the end of rows. A modest distance away from the front sits a line of pale women in Amish headwear. Their sturdy patriarch is planted beside them, his forearms crossed in front of his starched white shirt. Above our heads, suspended from the ceiling, two huge fans chew the heavy tropical air.

A local elder stands up and shuffles his way to the microphone. He is in his eighties, at least, and looks pale and fragile, like a drift of smoke. There is a squeal of feedback. He clears his throat. The sound of it bounces off the parquet floor.

'Ladies and gentlemen,' he says. 'Without further ado, it gives me great pleasure to, er, be able to introduce to you a man whose work I'm sure you're all familiar with. We've been looking forward to his talk for a long time now. He's, er, travelled a long way to see us tonight, so please give a very warm welcome to Mr John Mackay.'

Proudly, down the centre aisle, I watch him come: the man we all want to see. With his white prophet's beard, charismatic glimmer and wide-brimmed bushman's hat, he clutches in his right hand a thousand pages of visions, violence and lore, of science, sects and sorcery, all the wisdom of all the worlds, everything anyone needs to know about anything. Mackay walks slowly through applause, takes his place at the front of the hall and waits for the crowd to settle. Once silence is regained, he finally begins.

'Charles Darwin wrote a book,' he announces. 'Does anyone know what its name was?' His sparkly eyes scan the rows. 'The name of his book was *The Origin of the Species*. I have another book here.' He holds up his leather-bound volume, its pages, weary at the corners, flop open. 'It's called the Bible. Tonight, the choice you have to face up to is this – do you put your faith in Darwin, who wasn't there? Or God, who was?'

As Mackay speaks, the hands of the church clock, down in the town centre, clunk to 8.30. By now, the place is almost entirely deserted. That is what it is like up here, a hundred and sixty miles north of Brisbane, Australia, on the humid banks of the Mary River. It is a place of early closing and close community; of pineapple plantations, clapboard churches, empty roads and old Holden utes rusting in silent fields. The landscape itself is lush and strange, with its sinisterly christened creeks, monster cacti growing in gas-station forecourts and vast rock formations that jut out of the land like ancient tumours. The locals – dairy farmers, timber men and the descendants of gold-rush pioneers – know the town as Gympie, an Aboriginal word meaning Devil. It is actually named for a freakish native tree, a murderous hermaphrodite called the gympie-gympie, whose flowers are simultaneously male and female, whose fruit is a lurid, tumescent purple and pink and whose pretty heart-shaped leaves are covered with hairs that contain a toxin noxious enough to kill dogs, horses and sometimes men. The gympie-gympie is a hysterical nightmare of nature; evidence, I believe, of the conscienceless magnificence of biological evolution. But, right here, right now, I am in an intimidating minority of one. Because all of these people and tonight's main attraction – an international Creationist superstar and tireless prosecutor of the diabolical trinity Darwin, Dawkins and Attenborough – believe the gympie-gympie's malevolence to be a direct result of Adam eating forbidden fruit and introducing sin, death and nasty prickles to a perfect world.

Mackay clicks a button. An image of an enormous bird flashes on to the overhead projector.

'What's the name of that funny little chicken?' he says.

Nobody responds.

'Emu!' he says. 'They can't fly, but they can run like crazy. The interesting thing is, if you dig up their fossils, they used to be twice the size they now are. That's change, but it's not evolution.'

He allows the last sentence to unfurl slowly in the sweating air above him.

'If you take your Bible seriously you will notice that Genesis is emphatic that when God made the world there were no killers. Everything only ate plants. Now that is different to Charles Darwin's picture of evolution. Genesis one and two are dogmatic. God made everything very good. Do you realise that means there was a world where even broccoli tasted good? Can you believe that? That's what it's talking about. It meant no killers, no carnivores, no competition and no struggle to survive. But what is that catchphrase you learned in biology at high school? Survival of the . . . ? Fittest. But no such competition occurred back in God's world. There was no struggle to survive at all. Everything survived.'

Mackay presses his little button again and the famous silhouette depiction of 'the evolution of man' appears.

'You see the chimpanzee on the left?' he asks. 'You see the man on the right? That's the history of the world according to most high-school textbooks. You and I are just hydrogen and somehow or other we turned into people. But if you look at your Bible, it says that everything started perfect and went *downhill*. Man sinned, God cursed the ground and death entered the world.'

He turns to face his screen.

'Let's put that in diagram form.'

On the screen, a bar graph appears, consisting of biblical names and numbers.

'Do you know that Adam lived until he was nine hundred and thirty years old? Noah lived until he was nine hundred and fifty? Abraham drops off at a hundred and seventy-five. Anyone here a hundred and seventy-five tonight? No? Big difference in the world. That's change, but it's not evolution. We live in a world where life-spans are influenced by stress in the environment. I'm old enough to remember when the Vietnamese first turned up in Australia. They were tiny. They'd come from a nasty place. All they'd had to eat for fifty years was bullets and Americans.'

I shift restlessly on the hard wooden seat, my eyes settling for a moment on a blank page in my reporter's notepad. I see the lines there, ready to be filled with the descriptions and the strings of overheard dialogue and the thoughts that I'll think about these Christians, these *crazy* Christians; the words that will make up the story that will eventually be read by people just like me. I see the lines, and I already know what they're going to say.

Sighing, I glance down the row. I really am a very long way from home. It is as if I am in a rural town of the early 1950s, listening to the shibboleths of men from the 1400s. Strange to think that we are comfortably inside the twenty-first century, and John Mackay is neither a time traveller nor an idiot of the fringes. Rather, he is a famous Christian figurehead who has just flown in from a tour of America and Britain, where he has spoken to thousands of fellow believers and appeared on mainstream television shows. A veteran evangelist for the literal truth of Genesis – the book of the Bible that describes God building the earth in six days – he has come to north Australia to give a talk on the obsession that has run through his life like a burning wick: evolution and all the reasons it is wrong.

For Christians like Mackay, this is the Armageddon debate, the row to end all rows. Its logic is stark and indestructible: to accept evolution, they say, is to call the entire Bible a lie. Anyone who successfully proves that God didn't create the earth in six days is setting off a chain of explosions that starts at the very base of all Christian thought, bursts up through the architecture of its parables, prophesies and gospels, and ultimately blows off its roof in a vast Satanic mushroom cloud. 'How do you get rid of God?' Mackay asks. 'You can't shoot him dead. So you attack his authority – and his authority is that he created the earth.'

Indeed, Mackay believes that if Lucifer himself didn't come up with the theory of evolution, he is certainly behind its wild successes. 'You have to look at the theory of evolution as the basis of all anti-God morality in the West,' he says. Later, when I ask him whether he considers *The Origin of Species* to be 'a kind of Satanic version of the book of Genesis', he brightens, pleased by the analogy, and says, 'Yes, definitely. That's exactly what it is.'

Mackay's organisation, Creation Research – whose stated aim is 'to seek evidence for the biblical account of creation' – has offices in the US, Canada, New Zealand and the UK and his annual speaking tours have made his name notorious among those familiar with the debate. In the last few years, he has earned attacks from august scientific bodies such as the Royal Society and the British Centre for Science Education, which has even gone so far as to publish an MI5-style dossier on Mackay ('Appearance: Mackay likes to play the larrikin. His dress style could best be described as "outback casual".'). In 2006 the National Union of Teachers demanded new legislation to outlaw the Mackay-style school creationism lessons, which the National Secular Society described as 'verging on intellectual child abuse'.

When I sat myself down in the community hall, I was unaware of the full strangeness of the creationists' theory. Luckily for me, Mackay proves to be an excellent teacher. I learn that around six thousand years ago, when God made the earth in six days, the environment was perfect and, as a result, Noah had metre-long forearms. There was no suffering, struggle, illness or sorrow; there were no carnivores; all living things grew enormous and the temperature was permanently pleasant. But ever since the day that Eve allowed a snake to talk her into eating the apple and then shared it with Adam, the world has become harsher, its inhabitants have got smaller and sicker and human society has been thrashing about in ever more desperate throes. God tried to teach us a lesson when he made it rain for forty nights. We didn't learn. We are incapable: ever since Eve's crime, we've been born this way – outlaw failures, fucking and sinning with callous abandon as the planet we've been given withers around us.

As his talk progresses, two further facts become apparent about John Mackay. One, he likes to speak in questions. Two, he has a bit of a *thing* about David Attenborough. 'I know a question David Attenborough wouldn't ask,' he says at one point. 'If creation is true, what would the evidence be?'

Of all the questions ever, this is probably John's favourite because he believes that the evidence is on the side of God. By education and by thinking, Mackay considers himself to be a scientist. And it is by these rigorous and testable methods that he has promised to prove the creation hypothesis to me.

When his talk is over, the Gympie Christians begin to bumble out of the double doors, with a few getting snagged on small-talk and lingering in chatty knots here and there. It is obvious that nobody had a real problem with John's presentation. He was, literally, preaching to the converted, and his audience reacted to what he had to say in exactly the manner you would expect of a people who were, in effect, sitting through a six thousand-year-old news report. The only person I can find in the crowd who isn't wholly convinced is a young woman named Catherine Stipe. She admits to doubts about some aspects of creationism before quickly adding, 'But as long as God made everything I'm happy.' When I ask if she believes in evolution, she looks baffled. 'I wouldn't quite go *that* far.'

As the hall empties, Mackay patrols his merchandise – books, DVDs and fossils and crystals which are, according to a sign, useful both for demonstrating 'God's engineering genius' and 'combating new age lies'. Several of the DVDs are of debates with evolutionist academics, which poses an interesting question: If evolution is so demonstrably true, what is he doing debating with academics and then selling the resulting showdowns in sumptuously produced DVD twin packs for $50 a go? What is he doing behaving like a man who is winning?

'We frequently win public debates,' Mackay tells me when we sit down later on. 'In fact, for a long while it was impossible to get debates because the academics didn't want to be shown up. But then word went around, "They're making too much progress, we've got to debate them again." So in the last

7

few years we've had quite a lot and the reason they always fail to beat us is they presume they're fighting against theologians with no science degrees.'

Mackay, a geologist and geneticist who seems to possess an eager and audacious intellect, has most recently crossed ideologies with iconic atheist Professor Richard Dawkins – who, not incidentally, once told the *Guardian* newspaper, 'People like Mackay thrive by drip-feeding misinformation . . . we cannot afford to take creationism lightly. It's not an amusing diversion, but a serious threat to scientific reason.'

John recalls the meeting with a contemptuous sigh. 'He was trying to be David Attenborough,' he says. 'I think it's because he's been getting so much flak. People are sick of him. Do you know, if Dawkins is speaking at a university before me, the evolutionists get so disgusted with him they'll double my crowd? But I led him to a point where he said, "Evolution has been observed, it just hasn't been observed while it's been happening." And that's just a stupid statement. If it's not been observed, it's not science. And if it's not science, what is it? So I said, "This is your faith starting-point versus my faith starting-point, let's not pretend any different." He didn't like that.'

*

I saw the lines, and I knew what they were going to say. My role here in Gympie is the one that I have been playing for years. It is to be a counter of weirdnesses, a cataloguer of wrongs. I am to list them in a newspaper; to upload them to a website; to send these Christians' errors soaring across the planet, so that the peoples of far continents can read them and . . . well, what?

A confession. Most of the time, I provide no real answers; no solution to the mystery of how these false beliefs have emerged. Every now and then, I might unbury an insight into how my subject has come to be the person they are. Mostly, though, the thing remains a mystery and I find myself gazing at my subject, as if through a window in a distant building, thinking: *I have no idea how you ended up there.* The only thing that I have really understood was that we are divided by an inscrutable void and that, in being unable to bridge it, I have failed.

And yet there I go, again and again, on stories just like this one – small adventures with men and women whose beliefs about the world I find strange. I have explored the company of Furries, cryonicists, cult members, swingers, mediums, body-builders, vampire-detectives, a suicide cult and a couple who believe they once met the yeti in some woods outside Ipswich. I like to write about these people – it is like being a tourist in another universe. There is something noble about their bald defiance of the ordinary, something heroic about the deep outsider-territories that they wilfully inhabit, something comforting – in a fundamental, primeval way – about their powers of cognitive transport. They are magic-makers. And, beneath all of that, a private undercurrent: I feel a kind of kin-ship with them. I am drawn to the wrong.

These are things that I am not supposed to admit. The jour-nalist poses as a clean, smooth mirror, reflecting back undistorted truth. To serve the reader, I must be unbiased, sane. I am not permitted to take sides, or to confess that the reason that I enjoy interviewing people is that I find simple conversation so difficult. Journalism gives me the comfort of rules: permission to ask whatever I want, without concerning myself with making offence. I can stand up and leave when-ever I like, without risking my wife's frequent and bruising complaint that I cannot be trusted in social situations. I am also probably not supposed to tell you that the only other situ-ation in which I have experienced this kind of relief is in therapy, of which I have had plenty. Or confess the suspicion that, if I am drawn to the wrong, it is because that is exactly how I feel most of the time, and that I have done so since I was a child.

It is a background state; a vague, non-specific kind of wrongness. It is like radiation – an instability that underscores everything; my entire life. It comes, I suppose, from my unconscious. And yet, in the overt world of my opinions, I am as outspoken as anyone. I experience my beliefs with a measure of certainty that, as I grow older, I find myself becoming increasingly suspicious of.

I consider – as everyone surely does – that my opinions are the correct ones. And yet, I have never met anyone whose *every single thought* I agreed with. When you take these two positions together, they become a way of saying, 'Nobody is as right about as many things as me.' And that cannot be true. Because to accept that would be to confer upon myself a Godlike status. It would mean that I possess a superpower: a clarity of thought that is unique among humans. Okay, fine. So I accept that I am wrong about things – I *must* be wrong about them. A lot of them. But when I look back over my shoulder and I double-check what I think about religion and politics and science and all the rest of it . . . well, I know I am right about that . . . and that . . . and that and that and – it is usually at this point that I start to feel strange. I know that I am not right about everything, and yet I am simultaneously convinced that I am. I believe these two things completely, and yet they are in catastrophic logical opposition to each other.

It is as if I have caught a glimpse of some grotesque delusion that I am stuck inside. It is disorientating. It is frightening. And I think it is true to say that it is not just me – that is, we all secretly believe we are right about everything and, by extension, we are all wrong.

All of my beliefs cannot be right, and yet the effects that they have had on my personal life have been costly. Hardly spoiled for friends, I recently dropped contact with a colleague whom I liked and admired after he told me that he believed the US should invade Iran. I overheard another friend, this one Jewish, proudly announce that she would never share a taxi with an Arab. That was six years ago. I haven't spoken to her since.

I don't view these acts with any sense of pride. I know, logically, that there must be good arguments for these individuals' strongly held points of view, but when I think about assessing them carefully and fairly, I feel incapable. I don't fully understand this reaction. It is as if I am too angry, too weak to bear the challenge of it. And there is a fear there too, lying secretly among all the bluster: what if they're right? What if the truth alters me; fractures something essential?

So I am left with the lonely consolation of my righteousness. That is all that I have. And what does righteousness prove anyway? I hold my beliefs with absolute conviction – but no less conviction than John Mackay. These views have created ruptures in my life, painful states of estrangement.

I have watched as these personal battles have manifested in the wider world. The decade of terrorism we have just lived through had its roots, of course, in mismatched beliefs that are both political and religious. Those same years saw what has the appearance of an increasing suspicion of science. The white-coated priests of the laboratory, to whom we have granted custody of the truth for so long, are seemingly being treated with growing levels of doubt. We don't trust the MMR jab, we don't trust climate data, we don't trust genetically modified wheat or 'conventional' medicine or supermarket-bought beef. One response has been the cultural rise of the radicalised rationalists: celebrity atheists who have written bestselling books and sponsored anti-God advertising on the sides of London buses; groups of self-declared 'Skeptics' who toured sold-out concert venues like rock stars, defining themselves in opposition to the kind of anti-scientific thinking that they declared dangerous. Every one of these people, convinced they are right. None of them convincing the other.

John Mackay got me reflecting on all this when he recounted his conversation with Dawkins. 'This is your faith starting-point versus my faith starting-point.' As I sit alone in my Gympie motel room, with its cracked plastic kettle and its stained sachets of sugar, I decide to go back to first principles: why do I believe that Mackay is mistaken about the origin of our species in the first place? Well, I suppose I believe him to be wrong because people I admire, such as Richard Dawkins, tell me that this is so. But, honestly? All I really know about evolution, aside from the basics of natural selection, is that man is descended from the ape. Like so many people who hold strong opinions about it, I have never studied evolution. I have exercised no critical thinking on the topic whatsoever. I have simply put my trust in the people that culture has directed me towards. I have run to Richard Dawkins because I believe in his credentials as a scientist, and because his views coincide with mine – with my 'faith starting-point', in other words.

I lie back and open the pamphlet that Mackay handed me earlier. It describes what the fossil record would look like if evolution were true. It says that what we should find, as we dig through the earth's strata, is simple organisms gradually becoming ever more complex and diverse, sprouting wings and legs and hair and all the rest of it. Instead, what we apparently find are fully formed species suddenly appearing and then disappearing with no intermediate, semi-evolved beings at all. (If frogs turned into monkeys, goes a common argument, why aren't we digging up 'fronkeys'?) This, says the text, accurately reflects the creationist vision of God magicking creatures abruptly into existence. It also apparently echoes the concerns of Charles Darwin himself, who is quoted as pondering, 'Why then is not every geological formation and every stratum full of intermediate links? Geology assuredly does not reveal any such finely graduated organic chain; and this, perhaps, is the most obvious and serious objection which can be urged against the theory.'

*

The next morning, we meet up in the property of a Gympie mechanic. It is here that Mackay intends to prove that the biblical creation account represents the true history of the world. Currently, though, the land in which his evidence is buried is flooded. It will be another half an hour before the water is pumped away. As we wait in the mud, with the warm rain soaking our hair and the sound of the weather playing the gum trees like a ghostly instrument, Mackay begins to tell me something of his story.

It begins in 1947, the year he was born in Australia to Scottish migrant parents. He was raised outside Brisbane in a family whose father he describes as 'strongly pro-evolutionist and anti-Christian' and, as a boy, he became a budding scientist with evolution his central passion. At sixteen, he was reading yet another book on Darwin's epochal idea when he came across a chapter on why there is no God. Its inclusion outraged the young science fan. It felt like crude propaganda, an article of burning faith shoved into a book that should consist solely of cold reason. 'I was offended intellectually', he says. 'So I deliberately picked up a Bible and began at the beginning.'

Somewhere around this time, the quick conversion of John Mackay took place. Talking to him, it is impossible to isolate the precise moment that belief struck him. It seems as though the boy, for some reason, simply became bewitched by faith.

Mackay tells me that God's existence is scientifically testable, 'because he promises to dwell within his people and that's a testable thing.'

'But how, exactly, can you test it?' I ask.

'He says, "I will make myself known to you," and he did. I know Jesus Christ personally. It's something in me.'

'Is it something you feel?' I ask.

'It's not just a feeling, it's intellectual too. It affects the way you think. It affects everything.'

Whenever and whatever happened to alter the boy's view of the world so radically, from the moment that it happened, Mackay's story becomes one of subservience to the contrary will within him that he calls God. He sacrificed his life's ambition to be a practising scientist when he felt 'called' to become a teacher. Having studied geology and genetics at university, he joined the staff at the prestigious Brisbane Grammar School, where, after deciding that 'nine out of ten' students abandon Christianity after deciding that Adam and Eve never existed, he managed to inveigle creationism into his classroom.

'Brisbane Grammar was private,' he explains. 'So you have a lot of freedom. You can innovate all sorts of education programmes that would take reams of paperwork to get approved elsewhere. I said to my colleagues, "I've found a way to teach creation." They said, "You can't do that." I said, "Yes I can."'

Mackay formulated a lesson that he called 'How do we know what we know in the first place?', the official purpose of which was to explore the methods we use to separate fact from fantasy. The example he used was creation versus evolution and he used it to help the children answer his favourite question ever: If creation is true, what would the evidence be?

Word of Mackay's unit spread, and he was invited to teach it at church groups. He was a hit. He circulated class notes to like-minded colleagues and impressed many, but most portentously an ambitious young teacher called Ken Ham.

I am surprised to hear mention of Ham in all this. He is a Queensland-born scientist who is now resident in the US, where he has become famous for his creationism museum and his daily radio show *Answers . . . with Ken Ham*, which is syndicated nationally to over a thousand stations. I am interested in Ken Ham because he and Mackay co-founded the Creation Science Foundation in 1979 only for Mackay to be kicked out after making some unusually bracing allegations about a senior member.

'I wasn't actually *kicked out* of the CSF,' Mackay corrects me, when I mention it. 'But it was getting to that stage.'

'I heard you accused someone of witchcraft.'

'I did accuse a lady of being a "divisive Jezebel",' he says, carefully. 'Jezebel was a lady full of rebellion and the Bible says rebellion is the sin of witchcraft.'

'And did you also accuse her of necrophilia?'

'That wording comes from somebody else,' he says.

'But did you—'

'Yes,' he says, reluctantly. 'I did communicate that as well.'

'And was it true?' I ask.

'I couldn't say,' he says, wiping some drizzle out of his beard. 'I mean, how could you know?'

We pause to check upon the progress that has been made with the water pump. We are here to see a set of fossilised conifers which apparently contain crucial evidence for creationism. As we make our way through the sticky mud towards the gradually emerging treasure, John explains how the petrified remains of dinosaurs challenge the basic tenets of evolution.

'The first dinosaurs look like dinosaurs,' he says. 'The last ones look like dinosaurs too. So within that timeframe – even if you did put it at millions of years – they produce their own kind, just as Genesis says.'

'But hang on,' I say. 'If humans have been here since day one, that means we must have existed at the same time as dinosaurs.'

'Yes,' he says. 'When you look at so-called mythical stories of dragons, they're real. St George really did fight a dragon.'

'But there are no dragons in the Bible.'

'There are quite a few dragons in the Bible. Go to Job 41:14. It talks about a creature with huge teeth and a terrible mouth that breathed fire.'

'Does that mean that Noah had dragons on the ark?'

'Obviously.'

By now, enough water has been sucked out of the pit that working geologist Liam Fromyhr can use the scene to tell me why he is convinced that the majority of his colleagues are mistaken in their belief that layers of earth or 'strata' are laid down over millions of years. For creationists, of course, these trees and the strata that they lie in will probably be around six thousand years old.

Liam points to a fossilised tree, a beautiful coppery piece of rock in which it's still possible to make out individual rings in the ancient wood.

'This is a polystrate fossil,' he says, 'which means it sticks through several strata at once. This means the layers must've been laid quickly enough to cover the tree completely before it decomposed. We've got three metres of strata here. So conventional thinking would assume they were laid over three hundred thousand years. But as you can see, we've got a log sticking right through them.' Liam gives me a long, steady look. 'Now, logs don't hang around for three hundred thousand years.'

I turn to John.

'So if these fossils are six thousand years old, this must mean they're actual trees from the garden of Eden?'

He considers for a moment.

'Well, this is a tree which, due to some circumstances, has been catastrophically pulverised into sections. You can see another one over there that has gigantic cobbles up against it. The size of the cobbles tells you that the water has been going pretty fast.'

'Hang on,' I say. 'Are you telling me these trees were knocked over during Noah's flood?'

'Basically.'

I bend down again to look at them. These old conifers, I can't help but notice, are normal sized and not – as they should be, according John's theory – gigantic trees, grown to an awesome monstrous splendour in a nutritionally, atmospherically and environmentally perfect Eden.

'They're not particularly massive, are they?' I say.

'Oh, these are just fragments,' says John. 'Is this a small tree trunk or a branch from a big tree? You just can't tell.'

'You do expect to find some gigantic trees, then?' I ask, vaguely. 'At some point?'

His eyes scan happily over the trunks.

'Eventually.'

*

'I'm going to say some things that might stretch your little brains today,' John says from his lectern in front of the altar. It is Sunday morning and he has invited me to watch him preach at the Gympie Community Church. 'I'm going to be talking about homosexuals. Open your Bibles at Leviticus chapter 20 verse 13. "If a man lies with the male as with a woman, both men have committed an abomination, they shall surely be put to . . .? Death."'

Either side of John's head are large banners, painted in happy colours by the neighbourhood's children. One says 'Love'. The other 'Joy'.

'Isn't it true that today we have gay bishops?' he says. 'Isn't it true that we have lesbian preachers? But in the Bible it says homosexual bishops, lesbian preachers, thieves, extortioners, adulterers, murderers and revilers will end up where?'

On an adjacent wall are their companions, 'Gentleness' and 'Kindness'.

'Hell.'

The woman in front of me highlights the relevant Bible chapter in pink ink.

'Do you know what's going to happen to our moral basis?' he continues. 'There will be a shift. If homosexuality used to be wrong and now it's right, why not paedophilia? You watch. That's what you'll see.'

I look around at the congregation of young families, elderly couples and children. I am expecting expressions of outrage; at the very least surprise. But everyone appears benignly accepting, as if they are watching clouds drifting over sunny meadows. Their Bibles have special weatherproof jackets with pockets and zips and pen holders.

'You ask what gives God the right to determine what's moral or immoral? He made the world. No argument applicable after that point. God is an absolute ruler and he's not interested in your opinions. There might be a non-Christian here . . .'

Mackay looks out over the congregation. His eyes seem to lock on to mine. My heart gives a single, powerful thud.

'Do you realise the Bible is emphatic that you're going to hell?'

Today, he even looks different. The sun has reddened his skin and the two clumps of hair on the side of his balding head give a regrettable horn-like impression. As he finishes, his voice deepens and rings with fiery portent. 'When a homosexual bishop meets up with a lesbian preacher in hell and they're asking why they're there, the demons will laugh and say, "We didn't obey . . . *and neither did you.*"'

The congregation murmurs their approval and John is replaced at the lectern by the pastor.

'Just a reminder that Charlie and Beryl and celebrating their fiftieth wedding anniversary this week, they'd love you to join them for tea and cakes in the meeting hall.'

*

After the service I canvas the Gympie faithful for their opinion of John's sermon, hoping that perhaps, after all, John Mackay will turn out to be on the fringes of an otherwise pleasant and accepting country community.

'It was good,' says a kindly looking father. 'I believe what he was saying, as controversial as that is in the world today.'

'But I'm thinking most people around here wouldn't agree with it?'

He looks confused.

'Oh, yes,' he says. 'Yes they would.'

'I expect *you* didn't agree with what he was saying,' I say, smilingly, to a nearby eighteen-year-old named Levi.

'I agree very much with what he said,' he replies. 'It comes straight from the Bible.'

'But you probably have lots of friends who wouldn't agree?'

His companion Charlotte interrupts primly, and with raised eyebrows.

'Most of our friends would be just as against gay people.'

I give up.

Later, I find Mackay enjoying a cup of tea and some cake, down at Charlie and Beryl's do in the canteen. I decide to take the opportunity to get the entry conditions of hell straight, because he seemed to be saying that it is only unbelievers who end up in the abyss. So wouldn't this mean that lesbian nuns go to heaven?

'No,' he says. 'Because lesbian nuns are living in public disobedience to their creator.'

'So it's the fact that the lesbian nuns are refusing to repent by being straight that's sending them to hell?'

'That's what's sending them to hell,' he nods.

'So a lesbian nun who repents a week before she died would be okay?'

'As a nun, she cannot plead ignorance of the Bible.'

'So lesbian nuns are doomed?'

'Basically, yes.' He takes a nibble of his fruit cake. 'It's like treason.'

The conversation moves further into morality. John tells me 9/11 was a 'classic case' of God punishing a sinful nation, a comment which brings to mind a personal calamity that John and his wife suffered a few years ago.

'What about your miscarriage?' I ask him. 'By the same logic, could that be a punishment for your sins?'

'No,' he says. 'Because you and I reap the results of the things that went before us that are sometimes beyond our control.'

'Is gluttony a sin?' I ask.

'Yes,' says John.

I point to his belly, which rises into view from beneath his shirt like a mountain summoned by God.

'You've got some repenting to do, then.'

He replies slowly, 'I've got a thyroid problem.'

I close my eyes and try to absorb the irritation.

'Come on, John,' I say. 'Isn't this all just . . . just . . . *stupid?*'

He looks baffled. He crosses his legs. I go on.

'What I mean is, you claim there is a legitimate scientific theory that says there's a magic superhero who has created a planet full of people to tell him he's great and who get tortured by demons if they're naughty.'

'I don't think it's stupid,' he says. 'You have to have penalties for those who do injustice.'

'It's not just the hell bit,' I say. 'It's also the egotistical superhero.'

'Stop there,' he says, crossly. 'You're attributing your human nature to God. There's no reason to accuse him of being egotistical.'

'What's his motive, then?'

'Why does he need a motive?'

I have a sudden and overwhelming urge to whimper. What can you do when common sense doesn't work? When reason's bullets turn out to be made of smoke?

'When I sat there listening to you today going on about gay people,' I tell him, 'I thought you were evil.'

'That doesn't surprise me,' he says. 'It was tough stuff.'

'But can't you see, the people you're attacking – the pro-equality lobby – sincerely want to make the world a kinder place? If everyone decided you were right, there'd be a genocide against gay people.'

'Okay then,' he says. 'Let me make a prediction too, based on creation. The end result of all this will be an *increase* in turbulence. Homosexuals will get into a position where they'll start to impose their values.'

'We'll be forced to be gay by gays?' I say.

'Yep,' he replies. 'That's where it will go.'

'And do you seriously believe that acceptance of homosexuality will lead to an acceptance of paedophilia and necrophilia?'

'Even in the churches.'

'Priests having sex with dead people?'

'That's right.'

'But, John,' I say, 'the view that homosexuality is a sin is illogical, because it's not a choice. It's a state of being that you're born into. You can't be tempted to be a homosexual. I've been tempted to steal, I've been tempted to lie, but I've never been tempted to kiss a man.'

'They have made a choice, whether it's paedophilia or homosexuality or necrophilia. They are all in a rainbow of that which is an incorrect choice about sex.'

I tell John that I am completely convinced that he is wrong. Apparently, though, I only believe this because I have been fooled by Satan. 'The Bible warns that the devil is a liar and is out to trick us,' he explains. 'When God says something's wrong, the devil's out to do anything to convince us it's right.'

'But if you follow that logic,' I say, 'any thought we have that goes against the Bible is the devil. So we're not allowed to think for ourselves.'

'We are allowed to think for ourselves,' he says. 'Your first step is thinking that God's wiser than me so I will accept what he says, even if I don't understand it.'

This, it seems to me, is a remarkable admission for a man who considers himself to be a scientist.

'So that's all the thinking for yourself you're allowed?' I say. 'The decision to believe everything God says?'

'Yes.'

*

Two weeks later, I discover that the only thing I know for sure about evolution is completely wrong. I find this out in a back office at Sydney's Australian Museum, the place I have come to for the end of my story. Playing the white knight, the truth teller, the good guy is Nathan Lo, a thirty-five-year-old doctor of molecular evolution. Lo is going to assess Mackay's assertions and offer a counter-creationist perspective on who built the gympie-gympie tree. We talk at a bare wooden table, beneath a framed picture of an aphid and behind a sink full of bottles marked 'glycerol' and 'H2O'.

I begin by telling Nathan about the puzzling lack of betwixt species 'fronkey' types in the fossil record. But, apparently, this isn't how evolution works at all. 'One very common misconception is that we evolved from things that are on the earth now,' he says. 'We didn't. Humans, for example, didn't evolve from chimps. They both evolved separately from things that have shared characteristics, and that don't look like anything that exists today.'

'Oh,' I say. 'Right. And are these things in the fossil record?'

'There are many, many fossils that have characteristics that are like both chimps and humans,' he says.

I ask about the claim that the fossil record doesn't show creatures getting steadily more complex.

'That's completely wrong,' he says. 'Yes, things are relatively complex for three or four hundred million years, but before that they're much simpler. Fish start approximately four hundred million years ago and if you keep going back, you get to things like worms and then if you go back about eight hundred million years, there's nothing that has any complexity. Everything was single-celled.' And so it carries on: the polystrate logs can be explained by the earth – and therefore the strata – moving around; dinosaurs do not suddenly appear in the fossil record fully formed, and so on.

Nathan, it turns out, is the un-John, his life-story being an uncanny polarised version of the creationist's. Where Mackay was brought up in an anti-Christian house and read a book in his teens that turned him godly, Nathan was sent to a fundamentalist Christian school and read a book that turned him rational. Its author? Richard Dawkins.

'There are middle-class suburbs everywhere that are full of people like John Mackay,' he warns as we walk down the echoing corridors. 'I know. I went to school with them.'

He explains that scientists are especially infuriated with creationists because of their determination to have the subject taught in schools as a scientific theory that's the equal of evolution. And as Lo explains, it is creationism's very simplicity that makes it dangerously seductive to children.

'The main problem,' he says, 'is that creationism is a really easy explanation to understand, whereas evolution is complicated and takes a lot of time to get. Sometimes, people just want to go with the easier one. But they're being led down the wrong path in terms of the truth. And you also have to ask why people like your creationist do it. They feel threatened by rationalism and science. They want to keep their numbers up so they can stay rich. All preachers need to be paid.'

'No,' I say. 'I don't think you're right on that one. I think John and people like him really do believe they're correct.'

Nathan gives me a doubtful look.

'They believe they're doing the right thing,' he says, 'but ultimately their motive is to make more money.'

I thank him politely and walk to the exit, towards the blaze and stress of the midweek city morning, feeling itchy and irritable and disappointed.

2

'I don't know what's going on with these people . . .'

In the winter of 2001, I met a ghost-hunter who baffled me so thoroughly that he ended up inspiring my first book. After more than a year of reporting, I concluded that neither science nor the superstitious have satisfactorily explained the myriad phenomena that people report as 'ghosts'. I was sure, however, that science would offer one in the end. This seemed obvious. I mean, the idea that there might be an afterlife – a heaven or a hell or a purgatory that souls were somehow stuck inside – was so clearly stupid as to be unworthy of sensible consideration. *Stupid, dumb, ridiculous, stupid, stupid, stupid* . . .

I was angry about religion when I was writing that book. I had been angry about it for as long as I could remember. Angry at the teachers at the Catholic schools I had attended; angry at the priests at the church that I was driven to every Sunday morning; angry at my parents for believing it all so thoroughly. My father is an intelligent man – sometimes intimidatingly so. And so I used to think, *How could he?* I mean, everything, the whole lot of it, it just seemed so . . .

When my father read my ghost book – in which I wrote about how *stupid, stupid, stupid* I considered his religion to be

– he telephoned me at home. 'If you don't mind my saying so,' he said, with what I now understand to be admirable restraint, 'I think you have misunderstood the concept of faith.' Faith is a journey, he told me. Many thoughtful, senior Catholics agree that belief in God is complex, subtle and often elusive. I made some impetuous response about even archbishops not being really convinced and we left it at that. It was as if we had both reminded ourselves of the separation that exists between us, and silently agreed to a retreat.

Since then, I have written about many more people whose beliefs I consider strange. And when I really dig into the reporting of these subjects, I usually find things to be never quite as I expect. My work has taught me that the truth is always nuanced; that outrage is mostly born of misunderstanding and that, sometimes, black really can be white.

I have also been losing my faith in stupid. My father isn't stupid. Neither is John Mackay. People who dismiss believers in God in this way do so in error. And Nathan Lo was wrong too, I think. Mackay's motive isn't money. I am convinced that he really does believe what he is saying, and that his mission is sincere. And when he says that he feels God so absolutely within him that he is left with not a whisper of doubt about his existence, I believe that too.

Nathan Lo and I are of the same team. We see ourselves as the rational ones, the clean-sighted bringers of twenty-first-century reason. And yet both of us, I have come to believe, are mistaken. We are wrong about the wrong.

*

It is six months after my journey to Gympie, and I find myself submerged in the impossible puzzle once again. It all begins in the lounge of sixty-eight-year-old UFO expert (and no relation of John) Glennys Mackay, which is cluttered with mystical ephemera – a Native American wolf mirror, a framed diploma in urine therapy and a crystal ball dumped in an ashtray. It doesn't go well. As Glennys speaks, I frequently feel as if I am being chastened for my naivety; as if my ignorance of the minutiae of alien lore is giving her a migraine.

Our meeting started happily enough, with Glennys telling me that she saw her first UFO in 1948, on her parents' farm. 'It wasn't until April 1964 that one followed me home,' she says. 'I was in a car and these hands, these faces, came to the window. They smelled like eggs.'

'What did you do?' I ask.

'I said, "Oh my God, don't you smell?" I remember going on to the ship. They said they didn't mean us any harm. They look like us, but their skin's more translucent. They wear wigs. These "greys" that everyone talks about, they're really robots.' She crosses her arms and adds wearily, 'I don't know why people carry on about greys.'

'How do you know they're robots?'

'I just know it,' she says.

'But how?'

'It's just something I've been shown,' she snaps.

Glennys believes that humanoid, wig-wearing aliens are already mingling with people on earth.

'I was at a conference in the US and two females turned up. You could tell they were wearing wigs. It was quite obvious. What they do, they dress up and go to Las Vegas and wander around.'

'If you were in a casino and saw two aliens in wigs playing poker, would you be able to tell?'

She nods proudly. 'The average person wouldn't.'

Glennys goes on to explain that their abduction programme involves aliens 'taking cells and seeds and eggs from us and trying to produce a better race'.

'That's a frightening thought,' I muse. 'A bit like Hitler. Dangerous.'

'But look at what the scientists are doing now!' she says. 'They're dangerous too. Look at Monsanto!'

'Oh, come on, Glennys,' I say. 'Frost-proof wheat is one thing. Creating an alien master-race to enslave the planet is quite another. If the aliens had their way, *we'd* be the ones that get wiped out. Don't you think that's a bit of a worry?'

'It is a bit of a concern,' she concedes. 'But then, you've got to look at the people who are in power now. Are *they* aliens?'

A week later, I am sitting in a circle in the middle of a forest at midnight, attempting to induce a close encounter of the third kind with some bells. Moments ago Kay McCullock, the organiser of the UFO group that I have joined, finished her introductory talk.

'First and foremost, health and safety,' she said. 'If a UFO lands, you must wait until it's stopped completely before approaching. Only invite the ETs to come closer if it is absolutely safe to do so. If anyone gets zapped, the first-aid kit is in the back of my tent.'

Right now she is walking about in circles, half-heartedly ringing a gong. After a couple of minutes, she stops to bring up the question of what sort of mantra we should be chanting in order to entice the aliens. This is when the bickering begins.

'I don't see why we need a mantra,' says one. 'Just hold the thought in your head. We don't need to repeat it and repeat it.'

'I'm not saying it's a mantra,' says Kay. 'That was just the first thing that came into my head. It's more like an affirmation.'

'Well, affirmation, whatever. Why do we need it?'

'Because once you put words out there – they're a frequency. It's creating on every level,' says Kay.

'Well, I'm not doing an affirmation. There's no point. Just keep it in our heads. They'll pick it up.'

'I think he's right,' says someone else, nervously. 'They can use ESP.'

'Are you sure?' says yet another voice. 'If we do an affirmation, it's more certain. We should offer assistance. They're coming from a long way away.'

'Our thought-forms will be projected perfectly clear as it is. For God's sake, these beings are highly advanced. We're not talking about Plutonians here.'

'Plutonians don't have ESP? Why do you say that?'

UFO-spotters, I have learned, are extremely adept at bickering. Over the next sixty minutes, there will be low-level grumbling about all sorts of things, including the mantra, about the dire risks of 'projecting blasé thought-forms' and about whether or not it is racist to call Plutonians 'nasty'. As I am sitting here, under the magnificent stars, listening to these adults arguing about things that don't exist, I wonder if I have accidentally shuffled slightly closer towards an answer. There is a hint of something in these arguments that are taking place around me: a kind of process that is in evidence.

It starts with a small and friendly disagreement. That disagreement is challenged. The pitch is raised. The friendliness vanishes and the positions harden. It goes round and around. As the irritation builds, Kay seems ever more convinced that the chanting of an affirmation is essential while her opponents shed any sliver of doubt that the ETs will be able to hear their invitation perfectly clearly via ESP if they beckon them silently, in their heads.

Haven't we all done this? Hardened a particular position, not as a response to superior information, but because of anger? I think of John Mackay – the young evolutionist who was sufficiently piqued by the arrogance of the chapter on 'why there is no religion' that he picked up a Bible and allowed it to alter the architecture of his world completely. It seems that for Mackay, in those first few life-changing hours, it was nothing to do with sounder arguments and everything to do with anger. Here, right in front of me, I am witnessing strange beliefs being born by a mechanism that has nothing to do with reason.

*

I have chosen to visit Kay McCullock's group because I want to meet one individual in particular. I have been hoping that a man called Martin Gottschall will give me a more orthodox perspective on the subject of UFOs.

'UFOs have been observed coming towards a hillside, not slowing down and going straight into it,' he tells me, when we sit down together the next morning. 'They do a dimensional shift so they no longer interact with the matter of our dimension.'

Martin says this with absolute assurance, as if he is telling me how the carburettor in a bus works. The strangeness condenses further when we discuss his belief that the aliens are here to deliver a vital message.

'Typically, they tell people: "Look after the planet, don't pollute it with all the chemicals, don't go into nuclear power because there are better ways of making energy,"' he says.

I ask Martin if these aliens – who have supposedly harnessed the power of clean and limitless 'free energy' – have ever actually taken the trouble to tell us how it works, and thus finally release us from our destructive dependence on fossil fuels.

'No,' says Martin.

'It's weird that they've come all this way to preach to us about eco-fuels, and yet they refuse to give us the answers,' I say.

'They're more interested in our spiritual development,' says his wife Sheryl.

'Still, it's a little irritating,' I say, bristling. 'They're quite smug, the aliens.'

Martin leans forward with a look of endlessly patient sympathy. 'What you have to realise is these extraterrestrials have been living on this planet for ever,' he says. 'Most of our spiritual teachings have come from ETs. They couldn't tell us anything that hasn't been told before because we haven't yet got to the point of complying with what they've already told us.'

Martin Gottschall is *Dr* Martin Gottschall, a consultant mechanical engineer with a PhD who has been studying UFO lore for thirty years. I had expected that to make a difference, that his qualification might indicate a level of simple rationality. But once more, here I am – confronted with the counterintuitive notion that intelligence is no protection against strange beliefs.

My research into the creationists suggested something related, and equally as bizarre: simple facts and basic logic just don't work in the way I had assumed. Before I embarked on my trip to Gympie, I imagined that it would be simple to corral a successful argument against John Mackay. After all, that is how you change a person's beliefs, isn't it? With facts. But facts proved entirely ineffective, and they were ineffective to a spectacular and baffling extent. To illustrate my point, here are just a few of the answers to reasonable questions that are given, typically, by Mackay and his fellow creationist thinkers.

If all of God's people are on the earth, why did he go to the bother of making outer space? To tell the time. If Adam wasn't born of a woman, did he have a belly button? No. Who created God? God is outside of time so doesn't need a beginning. If there is no evolution, how do you explain those heavy-browed Neanderthal skeletons? They were ordinary humans with something called 'Jelly Bone Syndrome'. If *T. rex* was a vegetarian, why did he have such huge teeth? To eat water-melons.

As you can see, reason has zero effect on these people. What I want to know is, why? Humans are rational beings. We receive, assess and assimilate new information. Superior facts replace the inferior. That is how we progress. That is how we operate. Evidence for our incredible abilities in refining our understanding of reality are everywhere – in computers and cities and advances in healthcare and all of the million tiny miracles of civilisation. But intelligence apparently isn't the forcefield against wrongness that I had once assumed. Reason is no magic bullet.

After all these years of work, I remain mystified by how people come to believe unlikely things. I don't think stupid is the answer. But if stupid isn't the answer, what is?

*

Arriving home from the woods, I find myself reluctant to do any further research on UFOs. It all seems so pointless. As with God, I tend to summarily reject the idea of aliens. Even though I have no idea what a weather balloon is, I have always dismissed all UFO sightings as them. At some unknown point, I made an instant, unilateral decision that UFOs were daft and that no examination of the evidence was necessary. But then I did examine the evidence, and what I found surprised me.

The first thing was the sheer number of apparently sane people who have had an experience of them. There are hundreds of accounts of UFO sightings by people such as airline pilots, military personnel and police officers; individuals who actually know what a weather balloon is. More than that, though, I am surprised by the compelling simplicity of the argument. The existence of aliens themselves – for me, the first and most difficult claim to digest – turns out to be accepted by most astronomers and cosmologists. In describing the quantity of non-human life thought to be extant in the universe, the word often used is 'teeming'. It has been estimated there are over a hundred thousand billion potentially life-bearing planets in the vast out-there, many in solar systems in our own galaxy that are one billion years older than ours. Physicists such as Dr Michio Kaku, a holder of the Henry Semat Chair and Professorship in physics, say it is theoretically possible to travel the distances required of UFOs using shortcuts known as wormholes. He argues that it is only logical that alien scientists a billion years more sophisticated than ours could have created wormhole-capable craft: 'You simply cannot dismiss the possibility that some of these sightings are some object created by an advanced civilisation.'

Then, with increasing fascination, I read about Professor John E. Mack of Harvard University, a Pulitzer prize-winning biographer and psychiatrist who specialised in adolescent suicide and published his research into people who claim to have been abducted by aliens in 1990. Mack initially assumed all abductees to be delusional. But then he met some. Working closely with more than two hundred individuals, Mack quickly discounted the common 'sleep paralysis' theory due to the simple fact that many abductions are reported when the individual was awake. He eventually concluded, 'These people, as far as I could tell, were of sound mind, had not communicated with each other, were not getting details from the media – this is long before the great media rash of information on this subject. They were reluctant to come forth, they described similar stories in great detail and were shocked when they would

34

hear someone else had had a similar experience. The only thing as a psychiatrist that I knew that behaved like that was real experience . . . I would not say that, "Yes, aliens are taking people," but I would say that there's a compelling phenomenon here that I cannot account for in any other way, that's mysterious. I can't say what it is but it seems to me that it invites deeper, further inquiry.'

Mack published his research in 1990, in a book entitled *Abduction*. It was an instant bestseller and Mack became a minor celebrity. And that is when things became really fascinating.

The Harvard establishment reacted to all this with profound embarrassment. They decided to act. The Dean informed Mack that a committee had been appointed to 'investigate' his research, a move that could lead to the tenured professor's removal, something that had not happened in the history of the institution. This was the beginning of what Mack felt to be a sustained assault on his job and reputation that was to last for fourteen months. Mack responded by going public, accusing the university of trying to silence him with tactics that were 'Kafkaesque'. As the process took its course, Mack said the accusations against him changed frequently and details of the investigation's progress were kept secret. Most of the complaints evaporated when inspected. It only came to an end, Mack believed, because Harvard's administration came under public attack, for their attempts at suppressing his basic academic freedom to study what he pleased. Even when it was all over he felt marginalised by the university.

Mack, who died in a road accident in London in 2004, said of the Dean, 'He was a friend. He told me, "If you'd have just said this was a new psychiatric syndrome you wouldn't have gotten into trouble." The problem had to do with the fact that they didn't like what I was saying.' More recently, his attorney

Eric MacLeish told a BBC reporter that Harvard Medical School had distorted Mack's views. 'It was really outrageous that he had to go through this inquiry. The idea that Mack would put his own agenda above the interests of his patients was abhorrent. There was never any proof of it, and the evidence that we mustered was exactly the opposite. He was simply willing to listen. What this really was about was Harvard saying that, "We don't like this because you can't show any of this through double-blind placebo controlled study," and John was saying, "There's some real mysteries here. I don't know what's going on with these people but I can't dismiss them as mentally ill."'

There it was again – the battle in microcosm. An apparently strange belief being voiced, this one by an authority in damaged minds, and the response of the establishment, of reason and science, being a kind of vengeful and censorious fury. It seemed like such an inappropriate reaction, and something about it gave me pause.

Mack is clearly the underdog of this story. And yet a part of me couldn't help but feel some sympathy with the Harvard Dean. Having familiarised myself with the evidence I felt that I should accept at least the possibility of UFOs. But something underneath the level of my rational brain was unyielding in its resistance to doing so. It wasn't even a thought, it was a feeling, a prejudice: a great, dark lump of 'no'. No matter what anyone told me, I simply could not believe in travelling aliens. It was almost as if there were two versions of me – rival judges, battling for their preferred conclusion to win ultimate acceptance, and the one without access to any of the facts had won.

But at the same time, I couldn't help but think of Professor John E. Mack as a kind of hero. The way he was treated by his superiors was surprising: not as an intelligent colleague whose opinions differed from theirs, but as something infinitely more dangerous and threatening and dark. As a heretic.

Over the following months, as I dwell upon my time with the creationists and the alien-hunters, little events, names, slivers of dialogue and half-examined observations keep breaking the conscious surface. I am sure that, in among the white noise of those experiences, there are clues, patterns, shapes of meaning pulling themselves together; odd moments pregnant with hinted relevance that might yet help build a final understanding of the mystery. The fact of Mackay's angry lurch into belief; the curious reflection of his Road to Damascus moment in Nathan Lo's early life; the bickering and hardening of stances between the UFO-fanatics; Glennys Mackay's clean leap from alien-paranoia to Monsanto–GM-paranoia; the two conflicting versions of me; Lo's acid judgement of Mackay; its echo in that of the Harvard Dean's fight with John Mack; the mystery of the nature of the creationist's faith and the touching sincerity of the way he spoke of it. I don't know if any of this might lead me to an answer or, indeed, tell me anything about what is happening. But it all adds to the powerful impression that there is a lot more to be discovered about belief and its strange engines.

Perhaps it can be done by seeking out more heretics – stubborn individuals who are driven to defy the modern orthodoxy of science in the face of censure and scorn and ostracism. What powers possess them, and compel them to fight? What causes them to take such risks?

Belief is surely one of humanity's most dangerous forces. It ignites vast and ruinous battles; both 'culture wars' and real ones. It divides culture from culture; community from community; friend from friend; father from son. Belief is the heart of who we are and how we live our lives. And yet it is not what we think it is: not a product of intelligence or education or logic. There are invisible forces at play here. And I have no idea what they are.

3

'The secret of the long life of the tortoise'

I have to double-check, about half an hour after my arrival, because it has begun to seem so unlikely: could the true meaning of the ancient word 'yoga' *really* be 'unity'? So far, my experience of the most highly anticipated yogic event of the year has been indicative of anything but. I had expected that my particular ticket would buy me a superior position in the hall. It did, after all, cost £251. But in front of me, many hundreds of people have secured better spots than mine, closer to the stage on which their guru will be appearing. These, I will learn, are the 'VIPs', the 'VVIPs', the 'Corporate Members', the 'Founder Members', the 'Patron Members', the 'Life Members', the 'Dignified Members', the 'Respected Members' and, at the bottom, the lowly 'General Members' of the Patanjali Yog Peeth Trust and all of them are busy folding out foam mattresses and fastidiously marking their territory with bags, shoes and rolled-up socks. I, meanwhile, have been directed to a space halfway down London's vast Alexandra Palace by an assistant in a yellow sash. Trying to settle on the thin tartan rug that defines my tiny piece of land, I look at my watch. 06:20. Just ten minutes to go until the guru, Swami Ramdev, will appear.

I settle down and use the time to study my special booklet, which describes the basics of 'Yog' as taught by Ramdev – a vocal activist, it says here, against 'an Indian society divided by caste'. But it is hard to concentrate above the sound of his adjutants echoing around the walls as they prowl the margins of each sector demanding, 'Which pass are you? Which pass are you? Show me your pass. You are only a VVIP, you must move back. Let me see your ticket. Let me see your ticket. Is this a diamond ticket? This is only a gold ticket. You must move back.'

A few weeks ago, when I called the Divya Yog Trust to reserve my place, the woman on the telephone told me, 'The last time he visited the UK, local GPs noticed the impact on numbers in their surgeries.'

'That sounds incredible,' I said. 'How does it work?'

'The science that underpins the whole thing is that the body has the wherewithal to heal itself. You don't need external help. Breath is all you need.'

After six days, she promised, I would feel 'amazing'. Then she took my credit card details.

Yoga itself was being practised as long ago as 400 BC and possibly as far back as 3300 BC and, in its traditional form, it has eight 'limbs'. Each limb is a different set of instructions that you will need to follow if you fancy the sound of being liberated from all worldly suffering and the cycle of life and death. One of these limbs is the 'asana', which comprises the now well-known physical postures that have been isolated and appropriated by millions of Western women who are less concerned with breaking free of the cycle of life and death than they are with having smaller bottoms. Swami Ramdev believes that people have put too much faith in these postures and are missing the real action, which lies in the fourth limb, 'pranayama' or 'breath control'.

Back in India, Ramdev is held in such esteem that, on a domestic trip in 2011, four cabinet ministers were sent to meet him from his private jet at the airport. He has, he claims (somewhat unbelievably), one billion followers and two hundred and fifty million viewers of his TV show. His fame, over there, has made him almost as ubiquitous as the sun and his heat is becoming so powerful that it is now beginning to be felt in the West. This is to be the first stop on a UK tour that will also visit windily vast arenas in Coventry in the Midlands and Scotland. In London alone, three thousand people will attend daily sessions that run for almost a week. The last time he was in Europe he had a reception with MPs at the House of Commons and tea with the Queen, and addressed a United Nations conference at the request of Kofi Annan. This particular visit follows rapturous welcomes in the US and Canada. And wherever he goes, to whomever he speaks, he brings the same message – practise his seven yogic breathing exercises and your life will be transformed in myriad marvellous ways. Not only will you be happier and more respectful of your elders, Ramdev claims his regime of scientific breathing can cure afflictions as diverse as depression, baldness, obesity, asthma, diabetes and cancer. Pranayama is, in his words, a 'complete medication' and, in the words of one his senior assistants, 'like a miracle'.

Despite the fact that he describes himself as a 'swami' – a Hindu honorific title that literally means 'owner of oneself', a man who has total control over his body and urges – Ramdev boasts that he is proudly 'anti-superstition'. He is not a healer, saint or God-man, but a student of cold, academic rationality. The megastar ascetic, who is sponsored by Tilda Basmati Rice, insists that his theories are based on sound scientific research that has been carried out at his headquarters in Hardwar in northern India.

From my Western perspective, Ramdev's claims sound impossible. And yet they represent an interesting complication. Back in Gympie, John Mackay asserted that his belief is scientifically testable. 'God says, "I will make myself known to you," and he did,' he told me. When I enquired as to how, he said, 'It's something in me.' Meanwhile, when I asked his accidental namesake Glennys Mackay how she could be so sure that alien 'greys' were, in fact, robots, she replied, 'It's just something I've been shown.' For both Mackays, their conviction seems to be projected from the same place: the unconscious. Contrary to what John might insist, though, these beliefs do not represent any mode of proof. That is to say, John and Glennys might preach the reality of gods and greys, and many people might believe them. But they are not actually promising anything tangible, demonstrable or, indeed, testable to earn this faith. And yet Swami Ramdev is.

When he finally appears on stage at 06:30, we rise as one to greet him. A procession of acolytes files past to touch his skin and lay red roses at his feet. Then, accompanied by his three-piece band, he assumes a perfect lotus position and starts with his 'Ooooooooommmmmm'. His voice has an impressive timbre; it booms and unfurls and quivers your intestines. Sitting on the distant stage at the end of the colossal venue, in his orange robes with his feet on his inner thighs, he looks beguiling and beautiful.

With his theme song over, he jumps up and begins to bounce alarmingly, kicking one knee up at a time, almost to the height of his chin. Everyone copies him, beaming and giggling and panting. Then he starts walking on his hands. The crowd awkwardly drift back down to the safety of their tartan rugs. Ramdev reassumes the lotus and breathes in so completely it looks as if his stomach has been scooped out. It bulges into a giant ball, like a watermelon being pumped up.

He causes it to shimmer, with little waves of contractions running through it. And then, finally, the pranayama begins.

The seven exercises that Ramdev promotes are almost as effortless as breathing itself. There is one where you lie on your fists and breathe. There is another where you breathe in and stay breathed in for a bit. And there is one which involves breathing in slowly and then exhaling abruptly with a loud 'hhhfff' sound. This, we are told, expels 'toxins' from the body. And then there is 'the bumblebee', which is designed to 'balance dopamine levels' and sharpen memory and involves us putting our hands over our faces to prevent 'energy' leaking out of our eyeballs.

Respite comes during Ramdev's long lectures, which are delivered in Hindi. As he speaks, my concentration breaks. I notice that the hall is filled with subtle contradictions. Ramdev goes to great lengths to tell his fans that he is no quasi-god, but his promotional banners seem to imply a different message. There is the Swami floating on water with the sun coming out of his head; there is the Swami levitating on the sunset with his stomach hollowed out; there is the Swami parting the clouds to reveal a celestial white glow; there is the Swami with the sun shining out of his backside. And there he is beseeching his faithful to enjoy the benefits of 'the world's best basmati rice'.

Pushing myself painfully upwards, when the session is over, I decide to seek out someone who can speak to the truth of Ramdev's claims. I find Aasha, who has taken two weeks' holiday from her job as a tax inspector to be in charge of Ramdev's volunteer workforce. She gives the impression of embodying the very spirit of prim, precise orderliness. Her hair is soberly cut and perfectly symmetrical, her dead-straight fringe frames neat, circular spectacles.

'I am a rational person,' she says. 'I am very sceptical by

nature. But there's no mumbo-jumbo here. I would have walked out if there was any hint of mumbo-jumbo.'

She tells me that it was the death of her brother that inspired her journey into pranayama.

'He got Legionnaire's disease and was put on a ventilator,' she tells me, plainly. 'I made the decision to switch off the machine. I had to be strong for the whole family. I went into a depression. Very, very dark.' Her expression lifts into one of brightness and smiles. 'But when I saw Swamiji on the Asatha Channel he almost immediately took me out of it. I wanted to live for that. I wanted to be alive.'

'And is it true that he's cured cancer?' I ask.

'It is true,' she nods. 'It has been found that cancer cells cannot thrive in a highly oxygenated environment. When you do this type of exercise you flood your system with oxygen and this brings about huge biochemical changes. One of the exercises is the equivalent of chemotherapy and one is the equivalent of radiotherapy.'

Aasha walks me over to a table near the busy merchandise stalls and introduces me to sixty-three-year old Harita from Ilford in east London. Over the last decade, Harita has had cancer in her bowel, bladder and spine. She has had her uterus and half her bladder removed. She sits poised and upright in her cushioned seat, her hands squarely placed on her lap. Her weakness only becomes apparent when she speaks. She twists and pulls at an old paper handkerchief and her sentences tremble and break.

'Now is the fourth time cancer has come to me,' she tells me. 'They said they couldn't give me chemotherapy because it's not working any more and now they want to give me radio-therapy. But I said, "No. Give me one month. I want to see Swamiji. I will be better with this. Swamiji can cure every-thing."'

That night, in the chaotic Muswell Hill hotel that I have put myself up in, I lie in bed with a copy of the official Ramdev book *Yog: In Synergy With Modern Science*. Written by his colleague Acharya Balrishna, it makes for extraordinary reading. 'He has a dream of a disease free world,' it says. 'This, he plans to achieve with the science of Yog which he feels will bring an end to the unethical business of weapons and allopathic [i.e. conventional, Western] medicines.' Much of the text seems to be oppressively scientific – full of graphs, anatomical diagrams and dense paragraphs containing words such as 'neuro-endocrine system', 'limbic-hypothalamic' and 'spondylitis'. Mixed in with the jargon, though, are some fantastical-sounding claims. 'The person who follows celibacy with complete austerity develops incredible physical, mental and spiritual abilities'; 'The person who recognises the value of pranayam and makes it the very base, certainly wins over enemies,' and my own favourite, 'The slower the breath, the longer the life. This is the secret behind the long life of the tortoise.'

I also read some press cuttings that concern the controversies that have struck Ramdev, back in India. He owns a factory that manufactures over a hundred and sixty herbal treatments, including syrups, tablets and powered potions. In 2006 a senior politician accused him of using human bones and the testicles of an otter in his medication. This led to angry denials from Ramdev. His furious supporters gathered on the streets of New Delhi and burned effigies. During the disorder, twenty were arrested. Now officially exonerated, he blames a sinister conspiracy of multinational pharmaceutical companies who were threatened by both his commercial empire and his frequently stated ambitions for a world free of Western-style medicines.

The empire of the Swami suffered more significant trouble

over claims that pranayama can cure AIDS – a statement Ramdev denied ever making after he was threatened with legal action by medical NGOs and brought under pressure by the Indian government, who took the extraordinary step of publicly censuring him. It is an episode that seems not to have harmed his standing much. Ramdev remains, according to the biography in his book, 'famous for his medical research, practical approach to yoga and services in the field of cow breeding'.

I spend the next five days rising in the darkness, picking my way to my small square of tartan in the Alexandra Palace, doing my breathing exercises and feeling exactly as 'amazing' as you might expect after three hours of pre-dawn nose yoga and speeches delivered in Hindi by a man sitting very far away. I also spend a good deal of time badgering and whining at the organisers for a personal audience with the Swami. Their puckered smiles and dipping chins tell me everything I need to know about my chances. But then, unexpectedly, it pays off. I am finally granted ten minutes with Ramdev. We are to meet in a back room where the 'Founder Members', who have each paid more than £6,000 for their rarefied status, are queuing to meet their hero.

When the occasion arrives, I am made to wait for hours. We are in a messy fluorescent-lit area behind a large closed door that is strewn with wipe-clean tables and stackable chairs. I am watching an elegant lady in a sparkling sari and a golden, diamond-encrusted watch take her turn with the barefoot ascetic, when I see Aasha.

I say, 'Bearing in mind how he speaks out against divided India . . .'

'There is no division here,' she interrupts, smiling thinly.

'I'm sorry,' I say, 'but it seems to me that the more money you spend, the closer you get.'

The elegant woman kneels before Ramdev. An expensively healed foot pokes out of her silken robe.

'It might seem that way,' Aasha replies. 'But this is a family and once you enter, you are engulfed by his love.'

'You've only got to look at how much money these people have spent, compared to everyone else.' I give Aasha a doubtful look. 'Maybe that's a coincidence?'

Aasha considers the scene for a moment. She lowers her voice.

'To be honest, I'm not too happy with it myself,' she whispers. 'But I can see why he's doing it. Medical science will not accept anything unless clinical trials are carried out. That is what he's currently seeking to do and these trials are tremendously expensive. He needs to raise large amounts of money.'

More time passes. And then more. I find myself sitting next to the most beautiful woman in the room. Shipra is a clinical nurse and she informs me that, if I do eventually receive my promised audience, she will be translating. We watch in silence as Ramdev listens to a family's woes with an intense, hawkish expression that peers through the no-man's-land of skin between his beard and hair. Occasionally he breaks into an unsettling kind of laugh, which involves him throwing his head back as far as it will go while making absolutely no sound at all. Shipra, I notice, is finding it difficult to restrain her gaze.

'He's very charismatic,' she says. 'Spiritual people have their own aura. He's also very funny. He says, "You eat vegan food when I'm looking and then you go home and eat fried food." Ha! Ha!'

She looks at me and carries on laughing. 'Ha ha ha.'

I smile and nod politely as Shipra beams, and leans in towards me.

'You know,' she whispers, 'he's a sworn celibate.'

'That must be disappointing for his fans.'

'Yes,' she says, gazing directly at his mouth. 'Yes, it is.'

When the time finally comes, I settle down on a seat adjacent to Ramdev. Seeing the Swami treated as a kind of godhead for the previous few days seems to have had an unconscious effect on me, and I am surprised to find myself nervous. I begin by asking, just to confirm, that pranayama really can cure all diseases. He nods deeply, his beard pushing against his orange robe.

'Yes,' he says.

'So it can cure cancer?'

'Yes.'

'AIDS?'

'Yes . . . er, no!' he says, suddenly looking panicked, his eyes shining wide and white from the shadows of their hairy dens. 'No AIDS!'

'So it can cure every disease in the world except AIDS?' I ask.

'Yes,' he says. 'But even in AIDS it can help the immuno-suppressive system and lymphocytes.'

I move on to the reports that I have read in the Indian press of Ramdev telling children that Coca-Cola will turn their skin dark, a powerful message for vanity-conscious youngsters to whom pale complexions are desirable – and a statement that is unarguably wrong. I am curious to see if Ramdev will admit to saying this as, presumably, he is smart enough to realise that I know it to be untrue.

'Did you once claim Coca-Cola darkens the skin?' I say.

His eyes slide sideways, towards Shipra.

'Even in the USA, the government has banned it in schools,' he says.

'But did you claim it darkens the skin?'

48

'There has been scientific research that says it can be harmful to health.'

I put down my pen.

'But did you say it darkens the skin? I just want to establish, for the record, if you've ever claimed this.'

He looks towards Shipra once more. I watch as a hot conference takes place between them in Hindi. Eventually, she tells me, 'Swamiji just says that to the kids. It's not necessarily true.'

I decide to tell Ramdev about my meeting with Harita, and how she has put her faith in him, over conventional medicine, by delaying her cancer treatment.

'He never tells people to stop their treatment if they're not well,' Shipra says.

'But you do campaign for a world free of Western medicines,' I say.

Ramdev smiles delightedly. He says, in English, 'I want this!'

'But it would cause massive suffering,' I say.

The guru gives his mane a serious shake.

'Western medicines are very expensive and they do not cure diseases, they only control them. They have only existed for two hundred years. Before this people were still being cured and they actually lived longer.'

Just as I begin to dispute this, I am interrupted by another extended exchange between Shipra and the Swami.

'Swamiji is asking, how did you get these questions?'

I show him my notepad.

'I wrote them,' I say.

Shortly afterwards, the interview is terminated, my time apparently up.

The next morning, as I am walking into the arena for my final session with the Swami, I am stopped by an official who tells me that she has heard all about me. 'You were asking questions you shouldn't have,' she says.

*

A couple of weeks later, I am back in the warm arms of Sydney, Australia, where I am currently living and working. I decide to send a kind of greatest hits package of Ramdev's claims to Dr Rosanna Capolingua, who chairs the Ethics Committee of the Federal Australian Medical Association.

One claim is: 'It is an undisputed fact that people [who practise pranayama] get cured of diseases that are normally considered terminal. The evidence comes from the clinical examination of patients of cancer, hepatitis, and other serious diseases performed before and after pranayama.'

Another: 'The presence of cows wards off many ailments; the touch and contact of one increases our vision and betters the eyesight. Every part of the cow, from its pure milk to its urine has healing and beneficial qualities.'

Another: 'The celibate is never unhappy.'

Dr Capolingua emails me back, saying that the statements that she has seen are 'surreal' and 'not based on science'. When I speak to her on the telephone, she says, 'His claims are potentially dangerous to patients because he suggests breathing provides cures to a whole range of diseases, which we know is not the case. Targeting a market of patients who are frightened and seeking some form of miracle is very unethical. It's exploitation.'

Capolingua says that, contrary to what Harita told me, breathing deeply in an ordinary environment doesn't, in fact, raise oxygen saturation. And when I tell her about Harita and her radiotherapy, she says, 'That's dangerous. To delay that sort of treatment can have a very significant adverse outcome on the patient.' Of the book's claim that out of 1,233 new Western medicines developed since 1975, only thirteen are useful in hot, arid countries she splutters, 'Oh God, no, that's rubbish'; when I read her a passage in which he describes how food we have eaten comes into contact with oxygen, she actually starts laughing. 'That's not how it works at all,' she says. 'These processes are well understood and he's getting them wrong.'

All of which is useful to hear, but not entirely surprising. What intrigues me more is the remarkable scene that I witnessed on my final day at the Alexandra Palace. One ordinary middle-aged person stood up and joyfully announced, 'I had severe arthritis and now I'm better!' Another, 'I had severe diabetes and now I'm better!' Another, 'I had high blood pressure for twenty-six years and I am cured!'

This went on for some time.

I was witnessing something that my experiences with the creationists and the UFO-spotters did not offer. Results. Something that, at least in essence, is testable. And yet the miraculous proofs boasted of by Ramdev's London followers – claims of healing that are reflected in the testimony of many thousands of Ramdev acolytes all over the world – cannot have been born of his science-bereft breathing. So what is the truth? What has really happened to these people to make them so convinced that pranayama was the agent that made them feel so dramatically recovered? I was to find my answer in some invisible forces whose nature came as a surprise: in the phenomenon known as the placebo effect.

*

The seemingly magical powers of placebo were first effectively noted during the Second World War by a Harvard professor of anaesthesiology who found himself in southern Italy. Lieutenant Colonel Henry Beecher was working in a field hospital when he was astounded to witness a nurse who, having run out of morphine, instead injected salt water into a badly injured soldier – who apparently failed to notice any difference, feeling very little pain, and not suffering from the cardiovascular shock that might be expected of a man in his state. Months later, Beecher had the opportunity to dispense a placebo to one of his own patients. It worked. He made an ad-hoc survey of more than two hundred gravely wounded men and was amazed to find 75 per cent of them bravely declined the offer of morphine even though, before hostilities began, he had known them to be as sensitive as anyone else to even minor pain. Beecher formed a theory. Perhaps, after experiencing the violent trauma of the battlefield, these fighters had developed a new psychological perspective. Maybe their blasted limbs and shrapnel-spattered torsos didn't seem like such a big deal, after they had witnessed the grotesque deaths of so many including, very nearly, themselves. To Beecher, it seemed as if pain was affected, somehow, by perception. In 1955 he published a paper in the *Journal of the American Medical Association* on 'The Powerful Placebo'. Although it has since been demonstrated that Beecher's interpretation of the data contained within the study was, at best, highly careless, it would go on to affect the practice of medicine for ever.

Since the turn of the twenty-first century, placebo has been studied more than ever. It has been discovered that the anxiety dampener diazepam – also known as the multibillion-selling superhit Valium – only actually works when the patient knows that they are taking it. Experts such as psychiatrist Patrick Lemoine have asserted that between 35 and 40 per cent of *all dispensed medications* are actually 'impure placebos' – that is, they contain just enough genuine active ingredient so that doctors don't have to lie about what they have prescribed, but not enough that will have an effect. A 1998 study by researchers at the University of Hull found that up to 75 per cent of the effect of brand-name antidepressants such as Prozac might be down to placebo; Professor David Wootton of the University of York has written of one estimate that indicates that 'a third of the good done by modern medicine is attributable to the placebo effect'; while an acknowledged world expert, the University of Turin's Professor Fabrizio Benedetti, has gone so far as to state that 'Placebo is ruining the credibility of medicine.'

An individual's placebo response is dependent on their conditioning – their experience of similar past events – and on their perception – their expectation of what will happen. This is why expensively packaged brand-name headache pills work better than their supermarket equivalents, even when the cheap ones are identical in their ingredients; why zero per cent 'alcohol' can make you feel drunk; why completely fake drugs can benefit the symptoms of Parkinson's, arthritis, ulcers, hypertension, depression, panic disorders, sexual dysfunction and angina; why they can make athletes go faster, for longer and with less pain and convince asthma sufferers they're better, even when they're not. It is why four sugar pills work more effectively than two; why sham injections work better than sham capsules, capsules work better than pills, big pills work better than small pills; and why healing effects can be summoned from complicated but useless electrical equipment, pointless electrodes in the brain and an application of smelly brown paint. One study has even indicated that the *unspoken thoughts* of your doctor can alter the efficacy of pain-relief drugs.

More recent research suggests that the placebo effect might even work when we know that our medication is pharmacologically useless. In one small study, Professor Ted Kaptchuk of the Harvard Medical School arranged for thirty-seven patients with irritable bowel syndrome to take an inert pill, twice a day. Even though they were informed that the treatment worked only 'through the placebo effect', these participants reported almost double the improvement of a forty-three-strong control group, who received nothing. If this experiment proves satisfactorily replicable, it will suggest that even when we *know* a drug to be bogus, the very act of being treated, of swallowing something, of being caught in the ritual of science and authority and focused attention, can still trigger our body's various neurochemical healing tools.

Professor Nicholas Humphrey of the London School of Economics writes that the placebo response is 'a trick that has been played by human culture. The trick is to persuade sick people that they have a "licence" to get better, because they're in the hands of supposed specialists who know what's best for them and can offer practical help and reinforcements. And the reason this works is that it reassures people subconsciously . . . so health has improved because of a cultural subterfuge.'

Professor Humphrey eloquently describes the trick of placebo but he also unwittingly provides the most reasonable explanation for Swami Ramdev's healing powers that you might find. Of course, placebo effect is limited. It cannot shrink tumours, mend broken jaws or cure diabetes. But it can have remarkable effects on pain, for example, and inflammation, ulcers and anxiety. So when I ask myself why it is that reasonable, sceptical Aasha is convinced that her discovery of Swami Ramdev lifted her depression, I think I now know the answer.

Because it did.

4

'Two John Lennons'

One sunny Sunday afternoon in May, I was murdered. It was a vengeful lover that did it – or perhaps an elder brother, I can't exactly recall. I can, however, picture my attacker clearly. He was enormous and bald and had a hammer, with which he hit me several times in the throat. And then he killed the girl that I had been trying to protect; the girl I loved and who didn't love me back. My murderer had mistaken us for lovers. I had tried to stop him as he attacked the beautiful brown-eyed girl for whom I had longed for years. But he turned his hammer on me. And within two minutes, I was dead. Did I mention that this happened in Germany? In the fifteenth century? In a past life that I am, only now, reliving? This bloody and rather surprising memory has returned to me in the clinic of past-life regression (PLR) therapist, astrological counsellor, linguist and noted voice-over artiste Vered Kilstein.

Although she refuses to reveal her age, admitting only to being in her 'late, late forties', forty-nine-year-old Vered is prepared to admit that her work in the regression business stretches back for over a decade. It was the famous US expert Dolores Cannon who originally taught Vered the PLR method, and about its aim – which is to cure people of their physical and psychological maladies by hypnotising them and allowing their unconscious minds to drift into lives that they have lived before. 'This process can allow great shifts in a person's life,' Vered says. 'We can identify patterns of behaviour we've been repeating through lifetimes. Just seeing them is a release of that pattern.'

Vered's office sits in a row of high-end businesses, next to a plastic surgeon and a cosmetic dentist. Her front door is identifiable by the enormous stone Buddha's head that basks, bliss-eyed, beside it. Inside is a smart, calming room that is decorated with crystals, mystic books and a glass dodecahedron hanging off a bit of wood, which is on sale for £500. Vered herself is dressed in comfortably loose dark-green clothing and has hair that is perhaps best described as 'excited'. It is long and dark and has been pinned about her head with a complex arrangement of clips and gives the impression of being frozen, mid-explosion. It is, in fact, exactly the sort of hair you might expect of an individual who boasts of official qualifications in 'advanced past life regression', 'Jungian astrology' and 'de-hypnosis'. It is hair that has been told incredible secrets about the universe and is just bursting to tell you all about it.

'I'm very aware of myself as being an entity of consciousness across lifetimes,' she tells me, once I have sat down. 'I'm one of the millions who are here to help people move to a new consciousness.'

Before she puts her clients under, Vered likes to spend some time counselling them, exploring the issues that it is hoped the regression might solve. The issue that I am seeking help with concerns the invisible force known as the placebo effect. As with pranayama, I am wondering if it might also account for the perceived success – and therefore the belief in – dubious therapies such as this one? After all, there have been some incredible tests that have suggested that the benefits of *all* forms of therapy may be down to nothing more than placebo. For a 1979 study that has been widely replicated, academics at Vanderbilt University in Nashville took fifteen patients who had been complaining of depression and anxiety and sent them to see various psychotherapists. At the end of their treatment, they showed no more improvement than a control group who had been seen by fake therapists who had received no training whatsoever. Other academics have shown that, despite the fact that different varieties of therapy are based upon competing concepts of mind, it doesn't matter which one you choose to help you with your problems – they all have pretty much identical rates of outcome. Having controlled for the effect of what is known as 'regression to the mean' – a principle which, in this context, speaks to the tendency of our minds and bodies to heal anyway, whether we seek help or not – these studies really do offer evidence that placebo may be the secret of all talk-based cures.

For me, this was not a staggering discovery. I was barely out of my teens when I saw my first therapist, and fought to kill the particular unhappiness that was possessing me. Back then, I was at the mercy of invisible forces of a different kind: I was in love and it was all too much. Every Monday evening, I saw my counsellor, in a room not too different from this one. I would tell her stories about the week that had just passed and stories from my childhood. Stories in which I was never the hero. It didn't make me happy. After around two years, I stopped going. They wrote me a letter, urging me to recommence the sessions for my own 'safety'. And I would return, several years later. When I came back, it was invisible forces, yet again, that drove me there.

None of which is especially helpful for Vered at this moment. So instead I mention the other thing that has been on my mind of late: that grey veil of non-specific *wrongness* that I can't find a way to escape.

'I sometimes find life too difficult,' I say. 'I feel as if everyone's against me, like I'm doing something wrong all the time and I don't know what. It's exhausting. It gets too much.'

She purses her lips and makes some notes with a special pen that has a light inside it. It glows celestially down on her pad.

'Our thoughts create our reality,' she says. 'You seem to experience the world as aggressive and dog-eat-dog. A lot of people do.'

She makes some more notes. She frowns irritably, and then scribbles her special light pen frantically back and forth on her notebook. It appears to have run out of ink.

'Some people can deal with that world,' I say, ruefully. 'The go-getters, the businessmen.'

She puts the special light pen to one side and picks up a normal one.

'Do you feel there are people out there who achieve success without treading on people?' she asks. 'Are there any wealthy people who've achieved success in honourable ways?'

Suddenly, I feel embarrassed.

'No,' I begin. 'I mean, I don't think there are.' I pause for a moment. Vered looks at me, pleasantly. 'But . . .' I say. 'But . . . maybe that's a prejudice of mine. Because it's obviously not true.'

'It doesn't matter what the truth is. It's what you feel is the truth.' She makes another note and stops for a think before musing, 'There could be an issue here around worthiness.'

Before I am led to the couch, I ask Vered to explain what is about to happen. 'I don't really believe in linear time at all,' she tells me. 'We use terminology like "past", "present" and "future" because we're living in a three-dimensional reality.'

I probably look a bit confused.

'It's like a tuning,' she continues. 'Let's say that you and I, at this moment, are tuned into the same consensual reality. With this process, I can tune you to have a double focus.'

I think what she is saying is that we are all living lots of different lives at once. I just happen to be 'tuned in' to this one at the moment. During hypnosis, Vered is going to fiddle with my tunings and that will enable me to glimpse other lifetimes – or, as she prefers, 'time-space dimensions'.

'All I'm doing is helping you move into a deeply relaxed state,' she says, as I lie back on her massage table. 'Then I ask your subconscious, your "higher self", to take you to the most appropriate time-space. That can be in the past; that can be in the future.'

The hypnosis works surprisingly well. Vered asks me to picture a special place 'like a meadow'. I think, *Hmmmm, meadows* and imagine a warm, flower-filled pasture fringed with a dark, looming forest. 'This is the part of the mind we'll be working with today,' she says. 'The part that deals with images and memories. The part that's active at night. Can you see a cloud?'

'Yes.'

'Can you sit on it for me?'

I sit gingerly on the cloud.

'I'm on it.'

'This cloud can carry you over the mountains and over the valleys and over the oceans, drifting and floating, soft, protected, comfortable and safe, floating and drifting, drifting and floating, over the land, over the valleys, protected and safe. This cloud is like magic because not only can it carry you over the land and over the valley, it can also carry you back and back and back in time and space so I'm asking the cloud to move and carry you back and back and back in time and space, to another time, another place, where there's information we would like to find to help you.'

The cloud floats down and I see a cot. Vered asks if I have feet. She wants to know what age they are; what colour the cot is; what room I am in; what I can hear. But we don't get far in that life, so the cloud takes me to the 1920s, where I am speeding in a purple sports car following an argument. I crash into a tree. I am dead. Next up, it is fifteenth-century Germany and the murder with the hammer. And then I am in London's West End in the 1940s. This time, I am a woman. I am hurrying to work – behind a ticket-till in a Soho nightclub – when I am suddenly gripped by a powerful, almost psychic sensation that my husband, who is at war, has been killed. All night, at work with the girls on the cash desk, I keep my fears to myself – many of my friends really have been widowed by the Nazis. They are the ones deserving of sympathy, not me, with my silly, superstitious 'feeling'. Then it is 1945. I am in Portsmouth, watching my husband's boat disembark. He is not there. I run up to a young sailor on the gangplank. He insists that he knows nothing about my husband but I can tell by his sad, frightened eyes that he is lying. Then, in the same life, I am taken forward to the late 1960s. I am lying ill and heartbroken in the attic room of a boarding house. I have been living on baked beans straight from the tin. I am wearing my overcoat and stockings in bed to shield me from the devilish grey cold. I don't die so much as fade quietly away: after all, I have been dead ever since that rainy night in London's West End – dead of heart, dead of hope and possessed by that mysterious and melancholy knowledge.

'It was like opening the floodgates!' Vered declares, after I have come round. 'Your subconscious was so ready and ripe to allow the stories to rush out of your energy system. There was a beautiful, hungry flow. Especially in that last one. There was an intensity of emotion. I actually was getting chills in my spine. Your sadness was so overwhelming. But now – look at you! You look totally different!'

'How do I look?' I ask.

'Frisky and cheeky and alive!'

And the strange thing is, I feel it too: light and unburdened. And there is something else: a dangerous thrill at having been so intimate and vulnerable with Vered. Grinning helplessly, I ask her to recount some of her proudest successes. She tells me about a man who had persistent problems with a nerve pressing on a shoulder muscle. 'His was an almost textbook case,' she says. 'He told a very moving story of having been a knight in England. He'd come late to a meeting because he'd been cavorting in the forest with his beloved. His headdress wasn't on properly and the other members of the brotherhood of knights were furious. One of them hit him with a sword in that shoulder. We had to bring him to a place of forgiveness. He opened his arms, in armour, to the other knight and held him. And he never had that pain again.'

I ask Vered if it is her experience that a high number of clients turn out to have been heroes of some sort – knights or kings or celebrities.

'People who've had a profound effect on the world – the Cleopatras, the John Lennons – you could see them as sparks,' she explains. 'The soul has many sparks in it. So a lot of people may carry sparks of John Lennon.'

'Have you ever had a John Lennon?' I ask.

'I *have* had a John Lennon.' She thinks for a moment. 'Actually, I've had two John Lennons. And who's to argue with that? Others have had more mundane lives. One lady was a twig. During my first regression I experienced myself as a blade of wheat.'

'A blade of wheat?'

'I was literally a blade of wheat. It was a very, very moving experience. I was quite dry and yellow.'

'How did it feel to be a blade of wheat?'

'Vast and empty and alone.'

'And now you've experienced yourself as a blade of wheat, do you sometimes feel guilty eating wheat-based products?'

'I am totally wheat-intolerant!'

In the days following my regression, my thoughts keep returning to one innocuous comment of Vered's: 'The part of the mind we'll be working with today is the part that deals with images and memories. The part that's active at night.'

This, it seemed to me, was absolutely correct: my impression, as I lay on the couch, was that I was in a kind of dream state and that Vered was guiding me through it. What appeared to be happening was that my imagination, in its state of semi-consciousness, was not only producing images at Vered's command, but creating narratives: stories in which I played the leading role. They were vivid and memorable and emotionally compelling. Having learned about placebo, with its motors of expectation, ritual and the focused attention of authority figures, I could quite understand how PLR therapy could have beneficial effects for many clients.

Over the last few years, scientists have been studying the satisfied customers of counsellors much like Vered. For a 2007 paper, Maarten Peters and his team at Maastricht University told a cohort of PLR believers to recite a list of forty random names. Later, they were shown a new list that contained those same names again, but also a jumble of famous monickers and others they had not previously seen. Then they were asked, 'Which are the famous names?'

Compared to a control group of people with no belief in reincarnation, the PLR faithful were almost twice as likely to mistakenly conclude a name they had recited from the initial list was actually a celebrity. In other words, they had struggled to tell where the memory had come from. Did they know that person from out there in the world? Or was their name famil-iar because they'd seen it in that list earlier on? They had made what is known as a 'source-monitoring error'.

Psychologists at Harvard University led by Susan Clancy used a similar method to test the memories of people who believed they had experienced alien encounters. They re-cruited eleven people who 'remembered' being abducted, a further nine who believed they had been taken because of apparently mysterious symptoms, but couldn't recall anything specific, and a control group of thirteen. Both the alien groups were significantly more prone to make source-monitoring errors than the control. Although this result wasn't replicated in an attempt by UK researchers, led by Professor Chris French, he says, 'There have been quite a few studies since then, both published and unpublished, that support the idea that paranormal believers are more susceptible to errors in "reality monitoring", which is a general term used to refer to our ability to distinguish between events that take place in the outside world and those which are internally generated.'

This, it seems, is another striking unconscious effect – an invisible force that, like placebo, has the power to conjure false beliefs.

*

Before leaving Vered's clinic, I find another surprising con-nection between past lives and alien abductions. It happens when I ask her about the scientific basis for belief in past lives. She sighs, 'Oh, fifteen, twenty years ago I would've been very, very concerned about proving this within the empirical scien-tific realm, but now I'm in a place where I have no need to even go there. I don't even know what reality actually is.' Then she makes the link. 'But there are some amazing people that come from very, very conservative paradigms. Probably the person I most admire is Professor John Mack. He was a Harvard psychiatrist.'

It takes me a moment to place the name – then I remember. The heretic: the brave academic who was nearly thrown out by the Harvard Dean for studying areas that they had considered forbidden.

'John Mack did thirty years' research into the abduction experience and I admire the way he had the courage to write about his findings,' Vered tells me. 'He said, "These are very sane people. They're not psychotic or schizophrenic." Having said that, he thought that there were people who had abduction experiences who then became schizophrenic, because they couldn't deal with what happened to them.'

I don't know why, but I am rather disheartened to find that Mack had been embraced so wholeheartedly by Vered. Then, just before she closes the door behind me, she says something that will come to resonate for many months to come. 'I actually will suggest that when you're ready, you come for another session. Very often I don't, but I feel with you, we just touched the tip of the iceberg. I got the sense that your subconscious was saying, "Finally someone's going to acknowledge me! I've got things to say, I want to be heard!" It's like your conscious mind is so analytical, and your subconscious mind is saying, "What about me? I need to be addressed."'

And as it turns out, Vered Kilstein could not have been more right.

5

'Solidified, intensified, gross sensations'

A winter night in the Blue Mountains, 140 kilometres west, 1,065 metres above and many degrees of strangeness removed from the glories of Sydney, Australia. When the slow train that winds up the valley finally drops me off, I am surprised to discover that the compound I am heading for is a long hike out of the village of Blackheath. The road is narrow, empty and lined with tall trees that have become a gigantic wall of shifting shadows in the dark. I have never liked the Blue Mountains. Tourists seem to enjoy its views and its tearooms and its rainy, isolated towns, but whenever I have visited, it has always seemed to me to be an uneasy place, of bad memories, freezing mists and general human weirdness. You hear rumours of unkind people taking refuge among its epic forests, of suicides and dying walkers and long-ago massacres of Aboriginal tribes.

This is why, as I shuffle alone and slightly afraid up this unlit path, I am warmly anticipating the glad reception that will no doubt greet me when I arrive at the Vipassana Meditation Centre. Tonight, there is to be a welcome dinner and a get-to-know-you session and tomorrow will begin ten days of soothing and absolute silence. It is to be a retreat during which we will learn what is perhaps the world's most ancient form of Buddhist meditation. This, it is claimed, is the method perfected by Gotama the Buddha himself more than two and a half thousand years ago. Other varieties serve to focus the mind with the use of counting, mantras or visualisation, but these practices are dismissed by Vipassana teachers as crude 'concentration techniques'. Vipassana is not concerned with childish 'blissed-out states', but with moral and psychological purification. By observing 'the changing nature of body and mind' we will perform a 'deep, deep operation on the brain' and thereby 'experience the universal truths of impermanence, suffering and egolessness, penetrating ever subtler layers of mind until we reach the source of our misery'. And when we are done, in about a week and a half's time, happiness is going to follow us 'like a shadow'.

Unlike past-life regression, there is plenty of sound evidence for the efficacy of meditation. Like PLR, though, it does come shrink-wrapped with some strange beliefs – about reincarnation, for example, and karma and the universe consisting of thirty-one levels, one of which is inhabited solely by giants. Although it seemed to me that what tangible effects PLR had were likely to be a product of the placebo effect, I would be being unfair to Vered Kilstein if I was to dismiss *all* of her healing powers as accidental. She was, I thought, an analyst of genuine talent. When, after only a few minutes of talk, she asked me if there exist any wealthy people who have achieved success in honourable ways, I replied, 'No.' And in doing so I had revealed myself to hold an implicit belief that is every bit as prejudiced as the ones John Mackay had preached to the mild-mannered gay-haters of Gympie.

I experienced that nauseous, unmoored sensation again. There I had been, blithely assuming that the bigots were everywhere else and it had taken Vered less than ten minutes to demonstrate that I was one as well. Since meeting John Mackay, I have been mapping the wrongness of others, trying to track the trails of their cognitive errors back to some kind of source. But what about *my* beliefs, *my* wrongness? Doesn't the position I hold, with my Dictaphone and my notepad and my ability to always have the last word, depend on operating from a safe position of known sanity? Isn't that the assumption that I demand from you, the reader? Am I 'sane'? If so, why is it that when I look back upon my life I all too frequently see the actions of a man who is anything but? It was time, I realised, for some humility and reflection and pause. And that is what I am hoping to find here.

I turn the corner, off the road, and rush through the darkness of the car park towards the welcoming light of the canteen. The room is bare and dirty-white and crammed with trestle tables and men. All between their early twenties and late forties, every ethnicity seems to be represented. There are sporty ones with tracksuits, straight backs and gelled hair; slumping city types fresh from work with their collar buttons undone; solitary, lumpy, middle-aged guys; and an original hippy with orange trousers and a hat that is unnecessarily tall. And there is an atmosphere I wasn't expecting, too, of tension and of watching.

I walk to the registration desk, where a manager hands me a plastic ziplock bag. 'Place your wallet and your mobile phone in here.'

I do as he requests. He says, 'Do you have a mobile phone?'

'It's in the bag,' I reply.

'No other phones? You are forbidden from having a mobile phone on your person during the course.'

'It's in *there*!' I say.

He looks at the bag warily, then back at me. He hands me

a document, on which I have to provide details of my medical history and mental health and sign an agreement to say that I will abide by the 'code of discipline'. I brush my eye over it quickly. There is something about remaining silent for the duration of the ten-day course and blah, blah, blah something about not killing anyone.

I sign on the line and wander over to collect my meal. I sit, eyeing my food carefully. I can't work out exactly what it is – some lentil concoction.

'First time?' says the young man of Malaysian appearance sitting next to me.

I nod, forcing down a gobbet of green-grey sludge.

'Are you nervous?'

'No!' I say. 'Nervous?'

He nods at me, admiringly.

'Well, yeah,' he says. 'They say, by day eight you don't really feel the pain any more. It's like you're separate from it.'

I put down my spoon.

'*Pain?*'

But his attention has been taken by the arrival of a man at the front, who puts on an audio tape and instructs us all to listen. 'Apparently,' my dining partner just has time to add, 'most people don't last the first six days.'

From the cassette player, we hear a cold, aristocratic-sounding English voice. 'You must agree to abide by the code of discipline,' he says. 'You must make a decision now that you will remain here for ten days. You must not leave the compound. To leave early could be harmful.'

I glance around at the drab walls, the closed doors, the lentil pot, the drinking urns marked RAINWATER and the sign saying DO NOT FACE THE FEMALE SIDE. There is something about this place . . . it just doesn't seem like the blissful haven I was expecting. Vipassana, after all, is supposed to be an escape from the trials and tribulations of everyday life. I look down, worriedly, at the document I have just signed.

'WHAT VIPASSANA IS NOT: It is not an escape from the trials and tribulations of everyday life.'

Oh.

I turn the sheet and skim through the code of discipline. 'The foundation of the practice is sila – moral conduct. Sila provides a basis for the development of Samadhi – the concentration of the mind. Purification of the mind is achieved though panna – the wisdom of insight.'

I note that I have agreed to abstain from killing any living creature, from stealing, from sexual activity, from telling lies and from taking intoxicants. And it is not your standard silence that I will be observing, it is a 'Noble' one – which means 'silence of body, speech and mind. Any form of communication with fellow students, whether by gestures, sign language, written notes etc. is prohibited'.

I glance at the course timetable.

'Morning wake-up bell – 4 a.m.'

Oh.

When the tape has finished, we are led through the shadowy compound to a large pagoda, where we kneel in rows on the concrete floor. The lights are low and we are reduced to anonymous, hunched black forms in the gloom. I steal a forbidden glance to my right, where I can make out thirty or so other lumps – presumably, these are the women from whom we are strictly segregated. On a low stage in front of us, a man and woman are kneeling with closed eyes and perfect stillness, their heads just visible above huge blankets which cover their torsos and folded legs. It takes me a moment to work out what they are, whether they are real.

Once I have settled as best as I can on the dense rectangular cushion provided, a guttural moaning descends from above. It rolls and booms, magical and powerfully sacred, its impossible words petering out into long, drawn-out rumbles. When it is over, the voice – slow, rich, Indian-sounding – compels us to swear that we will stick to our promises ('I will refrain from sleeping on luxurious, warm, high, cosy beds') and warns us that we are here to perform a 'deep, deep operation on the brain'. 'This is not about breath control,' he says. 'That is a discipline called Pranayama. This is the complete opposite.' He advises us to 'Work hard, work seriously, work diligently, diligently, diligently.' Certain 'weak-minded' people sometimes ask to leave on day six, he adds, before instructing us to focus all our attention on the sensation of breath entering and leaving our nasal passages. There is no mention of pain, there is only the insinuation of it in my hips and knees and ankles. 'Resolve to remain for the entire period of the course, no matter what difficulties you may face,' he orders finally, before slipping into another spooky, primordial chant.

When it is over, it takes me a minute or so to rub the ache from my muscles and joints. I head off, careful not to look at any of the other men, and find my small white room. It contains nothing but some coat hooks and a narrow bed. I don't feel tired at all. What on earth can a lonely man *do* to fill a bit of time in a place such as this? I stand there, gazing through the open bathroom door at the roll of tissue paper hanging glumly from its holder in the low blue light.

No. It is forbidden.

I climb into my sleeping bag, zipping it all the way up so that my body is chastely separated from my hands and my right arm is distracted by the torch it is busy shining on some print-outs that I thought to bring with me. I read that this place was opened in 1983, is the second to be founded outside India and can accommodate a hundred and ten students, fifteen hundred of whom have their minds purified annually.

The voice that boomed about us from above was that of Vipassana's brain-excavator-in-chief Mr S. N. Goenka, who was born and raised in Myanmar. Once a wealthy businessman, he found the technique to be so wonderful that he devoted his life to it. Since settling in India in 1969, tens of thousands of people have completed the free courses that they offer at centres in Britain, Canada, the United States, New Zealand, France, Japan, Sri Lanka, Thailand and Nepal.

The next thing that I hear is a gong bonging outside my door. It is ten minutes before 4 a.m. I dress haphazardly and shuffle up the dark track towards the pagoda. Aware of other shufflers around me, I keep my head down and my silence noble. Collecting as many cushions and blue blankets as I can carry, I move to my allocated spot on the concrete floor. I lay down a large, thin foam block and put two rectangular ones on top of that and use it as a sort of seat. As I sit, I can feel the pain from last night returning. It settles itself grumpily into my lower back and body as I wait for the teachers to arrive and begin the lesson. Five minutes. Ten minutes. At twelve minutes, I glance furtively around the huge hall. Everyone has their eyes closed. They are sitting straight and still, breathing, concentrating. Oh *God*. There *are* no more instructions. We have started. This is *it*. Between now and lights-out, I realise, I have to spend nearly eleven hours thinking about my nose.

I feel as if I have been bolted inside a coffin. The impossible distances of the hours ahead induce the wooziness of vertigo. Time, petulantly demanding to be filled, turns on me, becoming both gaoler and gaol. The energy that my body has amassed for the day ahead swells, as if from a geyser. There is too much of it. There is nowhere for it to go. I begin to rock very gently back and forth, in the way I used to, to comfort myself when I was a child. I take a series of deep breaths before remembering that, according to Vipassana lore, this is not sufficiently 'real' and therefore forbidden. I gird my spine and rearrange my ankles, which have become numb and sore, and try to empty my brain. I sneak a look at my watch.

Three minutes have passed.

Two endless hours later, we are finally released by the sound of a mournful gong. Blinking into the freezing mountain dawn and moving carefully with painful legs, I can make the compound out for the first time. It is a complex of single-storey accommodation blocks linked by dirt paths. The pagoda is on one end, on the other is the canteen, which is set in a beautiful Japanese garden with winter-bare trees and a wooden walkway over a pond that is inhabited by koi and invisibly rib-bitting toads. I walk, obediently, with my head down, seeing only passing feet. I am starving.

I lift a tea-towel from a steel tray of toast. Each slice has only vague skid-marks of brown at its edges. I join the queue for the hot stuff and am spooned a ladle of grey porridge. A second helper adds a small dump of tinned prunes. It is a Buddhist breakfast indeed: entirely free of ambition, not desiring approval. I wander into the corner, swallow my food between mouthfuls of rainwater and wonder what I have got myself into. Why did I imagine it would be sensible for me to 'penetrate ever subtler layers of mind?' I am the *last* person . . . I mean, most of the time, when I think about my unconscious, I picture something angry, struggling to get out of a box.

And then, during the first afternoon session, something extraordinary happens. I catch glimpses of it, I think: hints and implications and strange visions that, I can only suppose, come from the mute parts of my brain – the secret regions that contain the invisible forces that produce belief in God and faith in aliens and the imagined biographies of all those John Lennons. I decide to pay strict attention. And in my struggling to stay awake during the process of going to sleep, I discover that I can watch my conscious mind falling into itself.

When my eyes have been shut for a few moments, my thoughts are just the usual nagging parade of recent memories and worries about the future. Then I start to notice the patterns behind my eyes. The longer I look, the more the monotone smudges take on crystal Technicolor form. Sometimes they appear to reflect what is going on externally; a tickle on my cheek will become a sliding wall of millions of laughing cartoon mouths. At other times they are gloopy, cut-out movies of whatever memory I am replaying. I will see faces from my past, images of places and irrelevant events. My internal monologue warps and switches. At one stage it turns French, saying, 'Continuez, continuez.' Then I hear a woman repeating 'Lamb's fry' in a whispering monotone. The breath deepens. I see a dog's back, a pair of female lips, an ocean wave and I assume this to be the outer atmospheres of the unconscious, because it is at this point that the devils of sleep add their enchanted cornflour and everything thickens into a proper dream. I see the start of a television commercial for a new Ford SUV. It spins on a revolving podium, its unlikely brand-name spelled out in glorious sparkling letters: MIND. My spine relaxes, my jaw sags and I snap awake just in time to save my body collapsing on to the concrete floor. Then I look at my watch – three or four minutes have usually passed – I shuffle my aching legs and begin it all again.

Over the next few days, the contents of these visions begin to worry me. The 4 a.m. wake-ups pull me out of some subterranean phase of sleep so abruptly that I can remember vivid details of my dream. One morning, I am walking in a red-light district when I see a girl who I know and love but who does not love me. 'I'm a prostitute,' she says. I ask her hopefully, 'Does that mean I can sleep with you?' She looks sorry for me, but resigned. 'I suppose so,' she sighs. 'It's £30.' During the mediation sessions, at the point just before I dissolve into unconsciousness and bolt myself awake, I begin to see the faces of women that I loved long ago. Sometimes it is a glimpse of a bare shoulder that I haven't seen for years. Sometimes it is a detail of a face or a length of hair. Sometimes they turn to face me and smile. Always, they make me feel sad.

My first memory of being in love is lying alone in a tent on a hot summer's day, feeling so scared and sick with dreadful emotion that I couldn't move. It was during a Scout camp. I was twelve years old and in the teeth of some invisible force that I couldn't understand. That was the beginning of what I would one day come to think of as my second madness.

*

The pain of Vipassana is not merely one of memory. As the ache of one day builds on top of the next, I begin to find it impossible to kneel upright for more than ten minutes. No matter how carefully I engineer my structure of cushions and blankets, I find no escape: the concrete beneath the padding always punches through. It begins, at the start of a session, as aches in my shins, ankles and the tops of my feet and then spreads and merges to form great tracts of agony, while my back – which, along with my head, must remain straight – hurts in such a way that I keep imagining that it has daggers of wood sticking out of it.

Equally unpleasant is the disorientation of being lost in time. The desperation for the session to end is such that I lose faith in my body-clock. After what seems to be a long period of shuffling and rubbing-away of pain, there always comes a terrible moment when I realise that half an age has passed and I have twice as long to go. *And it is still not over, and it is still not over, and it is still not over* . . . I come to hate the sound of the air conditioning shutting off at the beginning of a session, and the resulting silence. I dread it as if it is the closing of a prison door.

At the end of every day, a grainy video lesson from S. N. Goenka is projected on the back wall. Everything I am experiencing is, I think, to be expected. 'It would be wise to understand that what seems to be a problem is actually an indication the technique has started to work,' he says. 'The operation into the unconscious has begun and some of the pus has started to come out of the wound. Although the process is unpleasant, this is the only way to get rid of the pus; to remove the impurities.'

Following this, we are permitted to come to the front, to ask the resident course leader questions about our practice. One evening, I hear someone confess that he has been in so much pain that his entire body was shaking. He is advised to concentrate on his palms and the soles of his feet. Aside from that exchange, I have no way of gauging how I am getting along, comparatively speaking. I have come to understand, though, that I am annoying people. During rest periods, I keep accidentally sitting with my feet pointing towards the teacher, which is forbidden. My nostril keeps whistling, irritatingly. I fidget, and am ceaseless in my attempts at engineering an elaborate system of pulleys and ties with rolled-up blankets to ease the pressure from my painful limbs. Yesterday morning, I sneezed all over the back of the man in front of me. I am, I have decided, the worst meditator here.

The only person who rivals my position in the ranks of the abysmal is the man who walks about with his mouth wide open. When he kneels to meditate, I can see that he doesn't wear underpants. Sometimes he goes to sleep, right there in the pagoda. You can hear him snoring. The person nearest me, meanwhile, is the best practitioner of all. Of Indian appearance, he arrives early in immaculate sportswear and does stretching exercises in which he puts his ankle on a wall and bends his head to meet it. He is a vision of Zen perfection, whereas I am useless – fidgeting and sore and cowering from the ghosts of ancient lovers.

Sin, of course, requires other people. And so it is that, over these first few days, silence makes saints of us all. Without the ability to speak or even look at anyone, I begin to feel myself humming with a perfect, holy sila. Goenka is just about the only human we hear from and the sound of his voice begins to possess me, taking over my internal monologue. He has a habit of repeating various catchphrases and, at times, that is all I can hear in my head: 'Peeeerfect equanimity, peeeeerfect equanimity'; 'Aaaaasss it is, aaaaassss it is'; 'Work haaaaaard, work diligently; work seeerrrriously.' In my room, on a break one evening, I only realise that I have been chanting these mantras out loud when a deliberately loud cough in a neigh-bouring room breaks my trance. I stop, shocked at the realisation of what I have been doing, and notice a fly buzzing at my window. The urge is to kill it but – mindful of Goenka's teaching, that every time you break a rule you generate 'deep deep sankaras, deep deep sankaras and that means deep deep misery,' – I resolve not to. I have no idea what a deep deep sankara is, but I definitely do not like the sound of it. So I just sit there, on my bed, rocking gently back and forth. As I do, I become anxious about the rule that forbids writing anything down during the course. I have smuggled a pen and pad into my room in order to make notes. And then there is the $50 that I found in the coin pocket of my trousers. I'm not sup-posed to have money. Have I failed somehow? Will all this affect things?

My only relief comes during the periods following meals, when I wander the woods alone repeating Goenka's favourite lines over and over to myself, enjoying the noise of my voice and spooking the lizards, who I keep catching examining me coldly from behind dead leaves. I develop a routine. There is a little clearing that nobody else knows about. I go there after meals, just in time to let the rainwater that I drank earlier drain out through the fence, spraying into the bushland beyond. I remain in the clearing, walking in small circles, until it is time to drag myself reluctantly back into the pagoda.

The meditation gets no easier. I notice that there seems to be some sort of enforcement going on. One morning, I glance up to see a volunteer handing the pantless boy a piece of white paper. He is informed that the teacher wants to see him. When we return for the afternoon session, he is gone. All of his cushions have been cleared away. It is as if he had never been there at all.

Soon, we are issued new instructions. Instead of concentrating on the breath entering our noses, we are to focus on tiny sensations in our upper lip – 'biochemical changes' – and are forbidden from scratching our faces at all, even when we are not meditating. The difficulty, of course, is that as soon as one tickle realises you are letting him live, he whistles for all his friends. I picture them as tiny flies with multicoloured legs and fiery backs. I become practised at keeping five or six hanging off my face all at once. And then comes the day I have been worrying about. Then comes day six.

We were warned what would happen the evening before. Goenka informed us that we would henceforth be required to undertake three daily sessions of adhitthana – hour-long 'sittings of serious determination' – during which we are forbidden from moving at all. He went on to counsel us: 'It is very likely that one will encounter gross, solidified, intensified, unpleasant sensations. You have encountered such experiences in the past, but the habit pattern of your mind was to react. Now you're learning to observe without reacting. Pain exists, misery exists. Crying will not free anyone of misery.'

The first time I try, it hurts so much that I think I am going to vomit. Halfway through, someone walks out. I crack open my eyes to watch. I see only the material of his trousers as he passes – the places where his hands have been resting are wet. When it is finally over, and I push myself agonisingly to something approaching a standing position, I am almost surprised to see my legs looking normal. I was half expecting them to appear as they feel: swollen and twisted and bloody.

It takes several attempts before I am finally able to achieve the full hour without any movement at all. When it is over, I come around with a sense of soaring but vulnerable elation. I need hugs, congratulations. What I get is the teacher, unsmiling and distant at the front: 'Take rest for five minutes and start again.'

Lunch that day is edible. I think it is some kind of satay. I shovel in great, grateful spoonfuls of it, staring straight ahead, treat myself to two cups of rainwater and then head off to my clearing to be alone. On arrival, I begin urinating through the fence, as usual. Gazing blandly at my penis in action, I find myself repeating one of Goenka's favourite catchphrases in a loop: 'It rises, it passes away. It rises, it passes away.' Behind me, fearsomely close, there are footsteps. I freeze. They pause, then pass by. I take a moment. I zip up my fly and retrace the stranger's passage. I have no idea who that was, but there is no way that they did not hear me and see what I was doing. I go back to my room. There is another fly in there. I take my print-outs and roll them up and smash it *dead, dead, dead* against the window.

Over the last few days my tinnitus, which is always with me, has worsened dramatically. Last night, as I lay in bed, I could make out five separate tones, five mechanical cries, five blue lasers of searing din firing from somewhere in my cochleae to the deep interior of my brain. It is a sound that I cannot separate from the years that I was tortured by my own mind; the awful seasons of my second madness.

For reasons that still confuse me, from that day in the Scout tent to the evening when I began my relationship with the woman I would one day marry, I lived my life in a mode of almost constant romantic dereliction. Again and again, as a teenager I would fall into a powerful state of love that would always go unrequited. When, finally, I persuaded someone to go out with me, I was seventeen, she was fifteen, and we lasted for more than two years. I loved Jenny so much that I felt as if I couldn't physically contain it. I became fixated with boys she had kissed before me. I made her tell me about them, about what happened, about *what exactly happened*, over and over and over again. *So that's all that happened? Nothing else? Are you sure?* I became paranoid. Because she was so beautiful, you see, and every man out there was a dangerous rival and how could *I* compete with any of them? From waking to sleeping, I could think about almost nothing else. I became obsessed. I became intolerable.

And so, one afternoon in her bedroom, Jenny tried to leave me. I dug my thumbnail into my wrist with such force that it broke the skin. I had a kind of blackout. The next thing I knew, a lot of time had passed and my mother had arrived in her car. She had been called because I was incapable of catching the train home alone.

This behaviour, this madness, was to repeat itself again and again throughout my twenties. I was tormented by paranoia and jealousy and this feeling that love was an awful and gigantic magic, a black spider spinning rope around my heart until it crushed. I soon found that the most efficient tool for hammering the heart back together was the decibel. I came to rely on music. I found that it induced a kind of hypnotism through which the song and the hurt became indistinguishable. The music meshed with the pain and then it lifted it from me; it took its weight. And the louder the volume was, the greater the effect. Today, like a detuned radio picking up the distant echo of the big bang, I can still hear the noise of all that dead love. And I consider it only right and proper that it sounds like a scream.

In my dim and lonely room in the Blue Mountains, I sit on my bed, listening to my brain damage and examining the small scar on my wrist. I think about my madness and recall that my preferred band, during the Jenny years, were The Afghan Whigs – well known in the 1990s for exploring themes of guilt and self-loathing. I remember lines of one favourite song: 'Hear me now and don't forget, I'm not the man my actions would suggest. A little boy, I'm tied to you, I fell apart, that's what I always do.' Suddenly, it all seems relevant again.

I push myself to standing and leave the room. Walking to the pagoda, I am approached by one of the assistants. 'The teacher. He wants to see you.' He hands me a small white piece of paper. On it, written in pencil, are the words: WILLIAM STORR. I become frantic. This is it. I am going to be thrown out.

When my appointment finally arrives, I am let into a room to find the teacher waiting for me, lotus style, on a podium. I kneel obediently before him. He is British, perhaps sixty years old and has the expression of a man who has just discovered that all the raisins have been stolen from his muesli.

'I was just wondering how you were getting along,' he says.

'Fine . . .?' I say.

'You seemed a little distracted this morning.'

'Did I?' I say. 'I don't think I was.'

He says nothing. Then he smiles. I feel a powerful pressure beneath my eyes.

'I am finding all this – ' I look away – 'incredibly, incredibly hard.'

'A lot of people say it's the hardest thing they've ever done,' he says. 'Do you have anything you would like to ask me about your practice?'

I pause, nervously.

'These sankaras,' I say. 'I'm finding it . . . I just . . . How do you know they're *real*?'

'We have this obsession with proving everything in the West,' he says. 'The proof will be, does it work? Does it change your behaviour?'

'I also wanted to ask about this anapana – this process of pus coming out. Because things have been coming out. I thought I had forgotten about them a long time ago. It's been difficult for me.'

I look up at him hopefully.

'Those are *your* demons,' he says. 'You're going to have to deal with them.'

He nods again and smiles broadly. My time is over. I leave the room drunk with elation. In that moment, I really don't believe that I have ever been so happy. I felt as if I could follow my teacher anywhere.

*

It is the evening of day eight and she cannot stop crying. We have just had that terrifying moment, at the top of the adhitthana, the worst one, when the reassuring murmur of the air conditioning rattles and halts and gives way to a menacing silence and there is a woman at the back and she is sobbing and sobbing and sobbing. And we sit here, us compassionate Buddhists, and we listen to her falling apart. I should go to help. I would usually go to help. She is only over there. Why am I not moving? Because it is forbidden. There is nothing between me and her but empty air, no one to stop me but my teacher who is up there on the podium and yet, and yet . . .

After five minutes, she is taken outside. She starts screaming.

That night, after the curfew, I pull on my coat and my woolly hat and dig out my $50 and I walk back along the dark road until I reach the light of the town. I find a table for one in a crowded Italian restaurant and I eat a large meat-scattered pizza. I use some of the change to telephone my partner, Farrah, from a call-box on a Blackheath station platform. I tell her that I love her and that I want to come home. A taxi drops me back at the compound, a hundred yards from the entrance. I sneak along the bushes and tip-toe back to my room. By the time of the 4 a.m. gong the next morning, my perfectly maintained holy sila is lying spent, in a crusty tissue that I have tossed on the floor and in the swell of my dough-stuffed belly. *Bong! Bong! Bong!* I turn over in my bed. I go straight back to sleep.

*

'I'm not the man my actions would suggest.' The lyric is effective, because the plea it contains is not true. We are what we do, no matter how desperately we might try to insist otherwise. When I was a boy, despite my trying so hard, I would regularly steal – crisps from cupboards, pens from classmates, money from purses. My parents would catch me, again and again. I would have done anything not to be a thief any more. But something kept happening; some force would take me over. It was as if I would temporarily become another person. And then, the moment that the sin was committed, I would beg of myself, *'Why did you do it? Why can't you stop?* It was the same when

I was older and buried within the ropes of paranoid jealousy, and again when I developed an alcohol problem. During my years of madness, all of my actions suggested that I was a bad man; that I was, in some elementary way, *wrong*.

I felt these feelings return when I failed to assist the crying woman. It was as if I was not in control of my own actions. Throughout my battles in love, theft and drinking I came to know all too well that feeling of reason, of will, of better information, failing to influence my actions. And in the midst of it all, I always knew that I was being mad; inhuman. *That is not how humans behave.* We are in control of ourselves. We are not victim to convenient 'invisible forces'. We are one single person, with one set of values and one gallery of beliefs about the world. We are rational. We take in information about the world, we judge its worth and adjust our behaviour accordingly. We are agents of reason.

Everything we know about people tells us that this is so. It is this quality that elevates us above animals. It is the predicate upon which we evaluate the moral worth of other people. It is the basis of our legal system of judgement and punishment. But, as I kneeled in that pagoda, all of that seemed to break down. I wanted to go over there. But I didn't. I *couldn't*. Some devil overcame me. And I began to wonder, is it like this for other people?

Then I read about the events that spiralled from a single phone call to a Kentucky branch of McDonald's on 9 April 2004, and I discovered that it is.

*

It rang sometime after 5 p.m. and Donna Summers, the assistant manager, picked up the receiver. Straight away, she knew it was important. 'I'm a police officer. My name is Officer Scott,' said the caller. 'I've got McDonald's corporate on the

83

line here, and the store manager. We have reason to believe that one of your employees – you know: young, small, dark hair – has stolen the purse of a customer. Do you know who I'm talking about?'

Summers knew who it sounded like – Louise Ogborn, the pretty eighteen-year-old who was working to support her family, after her mother had fallen ill and lost her job. Officer Scott confirmed that it was indeed Louise and instructed Summers to fetch her, empty her pockets and confiscate her purse and car keys. She would then be required to perform a thorough search of the suspect. When Louise – a former Girl Scout and regular church attendee – was informed of what was about to happen, she began to cry. 'I didn't do anything wrong,' she said. 'I've been out there, working. You can ask anyone. I couldn't steal!' Summers instructed Louise to remove one item of clothing at a time and examined each as it was passed to her. When Louise was naked, Summers took the bagged garments outside, ready for collection by Officer Scott's colleagues, who would be arriving soon.

Louise had been detained, wearing nothing but a dirty apron, for more than an hour when Summers told the policeman that she had to get back to work. 'The problem is we're currently having Louise's home searched for drugs,' said Officer Scott. 'Do you have, say, a husband who can watch her for the time being?' Summers did not. But she did have a fiancé.

Soon afterwards, her partner Walter Nix Jr. – a churchgoer and youth basketball coach – dutifully arrived to guard Louise. Nix took the phone and followed Officer Scott's instructions precisely. He made Louise dance with her hands in the air to see if any stolen goods would 'shake out'. He made her open out her vaginal cavity with her fingers, in case anything was hidden in there. He made her turn around and touch her toes, stand on a desk. He made her kiss him, so he could check for

alcohol on her breath. When she refused to call Nix 'sir', Officer Scott demanded she be reprimanded with a spanking. Nix
did just that, for more than ten minutes. Two and a half hours
after the initial phone call, Louise was on her knees, tearfully
performing fellatio. It only occurred to any of them that
Officer Scott might be a hoaxer when the branch's fifty-eight-
year-old odd-job man became suspicious. He refused to take
over, despite being reassured by Summers that the whole
thing had been 'approved by corporate'.

Walter Nix Jr. has been described by a friend as 'a great
community guy . . . a great role model for kids' who 'had never
even had a ticket'. When he drove home, later that night, he
telephoned his best friend. He told him, 'I have done something terribly bad.'

This was not an isolated incident. Similar incidents had
been occurring for years. Ultimately, the scam was pulled in
more than seventy restaurants across the United States.

'The point is that this did not happen occasionally,' Philip
Zimbardo, Professor Emeritus of Psychology at Stanford University, tells me. 'If it happened just once or twice, you'd say,
"Gee, how dumb are these people? How gullible?." But it
worked most of the time. The scenario that was created was so
compelling that people got trapped in it.'

Zimbardo served as an expert witness in one of the trials
that related to the so-called 'strip-search scams'. He was called
because, back in the 1970s, he had become an authority on the
invisible processes which compel good people to do bad things
when he carried out a study that remains darkly notorious
among students of the psychology of evil. In an attempt to
examine the effects of prison life on ordinary individuals,
Zimbardo created a mock gaol on the grounds of his university and recruited the twelve most 'normal and healthy' young
men from a cohort of seventy-five applicants. 'We randomly

assigned half to be guards and half to be prisoners,' he recalls. 'I had to end it in six days because it was out of control. Normal healthy college students were having emotional breakdowns. Five of them had to be released early because of the cruelty and sadism of the guards towards them. It demonstrated in a powerful way how situations can overwhelm the best and the brightest.'

The Stanford Prison Experiment is a legendary study in the realm of what became known as 'situational psychology'. It helped to reveal a terrible flaw in the way humans typically view themselves. We tend to assume that we are in control of ourselves; that inner forces such as character and conscience captain our actions and define our behaviour. But the work of Zimbardo revealed the hitherto unimaginable power of outside forces to affect us. 'My research and the research of many social psychologists has demonstrated very powerfully that people can be corrupted into behaving in evil ways, often without the awareness of the power of the situation that they find themselves in.'

According to Zimbardo, there is a kind of recipe for creating evil. 'How did evil come about during the prison experiment?' he asks. 'It was people playing a role. You're assigned a role as a guard, a prisoner, a teacher or a military trainer – any of the roles we play in life. Although you start off thinking those roles are arbitrary and not the real you, as you live them, they become you. The second thing is the power of the group. You're a guard but you're in a cadre of other guards, so you put pressure on each other to be tough. Groups can have powerful influences on individual behaviour. Our guards were in uniform and they wore sunglasses to conceal their eyes. We call that de-individuation. You take away somebody's individuality. You make them anonymous. The next process is called dehumanisation, where you begin to think of other people as different from you and then as different from your kind and kin, and then as less than human. You take away their humanity. Once you do that, you can do anything to them – harm, hurt, torture, rape, kill. These were the basic processes operating in the abuses at Abu Ghraib prison in Iraq, which I studied at length because I was an expert witness for one of the guards.'

Of course, generating evil was not the intent of the Buddhists at the Vipassana centre in Blackheath. All the people who attend their courses do so voluntarily and a number of those present were returnees who evidently received huge benefit from their practice. When I look back upon my days there, I realise now that, psychologically speaking, I was unprepared, under-researched and weak. Really, I should never have gone. But listening to Zimbardo, I cannot help but wonder if situational forces had an accidental impact on my inability, despite myself, to stand up and attend to the screaming woman. Perhaps it was the role I had taken on, as serious, studious Buddhist; the pressure of the group to conform; the anonymity of the darkness and the prohibition against communicating with anyone. If so, I believe that there was also another powerful engine in play. When Louise Ogborn was asked in court why she did not simply leave the room in which she was being abused, she replied, 'I was scared, because they were a higher authority to me.' It was the same reason why her assistant manager and her fiancé behaved as they did. They believed that they were being instructed by someone senior to them.

'Excessive obedience' to authority is a flaw in humans that has been known to social psychologists for a long time. This is, in part, due to a set of extremely famous experiments carried out by Professor Stanley Milgram at Yale University in 1961, during which it was discovered that two-thirds of participants were prepared to deliver potentially fatal electric shocks to strangers, simply because they had been told to do so by a man in a white coat.

We are invisibly influenced not only by those in authority, but by those who populate our work and social lives. In a 2012 paper, neuroscientist Professor Chris Frith reviews a trove of well-replicated studies that demonstrate how, when we are in the company of others, we can automatically switch from 'I mode' to 'we mode'. 'We can't help taking into account the views of others,' he writes. 'The brain creates the illusion that we are all independent entities who make our own decisions. In reality there are powerful unconscious processes that embed us in the social world. We tend to imitate others and share their goals, knowledge and beliefs, but we are hardly aware of this. This is why strange narratives work best when they are shared by a group.'

In 1951, Professor Stanley Milgram's boss, Dr Solomon Asch, conducted a simple but devastating test that explored the ease by which we can let the opinions of others affect our own. He showed a hundred and twenty-three participants a series of two simple straight lines and asked them to say whether the first was longer, shorter or the same length as the second. Each person was in a group of eight and, initially, everything was easy. As you would expect, most of the time everyone gave the same answer: *the same, longer, shorter, shorter, longer, the same,* and so on. But gradually, for one person in the group, everything turned weird. Because all the others began to give answers that were wrong. What Asch wanted to know was this: when it came to their turn, what would that one person do? Go their own way and give the right answer? Or copy all the others?

This was a test to see if pressure from the group (who were actually actors) could compel individuals to defy the evidence of their own eyes. Asch found that around 70 per cent of people did just that. But as amazing and troubling as that finding was, it failed to answer a critical question: did the opinions of others simply intimidate the participant into calling it wrong? Or was his finding evidence of another, infinitely stranger hypothesis? That the group changed how the person actually perceived the line? It is a radical idea. Can it really be true? Can the view of the many actually *change the world* of the one?

It took the development of some advanced technologies before the tantalising beginnings of an answer could be sensed. In 2005, Dr Gregory Berns, a psychiatrist and neuroscientist at Emory University in Atlanta, conducted a test based on Asch's lines, which involved judging the 'sameness' of various objects while under social pressure to give the wrong answer. This time, however, the participants were in an fMRI scanner, having their brain activity recorded.

In Berns' study, people bowed to peer pressure 41 per cent of the time. But did they make a conscious decision to lie? Or were they somehow pressured into actually *seeing* the wrong answer? Were the situational forces so great that they altered their perception of reality? Checking the fMRI data, Berns' team found that in the moments prior to a participant giving their answer, there was no corresponding activity in areas of the brain that are associated with conscious decision-making. And yet there was corresponding activity in the area which is involved in the judging of spatial awareness. To put it simply, when these people were considering their response, it seemed as if they were not *analysing* their opinion, but *seeing* it.

Before we leap too high for our conclusion, it must be pointed out there has recently been a significant backlash, in scientific circles, against inappropriate levels of confidence in the kinds of things that fMRI scans can tell us. But if further research reinforces these findings, the implications will be weird and dazzling. In an interview with the *New York Times* after his paper was published, Berns said, 'We like to think that seeing is believing, but the study's findings show that seeing is believing what the group tells you to believe.' In his book *The Lucifer Effect*, Zimbardo writes that this test 'calls into question the nature of truth itself'.

*

They are everywhere, these invisible forces. In the effects of placebo, in the power of authority figures, in the awful physics of the situations that can push us silently into evil. What connects them seems to be some species of illusion. It tells us that these forces do not exist, that we are in control of who we are, what we do and how we think. Having spent ten days being menaced by proximity to my unconscious, it is clear where I now have to lead my search – to the place where all these forces work their magic, and where so many discomforting illusions are summoned. The brain.

6

'The invisible actor at the centre of the world'

The first surprise is how new brains are. The earth has existed for a full four and a half billion years, and yet it was just six hundred million years ago that the earliest of them began to form. It has taken almost all of that time for nature to work out the stunning mechanics of the human iteration. The first neurologically recognisable *Homo sapiens*, known as 'Mitochondrial Eve' (to whom, incredibly, genetic studies have shown that everyone on earth is related), lived only two hundred thousand years ago. Nobody knows what caused the human brain to accelerate its form and function until it was so dramatically in advance of our fellow creatures, but for some reason we gained an oversized prefrontal cortex, which enabled us to strategise, socialise and make lateral associations.

We left our sunny Eden in east Africa sixty thousand years ago and began colonising the world. Then, around forty thousand years ago, the next evolutionary mystery took place. For reasons that remain unclear, there was a sudden explosion in creativity that saw paintings springing up on cave walls from Australia to Europe and the crafting of intricate articles such as rope, oil lamps, drills and sewing needles as far away as

Siberia. We began painting our bodies, wearing jewellery and burying our dead.

It is for behaviours such as these that we humans like to flatter ourselves that we are made of a different metaphysical stuff than the animals. But our DNA does not lie. Even today, we remain a specific variety of African ape that evolved in the Great Rift Valley. The last survivors of the hominins, we once lived alongside at least four other varieties of nearly-humans. In terms of time alone, though, we are nowhere near the most successful hominin to have inhabited the planet. We might have been here for two hundred thousand years, but some of our cousins lived for more than two million.

From the confidence that is exuded by some neuroscientists, it might be easy to assume that the riddles of the brain have mostly been solved. But that is not so. How does it generate thoughts? How, exactly, does it store memories? How does it create that sensation of oneness, of coalescence, of having an identity, a narrative purpose, a soul? Although there are plenty of theories, the answers to all of these questions remain far from clear. In truth, this most magical of organs remains deeply mysterious.

It begins its formation in the embryo as a tiny fluid-filled tube. Pinched off in the centre as the foetus develops, one end of the sac becomes the spinal cord, while on the other grows – at the rate of two hundred and fifty thousand cells a minute – a piece of organic technology that is so advanced, and yet so wondrously strange, that nothing in the known universe is comparable. Built from what has been described by neuroscientist Professor David Eagleman as 'an alien kind of computational material', it is pink, has the texture of almost-set jelly, consumes 20 per cent of our bodily energy and is said to be capable of receiving millions of pieces of information at any given moment.

It might weigh little over a kilogram but, taken on its own scale, the brain is unimaginably vast. One cubic millimetre contains between twenty and twenty-five thousand neurons. It has eighty-six billion of these cells, and each one is as complex as a city and is in contact with ten thousand other neurons just like it. Within just one cubic centimetre of brain tissue, there is the same number of connections as there are stars in the Milky Way. Your brain contains a hundred trillion of them. Information in the form of electricity and chemicals flows around these paths in great forking trails and in circuits and feedback loops and fantastical storms of activity that bloom to life at speeds of up to a hundred and twenty metres per second. According to the neuroscientist V. S. Ramachandran, 'The number of permutations and combinations of activity that are theoretically possible exceeds the number of elementary particles in the universe.' And yet, he continues, 'We know so little about it that even a child's questions should be seriously entertained.'

Those still desperate for evidence that we are of a special category of being should start their hunt for clues in early childhood. Other mammals give birth to their young when their brains have developed enough that they can control their own body. But not us. We arrive into life, in the words of anthropologist Clifford Geertz, as an 'unfinished animal'. Our brains are so monstrously oversized that we are born about two years prematurely, at the point at which our skulls can still be squeezed agonisingly, bloodily and dangerously through a birth canal. We are then effectively useless for years, relying entirely upon a parent for survival until the gigantic computational device that sits on our neck is finally capable of running the body it is attached to.

Between the ages of zero and two, babies create around 1.8 million synapses per second. Throughout childhood, the brain is extraordinarily alive with the activity of warring neurons, fighting for connection space across its epic territories. Although it never stops changing, it remains in this heightened learning phase until late adolescence. In his book *Brain and Culture* Professor Bruce E. Wexler writes that 'During the first part of life, the brain and mind are highly plastic, require sensory input to grow and develop, and shape themselves to the major recurring features of their environment. By early adulthood, the mind and brain have a diminished ability to change those structures . . . much of the [brain] activity is devoted to making the environment conform to the established structures.'

It may have passed you by as you read it, just now, but what that rather formal, rather dry sentence is saying is amazing. It is the keyhole through which the first, fuzzy outlines of my answer can be spied. Although the context is neurological rather than psychological, it actually speaks to the whole picture: to the brain's form and the mind's function. To me, Wexler's words are an ancient spell, a revelation of long-hidden magic. They contain the essence of the brain's sly modus operandi – the organising principle behind the worrying fact that a central function of this wondrous machine is to deceive you. By the time you have reached adulthood, your brain has decided how the world works – how a table looks and feels, how liquids and authority figures behave, how scary are rats. It has made countless billions of little insights and decisions. It has made its mind up. From then on in, its treatment of any new information that runs counter to those views can sometimes be brutal. Your brain is surprisingly reluctant to change its mind. Rather than going through the difficulties involved in rearranging itself to reflect the truth, it often prefers to fool you. So it distorts. It forgets. It projects. It lies.

These untrustworthy processes run far deeper than the

realms of opinion and belief. Your mind contains internal models of everything, from the physical geography of the room you are sitting in to the rights and wrongs of the conflict in the Middle East. The brain loves its models. It guards them like a bitter curmudgeon, making adjustments only when it has to. It uses these models as a shortcut, in order to more easily conjure an illusion of a sane, whole and coherent reality. This illusion is so complete that we don't believe it is one. It is hard to underplay the brilliance of this lie: up to 90 per cent of what you are seeing right now is constructed from your memories.

Practitioners of lucid dreaming know how convincing these mental models of reality are. When writer Jeff Warren was trained to 'wake up' during a dream by expert Dr Stephen LaBerge of Stanford University, his mind's projection of the room that he had gone to bed in was so accurate he didn't realise that he was still asleep. 'It was my room, seamlessly modelled by my brain,' he writes in *Head Trip*. 'I could see the outlines of furniture from under the bottom edge of the mask, feel my bed underneath me, hear Kelly's breathing – everything was perfect. It even smelled like my room. At that moment there was no recognisable difference between my waking and my dreaming perception'. This experience is so common in students of lucid dreaming that Dr LaBerge teaches a variety of 'reality tricks' – such as looking at a clock's second hand to see if it is behaving predictably – to enable them to check if their eyes are open or closed. We all have these models. When we dream, and it feels real, it is because our models of reality are so detailed and textured and perfect it might as well be. It is all there: the sights, the noises, the textures and touches and scents. Our brains contain worlds. And it is mostly those worlds that we are seeing when we are awake.

If you are thinking that you must be misunderstanding all

this, because it is just too spooky, too grotesque, too much like a disturbing science-fiction film, then I am sorry to tell you that you are not. The truth really is this weird. We think of our eyes as open windows and our ears as empty tubes. We experience the *out-there* as if we are a tiny homunculus gazing from holes in our heads at a world that is flooded with light, music and colour. But this is not true. The things that you are seeing *right now* are not *out there* in front of you, but *inside your head*, being reconstructed in more than thirty sites across your brain. The light is not out there. The objects are not out there. The music is not out there. A violin has no sound without a brain to process it; a rose petal has no colour. It is all a re-creation. A vision. A useful guess about what the world might look like, that is built well enough that we are able to negotiate it successfully.

Of course, real versions of everything *are* out there – but not the versions that you are seeing. Those are merely your brain's impressions of how the world appears. Our eyes, skin, tongue and ears receive information, not as pictures, touches, tastes or notes, but as pulses of electricity. That is all we *really* know – the pulses. Your brain translates those pulses into a re-creation of reality that it can sensibly interact with. It is not known how all this disparate electrical data coalesces into the experience we all have of viewing some kind of inner television screen – but we do know that there is no television in your head; no single area, that is, which all the neural wiring leads to. We also know that the brain has a great many sleights and shortcuts and mirage-generating powers in its arsenal, and that it somehow manages to bring them together into one central, magisterial illusion: that reality and your place within it is simple, understandable and clear. Under its spell, you have become, in the words of neuroscientist Professor Chris Frith, 'the invisible actor at the centre of the world'.

96

We naturally assume that our senses are our principal source of information about what is happening at any given moment. They are not. They are mere fact-checkers. Consider your face as if it is a machine. There is barely a space on its surface that is not dedicated to the analysis of new information. When our environment is as we expect it to be, we mosey through life, wandering peacefully through the neurological illusion, thinking about the weather or the shops or the fight we have just had with our Internet provider. But as soon as we detect something unexpected, we become alert. The brain, concerned that its illusion might break down, is ever watchful for surprises. It directs the powers of the face and mind at the disturbance. Anxious to discover its source, so that it can integrate whatever it is into its projection of reality, it moves your neck so that you can focus squarely on the weirdness. Your skin, eyes, ears and nose are pointed towards it, your train of thought is interrupted as you seek to answer the question, 'What *is* that?'

Even when your surroundings contain no surprises, your brain is continually checking its guesses against what your senses are telling it. It uses them to make running adjustments to its projection, ensuring greater accuracy now and in the future. But because the brain is so heavily reliant upon what it already knows, it is difficult for us to experience things we have no prior knowledge of. In a startling 1974 experiment that tested these principles, cats were raised from birth in an environment where they only ever saw vertical lines. When a horizontal bar was placed in their cage, they walked straight into it. Until that painful point of learning, their visual cortices had never received any information about horizontal lines, and so to them the bars were invisible.

Humans, too, suffer when their brains have been deprived of information. When deaf people are successfully operated upon they can initially make no sense at all of the novel experience of hearing. Their brains have not yet learned how to translate all those new electrical pulses into their model of the world. Scott Krepel, who was fitted with a cochlear implant, enabling him to hear for the first time, told a reporter from the US radio show *This American Life*, 'It didn't feel like hearing; it felt more like a vibration in my whole body. I was sitting there and nothing was happening, except for like a little thing that was tingling throughout my body. But eventually, after a while, the vibrations localised to my ears. I didn't really know that it was sound at first. And eventually I came to realise, "Wait a minute, this must be it!" . . . I couldn't understand any of the sounds. It was just all noise.' After five years, his brain had still not caught up. Krepel abandoned his implant, preferring the safety and sanity of the silent world in which he had grown up.

As you might expect, it takes time for the brain to take its multi-sensory barrage of pulses and to process it into its grand illusion. Estimates vary, but the most dramatic that I came across had it that we are all living half a second in the past. The 'now' we appear to be experiencing is another illusion: a prediction that the brain calculates once it has received the already slightly out-of-date information from the senses. If a ball is thrown into the air, your brain predicts it will be slightly closer by the time you 'see' it and therefore 'moves' it to the correct place, enabling you to catch it.

Vision is of such importance to the construction of your virtual realm that one-third of the human brain is devoted to its processing. And yet your eyes themselves are nowhere near as good as you have been led to assume. Hold out your arm and look at your thumbnail. That is about the extent to which your sight is clear, coloured and detailed. Beyond ten degrees from this vivid centre, your vision is blurred, black and white and only able to detect potentially important information. It achieves the effect of showing you a detailed whole by building it up surreptitiously. Your eye darts at high speed around the scene that you are in and takes multiple high-definition snapshots of it. You are fooled into thinking your gaze is steady, still and under your conscious control but, in fact, these 'saccades' – which are the fastest movements made by the human body – happen up to five times per second. They are sensitive to change, patterns, contexts and textures – anything that might trigger a need for the brain to update its best-guess impression of the world. From what it shows you, it edits out the jarring motion of these saccades, as well as the blinks that happen every five seconds (it has been calculated that blinking makes us blind for a total of four hours per day). It also overlays a series of magnificent special effects, including colour and movement and filling in your blind spot and adding depth, generating a 3D version of what, writes neuroscientist David Eagleman in his book *Incognito*, is only '2.5D at best'.

The world appears to be coloured because, in the back of each eye, in an area of just one square millimetre, we have three varieties of cone that interpret incoming visual information as either red, blue or green. Every colour you will ever see is a blend of this triumvirate of basics. We assume that this is simply what the world looks like but, yet again, this is a lie. The atoms that make everything up have no colour. There are no colours inside the brain. Light waves are not coloured. So where are colours? They are another illusion, created in specific cells in the brain that have been located, so I am informed, in the visual area of the striate cortex V4. A fish such as a skate has no colour cones at all and so experiences the world in black and white. If you now feel superior to the skate and assume that you, the special human, have access to the full and fantastic panoply of shades that make up true reality, then I am afraid that I have to tell you that some birds and insects have four, five or even six colour receptors, compared to our sorry three. Their experience of the multi-multi-multi-coloured world is impossible for any human to even begin to imagine.

Because sight is of such pre-eminent importance to us, we assume that vision is the best way of negotiating the world. But this, too, is not objectively true. Dogs live, principally, in a world of smells; moles in a world of touch, bats in a world of noise and knifefish in a world of electricity. Their experiences of reality are specialised for their particular environments and survival needs, their perceptions profoundly different and no less valid than ours.

According to Professor Eagleman, 'Our brain is aware of very little of what is out there'. Its preoccupation is with presenting to us – and drawing our attention to – the things that might be important for our well-being. Our ears are only capable of hearing a small number of the sounds that are actually present in our environment; our eyes are blind to whole rainbows of visible light – less than a ten-trillionth of the spectrum is available to us. Right now, mobile-phone signals, soap operas, radio-broadcasted music and who knows what else are everywhere: in front of you, above your head, *inside* you. And yet you don't see them or hear them, because – much like a black-and-white television is blind to blue skies and green seas – you lack the equipment. In a sense, brains operate on a 'need to know' basis only. In *Making up the Mind*, Professor Frith describes the inexact and humble panorama that we inhabit as having a specific use: it is, he says, a 'map of signs about future possibilities'.

The world that you experience as objectively real is your own personal model of reality, and your brain tends to assume that everything new that you experience coheres to that model.

There are good reasons for this. It hardly needs to be pointed out that if the brain really is receiving millions of pieces of information (Professor Timothy D. Wilson of the University of Virginia quotes a figure of over eleven million, whilst in his book *Straw Dogs*, Professor John Gray has it at 'perhaps 14 million bits of information per second'), we are consciously aware of nowhere near that amount. As V. S. Ramachandran writes, 'The brain must have some way of sifting through this superabundance of detail.'

What are you aware of as you read this? The feeling of your back on the chair, an early rumble of hunger from your belly, the sound of nearby traffic, the fact that you need to get off the train at the next stop? It is not nearly eleven million things. Indeed, it is thought that the maximum number of points of information we are able to appreciate consciously at any one time is less than forty. One part of this sifting process involves the matching of incoming information with the personal belief system that you have about the world. Any information that fits is incorporated effortlessly into your experience of now. But what of the information that runs counter to your belief system? What then? 'One option is to revise your story and create a new model about the world and about yourself,' writes Ramachandran. 'The problem is that if you did this for every little piece of threatening information, your behaviour would soon become chaotic and unstable. You would go mad.' So instead we minimise, distort, rationalise and even hallucinate our way into disregarding this information. And the cost we pay for our feeling of sensible, sane and simple coherence? We lie to ourselves.

It is possible to catch the liar out. The brain may excel at making accurate predictions about what should be out there, but it sometimes gets it wrong. People who lose portions of their sight have been known to see cartoon characters, loved ones and historical characters romping across their blind spots, as their brains frantically try to guess at what should be in the darkened gaps. Ten per cent of elderly people who suffer from severe blindness or deafness experience hallucinations due to similar processes. Some stroke patients live, at least temporarily, in a state of complete psychological denial of their paralysis. A Dr Clarence W. Olsen has spoken of a patient who lost sensation and movement in her left side. Because her numb limbs now felt and behaved as if they belonged to someone else, her mind explained them in exactly this way – by telling her they actually belonged to someone else. Olsen has recounted, 'When she was shown that the limbs were attached to her, she said, "But my eyes and my feelings don't agree, and I must believe my feelings."' In his book *Altered Egos*, Dr Todd E. Feinberg writes of this and similar patients, including a forty-eight-year-old woman who, when asked about her numb side, grumbled, 'That's an old man. He stays in bed all the time.'

It is important to underline that none of these people are 'mad'. Their brains have simply failed to adjust to their catastrophic new realities. In most cases of this sort of denial, it takes between two and three weeks for their unpleasant situation to be absorbed into their working perception. Experiments on healthy individuals have revealed similar mistakes. Academics at the University of Wisconsin made an audio recording of a predictable sentence – 'The bill was passed by both houses of the legislature' – but covered a portion of it with static. Almost everyone who heard it said, 'Yes, I heard the words and the white noise.' But when asked where the static had actually taken place, a large proportion had no idea at all. Despite the fact that they weren't all present, they had *heard all the words*. Their brain had predicted what they would be, and produced them. It had lied. We tend to see and hear what we expect to see and hear, not necessarily what is there.

Other incredible insights come from people who have had body parts amputated and, because their brains have not correctly acknowledged the loss, continue to experience their presence as 'phantom limbs'. In his work, V. S. Ramachandran has come across tennis players 'catching' balls with phantom arms, women experiencing phantom breasts following a full mastectomy, phantom pain in a phantom appendix and even phantom erections in phantom penises.

The human realm, though, is not simply one of things that we see, sounds that we hear and vanished appendixes that feel sore. The University of Virginia's Professor Jonathan Haidt writes in *The Happiness Hypothesis* that our world is 'not really one made of rocks, trees and physical objects; it is a world of insults, opportunities, status symbols, betrayals, saints and sinners'. It is one of beliefs.

One result of this simple fact is that vast differences exist in the behaviours of human brains around the world. Some cultures, for example, experience emotions that are unique. In New Guinea, the Gururumba men have a mental state that is known as 'being a wild pig' in which they run around stealing things and attacking passers-by. Dylan Evans of the University of Bath writes that this emotion 'is seen as an unwelcome but involuntary event, so people suffering from it are given special consideration which includes relief from financial obligations'. He adds, 'The fact that different cultures can produce human beings with different emotional repertoires is testimony to the remarkable plasticity of the human mind . . . if your culture teaches you that there is an emotion called "being a wild pig" then the chances are you will experience this emotion.'

Many South Koreans are terrified of 'fan death', which they believe is a serious risk if you sleep in the same room as an electric fan. Panicked news reports about fan death are common during the summer and fans are sold with timer switches that automatically shut off after a preset time. In Iceland – a country that boasts a 100 per cent literacy rate – contractors carrying out huge public works, such as road building, have to consult with specialists to ensure that they bypass the homes of fairies and gnomes, while builders hire 'elf-spotters' to scope the land before work begins on a new house. In China people suffer from a condition known as 'koro' in which they feel their sexual organs – penises in men and vulvas and nipples in women – retracting into their bodies. They have a family member hold their shrinking part in place, all day and all night, for as long as it takes until the koro threat passes.

Even the nature of a state such as drunkenness is defined by where you come from. In the UK, Australia and the US we believe that alcohol is a disinhibitor, so we become flirtatious and aggressive and inadvisably honest when drunk – even when all we have had is a placebo cocktail. In Latin and Mediterranean countries, meanwhile, it is believed to encourage peacefulness and friendliness – and, for those civilised people, this is precisely what it does. 'The effects of alcohol on behaviour are determined by cultural rules and norms, not by the chemical effect of ethanol,' writes the anthropologist Kate Fox in her book *Watching the English*. 'The basic fact has been proved time and time again. When people think they are drinking alcohol, they behave according to their cultural beliefs about the behavioural effects of alcohol.'

It should not come as a surprise to learn that a good deal of our often faulty beliefs and tendencies come as a result of us being highly tribal. We remain, today, modern creatures with prehistoric thinking equipment. Which perhaps offers a clue as to why it was that – as Louise Ogborn discovered when she was compelled to strip in that McDonald's back office – we still have an instinct for obedience to authority. Studies by researchers in Switzerland have found that we are also programmed to punish, and to take pleasure in revenge. We have an additional, irresistible urge to divide the world into 'us' and 'them'. A study by three major US universities found that between 90 and 95 per cent of people have an unconscious racial prejudice. Others have observed that the only thing necessary to trigger tribal behaviour in humans is the creation of two completely arbitrary groups. Leave them alone in a room and watch it all begin: the people we identify with automatically become a part of our 'in' group. A series of unconscious biases flares up around then – haloes surround 'our' people, which magnify their virtues and minimise their faults. A dark, opposing magic happens to our view of those who are on the 'out'. But as damaging as it can be, we need prejudice. It is the shape of our models, the starting point for our guesses about the world.

When our brains are told things that contradict their models, we often enter a state known as 'cognitive dissonance'. In their book *Mistakes Were Made (But Not By Me)* social psychologists Carol Tavris and Elliot Aronson describe this as 'a state of tension that occurs whenever a person holds two cognitions (ideas, attitudes, beliefs, opinions) that are inconsistent, such as "smoking is a dumb thing to do because it could kill me" and "I smoke two packs a day". Dissonance produces mental discomfort, ranging from minor pangs to deep anguish; people don't rest easy until they find a way to reduce it.' As a result of dissonance, they say, 'most people, when directly confronted with proof that they are wrong, do not change their point of view or course of action but justify it even more tenaciously.'

We all know it. It is that feeling of tortuous thickness, of psychological scrap and spit, of internal obsession. We find ourselves chewing over something that we have done or heard or experienced. It can last for hours, days or sometimes longer. That upstairs agony, that bickering between the warring voices in our head – that is what it feels like to have your brain taking apart an experience and rearranging it in such a way that it doesn't have to rebuild its models. It doesn't stop until it has convinced you that *you* were right; until your hero status has been restored, rebuilt. It is the feeling of you lying to yourself.

It is a process that has been widely studied since the 1950s, when its existence was first hypothesised by Leon Festinger of Stanford University. One of the most egregious methods the brain uses to avoid the constipation of dissonance is with a thought-flaw known as confirmation bias. The pattern, which you may also recognise, goes like this. When confronted by a new fact, we first feel an instantaneous, emotional hunch. It is a raw instinct for whether the fact is right or wrong and it pulls us helplessly in the direction of an opinion. Then we look for evidence that supports our hunch. The moment we find some, we think 'Aha!' and happily conclude that we are, indeed, correct. The thinking then ceases.

Psychologists know this as the 'makes sense stopping rule'. We ignore anything that runs counter to our hunch, grab for the first thing that matches, think, *Yep that makes sense*, and then we rest, satisfied by the peerless powers of our fantastic wisdom. Perhaps the most embarrassing aspect of confirmation bias is the fact that we mistake the process of searching for favourable evidence as a fair survey of both sides of the argument.

Throughout the last few decades, a huge number of entertaining studies have been carried out that have revealed just how devious this delusion is. One of the neatest looked at unconscious sexism, and how the brain justified its secret, unpleasant prejudices to its owner. Participants were asked to consider candidates for the role of police chief. They had a choice: would a 'streetwise' man or a 'formally educated' woman be better suited to the job? The majority chose the man. When asked why, they said that they had thought carefully about this, and decided that it would be most useful for a police chief to be streetwise.

For a second group, researchers switched the genders. This time, the male candidate was 'formally educated' and the female was 'streetwise'. The majority chose the man. When asked why, they said that they had thought carefully about this, and decided that it would be most useful for a police chief to be formally educated. It is a discomforting thing, reading of these ordinary men and women, who presumably consider themselves to be kind and rational and fair, operating in such an unknowingly prejudiced manner. The study suggests that they had no idea why they believe what they believe, why they say what they say.

We deal with dissonant information using a variety of yet more devious cognitive stunts. Psychologist Deanna Kuhn found that participants in a pseudo-murder jury quickly compose their own story of *what I think happened* and then proceed, as they survey the evidence, to pay attention only to the facts that fit their narrative. In an earlier study, Kuhn found that the brain has a tendency to simply forget things that it considers contradictory to its models. But perhaps the most breathtaking trick of all is in how exposure to the opposing side of any argument often makes us *even more biased* towards our own beliefs.

Studies have shown that we tend to subject the evidence of our foes to much closer scrutiny than we use on our own. One had people reading two arguments about the death penalty – a first report that conflicted with their opinions and a second that agreed. Most of the participants concluded that the essay that agreed with them was a 'highly competent piece of work'. As for the document they disagreed with, they examined it with the eye of a prosecution lawyer until they found genuine flaws and magnified them, using even minor issues as the basis for disregarding the entire thing. As Thomas Gilovich writes in *How We Know What Isn't So*, 'Exposure to a mixed body of evidence made both sides even more convinced of the fundamental soundness of their original beliefs.' Confirmation bias is profoundly human and it is appalling. When new information leads to an increase in ignorance, it is the opposite of learning, the death of wisdom.

Recent studies have revealed even more unpleasant truths. In 2004, clinical psychologist Drew Westen and his colleagues used the bitter US election milieu to undertake an examination of the seductive power of the lies that we all tell ourselves. They took fifteen intelligent, educated Democrat voters and fifteen equally able Republicans and slid each into a brain scanner while presenting them with six pieces of 'information' (some made up by the psychologists) about John Kerry and George Bush. Each slide of information showed clear inconsistencies between the politician's words and deeds. They saw one, for example, that quoted John Kerry telling an anti-war constituent, 'I share your concerns. I voted in favour of a resolution that would have insisted that economic sanctions be given more time to work.' The next slide had Kerry writing to another voter, a week later: 'Thank you for expressing your support for the Iraqi invasion. From the outset, I have strongly and unequivocally supported President Bush's response to the crisis.' Each of the statements was written in such a way that any dispassionate observer would rate both politicians as duplicitous. Westen wanted to find out exactly *how* the brains of these ordinary voters dealt with this dissonant information.

After they had read the slides, the participants were asked to rate each politician's level of inconsistency on a scale of one to four. As Westen writes in 'The Political Brain', 'They didn't disappoint us. They had no trouble seeing the contradictions for the opposition candidate, rating his inconsistencies close to a four. For their own candidate, however, ratings averaged closer to two, indicating minimal contradiction.'

But that was just the beginning. Westen also had his scans to consult. He wanted to know exactly what happened on the neurological level when new data arrived that conflicted with internal models; when their minds were blasted into a state of cognitive dissonance. As he expected, the unpleasant emotion was soothed away quickly. 'But the political brain also did something we didn't predict,' he writes. 'Once participants had found a way to reason to false conclusions, not only did neural circuits involved in negative emotions turn off, but circuits involved in positive emotions turned on. The partisan brain didn't seem just satisfied in feeling better. It worked overtime to feel good, activating reward circuits that give partisans a jolt of positive reinforcement for their biased reasoning.'

We fall for the lies of our own brain. When we do, it rewards us. It seals its little mischief with a neurochemical kiss, drugging us into feeling good about what we have done. Of course, if we did carefully consider and fairly assess every new argument that we encountered, we would become confused, socially isolated and, quite possibly, insane. And mostly concluding that we are right about everything does have other benefits. As Tavris and Aronson so eloquently put it, 'Dissonance reduction operates like a thermostat, keeping our self-esteem bubbling along on high.' Indeed, a great many of the findings of decades of experimental psychology point to one grand and shameful conclusion: we are all deluded egotists.

Humans are subject to a menagerie of biases, a troubling proportion of which hiss seductive half-truths in the ear of our consciousness. They tell us that we are better looking, wiser, more capable, more moral and have a more glittering future in store than is true. One of my favourite studies involves participants trying to find a photograph of themselves that has been hidden in a panorama of hundreds of portraits of others. People tended to find their own image more quickly when it had been digitally enhanced to make them appear more attractive, suggesting that none of us are as good looking as we really think. Discussing a related experiment, behavioural psychologist Nicholas Epley told the *New Scientist*, 'When we ask people to rate how attractively they will be rated by somebody else and correlate it with actual ratings of attractiveness we find no correlation. Zero! This still shocks me.'

Another experiment had participants reading an essay about Rasputin – one set of readers were presented with the correct text while another group had a version in which the monk's date and month of birth had been altered to match their own. When questioned, the group with the similar birthdays generally thought more highly of the mad monk than the others, without having any clue as to why. Studies have also shown that we consistently overrate the quality and value of our own work.

Our ego acts upon the truth as a planet acts upon gravity. Reality warps as it pulls towards it. A cognitive error we all share, known as the spotlight effect, means that we go through our social lives convinced that everything we are saying, doing and feeling is being closely examined by those around us even though, in reality, they are all preoccupied with themselves, equally convinced the spotlight is on them. Gamblers rewrite their memories, crediting payouts to their excellent judgement and recalling their losses as near-wins or down to simple bad luck. Athletes tend to put their victories down to training, strength and stamina and their losses to unfortunate circum- stance; 74 per cent of drivers consider themselves better than average; 94 per cent of university professors think they are better than average. When husbands and wives are asked to guess what percentage of housework they do, their totals aver- age 120 per cent. Half of all students in one survey predicted that they would protest upon hearing an overtly sexist com- ment. When secretly tested, just 16 per cent actually did.

When we behave badly, it is usually because we were put in an unhappy situation. Circumstance has conspired against us. *Really, I had no choice.* When others do wrong, it is because of their character flaws. Professor Roy Baumeister, who spe- cialises in the study of evil, has found that even domestic abusers and murderers tend to view themselves as having acted reasonably in the face of unfair provocation. The Nazis believed that they were on a mission of good. He writes, 'The perpetrators of evil are often ordinary, well-meaning human beings with their own motivations, reasons and rationalisa- tions for what they are doing . . . many especially evil acts are performed by people who believe they are doing something supremely good.'

We love to judge others. We love to categorise. We love to divide. We are the good guys, they are the bad guys. We the hero, they the demon. Why? Because it fits the model. It bolsters the ego. It makes us happy. It has even been demon- strated that depressed people, with their dysfunctionally gloomy predictions about themselves and the world, are more accurate in their outlook than the mentally 'healthy'. The world, and your life within it, is far bleaker than you have been led to believe.

A final example should, I hope, offer some idea of the

brilliant power of the lies we tell ourselves. We typically have a bias that tells us we are less susceptible to bias than everyone else. Our default position tends to be that our opinions are the result of learning, experience and personal reflection. The things we believe are obviously true – and everyone would agree if only they could look at the issue with clear, objective, unimpeded sight. But they don't because they're biased. Their judgements are confused by ill-informed hunches and personal grudges. They might think they're beautiful and clever and right but their view of reality is skewed.

You might have read all of that thinking, *Yes, yes, I know people just like that. But I'm not really one of them, to be honest. I'm modest and humble and only too aware when I'm getting things wrong.* That's the sound of your brain lying to you. You *are* like that. If you are now thinking, *Yes, yes, yes, I hear what you're saying – but if you knew me you would realise that I'm not one of those people,* I'm sorry to say that you're still at it. Most of us think we are the exception. This most disturbing of truths has been widely demonstrated in study after study. When individuals are educated about these ego-defending biases and then have their biases re-examined, they usually fail to change their opinions of themselves. Even though they accept, rationally, that they are not immune, they still think as if they are. It is a cognitive trap that we just can't seem to climb out of.

Our prejudices and misbeliefs are invisible to us. They form in childhood and early adolescence, when our brain is in its heightened state of learning, when it is building its models, and then they disappear from view. We can think as long and as hard as we like about our biases – we can root about our own heads for hours, utterly convinced of our own objectivity, and still come up with nothing. They are inaccessible to the conscious part of our minds. The trick is so embedded – our warped sensations of right, wrong and truth are so folded into our fundamental sense of self – that we are immune from detecting them.

Just as the knifefish assumes his realm of electricity is the only possible reality, just as the hominin believes his tricolour palette allows him to see all the colours, just as John Mackay is convinced that lesbian nuns are going to hell, we look out into the world mostly to reaffirm our prior beliefs about it. We imagine that the invisible forces that silently guide our beliefs and behaviour, coaxing us like flocks of deviant angels, do not exist. We are comforted by the feeling that we have ultimate control over our thoughts, our actions, our lives.

There are seven billion individual worlds living on the surface of this one. We are – all of us – lost inside our own personal realities, our own brain-generated models of how things *really* are. And if, after reading all of that, you still believe you are the exception, that you really are wise and objective and above the powers of bias, then you might as well not fight it. You are, after all, only human.

7

'Quack'

Over and over again, they told her that she was being silly. But Gemma was convinced that her doctors were mistaken. You just *know*, don't you, when something is wrong, when the sensed systems inside your body nudge from their alignments. Strange shapes and colours would waft and form in her vision. She would fall asleep on the sofa and nobody could wake her. She was having difficulties in the office – her managers kept insisting they had told her what to do, but she had no memory whatsoever of them doing so. They had begun to treat her as if she was stupid. Gemma was not stupid. She had qualifications. A degree. But she didn't feel very clever when she sat in that chair in her doctor's surgery, desperate for him to listen. Every time she went, he would say the same thing. *There is nothing whatsoever to worry about. You're just a young girl, being silly.*

They found six small tumours, the size of thumbnails, on her brain. *Oh, it's nothing too serious*, they said. *They're benign. Some people live with these kinds of things for the whole of their lives without a problem.* But Gemma knew her own body. She knew her own mind. She knew that she was not the sort of person to sleep through her radio alarm clock, to courier files to the wrong office, to forget where she had parked her car. *You're panicking, being silly.*

The tumours grew. They conducted a biopsy. They drilled into her head. It took eight weeks for the results to come. You can't imagine the terror. Two months of it. Not knowing, wondering if you might die. When they finally arrived, they said they were benign. *Harmless. Fine. Silly.*

They found new tumours – these ones on her spine. She was alone when they called her. She telephoned her parents, but nobody was home. Her boyfriend wasn't picking up either. None of her friends were in. Evening had fallen before she was able to speak to anyone. All of those hours, alone with the news.

Chemotherapy made her sick. Over the course of a single weekend, all of her hair fell out. The tumours grew in size and threat. They gave her steroids. She gained four stones in one month. She had an extended stomach, a great big puffed-out moon face. She had to lift her eyelids with her finger if she wanted to see anything. Her bowels didn't move for weeks. She had a wheelchair, a stick. Her sight became so bad that she couldn't watch television or read. She had nothing to do but to lie there, terrified in her nauseous gloaming. She thought, *I'm only twenty-six. I'm the youngest of seven children. The youngest! It's not my turn.* Early in the winter of 1995, the oncologist visited her hospital bed. He said something strange. 'Okay, Gemma, these are your options. You can stay here, you can go to a hospice or you can go home.'

Gemma was groggy, confused. She reasoned, 'Well, sick people go to hospital. Dying people go to a hospice. And home – that's for fit people.'

She was delighted.

'Home, please!'

'Fine,' said the doctor, kindly. 'You've got those little pills and you've got him up there. Make sure you have a happy Christmas.'

What an odd thing to say. *Have a happy Christmas?* It was only October. It was some time before Gemma realised that this was her doctor's way of telling her that they had been wrong all along. That her tumours were, in fact, malignant. That she had cancer and would be dead within four months.

She felt betrayed. She had done everything they had asked of her. Medicine was like a, b, c, wasn't it? You got sick, they treated you and then you got better. It wasn't supposed to be like this.

Despite her bleak prognosis and her new medication, which now only treated her symptoms, Gemma carried on taking the 'little pills' that her oncologist had mentioned with his gently knowing smile. To her amazement, they seemed to work. By Christmas, her eyelids had opened up. Her bowels began to move. Her sight returned. And the more of the little pills that she took, the better she became. A year later, Gemma called her oncologist's office and asked why they hadn't been in touch. She was angry. She knew why – it was because they had assumed that she was dead. And who were they anyway? *They're not God. They don't decide when I'm going to die.* When her oncologist next examined her, he wrote in his notes, 'Gemma has made a remarkable recovery. Her case will remain a mystery.'

'But it's not a mystery to you, is it?' I say to Gemma, who has been telling me her story in the front room of her modest Sutton Coldfield home.

'Not to me,' she smiles.

The 'little pills' Gemma Hoefkens had been taking were homeopathic. She believes that they not only saved her life, they also changed its direction for ever. She is now a licensed homeopath who claims to have not seen a doctor for fourteen years.

The industry that Gemma works in is worth four million

pounds a year in the UK and billions in Europe and the US. Over fifteen thousand NHS prescriptions are issued for it annually, it sells in high-street chemists and user-satisfaction ratings in Britain score above 70 per cent. And yet Gemma's oncologist was not alone in his reservations over their efficacy. Throughout its defiant 230-year history, homeopathy has attracted the disbelieving fury of doubters from Richard Dawkins today all the way back to Charles Darwin, who wrote, 'In homeopathy common sense and common observation come into play and both these must go to the dogs.' Over the last few years, a campaign to stop the homeopaths has gathered into a truly damaging force. Questions have been asked in Parliament. In February 2010, the House of Commons Science and Technology Committee recommended the NHS cease funding the discipline. Even ex-Prime Minister Tony Blair has become involved, saying 'My advice to the scientific community would be, I wouldn't bother fighting a great battle over homeopathy.' But they do and, at least in Britain, they are winning: between 2000 and 2011 there was an eightfold drop in NHS prescriptions. It now comprises just 0.001 per cent of the NHS's annual drug budget. And Gemma has suffered personally at the feet of reason's furious armies.

In February 2010, she appeared on BBC Radio Five Live, to share the details of her recovery with the public. Afterwards, someone posted the interview on YouTube. On the video, every time Gemma speaks, a yellow rubber duck appears over her face with the word 'QUACK!' flashing out of its mouth. The video ends with a still photograph of Gemma herself. It is framed, in shocking pink letters, with the statement: 'DO NOT BE FOOLED. HOMEOPATHY IS A CROCK OF SHIT'. There is a blue speech bubble jutting from her mouth. It contains an additional single word rendered in bold yellow capitals. It says, 'QUACK!!'

I unfold a print-out of the yellow plastic duck and place it on the table in front of Gemma.

'Have you seen this?' I ask.

Her eyes flicker briefly towards it. She folds her arms.

'Yes.'

'How does it make you feel?'

She allows herself a moment to think.

'It makes me feel – how professional are they? They've got "quack" there and a yellow plastic duck. And how unprofessional is that? Who are these people who are so unprofessional? You know, who are they?'

I decided to find out.

*

In the upstairs bar of a dismal city-centre Manchester hotel, a pale platoon of anti-homeopaths is getting pleasantly drunk. These are members of the 'Skeptic' community, a large and swelling movement of activists and thinkers who campaign against people such as Gemma, and on behalf of science and reason. They meet in groups known as 'Skeptics in the Pub' and gather online to present podcasts, argue in chatrooms and compose outraged and unusually well-footnoted blogs.

They dress in comfortable jeans paired with strange polemical T-shirts ('Stand back, I'm going to try science', 'I reject your reality and substitute my own', 'Over 1000 scientists named Steve agree') or in dark-coloured knitwear, sleeves pushed up to elbows to regulate temperature. Huddling around low tables with pints of lager, they peck at Twitter with self-conscious frowns of concentration. The elder Skeptics – one or two of whom I recognise as speakers at this event – stand in fidgety groups by the bar, rolling back on their heels with fingers crooked over chins, listening earnestly to their neighbours. Everywhere I look, there are beards and little ponytails and cables dangling out of rucksacks. At least three of them look exactly like Dave Gorman.

This weekend, the Skeptics have gathered for the 'QED Conference' that has been organised jointly by the Merseyside and the Greater Manchester cells of Skeptics in the Pub. It will culminate in a mass international homeopathic overdose – a stunt that will seek to demonstrate that, as the campaign's marketing slogan has it, 'There's nothing in it'.

I am curious about the Skeptics because, from an outsider's point of view, their main hobby seems to be not believing in things. Psychics, homeopathy, chiropractors, ghosts, God – they don't believe a word of it and that is one of their favourite things to do. The fallibility of human belief is the base upon which the Skeptics build their activism. As bracingly incredible as it was to me, it is highly likely that the ordinary Skeptic would have discovered nothing new in the chapter that precedes this one. Confirmation bias, cognitive dissonance, unconscious ego-bolstering and the many illusions of vision are their foundational texts, their Matthew, Mark, Luke and John.

Skeptics rely on the findings of science, rather than the dubious anecdotes of individuals, to inform them about the world. They are knights of hard intellect whose ultimate goal is a world free of superstitious thinking. Do not make the mistake of doubting how seriously some take this task. Later in this event, an editor of the US's *Skeptic* magazine will note their responsibility as 'safe-guarders of the truth'. Another speaker will darkly threaten that, without their ever-watchful work, 'Nonsense will be allowed to reign.'

Much to the irritation of the Skeptics, homeopathy has been 'reigning', now, for more than two centuries. Its development, which began in 1790, is credited to German physician Samuel Hahnemann – who, just like Gemma, had grown disillusioned with conventional medicine. The theory says that illnesses can be cured by taking minute portions of substances which cause similar symptoms to those which ail you. So, if the bark of a toxic Peruvian tree causes symptoms similar to malaria, say, then a tiny dose of that can cure malaria. In Gemma's case, her many dramatic maladies were, she believes, cured by causticum. When I enquired as to what causticum was, she replied somewhat reluctantly, 'Er, you put it down drains.'

But Gemma was never in danger of being poisoned. The amount of causticum in one of her pills is really quite unbelievably small. In fact, if you buy a standard '30C' dose of any homeopathic treatment, it means the active ingredient has been diluted thirty times, by a factor of 100. That might not sound like too much, until you realise that your chance of getting even one molecule of the original substance in your pill is one in a billion billion billion billion. In his influential book *Bad Science*, Skeptic superstar Dr Ben Goldacre explained that you would have to drink a sphere of water that stretches from the earth to the sun just to get just one solitary, pointless molecule of it.

This is why their campaign's slogan insists that 'There's nothing in it'. Because there really is nothing in it. Homeopaths deny this, however, saying that when they dilute the substance, they first shake it (or 'succuss' it) which 'potentises' the water, causing it to somehow remember the active substance. The Skeptics reply that this is 'woo-woo', which is the word they use for nonsense.

I am quite comfortable in predicting that there is not a brain in this bar that would have been surprised to discover what happened when I broached the problem of empirical proof with Gemma. I began by asking about her practice as a homeopath, and whether the process of assessing which remedy to recommend to a patient was instinctive, or an exact science. She replied, 'It's an exact science. But it's something that the scientists don't understand yet.'

'I read that a sphere of water a hundred and fifty million kilometres in diameter would only contain one molecule of active ingredient,' I said.

'I'm not the best person to talk to about that.'

'What would your response be to a Skeptic who says it's diluted to such an extent that there's actually nothing in it?'

'I'd say go and look it up.'

'Look it up?'

'Yeah.'

'Have you ever read any scientific studies that have looked at the efficacy of homeopathy?'

'Yes.'

'Which ones?'

'Don't ask me that question.'

As I said, nobody in this bar would be surprised to hear any of that – and that is the central and unavoidable truth about the Skeptics. They are never wrong. Indeed, that is the whole point of them. And, as one of them volunteers, being right all the time comes with its own peculiar risks. When software engineer Bryan tells me that scepticism is the philosophy by which he lives life, he feels it necessary to make an unprompted addendum: 'It's not about calling people stupid.'

'Is that a common accusation?' I ask.

'You can come across as arrogant,' he says. 'Especially when you're in this type of environment, where people tend to be into the scientific literature.'

My next conversation is with a couple of not-that-friendly-looking-to-be-honest Skeptics named Bendt and Simon. Bendt, a bearded Swede in a leather trench coat, tells me that he came to the movement via loneliness and atheism. 'I was doing my PhD in Vancouver and looking for a social circle so I looked for atheists. From there, I went to scepticism.'

'And what was your PhD in?' I ask.

'Nuclear physics.'

Rob, meanwhile, was a schoolboy magician who became entranced by an individual who, like him, also began his journey into scepticism by performing simple magic tricks and marvelling at the ease by which you can fool a human. The man who inspired him, however, was to become a hero to rationalist campaigners all over the world. Now in his eighties, he has spent a long and celebrated life committing spectacular debunkings of psychics, spoonbenders and peddlers in woo-woo – a phrase that he invented. He is James Randi, king of the Skeptics, a near-legend in these circles. One of the many actions that Randi is celebrated for is his long-standing offer, made through his James Randi Educational Foundation (JREF), of one million dollars to any individual that can prove any aspect of the supernatural. That includes homeopathy. Indeed, one of his latest triumphs involves a high-profile Greek homeopath named George Vithoulkas, whose own 'Million Dollar Challenge' broke down just as his test was approaching. It is said that Vithoulkas dodged his judgement day by suddenly refusing to fill out the standard JREF application form, thereby triggering the collapse of the process. In a typically merciless statement that was published on Randi's personal blog (in which he also found room to call Vithoulkas a 'strange man', 'self-deluded' and a 'naif') he said, 'Many would-be applicants have considered themselves above such a simple requirement, but no exception has ever been made, nor will it be made.'

I meet another software engineer, named Colin, who credits Randi's debunking of Uri Geller – famous for his psychic spoon-bending – for his interest in critical thinking. 'He's a really big hero,' says Colin, who calls homeopathy a 'medical scam' and describes it as his principal interest. When I ask which homeopathy studies he has read, he dodges the question. 'I'm not a scientist so I can't really comment on the studies. But I'm fascinated by the absurdity of the whole thing.'

Conventioneer Dominic, meanwhile, is equally scathing. 'Homeopathy really is silly,' he chuckles. 'I look forward to taking part in the overdose.'

What is it, I wonder, that he wants to achieve with his campaigning?

'Just getting an awareness out there of how silly homeopathy is,' he says.

'Have you read any scientific studies into homeopathy?'

'Not personally.'

'I'm not sure I understand the point of it all,' I say. 'Isn't it just harassing a load of old ladies?'

'It isn't just a load of old ladies,' he says. 'Lots of people, if they take homeopathy and think it's real medicine, they might avoid going to an actual doctor.'

He makes a good point.

'Do you know anyone that that's happened to?'

'Not personally.' A moment passes, as he ponders the sceptical ramifications of this admission. 'Being sceptical, unless I know someone who has done this, I can't say for sure it has happened. But I have heard stories.'

'If you don't know anyone personally who has come to harm, then what makes you so angry about it?'

'Simply from a consumer-protection point of view.'

'You're interested in consumer-protection issues?'

'Yes.'

'And what other consumer-protection issues are you involved with?'

'I buy *Which?* magazine,' he says. 'And things like that.'

Finally, I settle down with Mark, who explains his interest in scepticism thus: 'It's incredibly important that people maintain a rational mindset, a sceptical mindset, with everything they approach in life and that they never get carried away with wishful thinking, with stuff they would *like* to be true.'

I sigh, my gaze emptying and slipping in the direction of the ugly carpet. I feel unaccountably depressed.

We talk on, and Mark says that his principal sceptical interest is in evolution, so I tell him about my time in Gympie with John Mackay, and about his opposite, the scientist Nathan Lo, who told me that much of the peril lay in the fact that the creationist story is simple to understand, whereas the science can be hard. But Mark, a twenty-five-year-old cinema employee, does not agree with what the doctor of molecular evolution had to say.

'I don't think it's difficult,' he says. 'In fact, the beauty of evolution is that it's incredibly easy to understand.'

I present the argument that, in essence, it is *all* faith – most of us do not look at the raw evidence for ourselves, but rely on charismatic leaders who reinforce our prejudices to do it for us. Mark nods approvingly.

'If you truly want the truth, you have to do it yourself,' he says.

'But who's got time?' I say.

'It's not about who's got time,' he says. 'It's about not trying to make reality fit what you want it to fit. We need to tell people to come to their own conclusions rather than what someone else tells them.'

'So, what evidence have you personally studied regarding evolution?' I ask.

'Well, there's *such* a mound of evidence with something like evolution,' he sighs. 'There are fossils in the ground that show a step by step picture of how we got to be how we are.'

'Fossils?' I ask.

'Fossils,' he nods.

'So you've studied fossils?'

'No, not personally,' he says. 'But, um, the fact that I've not studied fossils personally – the vast majority of people haven't studied fossils personally. Has anyone studied God personally?'

I don't understand exactly what Mark means, but as the glumness that has come over me is apparently not lifting, I decide that it is time for bed.

*

I don't know if there is any way back from the revelation that you are wrong and there is nothing you can do about it. But that, it seems to me, is the principal lesson of experimental psychology. We are blind to the effects of our own cognitive traps. You could even argue that it is these very traps – their unique patterns – that make us who we are. These days, when pondering matters of personal belief, the most appropriate question we can ask of ourselves is no longer 'Am I right?' but 'How mistaken am I, how biased?'

We have designed a system of knowledge to combat all this. Science is the opposite of religion. Its laws are not sensed in visions or divined by charismatics claiming access to a supernatural being. They are the result of sweat and fight and genius. Everything it knows, it has earned. The scientific process is what happens when you gather enough *Homo sapiens* brains together and give them time to think. It is astonishing: the greatest achievement of our species. The people gathered for this conference know this. They want to promote it; to celebrate it. As I keep having to remind myself mournfully, the Skeptics are *right*.

Why 'mournfully'? Why this gloomy sense? Why the

defensive feeling when I walked into the bar downstairs? Why are my instincts, in all their kneejerk ignorance, telling me that I should be on the attack, that these men and women are not of my tribe?

These are questions that journalists are not well practised in asking. We are similar to the Skeptics, in that we like to imagine ourselves as professional seekers of truth. We are led by facts, not prejudice or childish interpersonal likes and dislikes. I lie back on my hotel bed, recalling my behaviour earlier on – wandering about the place, speaking to Skeptics one by one and asking impertinently, 'What studies into homeopathy have you read? What studies into homeopathy have *you* read?'

Urgh.

When I was familiarising myself with the sceptical literature, I came across a book that contained an enlightening passage on John Mack, the Harvard heretic who had to go to war with his dean in order to defend his right to study alien abduction. Written by Dr Michael Shermer – founding publisher of the magazine *Skeptic* and director of the Skeptics Society – *Why People Believe Weird Things* closes with a devastating analysis of his beliefs.

Mack's cognitive journey reads like a perfect study in how the brain likes to rearrange the evidence of the outside world in order to match its inner models. (Not that Shermer doubts that Mack's patients were sincere: 'Knowing what we do about the fantastic imagery that the brain is capable of producing,' he writes, 'experiencer's experiences are nothing more than mental representations of strictly internal brain phenomena.') Mack had some tricksy cognitive dissonance to deal with: the lack of physical evidence that they had actually been taken aboard an alien craft. He acknowledged this was a problem, admitting, 'there is no firm proof that abduction was the cause of their absence', but then soothed the dissonance away by *dis-*

missing the entire notion of physical evidence. In an interview with *Time* magazine he complained, 'I don't know why there's such a zeal to find a conventional physical explanation. We've lost all that ability to know a world beyond the physical. I am a bridge between the two worlds.'

Here was a man as intelligent as you could hope for, who found re-imagining the nature of reality itself easier than admitting the obvious possibility that his patients were simply delusional. In his book, Shermer did a superb job on Mack. He was knowledgeable, sceptical, credible and wise. He was fantastic.

I found the whole thing really annoying.

Over the last few months, Mack has become a kind of hero to me. Despite his earlier caution, he ended up believing in amazing things: intergalactic space travel and terrifying encounters in alien craft that travelled seamlessly through non-physical dimensions. And when his bosses tried to silence him, he hired a *lawyer*. He fought back against the Dean and his dreary minions. He battled hard in the name of craziness. He was a heretic, an enemy of reason. He told a journalist from *Time* magazine, 'I am a bridge between the two worlds.' And I *loved* him.

But there it was – the miserable truth. I heard it downstairs, less than an hour ago: '*It's incredibly important that people never get carried away with wishful thinking, with stuff they would like to be true.*'

Mark the Skeptic was right, of course. And now that I have learned to mistrust myself, to realise that 'instinct' is merely ego-bolstering bias prancing about in the robes of wisdom, I am compelled to question why I would like so much for Mark to be wrong. I wonder if it relates to the truth hinted at by the university students who were asked to read the essay about Rasputin. The readers preferred him when his birthday matched their own. Without even being conscious of what was happening, something in their brains recognised a similarity and hugged the diabolical monk just a little bit closer. It seems to me that we spend our lives hunting for ourselves: we are moved by a novel when we recognise our experiences in those of the hero, just as we delight in the constellation of similarities that we discover in a new romantic partner. Perhaps we never really fall in love with someone else after all, and when we gaze into the eyes of our other half we are actually admiring our own reflection.

If all this is true, and my biases throb warmly when I detect pieces of myself, then why, on meeting the Skeptics, did I feel drawn to the defence of the homeopaths? What is the Rasputin trace that I sense in them, and in John Mack? I wonder if it has to do with the various madnesses that I once suffered. The delusional jealousy, the vandalism, the pathological drinking and theft. I wonder if it has to do with the fact that I was unhappy at school, that I made war with my teachers and that I had little in common with the kind of students who were good at science and mathematics. Am I, by instinct, with the irrationals? Are they my tribe? If so, that makes me an unreliable narrator. Which is not a good look for a journalist.

*

I am up on the balcony watching the three hundred assembled conventioneers enjoying a presentation about ghosts. A good proportion of them have come dressed in the white T-shirts that are being sold to promote tomorrow's homeopathic overdose. An even larger number have screens of various sizes in their laps and are managing to be sceptical about ghosts while interacting fitfully with their illuminated computer-extensions.

I recognise one of the panellists. Professor Chris French, a former editor of the UK's *The Skeptic* magazine and a professor of psychology who heads the Anomalistic Psychology Research Unit at the University of London. I once interviewed him, for the *Financial Times*.

The conventioneers laugh, as one, at a joke that French has made. I coldly survey the endless rows of chuckling white-shirted forms beneath me. *There they are*, I think. *All the Skeptics, all gathered together, all thinking for themselves.*

I have *got* to stop this.

I sit alone and try to rearrange my thoughts into something that resembles impartiality, but my biases are flexing madly. I am surprised, for a start, that so few of these disciples of empirical evidence seem to be familiar with the scientific literature on the subject that impassions them so. I am suspicious, too, about the real source of their rage. If they are motivated, as they frequently insist, by altruistic concern over the dangers of supernatural belief, why do they not obsess over jihadist Muslims, homophobic Christians or racist Jewish settlers? Why this focus on stage psychics, ghost-hunters and alt-med hippies? And isn't the scene before me precisely the kind of thing that the Stanford Professor Philip Zimbardo warns against? The first two steps in his recipe for evil – assign yourself a role, and become a member of a group. 'Groups can have powerful influences on individual behaviour,' he said. Weren't his doomed prison guards just like this: bonded by their fight, and their perceived superiority, in opposition to a common enemy?

One of the convention's organisers, Michael 'Marsh' Marshall, arrives. Charismatic, confident and eloquent, the twenty-seven-year-old marketing executive in the crisply ironed shirt seems at ease both on stage addressing the conventioneers and on television news shows, on which he has recently been in demand on account of his campaign against the homeopaths.

Marsh's journey into the movement began when he was a sixth-form student. 'I used to do palm-readings,' he tells me. 'I was pretty good at it, but I didn't believe it for a second. I just accidentally picked up some cold-reading techniques. It made me realise how easy it is to convince people of things that aren't true – and to convince yourself. I've been interested in psychics ever since, because there's a real harm in it. I had a reasonably well-documented tussle with a Liverpool psychic called Joe Power,' he says, recalling it with a smile. 'I went along to see him at one of his book signings and he didn't take too kindly to me questioning him and saying, "Well, if you can really do what you're saying then that's fantastic. Just test it first. If it turns out you pass the test, we're totally on board with you."' He shakes his head in amused disbelief. 'He just went mental at me. He called me every name under the sun.'

Unlike the Skeptics I met last night, Marsh is familiar with a case in which homeopathy has been harmful – and appallingly so. He recounts the case of an Australian baby who was diagnosed with eczema aged four months and ended up dying five months later after her father, a homeopathy lecturer, insisted on treating her with his highly diluted potions. When her parents were imprisoned in 2009, the judge blamed the girl's death on her father's 'arrogant approach' to homeopathy.

'I find cases like that really distressing,' Marsh says. 'Homeopathy is magic. That's what we're trying to get across with the overdose. We know we're not going to convince the hardened believers. It's the people who wander into Boots with a headache and say, "Homeopathy – I'll try that" that we want to reach. To those people, we want to say, "There is no evidence for homeopathy. The science has been done. It simply doesn't work."'

I can't help myself.

'Have you read any of the studies?' I ask.

'Yes,' he says.

I sit up.

'And understood them?'

'Yes.'

'Which ones?'

A touch of irritation becomes evident around the edges of his eyes.

'I can't quote their names.'

I ask Marsh if there is a risk that, with activists gathering regularly to agree with each other that the 'fringe sciences' are scams and their practitioners fraudulent or deluded, that something important might get missed.

There is a famous quote by William James, who spoke of the scientific gains that can be made by paying attention to the 'dust-cloud of exceptional observations' that floats around 'the accredited and orderly facts of every science'. What if some young academic who is interested in an esoteric subject such as homeopathy or ESP is intimidated by the roar of the crowd into ignoring his vocation? Maybe, in among all this junk science, some crucial anomaly exists, the study of which could lead to a fantastic breakthrough? But now it won't happen, because reason's fightback is too fierce, too gloating, too much of a threat to a young scientist's reputation. To be a Skeptic seems to involve signing up to a predetermined rainbow of unbeliefs. What if it slips into dogma?

'By definition to be involved in scepticism, you're someone who is critical of the world, is evaluating the world, and that in itself is a good inoculation against dogma,' he says. 'And anyway, decisions on that kind of stuff are not made on consensus or popularity, they're made on evidence.'

It is, in other words, a restatement of his message to the psychic Joe Power. As soon as anyone proves homeopathy, mediumship or extra-sensory perception, they will humbly admit that they have been wrong all along. The American rationalist-celebrity Rebecca Watson (another ex-magician who was inspired by James Randi) gives a typical definition of the Skeptic as one who is 'willing to examine their beliefs and [is] always open to new evidence, [and has] the ability to hold a belief and, if new evidence comes in, to completely change your mind.' This is why James Randi frequently rejects the title 'debunker', preferring 'investigator', and it is why, in the UK, there is a general preference for the American spelling, 'Skeptic': '"Sceptic" tends to get confused with cynic – de facto negativity,' explains Marsh. 'We like to emphasise that if stuff proves to be true, we'll believe it.'

Later that day, one of the world's most highly regarded sceptical activists will also claim a special immunity to dogmatic thinking on behalf of the warriors of science. Dr Steven Novella is a clinical neurologist from Yale University who presents the hit weekly podcast 'The Skeptics' Guide to the Universe'. 'This is an intellectual community,' Novella tells me. 'The reason why scepticism is incompatible with dogma and ideology is; it's very anti-dogmatic and anti-ideological at its core.'

I am startled to learn that Novella is so sceptical of homeopathy that he does not even accept its worth as an unusually sophisticated exercise in placebo theatre. He denies that placebo has any true physiological effect, insisting that it is purely psychological and that studies suggesting otherwise often fall victim to what is known as 'The Hawthorne Effect'. 'The act of participating in a clinical trial, of being observed, can make people feel better,' he explains. 'We have the data on this. People *think* they're feeling better, but they're not.'

The homeopaths themselves, says Novella, are a mix of the deluded and the knowingly fraudulent. 'There's always going to be a certain percentage of psychopathic con artists,' he says.

'In any system where people believe in magic, con artists smell that. It's like blood in the water to them. That aside, there's the people who are just profoundly naive. Then there are the promoters, like Dana Ullman [one of America's most active defenders of homeopathy]. They're really despicable because they get called out on the inaccuracy of the information they're providing. Then the next time they come around, they're peddling the same crap again.'

Before the day's proceedings close, I see Professor Chris French alone behind a trestle table that is piled with issues of *The Skeptic* magazine. I wander up to him to say hello.

'Oh, hi,' he says pleasantly. 'I really enjoyed your ghost book.'

'Thanks!' I say, beaming.

'But I have to say, you're not what *I'd* call a Skeptic.'

I sigh and wander off to spend the remainder of the day moseying in and out of talks. The final event of the evening is set by a sceptical musician from the US named George Hrab. As I leave the convention hall for bed, he is leading the crowd in a sing-along, the chorus of which goes: 'You won't believe what a Skeptic I am/I can't believe you believe in that sham/We disagree but I still give a damn.'

And in the morning, I overdose.

*

'Has everyone got the vial of pills we prepared for you?' says Marsh, up on the stage. On each seat there is a small plastic container with a white screw-cap, each one holding a palmful of pills. 'If you haven't got any, there are helpers at the back of the room who have spare pills so, don't worry, you will be able to overdose with us. In the time we've got before we're going to attempt to kill ourselves I'm going to take you through what's been happening over the last forty-eight hours.'

Marsh counts seventy cities in thirty countries across the world that are taking part in today's overdose. Then he proudly introduces a special video recording that has been made for today. He turns towards the huge screen, grinning, and suddenly – there he is. Gazing down at the crowd with his bright grey eyes, pink ears, bald head and famous white wizard's beard, it is the man Professor Chris French calls 'the patron saint of the Skeptics'.

'Hello,' he says. 'I'm James Randi.'

We watch in reverent silence as Randi talks of the times that he has overdosed in order to show that these 'scam medications' have no effect. 'Every day, parents of sick children are coming home from their pharmacy with fake medicine, leaving their children in distress because these manufacturers and these stores don't want consumers to know the truth,' he says. 'Every reputable study of these fake drugs has shown them to have no more effect than sugar pills.'

And then the moment arrives. The crowd shouts, '3, 2, 1, There's nothing in it!' And the sound of three hundred nerds crunching nothing fills the conference hall. Marsh happily surveys the room.

'Is anyone dead yet?'

*

Skeptic after Skeptic at the Manchester conference told me the same thing. Despite mostly admitting they were unfamiliar with the scientific literature, they all confidently insisted, 'There is no evidence for homeopathy.' James Randi himself has said that 'any definitive tests that have been done have been negative'. But this, I am subsequently informed, is not true. The website of the British Homeopathic Association notes 142 studies that have been published in 'good quality' journals of which just eight, it says, were negative. Meanwhile,

Dr Alexander Tournier of the Homeopathy Research Institute – who became an adherent when he was studying quantum physics at Cambridge University – tells me, 'If you talk to Skeptics they will acknowledge a paper that was published in the *Lancet* in 2005, which is known as "Shang et al.". That included a hundred and ten respectable studies of homeopathy, many of which were positive. You can't say that's nothing.'

I discover all this with a sense of woozy betrayal. I had put my suspicion of the Skeptics down to my own unfair prejudices. I believed every word that they told me. My irritation has a strange effect, coating the little facts with layers of emotion, exaggerating the mild intellectual sleight-of-hand until it seems personal – a conspiracy of enemies misleading me, mocking me. I am reminded of the bickering UFO-spotters who hardened their positions the moment that they were challenged. I think, too, of John Mackay's discovery of atheist propaganda in his textbook, and how this perceived mistreatment by ideologues threw him into the arms of the enemy. I know how he felt.

I decide to confess all to Andy Lewis, the author of the sceptical blog 'The Quackometer', who has agreed to guide me through some of the complex science that is involved in homeopathy. To my relief, he seems to understand. 'Yes, many Skeptics can be pretty lazy and say, "There is no evidence",' he writes in an email. 'A slightly better approach would be to say, "There is no good evidence". I can understand how you might have felt slightly misled.'

One of the most remarkable attempts at finding laboratory proof that homeopathy works began with the dramatic events of June 1988. That was when the world's most respected scientific journal, *Nature*, published a study that apparently demonstrated that water did, indeed, have a memory. The research team was led by a widely respected scientist, Dr

Jacques Benveniste – a senior director of the French medical research organisation INSERM 200.

Benveniste was initially sceptical of homeopathy. 'The first time I heard the word, I thought it was a sexual disease,' he said, in a 1994 interview for BBC TV. He had been working on allergies for fourteen years, when one of his forty-strong team claimed to have seen that some cells in a blood sample had an allergic response to an allergen that had been heavily diluted.

'I had the feeling of setting my foot in a completely unknown world,' said Benveniste. 'Something that was so strange that I couldn't even envision what was going on.'

Fascinated, he instructed his best researcher, Dr Elisabeth Davenas, to investigate. The culmination of this work was his *Nature* paper which caused an international sensation, despite its being published with two unusual conditions: first, that Benveniste obtain prior confirmation of his results from other laboratories; second, that a team selected by *Nature* be allowed to investigate his laboratory following publication. Benveniste accepted these conditions; the results were reportedly replicated by four laboratories, in Milan, Italy; in Toronto, Canada; in Tel-Aviv, Israel; and in Marseille, France.

But the 'editorial reservations' scandalised Benveniste. He was enraged, arguing that in his view the team that was appointed to investigate him was not appropriately recruited. It was made up of the *Nature* editor who had written the editorial, a fraud investigator and, of course, James Randi.

A replication was attempted. With everyone present, Dr Elisabeth Davenas – a homeopathy proponent who had interpreted all the original data – counted the number of cells that had been 'degranulated' by whatever agent it had been exposed to. At first, things looked good for Benveniste. When Davenas counted the blood that had been dosed with a homeopathic dilution and compared it with blood that had been treated with distilled water, the result was significant. But the investigators made Davenas assess the samples a second time – and this time, they weren't labelled. When Davenas counted now, without knowing which was the homeopathic-treated blood and which was not, the test failed. It was almost as if she was operating under some powerful unconscious bias that was affecting her judgement. When the result was revealed, some of Benveniste's scientists wept.

'His whole team was playing a trick on itself,' *Nature*'s editor, John Maddox, told the BBC. 'They very rarely made these measurements blind, which meant that anyone who knew what he was looking for could bias his own counting to get the kind of answer he expected.'

Their report was published in *Nature* in July 1988, under the headline, '"High-dilution" experiments a delusion'. It was devastating. They complained at the fact that Benveniste's lab was partially funded by a major homeopathy company and noted several potential flaws in his processes, while dismissing the claims of replication and describing homeopathy as a 'folklore' that 'pervades' Benveniste's laboratory.

Benveniste fought back, deriding the *Nature* team's 'mockery of scientific inquiry'. He was outraged that they had allowed one negative result to 'blot out five years of our work'. He described the investigation as a 'pantomime' during which 'a tornado of intense and constant suspicion, fear and psychological and intellectual pressure unfit for scientific work swept our lab.' The team, he said, 'imposed a deadly silence in the counting room, yet loud laughter was heard where he was filling chambers. There, during this critical process, was Randi playing tricks, distracting the technician in charge of its supervision.' Benveniste finished his grand defence, also published in *Nature*, by saying, 'Science flourishes only in freedom. We must not let, at any price, fear, blackmail, anonymous accusation, libel and deceit nest in our labs. Our colleagues are overwhelmingly utmost decent people, not criminals. To them, I say: never, but never, let anything like this happen – never let these people get in your lab.'

Two years later, he was fired.

The adventure of Dr Jacques Benveniste tells of a crucial principle of sceptical thought: that extraordinary claims require extraordinary evidence. If we are going to allow homeopathy, and therefore overturn much that is widely accepted in science, then we must reasonably expect the conclusions of its study to be exceptional. The tests must be painstakingly designed, and their results consistent, replicable and significant.

So what of the hundred and ten studies that Dr Alexander Tournier presented in his defence? Some of these may well conclude that homeopathy works, but are they any good? This is exactly what 'Shang et al.', the famous paper that Tournier referenced, sought to discover.

When different scientists tackle the same problem and produce conflicting results, one way of making sense of them all is to conduct a meta-analysis. You take the trials, use complex mathematical formulae to blend their data, and end up with what you hope is an ultimate conclusion. That is what Professor Aijing Shang's team, at the University of Berne in Switzerland, sought to do for homeopathy. It was an ambitious project and inevitably controversial: after more than two hundred years of ferocious argument, we would finally know: does homeopathy work?

To discuss 'Shang et al.', I call Dana Ullman, the US homeopath picked out as especially 'despicable' by Dr Steven Novella. I begin by asking for his thoughts on the Skeptics.

'They're a mixed and motley crew,' he says. 'They're medical fundamentalists and because they follow James Randi, who is a magician, they seek to purposefully misdirect the real issues in healthcare. Some are Big Pharma shills, others are just misinformed. A lot of them are science nerds. I have a science nerd in me, but the difference between me and the average science nerd is that many of them were abused as youngsters. They were hyper-rational and they had inadequate social skills and now they're on the Internet getting their venom out. They're bullying back. So my analysis of the reason why some of them are irrationally venomous – and you can use that term: I determine that many of them are *irrationally venomous* – is because they had a difficult childhood where they were abused and now they're getting back.'

We move on to Shang. His team began by looking for studies of homeopathy that were sophisticated enough to take into account the effects of placebo. Just as Dr Tournier told me, they ended up with a hundred and ten studies that looked at homeopathy's effect on a wide array of medical conditions.

They wanted to compare these with studies of conventional medicine. So, for each one of their homeopathic studies, they found a matching study from the world of mainstream medication that looked at treatment of the same disorder. So for every test of homeopathy on asthma, for example, they found a test of ordinary medicine on asthma.

First, they analysed the two sets of papers separately. They found that both conventional medicine and homeopathy showed a positive effect above placebo. Simply put, they *both* worked.

Next, they had a look at the quality of each one of those studies. Taking into account variables such as the number of people who took part in each test, they ordered them from the best to the worst and found that the better the study was, the worse the result for homeopathy.

Finally, they isolated the finest homeopathy studies in their pool of a hundred and ten . They found eight that were of the very highest quality. All of them concluded that the evidence for it was 'weak' and 'compatible with the notion that the clinical effects of homoeopathy are placebo effects'.

The result was damning. Homeopathy is nothing more than placebo. The *Lancet* published the study alongside an editorial headlined 'The End of Homeopathy'.

'Ha ha ha!' says Dana.

'You're laughing,' I note.

'Yes, I laugh at people who are sceptical of homeopathy and use Shang as their firmest body of evidence. People who do that have their feet planted firmly in mid-air. The ground that they're standing on is jello.'

Dana has several criticisms of Shang. He says that a series of studies that showed strong effects for homeopathy were unfairly ignored. He says that a subsequent critique of the study, published in the *Journal of Clinical Epidemiology*, accused Shang of 'post-hoc analysis' – that is, gathering his evidence first and then using it to find a way to prove homeopathy wrong. He says that some of the papers included were not intended to show whether homeopathy worked. Rather, they were exploratory 'pilot studies', carried out to test the design of a proposed experiment for potential problems before it is embarked upon properly. And yet negative results for pilot studies were taken by Shang to be conclusive, and therefore damning of homeopathy in general.

Finally, he disputes the entire basis of what Shang describes as a 'high quality' study. In science generally, it is taken to be logically sound that the more people who take part in a test, the more accurate the results will be. However, Dana says that this ignores the basic principles of homeopathy. When you visit a homeopath with stomach pains, say, that homeopath will not only take into account your chief complaint. Rather, he will talk to you for perhaps an hour about a wide range of subjects and take all sorts of apparently unrelated facts into his final decision in what potion or pill to recommend. Therefore, says Dana, the smaller studies are the most accurate, as these were more likely to be the ones in which an individual homeopath took the time to dispense an accurate remedy.

When I recount all this to Andy Lewis of *The Quackometer*, he chuckles knowingly. 'These are all things Dana has said before, bar the marvellous one where he says small trials are better trials,' he says. 'That shows quite a lot of chutzpah. What did you think of that?'

'To me, it makes sense,' I admit. 'Although I do appreciate that it leads us into dangerous territory.'

'But he's not telling you the whole truth.'

Andy takes me through Dana's argument point by point. He says Shang 'excluded all sorts of trials, and the reasons they were excluded were very specifically set out in the paper. He included a clear methodology because he wanted to make sure that he gave both sides a fair crack of the whip. If Dana could show that he had ignored their criteria, it would be a fatal blow. But no one's done that.'

Next, Andy tells me that the accusation that Shang was engaged in post-hoc analysis was not, in fact, published in the *Journal of Clinical Epidemiology*, which is an 'as good as you can get journal', but in a publication that deals exclusively with homeopathy. 'Oh, what can you say about that?' he sighs.

Of Dana's assertion that homeopathy will only work when 'individualised' he says, 'He's not being complete with the truth.' In fact, the father of homeopathy, Hahnemann himself, designed a scheme called Genus Epidemicus in which broad symptoms could be treated with the same medication. Indeed, that's why anyone can walk into Boots without an appointment and buy a homeopathic remedy for toothache. Also, Andy adds, there are lots of trials for individualised homeopathy. 'Forty or fifty at least. And the results for these as just as poor as all the others.'

Finally, of Dana's complaint that trials that were included were only exploratory, Andy says: 'The vast majority of homeopathy studies would be pilot studies. I don't think the inclusion criteria took that into account.'

'So does Dana have a point, then?'

'Um . . .'

'Would you go that far?'

'Dana is always wrong. So, no. I wouldn't go that far.'

*

Before his death in 2004, Dr Jacques Benveniste had begun an ambitious project. 'One day,' he said, 'we are going to be able to get our drugs on the phone. There is no reason why we can't have this, or have a whole pharmacy on a chip on our credit card.'

His words were prophetic. Today you can send a strand of your hair to a homeopath, who will dip it into a solution and beam its health-giving vibrations back to you through the air. You can buy machines that project homeopathic properties into blank pills. It doesn't require the actual original liquid dilutions – just get someone to email over the correct numeric code for, say, 'milk of the dolphin', 'dinosaur bone' or 'blood of the grizzly bear' and tap it in. Using this 'radionic' method, you don't even need pills. One proponent travels through Africa, handing mp3 files to people with AIDS.

Back in Sutton Coldfield, I wanted to discover a bit more about Gemma's practice. Despite the Skeptics' many campaigns, there are already laws in place that seek to stop homeopaths doing harm. The Cancer Act 1939 makes it illegal to advertise the ability to cure cancer. This made me curious about Gemma. Although her website makes no mention of the condition, I wanted to know how she dealt with patients while publicly crediting homeopathy with her own recovery. I asked if she had ever treated anyone who was suffering from it.

'Yes, I have,' she said. 'One with brain tumours. He was given two years to live. He came to see me, had some treatment, had a scan and they'd gone.'

'You realise that claiming the ability to cure cancer is illegal?'

'I don't treat the cancer,' she says. 'I treat the individual.'

'You treat the individual with cancer.'

'I treat people with diseases, but I treat them as an individual.'

'So if I came to you saying, "I've got cancer, I need medicine" you wouldn't treat that cancer, but the cancer would still disappear?'

She shrugged, 'Might do.'

'How do you know that your cancer didn't just go into remission?'

She looked baffled. Then angry.

'I was on my deathbed! And it suddenly changed, did it?'

We sat there, for a moment, in the space that now she uses as a consulting room. I took in the books, the pamphlets, the framed certificate in 'homeopathy and holistic healing' from 'The Lakeland College' and the large chart that explained what to do in various 'Homeopathy Emergencies' and I asked one final question.

'If you died and went to heaven and God sat you down and told you, "Gemma, I have to tell you – homeopathy is nonsense." Would you believe him?'

She answered in an instant.

'No.'

8

'Some type of tiny wasps'

It began in the way it often begins, so those that tell of it say: with an explosion of crawling, itching and biting, his skin suddenly alive, roaring, teeming, *inhabited*. A metropolis of activity on his body. This is not what fifty-five-year-old IT executives from Birmingham expect to happen to them on fly-drive breaks to New England. But there it was and there *he* was, in an out-of-town multiscreen cinema in a mall somewhere near Boston, writhing, scratching, rubbing, cursing. His legs, arms, torso – God, it was everywhere. He tried not to disturb his wife and two sons as they gazed up, obliviously, at *Harry Potter and the Order of the Phoenix*. It must be fleas, he decided. Fleas in the seat.

That night, in his hotel, Paul could not sleep. 'You're crazy, Dad,' said the boys. It must be tics, mites, something like that. But none of the creams worked, nor the sprays. Within days, odd marks began to appear, in the areas where his skin was soft. Red ones. Little round things, raised from his skin. Paul ran his fingertips gently over them. There was something growing inside them, like splinters or spines. He could feel their sharp points catching. Back home, he told his doctor, 'I think it's something strange.'

Paul had tests. It wasn't scabies. It wasn't an allergy or

fungus. It wasn't any of the obvious infestations. Whatever it was, it had a kind of cycle. The creeping and the crawling was the first thing. Then the burrowing and then biting, as if he was being stabbed with compass needles. Then the red marks would come and, inside them, the growing spines.

One evening, nearly a year after his first attack, Paul's wife was soothing his back with surgical spirit when she noticed that the cotton swab had gathered a bizarre blue-black haze from his skin. Paul dressed quickly, drove as fast as he could to Maplin's, bought a microscope and placed the cotton beneath the lens. He focused. He frowned. He focused again. His mouth dropped open. Dear God, what *were* they? Those weird, curling, coloured fibres? He opened his laptop and Googled: 'Fibres. Itch. Sting. Skin.' And there it was – it must be! All the symptoms fit. He had a disease called Morgellons. A *new* disease. According to the website, the fibres were the product of creatures, unknown to science, that breed in the body. Paul felt the strong arms of relief lift the worry away. Everything was answered, the crucial mystery solved. But as he pored gratefully through the information on that laptop screen, he had no idea that Morgellons would actually turn out to be the worst kind of answer imaginable.

Morgellons was named in 2002, by American mom Mary Leitao, after she learned of a similar-sounding (but actually unrelated) condition that was reported in the seventeenth century, in which children sprouted hairs on their backs. Leitao's son had been complaining of sores around his mouth and the sensation of 'bugs'. Using a microscope, she found him to be covered in red, blue, black and white fibres. Since then, experts at Leitao's Morgellons Research Foundation say they have been contacted by over twelve thousand affected families. Educational and support group The Charles E. Holman Foundation claim there are patients in 'every continent except Antarctica'.

Even folk singer Joni Mitchell has been affected, complaining to the *LA Times* about 'this weird incurable disease that seems like it's from outer space . . . Fibres in a variety of colours protrude out of my skin . . . they cannot be forensically identified as animal, vegetable or mineral. Morgellons is a slow, unpredictable killer – a terrorist disease. It will blow up one of your organs, leaving you in bed for a year.'

Since Leitao began drawing attention to the problem, thousands of sufferers in the US have written to members of Congress, demanding action. In response, more than forty senators, including Hillary Clinton, John McCain and a pre-presidential Barack Obama, pressured the government agency the Centers for Disease Control (CDC), to investigate. In 2008, the CDC established a special task force in collaboration with the US Armed Forces Institute of Pathology, with an initial budget of one million dollars. At a 2008 press conference, held to update the media on the agreed protocol for a scientific study, principal investigator Dr Michele Pearson admitted, 'We don't know what it is.'.

So, it is new and it is frightening and it is profoundly peculiar. But if you were to seek the view of the medical establishment, you would find the strangest fact of all about the disease.

Morgellons doesn't exist.

*

I have met Paul in a Tudor-fronted coaching inn, in a comfy executive suburb west of Birmingham. He arrived in a black Audi with leather seats, his suit jacket hanging on a hook over a rear window. There is chill-out music, a wood-fired pizza oven and, in the sunny garden, a flock of cyclists supping soft drinks from ice-clinking glasses. Paul is showing me pictures that he has collected of his fibres. A grim parade of jpegs flicks past on his screen – sores and scabs and nasal hairs, all magnified by a factor of two hundred. In each photo, a tiny coloured fibre on or in his skin.

'Is it an excrement?' he asks. 'A by-product? A structure they live in?' A waitress passes with a bowl of salad as he gestures towards an oozing wound. 'Is it a breathing pipe?' He shakes his head. 'It's just like something from science fiction. It's something that you'd see in a movie or in a book on aliens from another planet. It's out of this world.'

I nod and scratch my neck while Paul absentmindedly digs his nails into a lesion just below the hem of his khaki shorts. They visibly pepper his legs and arms – little red welts, some dulled to a waxy maroon, older ones now just plasticky-white scar tissue.

Paul has seen an array of experts – allergy doctors, tropical- and infectious-disease specialists, dermatologists. He has visited his GP more times than he can remember. None of them have given him an answer that satisfies him, or offered an end to the itching. His most recent attempt was at a local teaching hospital. 'I thought, *Teaching hospital! They might want to do a study on me.* Last week, I took them some samples of the fibres on a piece of cotton wool. But they discharged me. They said there was nothing they could do.'

Everywhere Paul goes, he carries a pot of alcohol hand-gel, which he has spiked with a traditional Middle Eastern parasite-killer called neem oil. In between his four daily showers, he steam cleans his clothes. The stress of it all leaves him exhausted, short-tempered. He has difficulty concentrating; applying himself at work. 'It affects my performance a bit,' he says.

'What does your wife think?' I ask.

His voice cracks.

'Frustrated,' he says. 'Sick of me being depressed and irritated. She wants her normal life back. And sometimes, without any progress coming along, I get depressed. Very depressed.'

'When was your lowest moment?'

He breaks eye contact. 'I don't want to go into that.' He stares into his half of ale, scratches his wrist and says, eventually, 'Pretty much feeling like ending it. Thinking, could I go through with it? Probably. It's associated with the times the medical profession have dismissed me. It's just – I can't see myself living forever with this.'

'Have you mentioned these thoughts to your doctor?'

'No, because talking about suic—' He stops himself. 'Things like that . . .' Another pause. 'Well, it adds a mental angle.'

Paul is referring to the pathology that clinicians and Skeptics alike claim is actually at the root of Morgellons. They say that what people like him are really suffering from is a form of psychosis called delusions of parasitosis, or DOP. He is, in other words, crazy. It is a view typified by academics such as Jeffrey Meffert, an associate professor of dermatology at the University of Texas in San Antonio, who has created a special presentation devoted to debunking Morgellons that he regularly presents to doctors and who told the *Washington Post*, 'Any fibres that I have ever been presented with by one of my patients have always been textile fibres.' It is thought that it is spread, not by otherworldy creatures but by the Internet. As Dr Mary Seeman, Emeritus Professor of Psychiatry at the University of Toronto, explained to the *New York Times*, 'When a person has something bothering him these days, the first thing he does is go online.' Dr Steven Novella of 'The Skeptics' Guide to the Universe' agrees: 'It is a combination of a cultural phenomenon spreading mostly online, giving specific manifestation to an underlying psychological condition. I am willing to be convinced that there is a biological process going on, but so far no compelling evidence to support this hypothesis has been put forward.'

But Paul is convinced. 'It is *absolutely* a physical condition,' he insists. 'I mean, look!'

Indeed, the evidence of his jpegs does seem undeniable. Much thinner than his body hair, the fibres bask expansively in craterous sores, hide deep in trench-like wrinkles and peer tentatively from follicles. They are indisputably there. Morgellons seems to represent a mystery even deeper than that of homeopathy. Its adherents offer physical evidence. Just for once, I wonder, perhaps the Skeptics might turn out to be wrong.

In an attempt to find out, I am travelling to the fourth Annual Morgellons Conference in Austin, Texas, to meet a molecular biologist who doesn't believe the medical consensus. Rather, the forensic tests he has commissioned on the fibres point to something altogether more alien.

*

In the spring of 2005, Randy Wymore, an associate professor of pharmacology at Oklahoma State University, accidentally stumbled across a report about Morgellons. Reading about the fibres that patients believed were the by-product of some weird parasite, but which were typically dismissed by disbelieving dermatologists as textile fragments, he thought, 'But this should be easy to figure out.' He emailed sufferers, requesting samples, then compared them to bits of cotton and nylon and carpets and curtains that he had found about the place. When he peered down the microscope's dark tunnel for the first time, he got a shock. The Morgellons fibres looked utterly different.

Wymore arranged for specialist fibre analysts at the Tulsa Police Department's forensic laboratory to have a look. Twenty seconds into their tests, Wymore heard a detective with twenty-eight years' experience of doing exactly this sort of work murmur, 'I don't think I've ever seen anything like this.' As the day wound on, they discovered that the Morgellons samples didn't match any of the eight hundred fibres they had on their database, nor the eighty-five thousand known organic compounds. He heated one fibre to 600°C and was astonished to find that it didn't burn. By the day's end, Wymore had concluded, 'There's something real going on here. Something that we don't understand at all.'

In downtime from teaching, Wymore still works on the mystery. In 2011, he approached a number of commercial laboratories and attempted to hire them to tease apart the elements which make the fibres up. But the moment they discovered the job was related to Morgellons, firm after firm backed out. Finally, Wymore found a laboratory that was prepared to take the work. Their initial analyses are now in, but the conclusions unannounced. More than anything else, it is this that I am hoping to hear about over the coming days.

It all begins an hour south of Austin, Texas, in the lobby of the Westoak Woods Church convention centre. Morgellons sufferers are gathering around the Continental breakfast buffet. From the UK, Spain, Germany, Mexico and twenty-two US states, they dig greedily into the sticky array – Krispie Treats, Strawberry Cheese-flavour Danish pastries, and Mrs Spunkmeyer blueberry muffins – as loose threads of conversation rise from the hubbub: 'I mix Vaseline with sulphur and cover my entire body to suffocate them'; 'The more you try to prove you're not crazy, the more crazy they think you are'; 'The whole medical community is part of this. I wouldn't say it's a conspiracy but . . .' At a nearby trestle table, a man sells pots of 'Mor Gone gel' ('Until There Is A Cure . . . There Is Mor Gone').

Many of the attendees that are moving slowly towards the conference hall will have been diagnosed with DOP, a subject that possesses a day-one speaker, paediatrician Greg Smith, with a fury that bounces him about the stage, all eyes and spit and jabbing fingers.

'Excuse me, people!' he says. 'This is morally and ethically wrong! So let me make a political statement, boys and girls.'

He dramatically pulls off his jumper, to reveal a T-shirt: 'DOP' with a red line through it.

'No more!' he shouts above the whoops and applause. 'No more!'

Out in the car park, Smith tells me that he has been a sufferer since 2004. 'I put a sweatshirt I'd been wearing in the garden over my arm and there was this intense burning, sticking sensation. I thought it was cactus spines. I began picking to get them out, but it wasn't long before it was all over my body.' He describes 'almost an obsession. You just can't stop picking. You feel the sensation of something that's trying to come out of your skin. You've just got to get in there. And there's this sense of incredible release when you get something out of it.'

'What are they?' I ask.

'Little particles and things,' he says, his eyes shining. 'You feel the sensation of something that's trying to come out of your skin.' He is pacing back and forth now. He is becoming breathless. 'You *feel* that. And when you try to start picking, sometimes it's a little fibre, sometimes it's a little hard lump, sometimes little black specks or pearl-like objects that are round and maybe half a millimetre across. When it comes out, you feel instant relief. It's something in all my experience that I had never heard of. It made no sense. But I saw it over and over again.'

Sometimes, these fibres can behave in ways that Smith

describes as 'bizarre'. He tells me of one occasion in which he felt a sharp pain in his eye. 'I took off my glasses and looked in the mirror,' he says. 'And there was a fibre there. It was white and really, really tiny. I was trying to get it out with my finger, and all of a sudden it moved across the surface of my eye and tried to dig in. I got tweezers and started to pick the thing out of eyeball. I was in terrible pain.'

I am horrified.

'Did it bleed?'

'I've still got the scar,' he nods. 'When I went to the emergency room and told the story of what had been going on – they called a *psychiatrist* in! I was like, "Wait a minute, what the heck is going on here?" Fortunately, he didn't commit me and after another consultation with him he became convinced I was not crazy.'

'So, it was a Morgellons fibre?' I say. 'And it *moved*?'

'Of course it was a fibre!' he says. 'It honest-to-God moved.'

Smith tells me that a Morgellons patient who finds unusual fibres in their skin will typically bring a sample to show their doctor. But when they do this, they're unknowingly falling into a terrible trap. It is a behaviour that is known among medical professionals as 'the matchbox sign' and it is used as evidence against them, to prove that they are mentally ill.

'The matchbox sign was first described in about 1930,' he says. 'They say it's an indicator that you have DOP. This is something that infuriates me. It has absolutely zero relevance to anything.'

Back in the UK, of course, Paul received his diagnosis of DOP after taking fibre-smeared cotton to his dermatologist. I tell Greg Smith that, were I to find unexplained particles in my skin, I would probably do exactly the same.

'Of course!' he says. 'It's what anyone would do if they had any sense at all. But the dermatologist will stand ten feet away and diagnose you as delusional.'

'But surely they can see the fibres?'

'They can if they look. But they will not look!'

'And if you try to show them the fibres, that makes you delusional?'

'You're crazy! You brought this in for them to look at? First step – bang.'

'But this is madness!' I say.

'It's total madness! It's inexcusable. Unconscionable.'

We speak about the CDC study. Like almost everyone here, Smith is suspicious of it. There is a widespread acceptance at this conference that the American authorities have already decided that Morgellons is psychological and – in classic hominin style – are merely looking for evidence to reinforce their hunch. Both Smith and Randy Wymore, the molecular biologist who arranged the forensic examination in Tulsa, have repeatedly offered to assist in finding patients, and have been ignored.

'Have you heard of the phrase "Garbage In Garbage Out"?' he says. 'It doesn't matter what conclusion that study comes to, even if it is totally favourable to the Morgellons community. It's not well designed. It's trash.'

As he speaks I notice Smith's exposed skin shows a waxy galaxy of scars. Although he still itches, all of his lesions appear to have healed. It is a remarkable thing. Sceptics believe that Morgellons sores are not made by burrowing parasites but by obsessive scratchers eroding the skin away. If Smith is correct, though, and the creatures are responsible for the sores, how has he managed to stop those creatures creating them?

'I absolutely positively stopped picking,' he tells me.

'And that was *it*?'

'Sure,' he replies, shrugging somewhat bemusedly, as if what he has just said doesn't run counter to everything that he is supposed to believe.

*

That evening, the Morgellons sufferers are enjoying a celebratory enchilada buffet at a suburban Mexican restaurant. Over the lukewarm feast, I have a long conversation with a British conventioneer – a midwife from Ramsgate named Margot. Earlier in the day, when I first met Margot, she said something that has been loitering in my mind ever since, wanting my attention but not quite sure why or what it is doing there. We were at a cafe, waiting for the man to pass us our change and our lunch. He dropped the coins into our hands and turned to wrap our sandwiches. As he did so, Margot sighed theatrically and gave me a look as if to say, 'Unbelievable! Did you see that?!'

I had no idea what she meant.

She rolled her eyes and explained, 'He touches the money, then he touches our food . . .'

Tonight, Margot describes a scene which ends up proving no less memorable: her, sat naked in a bath full of bleach, behind a locked door, wearing times-three magnification spectacles, holding a magnifying glass and a nit comb, scraping her face onto sticky office labels and examining the 'black specks' that were falling out. Perhaps sensing my reaction, she tries to reassure me: 'I was just being analytical,' she insists.

When bathing in bleach all night didn't help, Margot brought her dermatologist samples of her sticky labels. Shaking his head, he told her, 'I can't tell you how many people bring me specimens of lint and black specks in matchboxes.' She was diagnosed with DOP. Her employment was terminated. 'I'm a midwife,' she says, in her defence. 'I take urine and blood samples – specimens. So I was taking them a specimen. And that's what wrecked my life and career.'

As I am talking with Margot, I notice Randy Wymore, the molecular biologist I have been desperate to speak with, sitting at a nearby table. He is a slim, neat man wearing a charcoal shirt, orange tie and tidily squared goatee. When I sit with him, I find him to be incorrigibly bright, light and happy, even when delivering wholly discouraging news.

The first two samples that Wymore sent to the laboratory were not from Morgellons patients, but test fibres gathered from a barn and a cotton bud and then some debris from the filter in an air-conditioning unit. When the technicians correctly identified what they were, Wymore felt confident enough to submit the real things. And, so far, he says, 'We have not yet *exactly* replicated the *exact* results of the forensics people in Tulsa.'

Indeed, the laboratory has found Wymore's various Morgellons fibres to be: nylon; cotton; a blonde human hair; a fungal residue; a rodent hair; and down, likely from geese or ducks.

'That's disappointing,' I say.

He leans his head to one side and smiles.

'It is for the most part disappointing,' he says. 'But there was a bunch of cellulose that didn't make sense on one. And another *was* unknown.'

'Really?'

'Well, they said it was a "big fungal fibre". But they weren't *completely* convinced.'

The next day, nursing practitioner Dr Ginger Savely – who claims to have treated over five hundred Morgellons patients – leads an informal discussion in the hotel conference room. Around large circular tables they sit: the oozing and the itchy, the dismissed and the angry. 'I've seen a fibre go into my glasses' says one. 'I've seen one burrow into a pad'; 'One of my doctors thinks it's nanotechnology'; 'Check your clothing from China for nematodes'; 'Never put your suitcase on the floor of a train'; 'I was attacked by a swarm of some type of tiny wasps that seemed to inject parts of their bodies under my skin.'

I am writing the words 'tiny wasps' into my notepad when a furious woman with a terrifying itch-scar on her jaw says, 'I have Erin Brockovich's lawyer's number in my purse. Don't you think I'm not going to use it.'

'But who are you going to sue?' asks a frail elderly lady two tables away.

We all look expectantly at her. There is a moment of tense quiet.

'I don't know,' she says.

In a far corner, a woman with a round plaster on a dry, dusty, pinkly scrubbed cheek weeps gently.

Ten minutes later, I am alone in the lobby, attempting to focus my thoughts. My task here is straightforward. Has Paul been failed by his medics, or is he crazy? Are these people infested with uncommon parasites or uncommon beliefs? Over at the reception desk, a conventioneer is complaining loudly, hammering her finger on the counter.

'It's disgusting! Bugs! In. The. Bed. I've already been in two rooms. I had to drive to Walmart to buy fresh linen at 5 a.m. There's this *white* stuff all over the counter . . . '

When she has gone, I approach the desk and ask the receptionist if the weekend has seen a surge in complaints about cleanliness.

'Oh yeah.' She nods towards the conference room. 'And they're all coming from *those* people.' She leans forward and whispers conspiratorially. 'I think it's part of their condition.'

Satisfied, I retire to the lobby to await my allotted chat with Dr Savely.

'So, what do you think,' I ask her, 'about these tiny wasps?'

'Hmmm, no,' she says. 'But I haven't totally dismissed the whole genetically modified organisms thing. Something may have gone amuck.'

'Nanotechnology?' I ask. 'Some defence experiment gone awry?'

'If something like that went wrong and got out to the public . . .'

I decide to confess to Dr Savely my conclusion: that these people are, in fact, crazy.

'These people are not crazy,' she insists. 'They're good, solid people who have been dealt a bad lot.'

A woman approaches the vending machine behind the doctor. Between her palm and the top of her walking stick, there is a layer of tissue paper. We sit there as she creaks slowly past us.

'There's definitely *an element* of craziness here,' I say.

'But I truly believe it's understandable,' she says. 'For people to say you're delusional is very anxiety-provoking. Then they get depressed. Who wouldn't? Hello! The next stage is usually an obsessive-compulsive thing – paying attention to the body in great detail. But, again, I feel this is understandable in the circumstances.'

Not wholly convinced, I slip back into the conference room, where Margot is using her £700 wifi iPad telescope to examine herself. Suddenly, I have an idea.

'Can I have a go?'

Pushing the lens into my palm, I immediately see a fibre. The group falls into a hush. 'Did you clean your hand?' asks Margot. She fetches an anti-bacterial wet-wipe. I scrub and try again. I find an even bigger fibre. I wipe for a second time.

And find another one. Margot looks up at me with wet, sorry eyes. 'Are you worried?' She puts a kind, comforting hand on my arm. 'Oh, don't be worried, Will. I'm sure you haven't got it.'

*

Back in London, I find a 2008 paper on Morgellons in a journal called *Dermatologic Therapy*. It describes Morgellons patients picking 'at their skin continuously in order to "extract" an organism'; 'obsessive cleaning rituals, showering often' and individuals going 'to many physicians, such as infectious disease specialists and dermatologists' – all behaviours that are 'consistent with DOP' and also consistent with Paul. (For treatment, the authors recommend prescribing a benign anti-parasitic ointment to build trust, then topping it up with an anti-psychotic.) After finding fibres on my own hand, I am satisfied that Morgellons is some twenty-first-century genre of OCD that's spread like an Internet meme and the fibres are – just as Dr Wymore's labs are reporting – particles of everyday, miscellaneous stuff: cotton, human hair, rat hair and so on.

I am finalising my research when I decide to check one final point that has been niggling maddeningly. The itch. Both Paul and Greg's Morgellons began with an explosion of it. It is even affecting me: the night following my meeting with Paul, I couldn't sleep for itching. I had two showers before bed and another in the morning. All through the convention – even as I write these words – I am tormented; driven to senseless scratching. Why is itch so infectious?

For background, I contact Dr Anne Louise Oaklander, an associate professor at Harvard Medical School and probably the only neurologist in the world to specialise in itch. I email her describing Morgellons, carefully acknowledging that it is some form of DOP. But when we speak, Dr Oaklander tells me she knows all about Morgellons already. And then she says something that stuns me.

'In my experience, Morgellons patients are doing the best they can to make sense of symptoms that are real. These people have been maltreated by the medical establishment. And you're very welcome to quote me on that. They're suffering from a chronic itch disorder that's undiagnosed.'

To understand all this, it is first necessary to grasp some remarkable facts about itch. In 1987 a team of German researchers found itch wasn't simply the weak form of pain it had always been assumed to be. Rather, they concluded that itch has its own separate and dedicated network of nerves. And remarkably sensitive things they turned out to be: whereas a pain nerve has sensory jurisdiction of roughly a millimetre, an itch nerve can pick up disturbances on the skin over seventy-five millimetres away.

Dr Oaklander surmises that itch evolved as a way for humans to automatically rid themselves of dangerous insects. When a mosquito lands on our arm and it tickles, this sensation is not, as you might assume, the straightforward feeling of its legs pressing on our skin. That crawling, grubbing, tickling sensation is, in fact, a neurological alarm system that is wailing madly, begging for a scratch.

This alarm system can go wrong for a variety of reasons – shingles, sciatica, spinal-cord tumours or lesions, to name a few. It can ring suddenly, severely and without anything touching the skin. This, Oaklander believes, is what is happening to Morgellons patients.

'That they have insects on them is a very reasonable conclusion to reach, because, to them, it feels no different to how it would if there *were* insects on them. To your brain, it's exactly the same. So you need to look at what's going on with their nerves. Unfortunately, what can happen is a dermatologist fails to find an explanation and jumps to a psychiatric one.'

Of the obsessive investigations that Morgellons patients conduct on themselves, Oaklander says: 'When you feel an itch, what do you do? You look. That's the natural response. They may become fixated on the insect explanation for lack of a better one.'

But, she adds, that is not to say there aren't some patients whose major problem *is* psychiatric. Others still might suffer delusions in addition to their undiagnosed neuropathic illness. Nevertheless, 'It's not up to some primary-care physician to conclude that a patient has a major psychiatric disorder.'

If Oaklander turns out to be correct, it makes sense of the fact that Greg Smith's lesions healed when he stopped scratching. If the fibres *are* picked up by the environment, it explains how I found them on my hand. And if Morgellons is not actually a disease, but rather a witchbag of symptoms that might all have nerve-related maladies as its source, it squares something that Dr Savely said she is 'constantly perplexed' about: 'When I find a treatment that helps one person, it doesn't help the next at all. Every patient is a whole new ballgame.'

Thrilled at this development, I phone Paul and explain the itch-nerve theory. But he doesn't seem very excited.

'I can't see how that relates to my condition,' he sighs. 'I've got marks on my back that I can't even reach. I've not created those by scratching.'

It is a good point, perhaps, but one that I quietly dismiss. It now seems so likely that Paul is either delusional, or has some undiagnosed itch disorder, that I judge that he is merely looking for reasons not to believe this elegant and compelling solution.

Then, weeks later, I receive an unexpected email from a stranger in east London. Nick Mann has heard about my research into Morgellons and he wonders if I might be curious to hear about his experiences. When I arrive at his house, on a warm Tuesday night, and settle in his small kitchen with a mug of tea, I am doubting the wisdom of my visit. Probably, I think, I am wasting my time.

But Nick doesn't appear to be the kind of conspiracy-fixated, talking-too-fast, fiddling-with-their-fingers individual who usually gets in touch. Rather, he is a calm and friendly father of two who, he tells me, went for a walk a couple of years ago in the grounds of Abney Park Cemetery, just down the road from his home, when something unsavoury took place. It had been a sunny day and he had been wearing shorts and sandals. That evening, his legs began itching. Marks sprang up on his body. 'I was convinced something was on me,' he tells me. 'Something digging into my skin. Burrowing.'

Over the coming days, lesions began to open up on his skin. Running his fingertips over them, he could feel something inside: spines or fibres. He stripped naked in his kitchen and tried to dig one out. 'I stood there for three or four hours, waiting for one to bite,' he says. 'As soon as it did, I went for it with a hypodermic needle. There was one on my nipple.' He pales slightly. 'You know, I can't get that out of my head. It was so painful. I dug the needle in and felt it flicking against something that wasn't me. And I just carried on digging and scooping.' He carried on like this for nearly four hours. 'At one point my wife came in and saw blood dripping down from my leg and scrotum.'

By the end of the day, Nick had dug three of the 'things' from his body. They were so small, he says, 'You could only see them when they moved.' Tipping them from a Rizla paper into a specimen jar, he showed his wife, Karen. She peered into the pot. She looked worriedly at her husband. Karen could see nothing.

I put my pen down and rub my brow. Poor Nick Mann, I think. Just like Greg Smith, madly attacking his own body, trying to remove bits of fluff. And just like Paul – so convinced by the illusion of his own itch response that he became fixated on the fantasy that he had been invaded by invisible monsters. To get some general sense of how unstable this man could turn out to be, I try to discover a bit more about him.

'What did you say you did for a living?' I ask.

'I'm a GP,' he says.

I sit up. 'You're a GP?'

'Yes,' he says, brightly. 'I'm a doctor. A GP. At a practice in Hackney.'

'Right,' I say. 'Okay. Right. So then what happened?'

'I took the three mites I'd caught to the Homerton Hospital in east London,' he says. 'A technician there mounted one on a slide, put it under a microscope and said "Beautiful." Everyone gathered around saying, "Ooh, look at that." They had no idea what it was. They sent it over to the Natural History Museum, who identified it within a day. It was a tropical rat mite. What they do is go in through the hair follicles and find a blood vessel at the bottom. That's where they sit and that's what the fibres are – their legs folded back.'

It is astonishing. It seems to explain it all – the sudden itch, the fibres, even the lesions in unscratchable places. I discuss with Nick the sorry experiences that Paul had trying to get anyone to take him seriously. Nick admits that he was only able to have his samples examined by experts because he was acting as his own doctor. And if that hadn't happened, he says, 'I would have received exactly the same treatment that he did. Delusions of parasitosis.'

'Paul had the impression that his doctors were working from a kind of checklist,' I say, 'and if his symptoms weren't on it, he was just dismissed as crazy.'

'I'm afraid that's true,' says Nick. 'If none of the medical models fit, they're dismissed. The immediate conclusion is "medically unexplained symptom", which is a euphemism for nuts. It's a sad indictment of my own profession but I've experienced it first-hand. There used to a culture of getting to the bottom of the problem. There isn't that now. I find that really sad. And the idea that people with Morgellons are nutty – I really did nearly go mad with the itch. It was disturbing my sleep, there was barely a minute where I wasn't having to scratch or resist the urge to scratch. It's this constant feeling of being infested. It freaked me out.' As for the weird reasons that patients come up with for their condition – the nanotechnology, the tiny wasps – Nick is unsurprised. 'Of course, you look for answers, don't you?' he says. 'We need to find explanations for things.'

We need explanations. We need certainty. And certainty is precisely what I have been seeking over the last few weeks. Are Morgellons sufferers mad? Are they sane? Are they the one? Or the other? I never considered the possibility that they might be both. And, in this, I wonder if I can detect another clue, another soft point in our faulty thinking about beliefs and who we are.

This compulsion to separate everyone into absolute types is the first lesson of Christianity that I can remember learning: kind people go to heaven, unkind people go to hell. There will come a day of judgement and that judgement will be simple, sliced, clean, merciless. In boyhood, the law of the playground dictates that you mentally divide your cohorts into people that you like and people that you don't – in-groups and out. This doesn't change much in adulthood. The Skeptics that I met in Manchester thrived on this kind of binary division – and the combative homeopaths did, too. They both told their story, and cast each other as villain. We are a tribal animal. It is who we are and it is how we are.

The urge is to reduce others to simplified positions. We define what they are, and then use these definitions as weapons of a war. Nobody enjoys the restless unpleasantness of doubt. It is uncomfortable, floating between poles, being pulled by invisible forces towards one or the other. We need definitions. We need decisions. We need finality if we are to heal the dissonance.

When my father told me that I had misunderstood faith – that it was not a matter of certainty, but a journey – I was instinctively hostile to the idea. Perhaps it suited me better to think that Christians are foolishly convinced by childish beliefs; that they are stupid. It is a reassuring story that I told myself because, according to the models of my brain, Christians are Bad. Journalism, too, encourages just this kind of certainty. Facts, assessed and checked. Liars exposed, truth-tellers elevated. Good guys and bad guys. The satisfaction of firm conclusions, of nuance erased, of reality tamed. In my younger years, I was driven to the ends of my own sanity by the desire for this form of truth – an unthreatening, finished article that is cauterised and stitched and does not bleed. Does she love me? Is she faithful? Will she love me next week? Next year? Did she love him more? Does she desire him more? Will we stay in love for ever?

In my mid-twenties, I attended weekly group therapy sessions in north London with people who were much older than me. One evening, a woman in her mid-forties was talking contemptuously about her father, a university lecturer who, she said, had 'a crush' on one of his teenage students. I was scandalised.

'But he's married!' I said.

She looked baffled. What was my point?

'I mean, doesn't he love your mum any more?' I said. 'Are they getting a divorce?'

The adults around me shared a moment. Glances were exchanged. Sniggers were muted. As I write this, I can tell you that the shame is still alive. I can feel it slithering out from underneath the memory and into my skin.

I used to hold a fierce belief in binary love, of the kind that is promised in music, film and literature. You are in love, or you are not. They were absolute modes of being, like Christian or non-Christian, right or wrong, sane or insane. Today, my marriage is happy because I understand that true love is a mess. It is like my father's belief in God: a journey, sometimes blissful, often fraught. It is not the ultimate goal that was promised by all those pop songs. It lacks the promise of certainty. But it is its very difficulties that give love its value. If you didn't have to fight for it – if it was just *there*, reliable, steady, ever-present, like a cardboard box over your head – what would be its worth?

I used to expect love to be solid, sure, overpowering, *decided*. That is how we declare ourselves. When we get married, we promise faithfulness for ever. When priests talk about God, they say, 'He exists.' When the Skeptics talk about homeopathy, they say, 'There is no evidence.' When the medical establishment talk about Swami Ramdev's pranayama, they say, 'It doesn't work'; when they judge Morgellons sufferers, they say, 'They are delusional.' But what if pranayama works like homeopathy works, by brilliantly triggering various powerful placebo effects? What if these Morgellons sufferers *are* crazy, but they have been driven to these ends by itching caused by a variety of undiagnosed conditions and rejection by lazy doctors?

As I leave the home of Dr Mann, he kindly offers to see Paul so that he can check if his is an infestation of tropical rat mite. After their meeting, a few weeks later, Nick emails me to say that he found no evidence of it, but that 'he's certainly not delusional'. He sends some fibre pictures and one of Paul's videos to the experts at the Natural History Museum. They reply, 'It is our opinion that the fibre is a fabric fibre and it is only its curvature, and consequent variation in focus, that makes it appear to be arising from under the skin. The specimen in the video does look like a mite. It is not clear enough to be certain, but the most likely candidate is a member of the suborder Astigmata, for example, a species of the family Acaridae or Glycyphagidae. These mites are typically found in stored foods, but also occur in house dust.'

Theirs is a conclusion that will be echoed when the CDC study is finally published. 'No parasites or mycobacteria were detected,' it reports. 'Most materials collected from participants' skin were composed of cellulose, likely of cotton origin. No common underlying medical condition or infectious source was identified, similar to more commonly recognised conditions such as delusional infestation.' Commenting on the work, Steven Novella writes, 'The evidence strongly suggests that a psychological cause of Morgellons is most likely, and there is no case to be made for any other alternative . . . It is entirely consistent with delusional parasitosis.'

And Paul is back where he began.

The last time I speak with him, he sighs deeply down the phone.

'Are you all right?' I ask.

'Pretty crap actually. I've been forced out of my job. They said it's based on my "engagement level" and that's down to the lack of energy I've got at work. I can't sign myself off sick because Morgellons is not a diagnosis. There's no legitimate reason for me not to be operating at full speed. But, you know, I'm a fighter. I'm trying to rally against it but it's . . . quite upsetting, really.'

'How are you coping?'

'Well . . . lurching along the parapet of depression, I suppose. But I'm all right. You can put another line in your book – my job is another thing that has been destroyed by this disease. And all because Morgellons isn't supposed to exist.'

9

'Top Dog wants his name in'

King's Cross station, London, some time in the early eighties. A man on the end of a platform, shouting. Dirty, pale, young. Commuters backing away as two members of the British Transport Police approach him. They know what they are dealing with. Look at him. What a freak. What a lunatic. *What a fucking nutter.* They could never guess that, only three months ago, twenty-one-year-old Ron Coleman had been a successful investment banker working the futures market in the City and living in a beautiful flat in West Hampstead. Now here he is: broke, raging at phantoms and contemplating jumping in front of a train. Ron knows he looks crazy. But he can *hear* them. They're real! All talking to him, talking about him. He can *hear* them. And he can hear *her*, among the others: Annabel, his amazing, beautiful, blue-eyed Annabel, who he misses. Oh, he misses Annabel so much. He can hear her, saying, 'Go on, Ron. Why don't you jump?'

The policemen took Ron to the Royal Free Hospital in Hampstead. A psychiatrist told him that he had developed a disease of the brain called schizophrenia. But it was treatable. All he had to do was stay in hospital and take the medication. In ten days, Annabel's voice would fade.

Ten days passed and Ron did not feel better. 'I'm getting out of here,' he thought. But before he could reach the door, the nurse stopped him.

'Where are you going?' she said.

'Home.'

'Well, you can't.'

'Of course I can! The doctor said after ten days, it would work. It's not worked. So I'm going home.'

The nurse pressed a button. The ward went on lockdown. Ron Coleman was sectioned. It was a terrifying moment, and his first skirmish in a war of ideas that he has been fighting, now, for over thirty years. Since his sectioning, he has become an icon to an ever-growing group of voice-hearers who insist that, actually, there is nothing wrong with them. Voice-hearing, they say, is not a proof of mental illness. Like left-handedness or ginger hair, it is actually just a variation; another version of being human. Like homosexuals in the 1970s, they don't need curing of a psychiatric illness but rather liberating from a model that says they are sick. One day, they hope, the stigma of being a voice-hearer will vanish, and the world will come to agree with Ron's dramatic hypothesis: that there is no such thing as schizophrenia.

Most psychiatrists say that schizophrenia is a very real physical disease. They think this for several reasons – perhaps the most persuasive being that they can detect its presence in the brains of sufferers, using scans and post-mortems on deceased patients. But members of the Hearing Voices Net-work (HVN), of which Ron Coleman is a leader, dispute this. Along with a cadre of rebel psychiatrists, they have come to believe that people hear voices, not because of some disease in their brains, but as a result of traumatic experiences. Professor Marius Romme, the Dutch psychiatrist and the movement's intellectual godfather, suggests that auditory hallucinations are nothing more than the brain's attempt at offering advice following an emotional crisis. It is, he has said, 'a normal response to an abnormal experience'. If you go hunting for abnormal experiences that might have caused Ron's voices, you will find two.

He was born in Dundee, in 1958, and raised by good Catholic parents on a bad estate called Kirkton. He loved church and he loved rugby and it was after a match, drinking with his teammates in a notorious pub called the Clep, that he saw her. 'It was one of those love-at-first-sight things. She was *stunning*,' he says, still visibly flushed all these years later. Even in that part of Dundee, the Clep was known as a hard place. Nothing was allowed to distract from the alcohol: not a TV nor a telephone nor even a jukebox. All you got at the Clep were seats, beer and a place to piss. Women never drank there. And yet, there she was, up at the bar – a posh-talking girl with a black fringe and hippy bangles and bracelets, 'and jeans – very tight jeans. And she had these amazing, penetrating blue eyes. That's what really got me: those eyes.'

Ron was not quite sixteen. Annabel was twenty-five. He asked her if she wanted to go to the Hong Kong, a late-night Chinese restaurant that had a bar and a dancefloor. 'It's not that I was particularly confident,' he explains, 'it's just that it was *her*.' When she said yes, he was amazed. 'I had to ask the captain of my rugby team to have a whip-round because I didn't have any money.'

Ron and Annabel became lovers. 'We had a great time together. She showed me a new world. Classical music, rock music, art. She taught me what love was.' Two years into their relationship, they decided to marry. Then, one day, for reasons he declines to share, Annabel died. 'And my life became a total misery.'

Still, he had his rugby. He *needed* his rugby. He needed it because it was the only way he knew how to deal with his life's other abnormal experience.

As a boy, Ron had dreamt of becoming a priest. When he was ten, a man called Father Adrian joined his local church and quickly became a popular and respected member of the community. The man and the boy grew close. One morning, following mass, Father Adrian told him that they needed to pray. They knelt slowly in front of one another. 'You are a sinner,' said the priest, softly. 'You have led me into sin. What's going to happen now – it's because you've been tempting me. It's your fault. And, for doing this to someone like *me*, you deserve to burn in hell.'

When it happened, Ron felt as if he was looking down on himself. He remembers the smell of incense and Father Adrian's purple robe. He remembers thinking, 'Why does God hate me so much?'

The abuse went on for nearly a year, until Ron stopped attending mass. Instead, he would sit on Law Hill, staring down at the church and eating 'mushie' – the honeycomb sweets he would buy with the money that was supposed to go into the collection. He would expel his feelings of guilt and shame and rage by imagining his opponent in a rugby scrum was Father Adrian. 'Rugby wasn't a sport for me. It was a coping strategy,' he says. 'I'd picture his face and try to kill him.'

When he was twenty-one, Ron broke his hip. His doctor told him he would never play again. His coping strategy gone, he was in despair. Shortly afterwards, he was working on some analysis at work, waiting for the computer to finish its calculations. He was sitting there, bored, idling and doleful. And then Annabel said to him, 'You've done that wrong.' He froze. *What the . . .?* He looked around. There was no one there. 'So, being a good Scot,' he recalls, 'I went to the pub and got absolutely rat-arsed.'

He carried on drinking, day after day, more and more and more. In the chaos of his increasing dereliction, he stopped making money for the firm. After eight weeks, he was dismissed with a payout of thousands. He spent the money on alcohol, cocaine, amphetamines and Purple Hearts to help him come down. The voices worsened. Annabel would beg him, 'Come and join me, so that we can be a family again.' Father Adrian would barrack him, 'You're a bastard, aren't you? It's your fault. I told you: you deserve to burn in hell. You led me into sin and you fucking loved it.'

At first, Ron assumed that he was ill. But soon, he became less sure. When someone suffering auditory hallucinations hears voices, they really do *hear* them. They sound no different to a true voice. Sometimes they come from 'inside' your head, often they come from outside – exactly as if you were sharing a room with someone invisible. Sometimes they talk to you ('You're a cunt'), sometimes they'll narrate your every action ('Now the cunt is making tea'), sometimes different voices will discuss you ('Look at that cunt, he's got nothing left to live for', 'I know, look at him! No one loves him, he might as well just kill himself').

'It was just constant, constant, constant,' says Ron. 'You'd just want to get away from them. And the problem is, you start to think they're real. Because you can *hear* them. You wonder – why can other people not hear them?'

The doctors in the Royal Free Hospital told Ron that he should ignore the voices. 'You'd say to the nurse, "My voices are really bad, can I talk to you about them?" and she'd say, "Let's play Scrabble!"' He noticed that being labelled a 'schizophrenic' led to people patronising him. Like the time he was forced to attend a lasagne-making class. 'I said, "Look love, I might be mad, but I'm not fucking stupid."' A nurse followed him everywhere. 'Bathroom, toilet, the works,' he says. 'It's dehumanising. It starts the institutionalisation. You start to think, If that's what they expect, that's what I'm going to give them.'

'Give them what?' I ask.

'Grief,' he says, smiling. 'I started telling them to fuck off all the time.'

Ron was forced to take medication that threatened terrible side-effects: tremors, weight gain, sexual dysfunction and the increased risk of diabetes and cardiac arrest. 'The meds made me drool, slime coming out of my mouth, I'd be stiff. I'd say to the doctors: "You're just a fucking Nazi; just a pill merchant." But then one of the older hands had a word with me in the smoke room. He said, "You want to get out of here, yeah? You have to keep your head down. Just tell them you're feeling better." That's how I learned to lie.'

Eighteen months after his sectioning, Ron lied his way to release. He took the first coach out of Victoria coach station and ended up in Manchester. To avoid going back into the psychiatric system, he lived on the streets. When the voices worsened, a doctor gave him a three-month supply of medication. He used them to try to kill himself. He woke up four days later, sectioned once more, in a Manchester hospital. And that is where everything was to change.

A support worker told Ron about a radical-sounding group that was forming nearby. It was inspired by the work of controversial Dutch psychiatrist Professor Marius Romme, who encouraged members not to ignore their voices, but to accept their reality and actively listen to them. 'By now I'd learned not to rock the boat,' he says. 'So I told her it was the craziest idea I'd ever heard. She said that if I agreed to go, we could stop for a beer on the way back. And I said, "This is the best thing that's ever happened in psychiatry. Let's go."'

When Ron arrived at the fledgling Hearing Voices Network

meeting, he was told something that ran counter to all the psychiatric lore he had ever heard. His voices were not a disease. They were *real*. They had meaning. They were a part of him and he needed to listen to them. To Ron this made sense: his principal voices were Father Adrian and Annabel. It was as if the two most terrible events in his life had taken living form; as if he was being haunted, daily, by the saddest things that had ever happened to him. How could they be dismissed as 'irrelevant', just a symptom of schizophrenia, as a cough is to a cold? Father Adrian and Annabel *were* part of him. *Of course* they were. 'I felt total astonishment,' he says. 'My support worker and I sat in the car outside for hours just talking about that idea. We never made it to the pub.'

It was the beginning of a journey that led to Ron being drug-free and happy. By listening to his voices, negotiating with them and taking a firm parental line against them, he retook control of his mind. Within a year of that first meeting, he was made British national co-ordinator of HVN. He became known for his 'Mad Pride' stance and his 'Psychotic and Proud' shoulder tattoo. Today he says, 'Voice-hearers are not sick. We're just a variant, a variation, like people who are left-handed.' He also dismisses the idea that auditory hallucinations are a principal symptom of schizophrenia. 'There's no evidence that schizophrenia even exists,' he says. 'The diagnostics for any major mental illness are, in my opinion, completely subjective. You can see three different psychiatrists on the same day and get three different diagnoses. If you're hearing voices and you've got a straight face they'll call you schizophrenic. If you're laughing they'll call you manic depressive. If they don't like you, they'll call it a personality disorder. These are just catch-all terms that psychiatrists use when they're baffled.'

The story of Ron Coleman is both gripping and exceptional. On his telling, it appears to be a case in which the consensus view of the scientific establishment has been proved wrong – by a movement whose spokesman is categorically, unashamedly and literally mad. As Ron tells his story, I find myself rooting for him. It is as if the biases of my brain are reaching out towards him, a thousand arms, encouraging, cajoling, applauding. All of them are silently lobbying my unconscious to believe the *right* thing.

Just as Ron's mind contains ciphers of Annabel and Father Adrian, mine surely echoes with the felt emotions of Gemma Hoefkens and John Mack and my father and a hundred others. Do I want Ron to be proved right because I identify with the irrational ones? Is it because, as I have grown older, I have found an urge to defend my father, to excuse his religious beliefs rather than to scorn them? I ask the questions because I really don't know the answers. How could I? My biases are invisible to me – I feel them only as a wordless urge, an emotion, something inside me that fountains upwards when I listen to Ron speaking. I can't see these sensations or analyse them forensically. I can't locate their source. I can't alter them.

I wonder, too, if there might be a simpler reason for my unprofessional wish for Ron to be right. His is the perfect story: the kind, poor boy – a churchgoer! – who falls victim to tragedy and a powerful elite. He is locked up against his will. He fights back. At first, he fails. He *nearly dies*. And then he rises, resplendent, to take on the heartless operatives of psychiatry on behalf of an army of his fellow-repressed around the globe.

Stories are so central to our understanding of the world that their importance can be easy to miss. Like the cats raised in cages without horizontal lines, we are at risk of bumping into the fact that our own stories can lie to us if we are never given reason to consider it. I wonder how often we are seduced by attractive plots that we have happened across in life: tricked into faulty beliefs by our hatred of Goliath.

Gemma's story also told of a death's-door underdog, flirting with disaster at the hands of an unfeeling medical profession, only to fight back, then saving herself and, ultimately, others. The Skeptics pitch their battle as a crusade against evil stage psychics who exploit the bereaved and amoral chemists who knowingly hawk 'sham medication' as poor, sick children wilt in their beds.

Who are the heroes? Who are the villains? Jesus or Dawkins? Gemma or Randi? Are they of your tribe? Or are they of the repulsed and repulsive other? The explorers of neuroscience and experimental psychology tell us that we make these decisions instantly, underneath the surface of our awareness. Something happens, down there in the unconscious. Some mechanism, some switch, some electrical storm of cognition ranges across the strange territories where we keep our models of the world and where the restless, barracking ghosts of everyone we have met who has affected us still roam: mothers, fathers, lovers, dead wives, abusive priests. This is the place where beliefs are made and where madness gathers. It is the realm of the invisible forces that I have been hunting.

*

Professor Marius Romme settles slowly into his armchair on a late afternoon in winter. The room he has taken, during a teaching visit at the University of Durham's Institute of Advanced Studies, is darkening quickly as the ancient green and the chapel outside the window fade into the dusk. Even at seventy-seven, Romme is attractive: tanned, tall and fit, his grey hair waxed back in a charismatic sweep. Beside him, his longtime research partner Dr Sandra Escher sits forward, more anxious, alert and eager to please. Romme is the man that started it all, when he met a woman in Maastricht whose life was commanded by gods.

Back in the mid-1980s, Romme was a professor at the University of Maastricht who practised as a psychiatrist in the local Community Mental Health Centre. Then, as now, psychiatrists use one of two 'bibles' to diagnose their patients, the most famous of which is known as the DSM. It is like a catalogue of madness, and lists thousands of psychiatric diagnoses along with their accompanying symptoms.

Because of the gods, and all the things they forbade her, this patient had lost friends and the will to do very much at all. According to the DSM, if you are hearing voices and you are isolated and you lack initiative, that is three of the symptoms of schizophrenia – and three ticks means you have it. So that is what Romme told her: 'You've got schizophrenia.'

The patient was not impressed.

'Well, that's all very nice,' she said. 'But it doesn't help me. You've just given it a name. How can I learn to live with these voices?'

'I just didn't know,' Romme tells me. He arranged for her to meet with another voice-hearer, thinking it might, at least, help with her isolation. He was amazed when they understood each other's experiences so completely. 'It was clear that they really did hear voices,' he says. 'They didn't fantasise it.' He recruited more voice-hearers but, while they enjoyed meeting one another, they couldn't work out any real strategies for coping with their constant malady. Then Romme had an idea. His work with unusual humans had impressed upon him the almost infinite variety of experience there is out there. What if they made an appeal on television? It was a long shot, but perhaps they would find *one* person who heard voices and had somehow found a way to manage them.

When they went on a chat show, in 1987, they found not

one person who was happy hearing voices – they found more than two hundred. 'That was really shocking,' says Romme. 'My training told me that all auditory hallucinations are signs of pathology. But these people were perfectly happy.'

While interviewing these happy voice-hearers, Romme secretly tried to diagnose them by finding three DSM-listed symptoms to tick. 'And I couldn't,' he says. 'I was astonished. It was a totally new experience. These people were in no need of help.'

'What was the difference between the happy voice-hearers and the unhappy ones?' I ask.

'We found that non-patients are not afraid of their voices,' he says. 'Patients are, and they had more intense and frequent traumatic experience in their young lives. Eighty per cent of patients had experienced traumatic overpowering situations. For the non-patients, it was about forty or fifty per cent.'

These hugely significant numbers led Romme to his heretical hypothesis: what if hearing voices is nothing to do with a physical disease of the brain? What if it is a natural response, triggered by trauma? And it has a positive purpose, to be like an adviser? An encouraging presence, willing someone to look differently and more creatively at their problem? What if it is actually a *good* thing?

The objections to this are obvious. What about when they call you a worthless cunt? That doesn't seem very helpful. 'The voices reflect the way the person looks at their problem,' he says. 'If the person looks negatively at it, their voices join the negative side.' What about the voices that preach suicide? 'These voices are saying, "Do something to change your life, otherwise you'll be dead,"' he says. 'It's a metaphoric message.'

Romme soon came to doubt the rationale of medicating voice-hearers. 'If you've been sexually abused, that's the problem, not how you react,' he says. Although he concedes that anti-psychotics 'help a little bit' and that 'a small number' of patients stop hallucinating, he adds that they work by reducing emotion, which you need in order to learn how to live with your voices. They also kill one in a hundred. 'Is it worth it?'

Romme's superiors at the University of Maastricht were not impressed by all this wild heresy. In fact, they reacted in a way that is remarkably similar to that of the Harvard dean who led the attempts at silencing John Mack.

'They said I was going crazy,' says Romme. 'They accused me of hearing voices myself. It soon became clear that they were trying to get me out. I had challenged the medical model and it was not appreciated.'

It took a while, but Professor Romme eventually convinced some of psychiatry's leading thinkers that he wasn't insane. One of these academics is the University of Manchester's Professor Richard Bentall, who has been studying auditory hallucinations since 1985.

'I am a reluctant convert to what I am about to tell you,' he says. 'There is incontestable evidence that there's a wide range of bad things that can happen to kids, including sexual abuse, which increase the risk of psychosis dramatically. Contrary to what you'll find in virtually every psychiatric textbook and regular papers published in respected journals, the evidence for a genetic determination of these disorders to specific genes is wafer-thin. If there was a gene for schizophrenia they would have found it by now. What it looks like is that there are probably a thousand genes which each produce a small increase of risk. However – and this is also contrary to what you'll find in psychiatric textbooks – there is a massive amount of evidence of environmental factors playing a role.'

In his book *Doctoring the Mind*, Bentall quotes multiple surveys of psychotic patients who have experienced 'very high levels of sudden trauma, including violent incidents and sexual assaults, compared to the experiences of ordinary people'. A typical example is a 2004 paper in the *British Journal of Psychiatry* that found the rate of childhood abuse in adults suffering psychosis to be fifteen times greater than expected. He is currently preparing to submit a meta-analysis to 'one of the world's top medical journals' which will compile ten years of large-scale studies into the environmental causes of psychosis. 'Just to tell you what the meta-analysis will say – the odds ratio is three. That means that somebody who has been sexually abused has a three times greater chance of becoming psychotic than somebody who has had a healthy childhood.'

I ask Bentall what he thinks of Ron Coleman's contention that there is no such thing as schizophrenia. 'Isn't that a bit extreme?'

'I don't see it as extreme,' he says. 'I've said it myself. It's an utterly useless concept. It hasn't helped anybody. But there's a philosophical question to be asked about all this – how do we define mental illness? We don't have any kind of biological reference for psychiatric disorders in the same way that we do for, say, appendicitis. Even if we did, there'd be an issue of where we draw the line between a psychiatric disorder and not. Virtually all of them lie on a continuum with normal function. It's not you're schizophrenic or you're not – people are more or less schizophrenic.'

At some point in my journey, wherever the line into true mental illness actually lies, I suddenly realise that I have crossed it. I wonder when I did it, and with whom? Who amongst all the people that I have met are just ordinarily irrational? And which are the ones who are ill?

But inside the ermine robes of these lordly judgements hangs a soggy pocket of doubts. What qualifies me to act as this binary-thinking St Peter of the sane? Am I certain that I am on a different side of the line to Margot from Ramsgate?

When I was in my early twenties I would sneak back to the flat I shared with my girlfriend, two minutes after leaving for work, so convinced was I that she was having an affair with the man upstairs. I had no reason to suspect this. I didn't even know who lived up there. As I tip-toed to the door, I would tell myself, 'You're fucking *mad*.' And yet there I was, leaning in, listening for footsteps. It was the same as the occasions on which I would find myself helplessly phoning premium dating numbers in the local paper, to check if any of the women 'seeking love' were her. It was irrational. Delusional. One version of me knew it, while another couldn't help itself.

I do not consider myself mentally ill, and yet I have behaved in ways that I could neither control nor explain. I have had suicidal thoughts. When things become difficult, I often console myself that simply resigning from the game is 'an option'. In that moment I believe it to be a rational judgement – I have my models of the world and I understand it to be an essentially hostile place. If it overwhelms me, then I am overwhelmed. I have done my best and it didn't work. A decision simply to stop fighting seems reasonable. Fair.

And yet, as I write this, it seems like anything but. It is disorientating. I *know* that when I feel suicidal, I am convinced that it is my life and my choice and that I am making it in a clear and reasonable condition of mind. But now it seems equally obvious that this is the product of damaged cognition; that to leave my wife and family in this way would be cruel. There they are again, those two people – the one that believes in UFOs and the one that doesn't; the one that wanted to stop stealing and the one that couldn't help it; the one that wanted to help the screaming Buddhist and the one that couldn't; the one that knew the lover was faithful and the one that knew she wasn't. Which person am I? Am I two people? *More?*

Mental illness, says Richard Bentall, 'lies on a continuum'.

It seems to me that, on any given day, we all suffer mild symptoms of many of them. I might hear my wife's opinion of the fact I have left the washing up, just below the level of my conscious hearing; I might feel paranoid about an uncommunicative newspaper editor who has failed to acknowledge a submission; I might experience a light OCD when I triple-check that the iron is *definitely* off before I go out. Perhaps a full, debilitating mental illness occurs when one of these ordinary patterns of thinking takes over.

'That's exactly correct,' Bentall says. 'But the question still remains – when, exactly, do we decide it has taken over?'

I tell Richard that it is as if there are different versions of me, different agents with different opinions, all operating from within the same skull.

'There are lots of theories about multiple selves and, depending on how you define them, they're probably true,' he replies. 'The brain generates models of the world, and one of the things it does is generate a model of what sort of person we are, what sort of person we'd like to be and also what sort of person we fear becoming. So there are all these different versions of us swimming around in our brain. They tend to come to the fore at different times – you do something which you realise is a bit embarrassing and your feared-self rears up. It's not a nice feeling.'

'Is this related to the fact that you're one version of yourself with your father, and then another with your wife?'

'Absolutely,' he says. 'But it's important to remember that these are just models. They're conceptual systems which get activated at different times. Our various selves can be more or less in tune with each other or not. When they're not, that's associated with psychiatric problems. So depressed people in particular have a huge gap between how they see themselves and how they would like to be – their ideal self. If you're not the sort of person you'd like to be, that's how you get depressed.'

*

This endlessly human and private struggle that we all go through – trying to merge our many selves into one happy and real whole – is a notion that is central to the work of an ideological co-conspirator of Ron Coleman and Professor Romme. From his Bradford base, Dr Rufus May manages to be many degrees more controversial than them both. Not only is he an NHS doctor who encourages voice-hearers to come off their medication, he is also a diagnosed schizophrenic – a fact that he kept secret during his medical training.

Rufus picks me up from the station in his home town of Hebden Bridge, Yorkshire. It is a freezing November afternoon and as he drives me to the top of a hill, along a narrow cobbled road, I tell him what Richard Bentall had said about the different versions of us.

'We've all got them,' he agrees. 'We meet them in our dreams. We have dialogues with them. Most people can't hear them in waking life, but they might influence us – when you get angry, sometimes it's like you're taken over by a demon. In someone who hears voices, it's just a bit more real.'

We soon arrive at his house, where I am to meet Nutmeg the dog and one of his patients. Deborah is twenty-five, pale, meek and crowded with unwelcome personalities. Under Rufus's care, she has stopped taking anti-psychotic drugs. Rufus helps her by 'dialogue-ing' directly with the other consciousnesses that haunt her. He has promised that I can observe him as he works and, if things go well, I might even be allowed to interview one of Deborah's voices.

As the kettle rises to a whistle and Nutmeg bounces excitedly around my legs, Deborah pulls the sleeves of her jumper over her hands and studies the surface of the wooden table. In the corner, pouring the tea, Rufus tells of his own fascinating journey into madness, which began on his eighteenth birthday. 'I remember feeling like I needed to be somebody that I wasn't,' he says. 'I started to get lots of strange ideas. I lost my sense of who I was.'

Rufus had a talent for art and had taken a job, near his parents' home in Islington, north London, as a trainee draughtsman. 'I was copying plans of industrial buildings,' he says. 'It was really boring, mechanistic. It was like my mind said, "Forget about this, just imagine what else I could be." So I imagined I was an apprentice spy. When they asked me to deliver parcels, I thought, *Maybe they're secret messages.* I started to create a reality that was much more interesting.'

What began as a game slowly took on the sharp corners of a life that was real. It was the time of the Cold War and Rufus fantasised that he was being recruited by the British Secret Service as a junior spy. He had had his heart broken, recently, by a girl called Jane. 'I worked out that she was probably spying for the Russians.'

'So that was why she'd left you,' I clarify. 'Because the Russians had made her?'

'Yeah – and not because I was a crap boyfriend,' he says with a laugh. 'It protected me quite nicely.'

Rufus would stay up all night, roaming the West End of London with his dog, trying to find the safe house where he and Jane would be reunited. He looked everywhere for clues that he was, indeed, being recruited as a trainee spy.

'The more you look for evidence to back up your unusual beliefs the more you find them,' he says. 'I'd seen films where spies got special messages on the radio, so I'd twiddle around and try and find them. Like this . . .' He turns, switches on the radio next to his kettle and begins to randomly dial between clouds of white noise. The first voice we hear is stern, calm, in perfect Queen's English.

'. . . *The British government has a shoot-to-kill policy* . . .'

'Argh!' I say.

I jump up from my seat.

'See what I mean?' He grins.

'Was that really just on the radio?' I ask.

'That was just on the radio! That's exactly the kind of thing. So you see, once you seek, you will find.'

On the other side of the table, Deborah mutters, 'I'm a bit freaked out now.'

'Once you start looking, these little coincidences become really . . .' Rufus stops, unable momentarily to maintain his cool, and glances back at the radio. 'Fucking hell. Luckily, I didn't get that one.' He turns back to face me. 'So you can see – it's really exciting and stressful, which means you're staying up late at night, you're hypervigilant, and when you don't sleep, even more coincidences start to happen. My uncle was a Baptist minister. He used to say that God would communicate in strange ways. He'd see messages in advertising hoardings, or he'd open the Bible at random pages and see what the message for him was. I started to do that with driving manuals. I just made this rich fantasy world for myself.'

Rufus began to suffer chest pains. 'I thought it must be a gadget that had been inserted into my chest by the oppositional forces.' Oppositional forces meant Russia. And Russia meant Jane. When Rufus told his GP that his ex-girlfriend had placed a deadly gadget in his heart, she told him, 'You need to see a specialist.' He assumed that he would be referred to a specialist in spy-gadget removal. What he wasn't expecting was a psychiatrist.

'There's some history of paranoia and psychosis in my family,' he tells me. 'My mum's sister had a diagnosis of schizophrenia and heard voices and my grandad as well. So as soon as the doctors knew that, they were like – ' he rubs his hands together – 'job done. This is schizophrenia. It's a genetic disorder and you'll have to take this medication for the rest of your life.'

The medication made him feel empty, alien, dead. He could no longer draw a straight line. He could not achieve an erection. Against the advice of his doctors, he tried to halt the medication. The first two times, he ended up back in hospital. The third time, he succeeded. And then a friend of his committed suicide.

'She jumped off a building,' he says. 'She was probably hearing voices and all they did was keep increasing the medication. I was really angry. I thought, *I've found my mission*. I would infiltrate the psychiatric system. Go undercover as a psychologist and expose it from within.'

Rufus describes the voices as messengers who speak on behalf of an individual's ugliest experiences. 'Through emotional trauma, someone might split off different parts of their experience, different emotions, different stories that they might have to bury. They can come back as voices. So what I do is help somebody understand different parts of themselves. It's like a peace-making process. I turn the voices into allies.'

Before we begin the dialogue-ing, Rufus wants to confirm our prior agreement, that I will not only change the name of Deborah in my book, but all of her voices. 'Is that okay with you?' Rufus checks with Deborah.

She sits silently, for a moment, as her voices report back.

'They're all fine with that apart from Top Dog,' she says. 'Top Dog wants his name in.'

Top Dog is Deborah's dominant voice. He is, says Rufus, 'a cross between the Godfather and a Kray twin'. He has threatened to kill Deborah many times. He has tried to convince her into suicide, saying, 'If you don't kill yourself, I will kill people you love.' Rufus defends this behaviour, saying that Top Dog is 'like a bodyguard. He was trying to protect her by getting her to kill herself, because he thought that the world was a cruel place and not worth bothering about.'

'Hmmm,' I say with a nod.

Earlier this year, Deborah nearly went through with it, before changing her mind at the last moment. The next day, a friend of hers died of cancer. Top Dog told Deborah, 'I killed her because you didn't kill yourself.' Deborah believed him. When I ask now if she realises that this cannot be true, she replies, 'I'm still working on that one. It just seems a bit too much of a coincidence, really.'

As well as being a near-constant presence in Deborah's waking life, she even sees Top Dog – hallucinates him, so that he stands in front of her. He has silvery hair and claims to be thirty-five, but looks, to Deborah, closer to forty. They meet each other in her dreams. When Deborah was being medicated – her doctors' attempts at murdering Top Dog with powerful anti-psychotics – he would tell her that if she didn't stop taking them, he would kill her family. It's not as though she needed much encouragement – the drugs made her fat, lifeless and incontinent. She used to fall asleep at the dinner table. 'They were humiliating,' she says. 'Dehumanising.' But whenever she tried to go clean, 'My voices got really angry. I would basically go insane.'

Now, with the help of Rufus – and against the advice of her doctors – she is off all medication. And slowly, she says, Top Dog is becoming easier to live with. He has even 'kind of' admitted that he didn't kill Deborah's friend. This, according to Rufus, is a result of his controversial dialogue-ing. 'Psychiatry will say, "Don't talk to the voices, because you'll make them more real,"' he says. 'I say it's already real. There's a real relationship going on and we need to understand it. We had a breakthrough a couple of weeks ago where Top Dog agreed to be less threatening about killing people and stuff like that,' he adds cheerfully before turning to Deborah and everyone else. 'So, welcome, Top Dog. How are you doing?'

'I thought you'd never ask,' says the phantom. 'You've been talking about yourself all day.'

'How do you feel it's going, this new relationship you and Deborah have got?'

'Sometimes it goes well,' says Top Dog. 'Sometimes I get angry with her. It drives me fucking nuts when she keeps secrets. And she's always thinking about other people first. People only care about themselves, anyway.'

'So you're a good reminder for her to put herself first. How are you finding your new role of adviser?'

'I'm starting to wonder if it's a good idea. Sometimes she doesn't cooperate.'

'Well, thanks for hanging in there,' says Rufus. 'I think you're learning patience. That's where we have a friendship – we're both trying to get Deborah to speak her truth.'

'Easy on the "friendship".'

'Do you get angry when she's too caring towards other people?'

'She needs to tell people to fuck off.'

'Perhaps she can learn from your directness.'

'Too fucking right.'

'I wonder if Will would like to ask Top Dog any questions,' says Rufus.

I lean forward, excited and fascinated, and a series of questions fires out.

'Are you part of Deborah?' I ask. 'Where do you live? Who are you?'

'I'm not too fucking sure myself at the moment.'

'Are you her friend?'

'I'm not her friend. I'm here to make sure she does the right thing.'

'That implies that you care about her.'

'Care's a strong word.'

I swallow drily. Top Dog, I begin to realise, is a bit of a prick.

'You're always encouraging Deborah to be direct and not keep secrets but you seem reluctant to admit your own truth. The things that you say imply that you care about her a lot.'

Deborah's face changes. She looks alarmed. Then embarrassed.

'He's being a bit rude about you,' she says.

As a child, Deborah used to have imaginary friends that were so vivid that she could see them. When I ask about the trauma that caused the voices, she tells me she was sexually abused, between the ages of eleven and twelve, by a man at her riding school.

'And when did you hear your first voice?'

'When I was nine.'

'So the abuse started when you were eleven, but you heard your first voice at nine?'

'Yeah.'

I look at Deborah. I look at Rufus. They look back at me happily, apparently untroubled by this revelation and what it implies about their theory.

'So trauma didn't cause your voices,' I say to Deborah.

'Oh, there were other sorts of things I went through before that, that were quite stressful.'

'What were they?'

'I was in a state school and I moved to a public school and so my parents were putting me under a lot of pressure to do well academically and, before that, we'd moved house and everything. We'd moved to public school and it was quite scary, there were older boys, um, fourteen, fifteen, and they were just, quite scary, you know.'

I am unconvinced. And I was alarmed earlier, when Rufus casually admitted that close relatives of his suffered from paranoia and schizophrenia. Surely all of this powerfully suggests a genetic cause?

Rufus says, 'There's lots of teachers and preachers in my family as well. Is that all genes?'

'You're being flippant,' I say.

'What I'm saying is, patterns of behaviour do run in families,' he says. 'Yes, nature plays a role. But it's not a genetic vulnerability, it's a different way of coping with stress. One person might respond to bullying in an anxious way, another in a dissociative way. Society says that it's more acceptable to be depressed than it is to be living in a fantasy world. But they're not better or worse, they're different.'

Before I travelled up to visit Rufus, Deborah and Top Dog I spoke with Dr Trevor Turner, consultant psychiatrist at St Bartholomew's Hospital in east London. Turner – author of books on schizophrenia and an ex-Vice President of the Royal College of Psychiatry – told me that encouraging schizophrenics to ditch their medication is 'extremely dangerous'. He admits that Romme and Coleman's Hearing Voices Network have been responsible for some good work in 'improving patients' positive feelings about themselves' and acknowledges that trying to turn the voices into a friend is 'absolutely right'. But he also has an interesting take on Professor Marius Romme's complaint that one in a hundred people die on the medication. 'That's pretty good, actually, because fifteen per cent of people with schizophrenia die from self-neglect or suicide because of the awful nature of their experiences.' The reduction in the suicide rate of medicated patients is, he says, 'fantastic'.

Voice-hearing itself, according to Turner, is the dominant symptom of 90 per cent of schizophrenics. 'It's a bit like having a temperature is a symptom of infection. It's showing your brain's overactive and is trying to pick up sounds that aren't there. It's playing tricks on you. It's increasingly well established that schizophrenia is a disease. There's evidence aplenty. When you give people anti-psychotics, their voices melt away and they become better again. You can do examinations of brains that show clear abnormalities in what's called the third and fourth ventricle. Scans have shown significant brain shrinkage in people with schizophrenia as well.'

We know that schizophrenia is a physical disease, then, not only because we can see evidence of it in the brain, but because the drugs for it work: anti-psychotics block the chemical dopamine, and this demonstrates that schizophrenics either have too much dopamine, or have too many dopamine receptors. But psychiatrists such as Professor Richard Bentall meet all these arguments with the same objection. How do we know these brain abnormalities and the dopamine-system faults are triggered by disease? Perhaps they are caused by traumatic experiences. 'There's compelling evidence that traumatic experiences can alter the structure of the brain [in these ways],' says Bentall. 'There's also compelling evidence that the dopamine system can be affected by experiences of unpleasant events. And there's very good evidence, that has appeared in the last two years, that shows that brain volume shrinks with a lifetime dose of anti-psychotics.'

When I mention Bentall to Turner, I am startled by his reaction. What follows may seem rather mild to the casual observer, but as criticism from one scientist to another, it is on the sharp end of serious.

'Bentall's highly selective in his sources and he generally uses individual anecdotal case results rather than carefully structured studies,' he says. 'People like Bentall are stuck in the belief system that it all derives from childhood experience. That's the credo of analytical thinking like his. It's a well-known trope in the history of anti-psychiatry. The most anti-psychiatry people on the planet are the Scientologists, who regard us as torturers, murderers, Holocaust-deniers. That, to some degree, is where this notion comes from. It's anti-medical. It's a belief system, not a scientific one.'

When I bring up Romme's study, in which he claims to have found that 80 per cent of voice-hearers have suffered significant early trauma such as abuse, Turner replies flatly, 'That's completely untrue. There's no evidence for that at all. The prevalence of child abuse is in debate anyhow. You can't find it, you can't see it, you can't smell it, you can't touch it but sometimes, if you spend enough time digging around in therapy, you can get someone to think of things. Thirty per cent of our memories are false memories anyway. It doesn't matter who we are.'

As Turner has wandered off the point, slightly, so has my concentration. I have a moment of panic when I think I have misheard him. I have to double check what he just said, because I can hardly believe it.

'Did you just say thirty per cent of our memories are false?'

'If you look at psychological studies,' he says, 'about twenty to thirty per cent of what we think are real memories are probably false.'

I make a hurried note. If this is true it represents a potentially crucial lead in my search for the source of irrational beliefs. Before I let Dr Turner go, though, I have one final question.

'Have you heard of Dr Rufus May?' I say.

'He's one of these self-appointed-guru-type people who thinks he knows better than everyone else,' he says. 'He's a liar and a charlatan.'

Up on the crest of a rain-soaked Yorkshire hill, the phrase 'he's a liar and a charlatan' clatters to the floor of Rufus's kitchen like a hundred saucepans hitting the tiles.

'Wow,' says Rufus. He takes a moment to gather himself. 'I guess we're just pushing in completely different directions. He's kind of managing people's distress. I'm trying to help people heal.'

I tell him that Turner said that the voice is a symptom, like a temperature. He turns to Top Dog.

'How do you feel being likened to a temperature, Top Dog?' he asks.

'I want to find this man. He needs to be very afraid.'

Richard Bentall is somewhat less equanimous than Rufus. 'Turner's an idiot, frankly,' he says, when I call him. 'His comments are stupid on many different levels. Let's start with one of them. There is no such thing as "the cause" of psychosis. There's not one cause, there are many interacting causes. I'm not claiming that sexual abuse or trauma is "the cause", what I'm claiming is that it is a major causal factor.'

For his meta-analysis – which, at the time of writing, is still undergoing peer review – Bentall found nine studies that looked at the question of whether there is a 'dose–response relationship' between abuse and psychosis. That is, do increased 'doses' of abuse reflect an increased likelihood of breakdown? 'All but one of the studies finds a dose–response relationship,' he says. 'That is very powerful evidence of cause. So for him to say that I'm being unscientific – he's being a completely unscientific idiot.'

'Okay,' I say. 'Sorry, I don't want to cause . . . but I have to . . . Trevor also said that you value anecdote over careful study.'

'I'm not talking about anecdote at all!' he says. 'I'm talking about rigorous epidemiological studies. But anecdotes are important – if he listened to a few anecdotes from his patients he might be more convinced himself. The great tragedy about this is that traditional psychiatrists don't listen to their patients at all. Turner is a very annoying person.'

'This is the last one. He said hearing a voice was like having a temperature.'

'I shudder, basically. I really shudder.'

*

From its roots in Maastricht and Manchester, HVN has gone on to help thousands of patients in twenty-two countries get off medication and in control of their voices. Today, you'll find Ron Coleman about as far away as you can get from that King's Cross platform without leaving the British Isles. On a far northern corner of Lewis, in Scotland's Outer Hebrides, he lives with his dog and his chickens and his wife and two children and the other invisible people that he carries around in his head. Rather than submitting to a medicated life in the psychiatric system, he instead sought counselling for the guilt that he felt around his abuse.

'I found myself innocent,' he says. 'And things got better.' He began negotiating with his voices: telling them to pipe down; you're wrong; I'll give you fifteen minutes this evening if you'll behave for the rest of the day.'

They're mostly gone now. But not entirely.

'The priest's still there,' he says. 'When I hear him, I know I need a break. His power used to be rooted in the guilt, so I can make him go away pretty easily.' Other voices are more welcome: they remind him of facts he has forgotten and offer him helpful references when he's doing his talks. 'That happens regularly.' But there is another voice, too. One that he has no desire to shoo away.

Every year, on the anniversary of Annabel's death, Ron will take a gin and tonic to a private place and sit alone and catch up with her. 'We just talk about how things are; how my life is,' he says. 'I'm happily married now, and I love my wife, but that doesn't mean I've stopped loving Annabel. My wife understands that. If madness is a lifelong condition then love certainly is.'

'It must be a bit heartbreaking, though?' I ask.

He sighs, and looks off into the deep horizon, where the blue, domed sky kisses the cold northern sea. 'I guess there is that element to it,' he says. 'But it's what everyone does, isn't it? If they've lost somebody, they still talk to them. The only difference with me is that mine talk back.'

10

'They're frightening people'

It took just one minute, on a Thursday morning in the middle of July. One minute, on a grey humdrum day in a small Manchester office. One minute, for the safety and safe memories of a family to be breached.

There were two men in separate rooms, each working quietly at their computers. At 09:02, the phone rang. The elder man, who had been checking his emails, lifted the receiver.

'Hello, this is Richard Felstead.'

'Is this the brother of Carole?' asked the caller.

'That's right, yes.'

'I'm calling from the coroner's office in Battersea. I'm very sorry to tell you that your sister Carole was found dead in her flat on the twenty-ninth of June. I'm sorry it's taken so long for us to get in touch. Carole's next of kin – she told us there was no family. But a letter was found, in her flat. It was from you. So I thought I'd let you know.'

It was 09:03. Richard was breathless with crying.

'I'll . . .' said the coroner's assistant. 'I'm sorry. I'll call back later.'

Richard walked to the next-door office, where his brother David was entering addresses on a database. When he told him the news, David didn't turn around. He stopped typing, he leaned his head all the way back and he said, very quietly, 'Oh.'

The telephone rang again. It was a different caller – a woman, but this one was speaking in a strange voice.

'Are you Richard?'

'Yes.'

'I know you're not one of the ones that harmed Carole.'

'Who is this?' said Richard.

She sounded slow, drawn out, modulated.

'I'm Carole's next of kin.'

She sounded *weird*.

'Yes, but who are you?'

'That's not important.'

'Do you know how Carole died?' said Richard.

'She had a very difficult childhood.'

'What was wrong with her? Was she sick?'

'As I said, she had a very difficult childhood.'

'No, no, hang on a minute. That's a lie. Carole had a great childhood. Who is this?'

'I've already told you. I'm Carole's next of kin.'

She was patronising now, like she was admonishing a naughty child.

'But – give me your name.'

'My name is not important. I just wanted to tell you that it's Carole's funeral tomorrow. She's being cremated. People have taken time off work. It's *very important* that the cremation goes ahead.'

Richard became furious.

The phone went dead.

Richard and David drove to Cheadle to collect their father, Joseph, from the factory where he was employed as an engineer. They knew many of the men that Joseph worked with. As they walked past their tool-strewn benches, his colleagues tried to say *hello*, *all right?*, *mornin' boys* but it quickly became obvious that something was wrong. They watched the brothers approaching Joseph's bay, where he was busy welding. When he saw his sons, he smiled and wiped his hands clean. His face fell when he registered their expressions. And then they had to tell him that his daughter was gone.

When the three men arrived at the family home in Davenport, half an hour later, their mother was delighted to see her husband. 'Oh, Joseph!' she beamed. 'Have you come to take me shopping?' The other two Felstead brothers soon joined them – first Anthony and then Kevin, whose lasting memory of that morning is the sight of his mother: 'Finished. On the floor. Drained. Shattered. Gone.'

The family began talking. Nothing made sense. Who was the mysterious caller who said she was Carole's 'next of kin'? Why did she talk of a 'difficult childhood' when Carole was happy, popular – *spoiled*, if anything? And how could Carole die? She was in the midst of a successful nursing career down in London. She was only forty-one. Why had it taken two weeks for the family to be informed? And how could there be a funeral taking place *tomorrow*?

Joseph stood up.

'She's not getting cremated tomorrow,' he said. 'I'll put a stop to it.'

'You can't stop a funeral, Dad!' said Kevin. 'How do you stop a funeral? What, are you going to march in there and take the coffin?'

Joseph telephoned the coroner's assistant. She brusquely informed him that now the family had been discovered, the funeral would be halted regardless. But instead of relief, Joseph felt troubled. Why was her tone so short? So *angry*? The coroner told him: 'We've been handed a life assessment that your daughter wrote. It's very upsetting.' It was six pages, typed. It said: 'My parents were abusive in every way imaginable: sexually, physically and emotionally. I grew up in constant terror. At three years of age, my mother smothered my sister. She sat me on top of her and then set the house on fire.'

Joseph was astonished.

'No, no, hang on a minute,' he said. 'Had she been ill or something? Had she been sectioned?'

The coroner's assistant said, 'Yes.'

Throughout the coming weeks, there came more questions. Officials dealing with Carole's death kept mentioning a 'psychiatrist friend' who accompanied her to many of her medical appointments and seemed to have some role in the cancelled funeral. And then there was this mysterious 'next of kin', who, to the family's fury, emptied Carole's flat of her possessions. On 6 August, Joseph was in conversation with the police inspector who was involved in the case when something occurred to him. 'This psychiatrist and this next of kin,' he asked. 'Are they the same person?'

'That's right,' said the inspector. 'Dr Fleur Fisher.'

Shortly after the call, Joseph searched the Internet for her name.

Most recently (1991–1996) she has been the Head of Ethics Science and Information for the British Medical Association.

*

When he was discussing the notion of sexual abuse causing people to hear voices, Dr Trevor Turner said something that – even after learning all that I have – managed to stagger me. 'Thirty per cent of our memories are false memories anyway. It doesn't matter who we are.'

If Turner is correct it suggests that all of us are far closer to that fuzzy, imaginary line than I could have imagined. I used to think of creationists as existing on one distant end of the continuum, with the bland massed-army of the scientists on the other. Now, in my mind at least, they have all shuffled a little closer. I am sure that the doctors Nick Mann and Annie Oaklander are correct, in that many Morgellons patients have been incorrectly diagnosed as suffering from DOP. Those sorry souls are victims of the kind of binary, dismissive thinking that I worry is evident among some Skeptics. In their haste to dismiss the ranting, scratching dispossessed, subtler truths are being missed. The itch might not be caused by tiny wasps, but in many cases, it does appear to be caused by *something*. Just because they are wrong about one thing, it hasn't necessarily followed that they are wrong about it all. And yet they are crucified for making one mistake. They are denounced as crazy and crazy is what many have become.

Ron Coleman's long battle against the scientific establishment is brilliantly illustrated in his observation that, 'In 1994, the Royal College of Psychiatry called the Hearing Voices Network "the most dangerous organisation in psychiatry". In 2000, they described us as "one of the most important".' Just because he was mad and biased by his own experiences and fighting against senior scientists and years of consensus and orthodoxy, it didn't mean that he was wrong. Indeed, what consensus there is among experts in schizophrenia these days says that both extremes have a point – that environmental *and* disease causes are probably involved in ways that have not yet been precisely fathomed. The psychiatric establishment have felt the lunatic's embrace and, over the last twenty years, have slowly yielded.

Most humans, not least myself, are an incoherent mess of madness and sanity. It is not as simple as I had once believed, judging who is rational and who is not. And what I am to learn over the many weeks that I will spend investigating the strange death and even stranger life of Carole Myers is that, when everyone believes they are telling the truth, and yet you are submerged in a milieu of dangerous delusion, it can be especially hard to tell.

The Felstead family's search for answers to the many mysteries surrounding Carole's decline is now in its sixth year. Endless letters, phone calls, hours of legal research and long nights on the Internet have resulted in the collection of hundreds of documents and the generation of yet more questions: angry ones about individuals they believe to have been malign presences in her life; strange ones about startling and little-known corners of human psychology; sad ones about the life and death of the kind and sparky woman that they still miss every day.

When I first contact the Felsteads, to ask if I can write about Carole, they pass me a telephone number. Discovered in Carole's phone records, it belongs to the woman whose role in the tale is, they are convinced, central: that of the 'next of kin', Dr Fleur Fisher. The day before I travel to Stockport to meet them, I dial it, nervously. A confident-sounding woman answers.

'Is that Dr Fleur Fisher?' I ask.

'Yes?'

I tell her that I want to talk to her about Carole.

'I'm very leery about putting my head above the parapet on that subject. And, if you don't mind my saying so, it's not wise for you to be involving yourself in this story either. That family, they're bloody terrifying.'

'You're frightened of them?'

'Of course I'm frightened. They're frightening people. And the things they've been saying about me!' she says, adding confusingly, 'I'm not a psychiatrist! I'm not a therapist!' She rings off, warning me darkly: 'Tread carefully.'

*

The building in which Joseph Felstead lives is a red-brick terrace, whose heavy net curtains, draped in low, funereal arcs across its front windows, block the gaze of strangers, as well as most of the light. The rooms inside are painted mauve and dark-red and are tall and shadow-struck and quiet. They are decorated with golden candlestick holders, old family portraits, strange urns and statues of dogs, birds and deer. Walking in from the street, the change is sudden and enveloping. The atmosphere has a halting, crowding quality.

Today Joseph sits glowering in the lounge, his muscular patriarch's hands gripping his armchair. Kevin – a softer presence – informs me that Richard's at work, and Anthony's too distraught to speak. Their mother, Joan, passed away last year. David is here, though, friendly yet possessed of an anxious, wiry tension. Over the coming hours, he will answer questions with flumes of facts and furious analysis, fossicking in boxes for the relevant document to illustrate his point.

For these men, Carole's life is as much of a mystery as her death. She had been a friendly, bolshie and academically successful teenager, who loved watching M*A*S*H and wearing the tartan shorts beloved of her favourite band, the Bay City Rollers. She was popular at school and had a noted instinct for caring, going out of her way to play with Michael, the neighbour with Down's syndrome, and spending long hours with a lonely old man down the road. At fifteen she got a weekend job in a home for the disabled. At twenty-one she qualified as a nurse at Stockport College and rented a nearby flat, making frequent visits back to Mum and Dad to borrow milk and money, and sunbathe in the garden. And then, in the mid-1980s, there began a silent drift away from the family.

'Her attitude became hostile,' says Joseph.

'What did she say was the problem?' I ask.

'We didn't have any conversations about it,' he says.

'But you must have been worried?'

Joseph shifts in his seat. 'I was more cross than anything,' he says, glancing away. 'It just seemed indifferent, that's all. Nothing sinister. She was our daughter. We'd spoiled her. And then to being almost anti-social? It was ill mannered.'

In 1986 the family discovered that Carole had moved to Macclesfield. She would still send Christmas cards and ring occasionally, assuring them that her career was going well. But by 1992 she had moved to London and changed her name from Carol Felstead to Carole Myers. They had to accept that, for some reason, she had chosen to stay away.

After her death, they began searching. It was slow, at first, but the family fought. Angry letters were written, court orders were threatened, freedom of information requests were made. They discovered that Carole had become mentally ill. Her medical records were a grim, broken history, told in photo-copied doctors' letters and psychologists' reports, of self-harm, alcohol abuse and stretches in psychiatric wards. She had frequently been suicidal. Over the years, she had been seen by a series of mental health professionals and had, in 1992, been diagnosed with multiple personality disorder.

The family were informed that Dr Fleur Fisher had no legal right to claim to be Carole's 'next of kin'. They also learned that a strange call had been made from Carole's flat, eight days after her death, to a company called Diamond Insurance. They requested a recording of it and today, they gather around an old boxy portable hifi to play me the cassette. It turns out to be a woman, getting herself insured on Carole's car – the one that went missing: 'I'm dealing with her flat and possessions,' says the caller. 'I need to drive down to Plymouth . . . She was the survivor of brutal family abuse over many years . . . I'm a consultant in healthcare ethics . . . My name? It's Dr Fleur Fisher.'

The family's fury and suspicion towards Dr Fisher grew, like roots, through their sadness and their outrage at the claims Carole had made in her life assessment. She said that she had been abused by Joseph and his wife, who were the high priest and priestess of a satanic cult, and that during her teens she had given birth to six children – some fathered by Joseph – that she had been forced to kill. She also said that a childhood friend that she had confided in had been murdered in front of her.

The most extreme of Carole's charges are easily proved to be false. The sister, whose murder she had apparently witnessed, actually died of a heart condition two years before Carole was born. The house fire, too, predated her birth. And yet Carole's medical records showed that the mental-health professionals involved in her case rarely challenged the grotesque visions of her memory. Most concluded that Carole's psychological problems came as a result of family abuse. But the Felsteads point the blaming finger straight back at the clinicians.

They believe that Carole came to have these recollections only after receiving treatment known as recovered-memory therapy. RMT is predicated on the Freudian notion that traumatic experiences are somehow repressed by the brain and that these festering, forgotten memories can cause psychological and physical problems later in life. They can only be treated, says the theory, if they are brought to the surface with the aid of techniques such as dream interpretation and hypnosis, which critics believe can sometimes create false memories. The Felsteads think that blame for Carole's psychological downfall lies with satanist-obsessed therapists who implanted these ideas in Carole's head and helped her black fantasies to flower. After all, they point out, something similar has happened before – most famously in Orkney in 1991, when nine children were forcibly removed from their homes following interviews with social workers, who were led by an individual who has subsequently been accused of being 'fixated on finding satanic abuse'.

I ask the Felsteads when the first mention of mental-health problems appear in Carole's medical records. A letter of December 1986 refers to his referral for therapy, in August 1985, for insomnia and nightmares related to 'family abuse'. A letter written in November 1986 mentions further 'psycho-sexual counselling' by someone whose name sends a cold stun of recognition through me. It is her: the next of kin; the woman who baffled me by insisting, 'I'm not a therapist!' It is Dr Fleur Fisher.

But despite all this evidence, as I leave the Felsteads' home, I remain troubled. Can what they are saying be true? Can it really be possible for someone to develop memories that are entirely false, and yet overwhelmingly rich, dramatic and powerful – so much so that they caused a bright young woman to separate from her family and be slowly driven mad?

*

As part of an assignment set by Professor Elizabeth Loftus, of the University of Washington, a cognitive-psychology student named Jim Coan asked his fourteen-year-old brother Chris to describe the occasion when he became lost in the University City shopping mall in Spokane, Washington. Chris did as he was told. 'I went over to look at the toy store – Kay-Bee toys,' he remembered. 'And I thought, *Uh-oh. I'm in trouble now.*' He became scared – 'I thought I was never going to see my family again' – but luckily, a 'really cool' elderly, balding man wearing spectacles and a blue flannel shirt arrived, and helped him to find his parents. The strange thing was that Chris had never been lost in that mall. He had never been rescued. The cool old man in the blue flannel shirt did not exist. His brother Jim had simply told him that he had once gone missing, on the instructions of Professor Loftus.

For the study, Jim had asked his brother to recollect, in as much detail as he could manage, four events from his childhood – and one of them was an invention. Over five days, as he was asked to provide more and more information about these events, Chris's false memory became richer. Weeks later, when asked to guess which one of the occasions was false, Chris picked a real one.

Professor Loftus was interested to see whether it was possible for a therapist to generate a memory of an event simply by suggesting it. In a further study, she gave twenty-four adults a brief description of four past events that they were told had been supplied by a close family member and asked to write about them. Unbeknown to them, one of these events was false. Six of them – 25 per cent of the group – actually *remembered* the false event. When asked to choose which of their memories was fiction, five got it wrong.

Professor Loftus tells me that she began studying memory in 1970. 'I decided to study the process by which I believe therapists are leading people into these very rich false memories,' she tells me. 'Since the "lost in the mall" study was published, I and many others have planted more bizarre and unusual false memories: of accidents, of being attacked by an animal, of nearly drowning, of witnessing demonic possession. What we have found is absolutely stunning. These memories can be very detailed, and people can be very emotional about them. A lot of these therapists say, "I believe she was abused because every time she talks about it she cries," as if somehow the emotion is proof that it's true. It's not.' False accusations are typical, she says, in people who unconsciously seek to blame shortcomings in their life on others. 'Abuse is a much more palatable explanation for the problems in your life,' she says, 'and that's why it's so appealing.'

Just like the myriad healthy biases in our brains, the memories Loftus speaks of tend to serve us in one direction: to bolster our sense of self; to tell a better story about ourselves. It is curious, when you consider the different genus of false memory that I heard about in the counselling room of Vered Kilstein: all those past-lifers who had been brave knights and Cleopatras and principal members of the Beatles. All that twisting, weaving brain-work creating all those heroes.

When I tell Professor Loftus the Felsteads' theory of what happened to Carole, she does not react with any great expression of surprise. In her experience, as an expert witness in US courtrooms, she has come across many instances of this kind of thing: false memories of ritual abuse, false memories of incest, false memories of rape. They have led to untold numbers of miscarriages of justice; shattered countless families and friendships. And they come about by surprisingly easy means. They don't even require a therapist. Any trusted source – a book, a friend, a TV personality – can suggest the possibility of abuse. Your mind might then produce a fragment – an image of something bad happening. What was that? You recall it again. You fill in the details. 'Repetition makes it more vivid and familiar,' Kimberley Wade, Associate Professor of Psychology at Warwick University, tells me. 'It'll start to feel like a memory.'

I mention to Professor Wade the suggestion in Carole's medical notes that she had been treated by therapists known to have a belief in satanic cults, and who practised various relaxation techniques. 'Using hypnotherapy encourages you to imagine,' she says. 'And did her therapist encourage her to not have contact with her family?'

'It's impossible to say,' I tell her. 'But she did cut them off almost entirely, at around the same time that she was being treated.'

'That's interesting,' she says. 'When we do studies implanting false memories, we tell our participants they can't talk to family members about their past. We think it contributes to the process if they've got no one to counter the suggestions.'

In conversation with these academics, I am struck by the understanding that everybody, to some extent, has untrustworthy memories. 'Every time you recall something from your past, it's reconstructed,' explains Wade. Just as the schizophrenia expert Dr Trevor Turner implied, the people studied by these scientists are not 'crazy'. 'These are healthy people without any mental impairments or psychological issues,' she says. But Dr Turner seemed to make an interesting mistake with his numbers. Professor Wade is famous in academic circles for generating false memories by giving people childhood photos that have been doctored, so that they show them in a hot-air balloon that they never rode in, for example. When asked to describe the memory in her fake pictures, she has found that 'On average 35 per cent of participants develop a rich memory of their fake event. They describe how it happened, where they were, how they were feeling.'

This, it seems to me, is the most likely source of the number that Dr Turner was referring to when we spoke. But I think he made a subtle error – not a third of our memories are false, as he had claimed, but a third of the population are susceptible to easily developing rich false memories. Although I have no doubt that Dr Turner made this apparent mistake in all innocence, it is interesting to note how it tended in the direction of the argument he was seeking to make – that people who hear voices may be recovering false memories of abuse during therapy. Having learned what I have about the sly operations of the brain and its treatment of evidence that might bolster or threaten our beliefs, I wonder if some unconscious mechanism might have fooled him.

To accept that a true recollection of satanic abuse could emerge during RMT, we would first have to know whether or not it is possible for memories to be 'repressed' at all. Professor Chris French – the Head of the Anomalistic Psychology Research Unit at the University of London, and the former editor of *The Skeptic* magazine that I last met at the Manchester conference – tells me that this idea is extremely controversial. 'There's quite a schism on this in psychology,' he says. 'Experimentalists and the neuro people tend to be quite sceptical, while the clinicians are more accepting of it. There's quite a clear divide. The people who appear to recover these memories relive the traumatic experiences, and the emotion that they go through is very very real. And that can be extremely compelling. The typical human reaction would be to think that this is true. But the same methods are used in the context of alien-abduction claims and past-life regression. So, logically, if you're going to accept that these recovered memories of childhood abuse are true then you should also accept the alien claims.'

French goes on to tell me that the British False Memory Society's files are 'full of cases' in which people have been wrongly accused of rape or abuse. 'A lot of people will go to their graves never being reconciled with their friends or family members,' he says. 'I think it's tragic.'

When I mention one of the therapists that appears in Carole's medical records, his reaction surprises me.

'Valerie Sinason?' he says.

'That's right,' I say. 'Do you know her?'

He lets out a deep sigh.

'Oh, *God*,' he says. 'She's got such a huge influence. Valerie Sinason is a dangerous woman.'

*

If the Felsteads' theory is correct, Carole must have received recovered-memory therapy in the mid-1980s, around the time that her relationship with her family began to pall. One letter in their cache comes tantalisingly close, noting that in 1985 'she was unable to describe the abuse in anything other than superficial terms' and that she subsequently underwent 'a number of sessions concentrating on relaxation training and thought stoppin procedures . . .'. But the only person I know who might have witnessed, first hand, what happened back then is Dr Fisher. But since our last conversation, she has vanished. She has changed her mobile number and has ignored several emails. Instead, I arrange an interview with Valerie Sinason, who, according to the records, saw Carole for psychotherapy every two weeks for eight months in 1992. I want to know if she will fit the description that Professor Loftus gave of the therapists she has come across in legal cases – that of an individual who is highly credulous of satanic abuse and has a tendency to believe ritual damage in patients. I am curious to know, do the individuals that she treats come to her with all their memories firmly in place? Or do their recollections arrive suddenly – suspiciously – during the therapeutic process? Will she see 'warning signs' of satanism everywhere? Or will she turn out to be soberly minded and rigorously sceptical, conceding that it happens only when there is evidence that compels it, and even then in rare, isolated cases?

*

There are two glass heads wearing sunglasses in Dr Valerie Sinason's lobby, and a basking lizard, and a statue of Sigmund Freud, a geisha, a large wooden eagle flexing its wings and a single bongo, on the floor, next to a tribal carving. On the wall, framed in wood, a topless woman arcs her back in lascivious, fleshy pastels. The consulting room contains two deep and squashily inviting sofas and many hundreds of books – a confusing library that ranges over a vast coven of subjects, including mind, language, conspiracy, reality, radar: Steven Pinker, Opus Dei, cybernetics, social cognition, *Understanding Radar, Radar Principles*. There is a small television with a selection of children's DVDs, steel bowls filled with plastic toy figures and a chaise-longue with a crowd of teddies resting in its crook. On the floor, shoved beneath a table, a large cloth boy gazes sadly into space.

This is Dr Sinason's NHS-funded 'Clinic for Dissociative Studies', which she runs from a large house in Golders Green, north London. Dr Sinason is well known in mental-health circles: she has written and edited books, is an in-demand speaker at international conferences, has co-authored a study about abuse for the Department of Health and is a frequently cited spokesperson in the broadsheet newspapers on issues as wide-ranging as the Bulger killings, Chris Langham and, of course, the controversial condition known as multiple-personality disorder or 'DID'.

She arrives tanned and relaxed in a loose smock, dark leggings and light trainers. We are joined by her husband David, who takes notes throughout our talk and interjects every now and then. I will discover later that she has brought him in for back-up, as she is suspicious of my motives. This might be because I have been deliberately vague about my reasons for being here. Concerned that mention of Carole's name might cause Dr Sinason to become guarded, I have told her only that

I am investigating allegations of ritual abuse in the north of England.

Over mugs of tea and a bowl of vegetable crisps, she begins by explaining that ordinary child abuse was once thought to be extremely rare. 'Back in the early 1980s, there was something like four hundred and eighty-six children on the child protection list,' she says, noting that she was one of the first clinicians to realise that incest was a bigger issue and to agitate for it to be taken more seriously. 'Thousands of reasonable professionals had something staring them in their face and didn't recognise it. But then the problem comes. If you start recognising abuse by the stepfather when the rest of the population is still thinking that maybe a stranger might do this to a tiny number of people – when they're on stepfather you're on father. When they get to father, you're on mother. When they get on to mother, you're on siblings. When they get on to siblings, you're on organised abuse. When they're on that, you're on dogs and animals and, then, ritual abuse.'

'So you've always been one step ahead of the curve?' I say.

She nods. 'And that's horrible. Because you know you're going to get bashed up.'

Dr Sinason's father was Stanley S. Segal, a campaigner on behalf of children with learning difficulties. His influential book *No Child is Ineducable* is, she proudly tells me, 'the reason why disabled children go to school today, instead of hospital. His motto, which I put to treating survivors of satanist abuse, was "I shall not pass them by, nor throw them crumbs". If you know something's true, you can't turn your back. You're a witness.'

'So the great lesson of your family is: listen to people,' I say.

'Absolutely,' she says. 'Absolutely. Everybody can say something of their history. We must bear witness.'

Carole's medical records contain a letter, written by

Sinason, that says she was 'the first patient Rob Hale and I worked with who had experienced chronic sadistic abuse'. Without mentioning Carole's name, I ask her about her 'first patient'. She describes a visit by two medical professionals – one a nurse with a limp, the other a psychologist.

'I just had that nasty feeling,' she recalls. 'It's her. It's her, and she's been hurt by them.'

'You could tell that from the *limp*?' I ask.

'Yep.'

Dr Sinason insists that she does not practise recovered-memory techniques. 'I don't use direct questions,' she says. 'I'm an analytic therapist. The idea of that is someone showing, through their words or behaviour, that all sorts of things might have happened to them – things that there might not initially be logical words for.'

For Dr Sinason, signifiers that a patient has suffered at the hands of a satanist might include flinching at green or purple, because those are the colours of the robes of the high priest and priestess. Another is when patients say, 'I don't know.' 'What they really mean is, "I can't bear to say."' Dr Sinason also goes on high alert when she judges that a patient is praising their family with too much enthusiasm. 'The more insecure you are, the more you praise. "Oh, my family were wonderful! I can't remember any of it!"'

'And that's a sign?' I say.

'Absolutely.'

I tell her that campaigning organisations, such as the British False Memory Society, deny that satanist abuse even exists.

'You've got to remember that it's allegedly "innocent" parents that join false memory societies,' she says. 'Among the groups that very loudly say "this isn't true" there are, of course, a certain percentage of abusers. They're in all the professions as well.'

'Which professions?'

'Every profession.'

As well as ritual abuse, Dr Sinason is an expert in people who claim to possess multiple independent personalities which they apparently switch between helplessly, with each personality often being unaware of the others. Known as 'dissociative identity disorder' it is a condition which many mainstream psychologists, such as Professors Chris French and Elizabeth Loftus, insist doesn't actually exist, but from which Carole supposedly suffered. At first, I am unsure if multiple personalities are even relevant to the allegations of satanism. I begin to detect a link, though, when I ask Dr Sinason what happens when she reports her clients' claims to the police.

'The problem with going to the police is that if somebody has a dissociative disorder, it's no good if one person comes to you and says, "I want to go the police because this has happened," because you don't know if there are other personalities that will then contradict the evidence.'

'So when the police arrive to take evidence, another personality emerges?' I clarify.

'And says, "It's all lies," and the police give up,' she nods.

Dr Sinason admits that some of her patients initially have no memory of satanist abuse. This, she says, is because 'Someone's main personality can be functioning perfectly. They can go to therapy for years and all the trauma is buried in other states of mind.'

'So you might have one personality with no memory of ritual abuse and another with all the memories?'

'Exactly. Exactly.'

I ask Dr Sinason about patients who make impossible claims, such as being raped by world-famous individuals. 'It could be misinformation,' she says, and offers an example of a patient of hers who insisted that she had been raped by

Margaret Thatcher. 'From the way she described it, I could see this had been deliberately done,' she says. 'She'd been drugged and people used *Spitting Image* masks. Just like some of the children I saw who had been abused by people wearing Mickey Mouse masks.'

Suddenly recalling 'lost' memories of satanic abuse, claiming to have been raped by Margaret Thatcher, confessions to the police that 'it's all lies' – it all might lead the dispassionate observer to conclude that the patient is unreliable: lying or delusional or developing false memories. Not for Dr Sinason. For her, with DID fully inveigled into the story's plot-line, it comes to represent powerful evidence that they have multiple personalities and that satanists are canny.

I have no doubt that Dr Sinason believes what she is telling me. But everything I have learned so far about the brain's capacity to embrace evidence that reinforces its precious models, and dismiss everything that doesn't, makes me suspicious of all this. I am fascinated, too, by what I can sense of her personal mission. Her father, a hero – responsible for saving a generation of children with learning difficulties from hellish hospital lives. And so, the family quest: to serve those who have historically been dismissed by the mental-health establishment. To 'bear witness'. To defend the dispossessed. To *believe* them.

But perhaps sceptical voices are too quick to dismiss the reality of ritual abuse. It is known, after all, that paedophiles occasionally meddle with pagan rites and symbolism. Satanic threats could feasibly be used to scare victims into silence. Perhaps Dr Sinason's description of what exactly goes on at these events will actually turn out to be sober, realistic and credible.

When I ask her to describe some, she tells me that children are stitched inside the bellies of dying animals and are then 'reborn to Satan'. 'Another one is being passed around the room and anally raped by everybody,' she says. On other occasions, they are 'made to eat faeces, menstrual blood, semen, urine, babies being cannibalised'.

'So the cannibalism – that's foetuses?' I ask.

'Foetuses and bits of bodies.'

'Raw or cooked?'

'The foetuses are raw.'

'Not even salt and pepper?' I ask.

'Raw. And handed round.'

'For everyone to have a nibble on? Like a cob of corn?'

'Like communion,' she says. 'On one major festival, the babies are barbecued. I can still remember one survivor saying how easy it is to pull apart the ribs on a baby. But adults were tougher to eat.'

She goes on to describe large gatherings in woodlands and castles, which involve huge cloths being laid out. 'That's normally when there's a sacrifice,' she notes, 'and because the rapes are happening all over the place. There's a small amount of cannon fodder in terms of runaways that are drug addicts, prostitutes, tramps that are used.'

'Tell me about the sex' I say. 'What happens?'

'Everything happens. Sex with animals. Horses, dogs, goats. Being hanged upside down. In the woods, on a tree.'

'How do they get an animal to have sex with a human?'

David thinks for a moment and says, 'Well, plenty of dogs have a go at people's legs.'

'True,' says Dr Sinason, adding poignantly. 'However horrible it sounds, the dog, at least, is friendly afterwards.'

'Because at least the dog has a good time,' I say.

'And the child loves the pet,' Dr Sinason nods. 'The pet is made to have sex with that child – but the pet, at least, is still their friend.'

*

Having sat in the centre of the Sinasons' wild kaleidoscope of beliefs, it seems obvious to me that the Felsteads are right in suspecting that Carole's therapists had some unlikely views. But Sinason doesn't enter Carole's story until the early 1990s. Her abuse 'memories' – at least the initial ones – cannot be blamed on her. There is only one person that I know of who knew Carole during that period. I am convinced that Dr Fleur Fisher would know if Carole had received recovered-memory therapy. But I have tried and I have tried. She has vanished.

Then David Felstead gives me another lead. In among Carole's phone records, he finds a possible home number for Dr Fisher. When I try, it goes to the answer-phone of another family. A few days later, in an act of utterly irrational desperation, I dial it again. This time someone picks up. To my astonishment, she says: 'Oh yes, people call for Fleur Fisher sometimes. I'll give you her number.'

Dr Fleur Fisher answers the phone with the all the head-mistress-like authority you might expect of a former head of ethics at the British Medical Association. Sometimes confident, sometimes wary, sometimes maudlin and resigned, she actually has good reason to fear the Felsteads. After discovering she had taken Carole's possessions, they reported her to the GMC and the police. Neither found sufficient evidence to act against her.

She admits that she had no legal claim to be Carole's 'next of kin', but denies the Felsteads' accusations that she stole her belongings. She emptied the flat, she says, because the property managers were demanding it. As she cleared up, she found the letter from Richard. 'Honourably, I gave it to the police,' she says. 'Otherwise the family would never have known. Never, never, never!' The clear-out happened on 7 July 2005, a date, of course, that became known as 7/7. The terrorist explosions crippled the public-transport network, which is why she needed to take Carole's car to get home. It was soon returned to London.

I ask why she phoned Richard on the day that the Felsteads were informed of the death. She did so, she says, because the coroner mentioned how crushed he had sounded. It is an act that she now regrets. 'Concern for somebody else's distress sometimes overcomes you,' she says. 'I was foolish. Unwise.'

Ironically, it was Dr Fisher's discovery of Richard's letter that led to the cancellation of the funeral. Was she upset when she heard it had been halted? 'You can't even imagine,' she says. 'I was giving a talk with the Bishop of Oxford. I just screamed and screamed.'

Finally, we get to the question of whether Carole's memories of satanic abuse were recovered. Initially Fisher refuses to speak about Carole. 'I have a duty of confidentiality, even after a patient has died. I was never her psychiatrist or psychotherapist or anything like that.' She raises her voice. 'I'm not a psychotherapist, for God's sake!'

'According to her medical notes, she saw you for counselling,' I say.

'No.'

'I have the letter here. It's dated 27 November 1986 and it says: "She required to see Dr Fisher for psychosexual counselling."'

There is a silence.

'Psychosexual is the wrong term,' she says.

'What's the correct term?'

'Uh, I really don't know. People come and tell you things that have happened to them.'

'Things like abuse?'

'Things that have happened to them,' she repeats, crossly. 'I'm not saying anything else. It's not right that this woman's

219

privacy should be breached in this way.' She is shouting now. 'She's dead! She's goddamned dead!'

'Were you ever worried that Carole had lapsed into fantasy?'

'Never,' she says.

By 1997, I tell her, Carole was claiming that a former Conservative cabinet minister had anally raped her with a claw hammer in Conservative Central Office.

For a moment, she doesn't speak.

'That's not something I knew about. It may have been fantasy,' she says, adding darkly, 'but I couldn't say.'

'Are you aware of any evidence that any of Carole's claims actually happened?'

'I never looked for any evidence.'

'Then what made you believe her?'

'She's not the only patient I've had who told the same kinds of stories.'

'About ritual abuse?'

'It turned out to be that, yes. The people didn't remember at first. They weren't aware. They were memories they'd had a long time and they just came out.'

And that, I decide, is all that I need to know. Before I ring off, I ask Fisher what Carole was like. 'She was a feisty, brave, intelligent woman. She was funny. A good laugh.' And then, softly at first, she starts crying.

*

As delusions and paranoias such as the ones Carole suffered are a common facet of schizophrenia, I seek the counsel of Dr Trevor Turner, the psychiatrist who mentioned false memories to me previously. 'One of the classic symptoms of schizophrenia is the idea that your body has been interfered with,' he tells me. 'And it's very common for people to develop extraordinary delusional beliefs. If you talk to families of people who have got schizophrenia, the number of them who have been accused of things is huge.'

If Turner's observations are correct and Carole was schizophrenic, I wonder what effect it might have had on her, having therapists validate her darkest delusions. What would it be like for someone with paranoid fantasies to have it confirmed that, yes, there really *are* satanists out there, trying to get you? 'Absolutely terrifying,' he says. 'It's highly likely it would make it worse.'

I want to put this directly to Dr Valerie Sinason. So a week later, I return to her Golders Green sofa. I tell her, for the first time, that I am investigating Carole Myers.

'Ha ha,' she says. 'Ha ha.' There is a silence. 'This is very helpful because you're now truthfully admitting where your position is.'

I ask if Carole was the 'first patient' she had described, with the limp. She denies it. Despite what it says in the medical records, she insists that she never treated Carole, admitting only to having seen her as part of a study into ritual abuse for the Department of Health. 'There is so much I could say about Carole,' she tells me. 'But it's totally against any ethical code to speak about patients.'

'Talking generally, then – why do you believe your patients are telling the truth, and are not delusional?'

'I've now seen over four hundred survivors that have all given ludicrously similar testimony,' she says. 'You know when someone is speaking, and it sends a chill down you – there's a very big difference between someone who's got a fantasy and utter terror.'

'But Carole was delusional,' I say. 'She said a cabinet minister anally raped her with a claw hammer.'

'I wouldn't be at all surprised by misinformation, someone being drugged up and shown newsreels to make them—'

'But isn't this the problem?' I interrupt. 'All the stories that are obviously nonsensical, you dismiss as planted misinformation. If you can accept that some of it's not true, how do you know *all of it's* not true?'

'The job of a therapist is not to be judge or jury or police force.'

'Do you not accept that if a patient is delusional, a therapist who colluded in that delusion – who said, "Yes, there are satanists who are out to get you" – could be causing huge damage?'

'That would cause real damage,' she says. 'But the purpose of therapy is hearing where a patient is.'

By now, I am getting cross.

'When someone is saying they've been anally raped with a claw hammer by a Conservative cabinet minister, that, *indisputably*, is someone suffering from a paranoid delusion.'

David pipes up: 'Well, have you asked him whether it happened or not? We've been shocked by some of the stuff that's proved to be true.'

I turn to Dr Sinason. 'So you're saying, maybe I'm wrong about the minister?'

She looks blankly at me.

'Maybe.'

I leave the conversation feeling angry yet satisfied. For me, the case is closed. But then I have a conversation that rattles me. I am speaking with Professor Richard Bentall, the madness expert who believes that sexual abuse is a major cause of people hearing voices. When I mention the case in passing, he says, 'Not Valerie Sinason?'

'Yes!'

'I read one of her case accounts and it just seemed amazingly familiar. Obviously, I've not met the patient, so couldn't say for sure. But, to me it sounded like somebody with psychosis.'

I tell him about Carole Myers.

'Jesus Christ!' he says. 'She's had a paranoid psychosis, that's what's happened! I don't know this person, but I always say, with paranoid patients – you have to bear in mind there's usually a nugget of truth in their paranoia. I think it's certainly the case that some therapists with their own agendas are capable of encouraging a distorted memory of events, if you follow what I'm saying.'

I spend a moment struggling to absorb what he has just told me.

'You're saying, Carole might have been abused?'

'You've been asking, is this satanic abuse, or is she imagining it? But there is a third option. She got abused – although not satanically – and then had a psychotic interpretation of it.'

'I'm sure the family are innocent,' I say.

'A hell of a lot of abuse is not by family members,' he says. 'Maybe she had been abused by somebody outside the family and developed a distorted memory of it. This is one of the horrible cases where we just don't know what really happened.'

*

On 21 June 2005, after years of silence, Carole unexpectedly phoned her brother Richard. She told him that she was lonely in London and that she had no friends. She had decided, after all this time, that she wanted to move back to Stockport to be with the family. On Wednesday the 29th, the day that Carole mysteriously died, Richard wrote the letter that would be discovered by Dr Fisher and would eventually trigger the family's search for truth. He recounted the latest news – about his business, his brothers, his dad's heart attack – and finished with a flourish that, in retrospect, seems haunting and prescient. 'One shouldn't maintain too great a distance,' he wrote, 'as once the moment is gone, it is gone.'

11

'There was nothing there, but I knew it was a cockerel'

So now we know. The men and women of science have delivered the shaming news and humanity has responded, in the main, by ignoring it. Of course it has – this is just what you would expect from brains that have evolved to project an image of reasonable, wise, clear-sighted coherence and yet whose decision-making engines run on a slick conjuration of illusion, prejudice and ego-bolstering sleights of truth; a system of irrationality that includes a kind of neural blacksmith's workshop for dealing with uncomfortable facts – there the furnace for softening them up, there the hammer and tongs for reshaping them, there the window from which to toss them out.

But all this is not enough. Cognitive dissonance, confirmation bias, the brain's desire to have the outer, real world match its inner models of it – it takes us part of the way there. It tells us that a properly functioning brain cannot be trusted to think rationally and, because our minds play these tricks without telling us, that owners of brains cannot be trusted to judge their own rationality. But since meeting Gemma the Homeopath, I have come to suspect that there is something else going on – some crucial process that I have missed.

Gemma had one fact that required explanation: her belief that homeopathy cured her cancer. When I asked her to explain this belief, she gave me far less than any respectable scientific study could offer – no data, no proof. And yet she also gave me *more*. Gemma told a compelling tale. A young woman on her deathbed, a hapless medical service, scenes of lonely devastation, of falling hair and swelling moonfaces, of a deathly oncologist and a sensational recovery just in time for Christmas. Crack open the belief and something magical bursts out. A story.

The model-defending brain tells of an organ that is, naturally enough, defensive. But before it has any models to defend, it has to actually build them. If I am to track the source of faulty beliefs, I need to discover how they become a part of the model in the first place. I have to understand, not just the brain's destructive powers, but also its creative ones. Creativity is, after all, a defining quality of humanity, and my journey has already found great glittering piles of it. Many thousands of followers of Swami Ramdev benefit from what I believe to be the placebo effect, and yet spin tales about ancient Eastern wisdom battling evil Western medicine. Buddhists feel the proven effects of meditation and yet run far from those safe lands, towards karma, reincarnation and extra-mortal realms inhabited by giants. Men and women feel an unexplained itch and weave a plot atop their welts that tells of nanotechnology and tiny wasps and a medico-industrial conspiracy. John Mackay experiences life in the world, and the mystery of its being here, and explains it using creation myths from the deserts of the old Middle East.

These are stories, and they seem to have a terrible effect on truth. With their narratives of good and evil, heroism and villainy, they are neural seducers, coaxing people ever deeper into the darklands of craziness. For Rufus May, this happened literally. He was bored and unhappy and began to tell himself an exciting tale in which he was being recruited as a trainee spy. Partly through a process which has the appearance, at least, of a pathological cousin of confirmation bias, he began to see evidence for this narrative everywhere. The story became the truth and Rufus became mad.

Whether Rufus May's experience has anything in common with that of the alien abductees is not clear. There is no consensus on if and how ordinary self-deception overlaps with the dangerous delusions of psychotics. But in a paper published in the *Journal of Philosophical Studies*, Lisa Bortolotti and Matteo Mameli point to the 'considerable continuity' that is evident between them. Both, they write, 'serve to either preserve positive emotions, deny unpleasant or disturbing facts or satisfy some other pressing psychological need'. Psychiatrist Robin Murray, meanwhile, says that schizophrenia can be seen as a 'salience disorder' in which random events in an individual's daily experience are soaked in too much significance. 'Everything seems important. Why are there all these red cars? Why are all these people wearing red jumpers? Could it be because someone has hired them to follow me? Could it be because I'm very important? Or could it be because they're all out to get me?' It is as if the mind of the schizophrenic is suffering from an excess of stories. This, I have come to suspect, is not a coincidence.

We humans are creatures of story. And the story of story begins in the unconscious.

*

To reveal the secrets of the storytelling brain, we need to lead our search backwards in time. Throughout childhood and until late adolescence, our brains are building their internal models of what is out there and how it all works – physical, social, emotional and so on. After that, our core beliefs harden and we find change, according to Professor of Psychiatry Bruce Wexler, 'difficult and painful'. The power of our many cognitive biases skews our view. We attack unwelcome information. The gravity of our personal worlds attracts us to other, similar worlds – people who 'see it like we do', whose opinions give us the warm, reassuring pleasure of comfort, familiarity, safety. It all thickens the illusion that our way is the *true* way. And some take it even further. In their heroic, heretical and wonderfully human way, they get up and get out there and attempt to change the models of other people so that they match their own. They write, they blog, they preach, they *create*.

But before all that, our models must be built, and it is in this building that the first awakenings of our need for storytelling can be discovered. Developmental biologist Professor Lewis Wolpert writes that babies 'construct reality through converging lines of sensory and motor information' – by interacting with the world and learning how causes create effects.

Cause and effect is at the core of belief. It is at the core of thinking, the core of being human. It has to be. Cause and effect is what we do – we just *have* to make things happen. It is sometimes known as the 'effectance motive' – the urge to learn by interacting with the world. Psychologist Jonathan Haidt has called effectance 'almost as basic a need as food and water'.

Our understanding of the law of cause and effect is so fundamental that our brains are wired to spot it everywhere, even when it doesn't exist. In *Thinking, Fast and Slow*, Professor Daniel Kahneman invites his readers to observe two words: 'bananas' and 'vomit'. 'There was no particular reason to do so,' he writes, 'but your mind automatically assumed a temporal sequence and a causal connection between the words *bananas* and *vomit*, forming a sketchy scenario in which bananas caused the sickness.' Professor Wolpert, meanwhile, writes of studies in which people who view moving discs on a computer screen cannot resist the belief that they are bouncing off one another. Similarly, moving dots often appear as if they are involved in a chase.

Our models are built by ever more complex observations that are based on a simple question – if you do *that*, then *what* will happen? This is why emotions are so crucial to thinking. They tell us the answer. They are the strange, ancient whale-songs of your models communicating with you, predicting the effect that will follow the cause. They represent a mode of language that is millions of years older than any human one. It is a form that we have been using since before we *were* human. If you are about to do something that your models predict will be good, you will get a subtle encouraging hit of pleasure. If you are about to do something inadvisable, you will feel bad. We are assailed with a constantly shifting sense-scape of complex feelings: disgust, pride, hate, hope, love, lust, rage and all the rest of them. Everything we come across – every sight, every smell, every person, every idea, every*thing* – comes coupled with a feeling, no matter how subtle. These feelings are your models – your unconscious mind – speaking to you. Professor Michael Gazzaniga writes that 'All decisions we make are based on whether to approach or withdraw, including our moral decisions.' Without emotions, we would be incapable of making these decisions.

Emotions guide all of your behaviour. In essence, they work by rooting through the past to tell you stories about the future. In their silent language of feelings, they are your constant adviser, hitting you with dread or desire or any one of their other terrible, shimmering, beautiful states in order to guide your thinking.

The old notion that there are two simple states of mind – conscious and unconscious, rational and emotional – remains useful for describing these ideas, but is now known to be radically simplistic. Recent theory on the unconscious – where those other simplified objects, the 'models', reside – says that it is not a single thinking-centre but, in the words of Professor David Eagleman, 'a combination of sub-agents' who often want different things and challenge each other for control of your actions. The mind, he writes in *Incognito*, is 'built of multiple over-lapping experts who weigh in and compete over different choices' and are 'locked in chronic battle'. What you decide and how you act is mostly (possibly *completely*) determined by the outcomes of these fights. 'Your behaviour – what you do in the world – is simply the end result of the battles.'

The point at which you sense that emotional hit, then, is usually the point at which these fights have been fought and won. We have many models of the world, which offer many predictions about the future, many different answers to the simple question: 'If I cause this to happen, what will be the effect?' The emotion that you feel when trying to make a decision – approach, withdraw – is a kind of match-report, informing you of the outcome of this complex debate between experts.

We have experts inside us, we have competing models of the world and we also have other people. When we are young and building our models through observations of cause and effect, we are not just seeing what happens when we shake a rattle. We are also creating models of human relationships, by interacting with others. Professor Bruce Wexler writes that the psyche is seen 'as an emerging organisation that evolves through increasingly complex interchanges with people'. He describes the psychoanalytic theory that we are prone to identifying not just with humans, but with animals, the 'heroes of a previous generation', long-dead ancestors and even characters from fiction, internalising them, so that they ultimately become components of ourselves. In *Brain and Culture*, he offers the example of young Native American men who, on reaching sexual maturity, are given the names of certain animals with the intention that they will assume 'important qualities of that animal'. Reading about all this, I cannot help but recall Ron Coleman and the frighteningly vivid models his brain contained of the criminal priest and of his lost love, Annabel.

Along this journey, I have given descriptions of our limited perception, cognitive biases and faulty, bickering models. Because the focus has been on our flaws, it might be easy to conclude that the brain is not particularly good at its job. This is not so. The models it creates and the predictions it makes *have* to be largely effective, otherwise we would simply not be able to operate. Indeed, there is a good chance that you have no idea how clever you really are. This is because you have no direct access to your unconscious models – the bits of yourself that are the most brilliant, mathematically, analytically and creatively. In fact, the part of your mind that you do your conscious thinking with is, in the words of Professor David Eagleman, 'not at the centre of the action in the brain, it is far out on a distant edge, hearing but whispers of the activity'. These whispers very often tell of wisdom and calculation whose sophistication might astound you.

Scientists at the Monell Centre, Philadelphia, had participants in a study smell gauze pads that had been worn under the armpits of people who had watched various films. *Without knowing why*, many of the sniffers could detect which pads had been worn during comedies and which during horrors. Then there are the amazing chick-sexers. When chickens are born in industrial hatcheries, they have to be separated by gender.

Because newborn chicks look identical, professional sexers are hired to do the work. Unfortunately, the professionals cannot tell you what the difference between a day-old male and a female chick is either. In order to learn, an apprentice sexer just starts working, examining each young bird and *guessing*, while an old master tells them when they are right or not. Somehow, a part of their brain eventually just *gets* it. Researcher Richard Horsey says, 'They just look at the rear end of a chick, and "see" that it is either male or female.' He quotes one former sexer who says, 'To be close to 100 per cent and accurate at 800 to 1200 chickens per hour, intuition comes into play in many of your decisions, even if you are not consciously aware of it. As one of my former colleagues said to me . . . "There was nothing there but I knew it was a cockerel." This was intuition at work.' By trial and error – cause and effect – these sexers develop brilliant models for male chick and female chick. Their unconscious minds use the sight of a chick's backside to compare it with their models, then use emotion to 'tell' the sexers the answer.

In an experiment that looked at just how intricately advanced 'intuition' can be, a team led by Professor Antoine Bechara gave participants $2,000 in play money and four decks of cards and told them they were to use them in a game. Different individual cards won or lost different sums of money. They should just go ahead and turn the cards and try to win as much money as they could. But the cards were not random. In fact, some of the piles were far more profitable than others. On average, it took the gamblers around fifty card-turns before they began to report a conscious 'hunch' that some of the decks were more profitable. But when their behaviour was analysed, Professor Bechara discovered something remarkable. Measurements of the electrical conductance of their skin, which can reveal levels of anxiety and nervousness, indicated that their emotions were subtly warning them against the bad decks after *just ten turns*. Their unconscious mind had worked out what was happening far quicker than their conscious minds and had warned them with a hit of *bad feeling*. They knew before they knew.

All of this seems to border on magic. But the brain, as we know, is also an organ of bias and prejudice whose rapid responses are made possible by its models – stubborn approximations of how the world works. Studies have established that qualified yet overweight job applicants are often assumed to be less intelligent, lazier and more immoral than their thinner counterparts. One sad experiment demonstrated that interviewers can unconsciously attach negative qualities to an applicant after they have seen them *sitting next to* an overweight person in the waiting room.

These unpleasant decisions are compounded by the fact that we usually don't even know we have made them. If we did, we might be able to use our rational minds to suppress them. But those instances are rare. Most thinking is emotional, and happens without you even being aware of it. We can't question ourselves, either. The great electrical thinking-galaxies that bloom and churn behind the eyes of the mind cannot tell us why they have decided that sitting beside an overweight person is bad. They cannot speak.

All of which leads us to an intriguing and essential problem. If our unconscious is mute, and yet driving most of our decisions, then how can we explain our own behaviour? As Professor Leon Festinger and his co-researchers into confirmation bias found: when confronted by a new fact, we feel an instantaneous, emotional hunch that pulls us in the direction of an opinion. We then look for evidence that supports our hunch until we hit the 'makes sense stopping rule' and our thinking ceases. Our mind completes the process by fooling us into believing that we have made an objective survey of the arguments, then gives us a pleasurable neurochemical hit of *feeling* as a reward. But all we have really done is confirm the hunch, silence the dissonance, reinforce the model.

If this is so, and all we are doing is defending the conclusion that our mute unconscious has already come to, it suggests something terrifying: that we don't know why we believe what we believe; we don't know why we do what we do. It says that all we are really up to when justifying our actions and beliefs is guessing. All we *really* know is how we feel, and our explanations for how we feel are inventions. They *must* be – because we cannot talk to the parts of our minds that have made these decisions. A homophobe cannot ask his own unconscious why he believes that homosexuality is evil. All he knows is that, when he thinks about gay people, his emotions say 'withdraw'. He feels disgust. Then he weaves a narrative that explains his disgust. He tells a story.

As we grow – and our knowledge of causes and effects become ever more sophisticated – so too do our natural abilities as storytellers. As Professor Timothy Wilson writes in *Redirect*, 'One of the main differences between us and the rest of the animal kingdom is that we have a large brain with which we can construct elaborate theories and explanations about what is happening in the world and why.'

At its most basic level, a story is a description of something happening that contains some form of sensation, or drama. It is, in other words, an explanation of cause and effect that is soaked in emotion. Human thinking must take this form because we are biologically incapable of removing the *feeling* from it. That is how our thoughts are delivered.

And complex brains create complex stories. In *Six Impossible Things Before Breakfast*, Professor Lewis Wolpert writes that, aside from their understanding that germs and food can cause sickness, 'there is a quite widespread belief among children that illness is a punishment for wrongdoing.' From an early age, a simple observation of a person falling sick is liable to become a narrative of good and evil and vengeance for sin. We are natural-born storytellers, who have a propensity to believe our own tales.

A series of remarkable scientific discoveries, going back to the nineteenth century, have bolstered this view. They have assigned it a word, which describes what we do when we unknowingly invent explanations for behaviours and beliefs whose causes we are actually ignorant of: confabulation.

In 1889 the German psychiatrist Albert Moll recounted telling a hypnotised woman, 'After you wake you will take a book from the table and put in on the bookshelf.' When she came too, she had no conscious memory of having been given this instruction. And yet she dutifully picked up a book and slid it into a space on the shelf. When Moll asked her why she had done this, she said, 'I do not like to see things so untidy. The shelf is the place for the book, and that is why I put it here.' She had confabulated a reason for her behaviour, which was actually caused by Moll's instruction. She thought that she knew why she was putting the book away, but the reason she gave was just a story that her brain had told her, and that she had believed.

Seventy-three years later, researchers at Columbia University injected epinephrine into some study participants which, unbeknown to them, would make their heart race, their face flush and their hands tremble. Some of the participants were then placed in the company of an angry person, others in the company of someone happy. The subjects with the angry person reported feeling angry, confabulating a fake reason for their heightened physical sensations. The happy ones did likewise. A control group, who *had been* informed about the effects of epinephrine, correctly put their bodily responses down to the drug. The other participants, though, experienced identical physiological effects and yet confabulated themselves into completely opposing moods. Writes Professor Michael Gazzaniga, 'If there is an obvious explanation, we accept it. When there is not an obvious explanation, we generate one.'

The most startling revelation of confabulation, though, has come from the study of people who suffer from such severe epilepsy that, in order to prevent them having potentially catastrophic global attacks, they have the two hemispheres of their brain surgically separated. These 'split-brain' patients have been the subject of a series of profoundly remarkable experiments by the celebrated neuroscientist Professor Michael Gazzaniga. They revealed the disorienting extent to which we all confabulate, all of the time.

It is a peculiarity of our neural architecture that each half of the brain receives information from, and controls the actions of, the opposite side of the body. The left is master of the right, the right is master of the left. Why this is remains a mystery (although some speculate that it is a mechanism for helping us move the appropriate limb towards sources of light). The hemispheres are not identical. In the majority of people, the left side is specialised for language and verbal communication, while the right is effectively mute. By itself, the right hemisphere can take information from your senses, but it lacks some essential word- and speech-generating circuitry. This means that it cannot, by itself, 'talk'. In normal brains, this doesn't matter as the two hemispheres are connected and information can travel freely between them. But the right hemisphere of a split-brain patient cannot speak. It is, in effect, silenced.

Because this is a slightly complex idea to explain, I'm going to use some colloquial language that some science-literate readers might object to, because of its imprecision. For those people, I should acknowledge that, very strictly speaking, regions of the brain don't 'talk', only people do. Furthermore, no implication should be drawn from what follows that the left hemisphere equates to consciousness whilst the right does not. Anyhow, for everyone else . . .

In order to study confabulation, Gazzaniga developed a method of communicating with only the 'silent' right hemisphere of a split-brain patient. He began by showing it a picture of a hat. When the professor asked the patient what he had seen, he said that he didn't know. Because the right hemisphere lacks this critical language and speech circuitry, it could not 'tell' the man that it had seen the hat, so he didn't know that he had. But when Professor Gazzaniga asked the patient to point with his left hand (which is controlled by the 'speechless' right hemisphere) at what he had been shown, it correctly fell upon the hat. The patient knew, but he did not know.

You might be pausing, now, unsure whether you have understood that correctly. This person felt no awareness of having seeing the hat – he had no apparent memory of it whatsoever – and yet, when he was asked what he had seen, he pointed straight at it? That is correct. It really is that strange.

It gets weirder. In his most famous test, Professor Gazzaniga flashed a picture of a chicken claw to a man's left hemisphere and a car covered in snow to his right. He then asked him to point to images that represented what he had seen. One hand went to a chicken, the other to a shovel. Remembering that the patient didn't realise that he had seen the car covered in snow, and therefore no clue as to *why* he was pointing at the shovel, Professor Gazzaniga asked him to explain his choices. 'Oh, that's simple,' he said. 'The chicken claw goes with the chicken and you need a shovel to clean out the chicken shed.'

He instantly told a story that explained his inexplicable behaviour – a story *that he believed*. It was a confabulation that would go down in neuro-scientific history.

It did not end there. In further brilliant examples of confabulation, Gazzaniga flashed the command 'Walk' to a patient's right hemisphere. When he did just that, and the researchers asked him why he had got up, he replied, 'I'm going to the house to get a Coke.' Using the same methods, the professor triggered various moods in patients. When he told the right hemisphere of split-brain patient 'JW' to laugh, she laughed. When Gazzaniga asked her why she was laughing, she said, 'You guys come up and test us every month. What a way to make a living.'

These split-brain patients were special only because the communication between their two hemispheres had been severed. The instant confabulations that they were making – I'm walking because I'm thirsty, I'm laughing because you're idiots – were not caused by this surgery. The surgery simply enabled Gazzaniga to catch these brains in the act. We *all* confabulate in this way. First we behave. Then we explain. What Gazzaniga's experiments revealed was the profoundly disturbing fact that our own explanations for our own actions and beliefs can have no basis in truth – and yet we believe them utterly. We are storytellers. That is what we do.

Gazzaniga theorises that the verbal left hemisphere of our brain contains an 'interpreter' that is driven to constantly narrate our actions, explaining them even though it has no access to the reasons why we are behaving as we are. Recalling a test where a visual stimulus was used to put a patient in a bad mood, only for her to blame her bad feeling on the experimenter, Gazzaniga writes, 'Ah, lack of knowledge is of no importance, the left brain will find a solution! Order must be made. The experimenter did it! The left-brain interpreter takes all the input coming in and puts it together in a story that makes sense, even though it may be completely wrong.' In his book *Human* he adds that the right hemisphere bases its judgements on 'sample frequency information, whereas the left uses the formation of elaborate hypotheses . . . [but] the left's tendency to create nonsensical theories about random sequences is detrimental to performance. This is what happens when you build a theory on a single anecdotal situation.' You could also say that this is what happens when you take a homeopathic remedy, begin to feel better and conclude that the remedy worked. Your interpreter module has told an invented story about cause and effect that you believe. Your surely held belief is a confabulation.

There appears to be a lack of consensus on exactly how much of our conscious reasoning is confabulation. Opinions range from those of Professor David Eagleman, who says that 'the brain's storytelling powers kick into gear only when things are conflicting or difficult to understand', to those of Harvard Professor of Psychology Daniel Wegner, who argues that even our sense of having free will is a confabulation – a story that seeks to reassure us by giving a sense of agency and purpose. Eagleman, meanwhile, writes that if we do possess free will, it 'can at best be a small factor, riding on top of vast neural networks shaped by genes and environment. In fact, free will may end up being so small that we eventually think about decision-making in the same way we think about any physical process, such as diabetes or lung disease.'

When I ask Professor Jonathan Haidt what he believes, he tells me that his position is 'nuanced. We don't have free will in the strictest sense of "I am the uncaused causer of my behaviour." That's a kind of craziness. Our behaviour is caused largely by forces we're not aware of. On the other hand, we're not puppets that are just dancing around to external causes. Our actions are shaped by forces that we would endorse as legitimate, such as our values.' I wonder what he thinks of the narrower question, of whether or not we have free will over the things that we believe. Using the example of climate change, I put it to Professor Haidt that our opinion on whether or not it is man-made could actually have an entirely emotional source and be nothing to do with reason. 'That's true for partisans,' he says. 'If you come to the question already on the left or the right, then that's correct. But there are surely some people who are not part of any team who have looked at the evidence and come to their conclusion – I don't doubt that.'

But regardless of whether or not we have free will (and the arguments for it seem – to me, at least – to be distressingly thin), neuroscientists and psychologists widely agree that confabulation is real and universal. To ever *really* know ourselves is simply not possible. We tend to generate stories to explain the mysteries of what we do and believe. When called upon to justify our beliefs we automatically become confabulators – innocent liars defending unconscious decisions that we were not even aware of making.

The principles of confabulation – if not its narrowest academic definition – can be found lurking in other crucial areas of the human condition, too. The shapes of its engineering can be found in the mechanisms of memory, in morality and in dreaming.

A 1962 study by Professor Daniel Offer demonstrated how vulnerable our autobiographical memories are to being re-written. Offer's team interviewed more than seventy male teenagers about their lives, before revisiting them thirty-four years later to check how accurate their recollections were. What were they like back then? Confident? Shy? Curious?

Academic? What were their beliefs about the world? 'Remarkably,' concluded the team, 'the men's ability to guess what they had said about themselves in adolescence was no better than chance.'

Social psychologists Carol Tavris and Elliot Aronson believe that we use 'confabulations of memory' to 'justify and explain our own lives'. In *Mistakes Were Made* they write that our sense of personal autobiography only seems coherent as a result of 'years of telling our story, shaping it into a life narrative that is complete with heroes and villains, an account of how we came to be the way we are . . . the problem is that when the narrative becomes a major source of self-justification, one the storyteller relies on to excuse mistakes and failings, memory becomes warped in its service.'

Warped indeed, and invented. Whether they are generated in ordinarily healthy individuals or psychotic patients, completely false memories are easily formed and can be dreadful to those whom they haunt.

In further unwelcome developments, Professor Haidt has demonstrated that our explanations of our own moral beliefs are also mostly confabulations. To test this, he wrote a series of quick stories that involve 'harmless taboo violations'. One, for example, involves a man buying a chicken from a supermarket, and having sex with it before cooking and eating it. In another, a woman cuts up an American flag and uses it to clean her house. When Haidt told these tales, people generally experienced disgust for the man's actions and felt that the woman had been disrespectful. Their emotions had formed powerful responses. The models in their unconscious minds had given their verdict – now they had to confabulate their reasons for it. But these were victimless offences. How did people justify their negative feelings? Many simply invented victims. After 1,620 harmless offence stories were read out, 38 per cent of people insisted that someone actually *had been* harmed. In his book *The Righteous Mind* Haidt recalls that when he and his colleagues would politely remind them that there *were* no victims, they would 'say things like, "I know it's wrong, but I just can't think of a reason why." They seemed to be morally dumbfounded – rendered speechless by their inability to explain verbally what they knew intuitively.'

Professor Haidt is perhaps *the* foremost expert on the psychology of moral reasoning. He writes that, rather than it being a process that we use in order to discover truth, 'moral reasoning is part of our lifelong struggle to win friends and influence people . . . Don't take people's moral arguments at face value. They're mostly post hoc constructions made up on the fly . . . We are selfish hypocrites so skilled at putting on a show of virtue that we fool even ourselves.'

The brain's powers of confabulation can be experienced vividly when we are asleep. Sometimes, an area of the brain stem causes a 'myoclonic jerk' – thought to be a release of muscle tension. Your brain will likely weave a dream to explain this sudden spasm, and you will find yourself falling – down stairs, off a tabletop, on black ice.

Of course, it should not be a surprise that we confabulate when we are asleep. As we have already discovered, one of the most disturbing revelations of neuroscience is that our sense of being 'out there' in the world is an illusion. We are stuck inside our skulls and the rich sensory landscape of sights and sounds and colours and smells that we think we are moving about in is actually a reconstruction. As neuroscientist and sleep expert Dr Stephen LaBerge has said, 'Asking why we dream is like asking why we are conscious. We dream because the brain is designed to make a model of the world whenever it is functioning.'

In *The Ego Tunnel*, neuroscientist and philosopher Thomas

Metzinger notes that 'the dream ego does not know that it is dreaming . . . The dream ego is delusional, lacking insight into the nature of the state it is itself generating.' In this sense, the 'dream ego' is little different from its daytime version. Whether awake or asleep, we are deluded into believing that we are 'the invisible actor at the centre of the world'.

Our brains create the world in which we exist – they also create us. Perhaps the greatest model that the brain creates is that of *you* – the 'I', the coherent individual, the soul who inhabits the body.

Starting with its basic lessons of cause and effect, the brain builds its models and uses them to create a virtual reality for us to exist in. This virtual reality is, in important respects, highly accurate. But it is narrow: our limited senses mean that we are unaware of most of the sounds and sights around us. It is biased: our intellectual worlds are skewed, primed to see and favour 'pre-approved' information. It is emotional: our feelings largely define our thinking. It is prejudiced: we remain a tribal species. It is selfish and egotistical: we are fooled into believing that we are wiser, more moral, more capable, better looking and with more hopeful futures than is true.

Our brain generates a model of a simply experienced, physical body that is moving through space. It imbues that body with a thinking mind that believes it is a single, coherent whole, but is actually a conglomeration of warring parts. It suspends that 'self' in a world that is simultaneously physical and emotional. It gives it memories and hopes – a place in time, in past and future. It covers many of the cracks with confabulation – innocent lies that we tell ourselves to keep the illusion steady, and ourselves happy.

We confabulate tales that make us believe that the 'I', and not all those frighteningly uncontrollable external causes, are the commanders of our behaviour. We confabulate tales that explain how Pranayama made us better; to account for the transformative effects of meditation. We confabulate tales to justify our emotional conviction that there really *are* satanic baby-eating cults. When he was in his psychotic state, Rufus May confabulated a tale about being recruited as a spy that made sense of the extra dopamine in his brain. Dopamine is a neurochemical that is implicated in the identification of 'prediction errors', or surprises. When we experience something that conflicts with our neural models we need to explain it by grafting it into the narrative that we tell of the world. Dopamine helps to tell us when our models need updating. Rufus's excess dopamine resulted in his attending to lots of extra-vibrant, vital, salient detail. He had become too sensitive to stories.

The benefits of story-making have been explored by Professor of Psychology Timothy Wilson. In *Redirect*, he considers how disturbing it has been for the human species to have gained the unique ability to ponder concepts such as hopelessness and death. 'It is so unsettling to think such thoughts,' he writes, 'that we have developed narratives that provide comforting answers . . . worldviews that explain creation, the purpose of life, and what happens after we die, thereby helping us deal with the terror of gazing into the sky and seeing ourselves as insignificant specks . . . many studies show that religious people are happier than nonreligious people.'

Analysis of one hundred such papers by researchers at Duke University Medical Center in North Carolina found that seventy-nine concluded that religious believers have more positive emotions and show a greater satisfaction with their lives than others. Anthropologists at the University of Connecticut found that Israeli women who recited psalms during the second intifada experienced less anxiety and an increased sense of control compared with those who did not.

Professor Wilson believes that a central benefit of story-making is the sense of certainty it offers. He tells of an examination of a group of people who had a 50 per cent chance of developing fatal Huntingdon's disease. They were given the opportunity to discover their fate using a simple test. Some participants took the test, while others chose to remain in ignorance. Those who tested positive were devastated: they would likely die in middle age. When they were seen again, though, six months later, their happiness levels had lifted back to normal. After a year, they remained stable. But the group who had chosen not to find out were significantly more depressed.

Surprisingly, the individuals who knew that they would die young were happier than those who were not sure. Says Professor Wilson, 'Those who had learned that they had inherited the Huntingdon's gene found a way to come to terms with it, by incorporating this news into their narratives and finding some meaning in it . . . those who remained uncertain about their health status could not undergo this restorative process of narrative change.'

We create stories because they make us happy. They are how we learn about the world. They are how we predict the future. They provide certainty. They are a source of power and motivation. They tell us why good things happen and bad things happen and why we are better than most. They are arks of meaning, the method by which we navigate our lives through a dangerous and confusing world. At every moment, night and day, we are acting in our own first-person narrative dramas. Not only do our brains make a world for our story to play out in, they also create its hero. Us.

12

'I came of exceptional parents'

I cannot work out what it is with that shirt – but it is *beautiful*. Its top button is unfastened and its pristine cotton is firm and yet soft. It is behaving in all the right ways – in all of its angles, in the soaring confidence of its collar's upright points, in the inviting shadows that it is painting on its owner's skin. How does a simple white shirt come to look so elegant? What, exactly, is it that makes it so different from any of mine? Probably, I think, it is expensive. The young man who is wearing it certainly *looks* expensive. He sounds it, too. The whole carriage can hear him. Whereas everybody else has spent this journey looking softly out of windows or quietly reading, he has spent it on his phone, cufflinks flashing, talking volubly about his many and important activities at university at Oxford, which is where this train terminates. 'I really don't know what his problem is with me,' he says, at one point, and I think, 'I bet I could tell you. I bet I could give you a fucking *list*.'

I watch him, through the heads of the passengers in front of me. He is one of those men who are *almost* handsome. He is an impersonator, executing a flawed performance of beauty – mimicking perfection and failing just enough so that your attention is drawn to his essential flaw. It is his mouth. It is too wide and juts upwards at the sides. Thin lips and billboard teeth give his face a note of imperiousness and cruelty. I wonder about the years he has ahead of him. The gilded, almost-perfect life. I realise that I am staring at him again. He looks at me directly, this lucky prince, this *student*, and I glance shamefully away.

I am an hour early for my meeting with the famous climate-change sceptic Lord Monckton, so I button up my coat and wander the city. I am in a pedestrian precinct, ten minutes from the station, when I am startled to recognise the scene in front of me – a Tudor-looking building that now houses a chemist. My father has a framed etching of it at home, hanging in the corridor that leads from the bathroom. Ten minutes later I see a magisterial, columned edifice with a distinctive circular frontage. I grew up looking at that one too. Scenes from this city surrounded me when I was young. Oxford University. It is part of my father's story. I try to picture him – young and thriving, perhaps still with his Yorkshire accent – walking these streets in the 1960s. I wonder what he was like, back then. Which college did he go to? I begin to squint up at the black and gold painted walkers' signs as I pass them. Christ Church? Was that it?

I am about to enter Christ Church when a man in a booth blankly meets my eyes. There is a smartly painted sign in front of me, declaring this to be a private entrance. Two students move through unimpeded. Flush-cheeked, with big hair and scarves and confident, in their gait and in their echoing chatter, which concerns an audition for a part in a play. They turn off into some secret corridor. I stand in the wind and watch them go.

University is a part of my story too. My parents wanted me to go to a respected one such as this, but I never doubted that their ambition was hopeless. Even towards the end, they seemed convinced that I had a chance. The last time I was in

Oxford was for a university open day. My father had sent me there praying, I suspect, that by witnessing the glories that were ultimately possible, I would be inspired, finally, finally, after all these years of trouble, to actually do some *work*. My only memory of that trip is of sitting in the room of an English professor, who said, 'Tell me about your favourite Tennessee Williams.' I don't recall how I answered. But I do remember the emotion of the moment; the shame that I had no idea at all what a Tennessee Williams was.

When I was at school, I would always argue with my disappointed parents and harried teachers that I wanted to write and that writers don't need qualifications. I made no attempt to pass my A-levels and when I failed them all, I happily took a job in a record shop and the editorship of a local music fanzine. While my ex-school friends were lounging around student bars, I was working eight-hour days, with four weeks off a year, keeping my spare time for interviewing bands, hustling advertisers and folding thousands of photocopied pages. I spurned university. I never went. I always said I wouldn't need it to succeed, and I didn't.

That is my university story. It is the one I tell everyone, and it is untrue. I didn't fail all my A-levels, I scraped an E in geography, on account of a project I did on the pH levels of some soil on a Scottish hill that I really quite enjoyed doing. I did attend university – in Luton. My leaving (which took place a matter of weeks into my course) was motivated less by the opportunity of an editorship and more by the fact that I missed my girlfriend, Jenny, so much that I felt as if I was being crushed underwater. I moved in with a drug dealer in Tunbridge Wells, discovered amphetamines and got sacked from the shop when they caught me stealing. I ended up back in my childhood bedroom, for a while, claiming the dole.

In the narrative that I tell everyone, I am the hero, defiantly fighting the authorities at school and at home, bravely choosing the harder path and winning. In the true version, I am an academic failure and a petty criminal. Cognitive psychologist Professor Martin Conway believes that when we recall the events of our lives, we become the accidental victims of a fight between the different ways in which the brain rebuilds memories. It takes sensory information – how we felt in that moment – and combines it with dry facts – dates and so on. But these two processes are in conflict. The rational side wants the truth while the emotional side wants a story that works in service of the ego. And mostly – unsurprisingly – it wants to rebuild you into a hero. I am not sure if I can blame my university myth on these unconscious processes. But the strange thing is that a part of me – most of me, in fact – has somehow come to believe it.

The public entrance of Christ Church takes you past a sign that tells of Lewis Carroll and Albert Einstein and the thirteen prime ministers who have studied there. The college building is fatly magnificent, with its arched windows, carved stone balconies and towering roofs. I wander up and down for a while, just looking, imagining. It costs seven pounds for a non-student such as me to enter. I buy my ticket and follow the strictly laid-out tourist route, prevented by bowler-hatted guards from wandering the parts from which the public are prohibited. Grand portraits of centuries-past alumni look down at me – pale faces emerge from dark oils as if looming out of death itself. Long fingers, long noses, raised chins, impressive and imperious and gloating. I walk through the dining hall, with its leather seats, its golden lamps and its lit log fires, to see grown men and women shuffling about anxiously in silver-service uniforms, waxing the floor and polishing knives and forks and special little spoons in preparation for the arrival of these miraculous and perfect teenagers, in their miraculous and perfect shirts, who will soon be ruling the world.

Suddenly unaccountably irritable, I decide to leave. On the way out, I hear the sound of an organ coming from the chapel. I pad in quietly, unsure whether or not I am allowed to enter. I find the source of the music – a stunning array of pipes that float high in the medieval shadows – and stand before it. This is the sound of my childhood. My father was – is – obsessed with playing the organ. When he retired, he had one built in a small upstairs room of his house. It was his version of buying a Ferrari, I think – a dream come true. He had to have the floor reinforced.

When I was growing up, I was obsessed with music too. But my father couldn't bear the pop that I listened to before my adolescence or the heavy metal that I stomped towards when I became a teenager. The records that I would buy, the posters that I would pin to my walls, were the cause of terrible fights. It was all symbolic to him, I think, of my failure at school, my thieving at home, my drinking, my lack of respect for *civilisation*. My parents hated my music, and they loved God. They worked in education and believed passionately in its principles. I rejected education and God and believed passionately in Zodiac Mindwarp and Faith No More. It made for an uneasy childhood.

Our beliefs and tastes are much more than they are. They signal to distances that lie far beyond their own limits. They are markers, signs that display the culture and moral structure that we have adopted for ourselves to live within. They are chapter titles in our story about the world. My father read the signs that were hidden in those posters, T-shirts and record sleeves, and he did not like what they told him.

Yesterday, I met Dr James Garvey, a secretary of the Royal Institute of Philosophy, at a cafe in the British Museum. He has written a book on the ethics of global warming, and been called a religiously minded eco-fascist by climate-change sceptics because of his refusal to explore the notion that it is all a hoax, or to read obscure papers by non-scientists. He told me that this kind of thinking represents 'a way of seeing the world. In order to be a conservative person in America you have to be anti-abortion, pro-guns, pro-death-penalty, small government, no regulation – and climate is in there too. If you look at that set of beliefs, that's an identity. And you can't change an identity with facts.'

I have begun to realise that I used to blame my parents for their beliefs. I took it personally that their identities did not resemble mine. What I didn't understand was that we cannot choose the worlds we live within. Dr Garvey told me, 'David Hume says, "nature hasn't left it up to us what we believe". You can't pick your beliefs. You can, to some extent, have an influence on them, if you are especially open. But evidence cannot shift almost all the things you believe.'

My father's anger at my music, mine at his spiritual convictions. If these were just confabulations – stories spun atop mute emotional responses – then which emotion was it? Fear, perhaps. My father's fear of my failure, mine of his rejection. Inevitably, naturally, as I have grown older I have found myself becoming more like he was back then. And so the distance lessens, the understanding gathers itself up from the edges and with it comes empathy and love. It strikes me, as I stand here, that there was a time when the sound of an organ playing would make me fearful. Right now, I find it beautiful.

It is nearly time. I leave the hushed chapel and walk to the Oxford Union, where I have an engagement with the 3rd Viscount Monckton of Brenchley. It is Dr Garvey's 'identity' problem that has brought me here, to meet one of the world's most controversial climate-change sceptics. What fascinates

me about Lord Monckton is not his explosively heretical defiance of the scientific establishment's now inarguable case for
the dangers and reality of man-made climate change. It is that
so many of his views seem to coalesce on the political right.
Why do constellations of belief tend to fall so reliably on the
left or right wing? Why, for example, would a person who votes
for the privatisation of public services also often be a supporter
of the foreign policy of Israel? Why would their opponent tend
to agitate on behalf of women seeking abortions and also for
cheaper fares on local buses?

In Lord Monckton's case, he is head of policy at the
right-wing UK Independence Party, an anti-European, anti-
regulation Christian, one-time adviser on scientific and
domestic policy to Margaret Thatcher and a popular speaker
with America's Tea Party movement. He has labelled climate
science the 'largest fraud of all time', believes that 'the Hitler
Youth were left wing and also a green organisation' and has
compared 2009's Copenhagen Climate Conference to the
Nuremberg Rallies.

Monckton's position on climate differs from that of the
mainstream in that he believes that 'very little' warming of the
earth will take place given the anticipated increase in carbon-
dioxide concentration. When the presentation that he gives in
service of this opinion was heard by Professor John Abraham
– who has published more than eighty papers on heat transfer
and fluid mechanics – he spent eight months tracking down
'the articles and authors that Monckton cited. What I discovered was incredible, even to a scientist who follows the politics
of climate change. I found that he had misrepresented the science.' Monckton responded by accusing Abraham of issuing
'venomously ad hominem . . . artful puerilities', said he had a
face like an 'overcooked prawn' and promptly declared legal
action.

Our modern notion of 'left' and 'right' beliefs has its genesis in the 1789 revolution in France, when defenders of the aristocracy, Church and crown placed themselves on the right side of the chamber at the French Assembly, while supporters of the revolutionaries sat opposite. It is remarkable to think that conservatives and progressives still tend to align in this way, as if magnetised. If emotions – unconscious hunches – drive the great mass of our beliefs, then what is the emotional cause of these disparate sets of positions collecting at opposite poles? And why, in the words of clinical psychologist and political strategist Professor Drew Westen, is 'the biggest single predictor of party affiliation – and of the broader value systems associated with it – the party affiliations of our parents'?

In preparation for my encounter with Lord Monckton, I spoke with Professor Jonathan Haidt about the source of our moral and political beliefs. 'The place to begin is with these amazing twin studies in the 1980s,' he told me. 'They said that every aspect of your personality is partly heritable – what kind of music you like, what food you enjoy, everything. So if your identical twin is separated from you at birth, they will probably have the same politics as you forty years later, and how it works is to do with your genes. You have a particular genome which sets your initial direction – the first draft of your moral and political mind. Your genome does not specify the final form of your brain, it really just specifies the starting conditions. Then, by this mysterious process by which brains are created *in utero* and run throughout life, you emerge with a *certain kind* of brain. Brains are what you call "experience expectant". Evolution, in a sense, knows that we're going to get lots and lots of experience about what kinds of animals are dangerous, whether society is stable or unstable, hierarchical or egalitarian. So we get all kinds of information from the environment; our brains are expecting that information. As they continue growing, they incorporate that information. So you have to take a genetic view, a developmental view and a cultural view. You have to take all three views at the same time to understand why people end up where they end up and if you leave any of these three pieces out you won't have the whole story.'

In *The Righteous Mind*, Haidt writes that genes account for 'between a third and a half of the variability among people on their political attitudes'. An analysis of thirteen thousand Australians has indicated that a key commonality among many of the genes that separated conservative from liberal was involved in their responses to threat and fear. 'Individual genes have tiny effects,' he writes. However, 'genes collectively give people brains that are more or less reactive to threat and more or less open to new experience.' Very broadly speaking, the open ones are more likely to wander leftwards. The fearful, meanwhile, run to the right.

We can be born, then, with a kind of pre-set 'mood' – open or fearful. Depending on what happens to us during childhood, aspects of this mood can be counteracted or encouraged. Our behaviour influences the behaviour of those around us which, in turn, re-influences us. Growing up, our personality draws those of a similar nature closer into our circles. Professor Chris Frith has already told me how we are barely aware of our automatic tendency to imitate the people around us, and absorb their goals, knowledge and beliefs. ('This is why strange narratives work best when they are shared by a group,' he added, significantly.) As an adult, these crucial choices – where we live, how we socialise, the newspapers we read – create yet more feedback loops.

In this way, our moods create our worlds. Although our destinies are not written in the codes of our genome, we are aimed in a certain direction before we are sluiced from the womb. Our emotions weave a breadcrumb trail of *advance* or *withdraw* responses, which we can hardly help but follow. They influence our experiences, which influence the way we understand the world. Unless dramatic life events intercede, we have a tendency to become what we are.

The stories that we tell ourselves are another essential component to all this. The model of the world that we build for ourselves to live within is made of observations of cause and effect that are soaked in emotion. These micro-stories, whose purpose is to explain and predict the world, can grow into staggering tales of magnificent drama and complexity. In *The Political Brain*, Professor Westen writes 'research suggests that our minds naturally search for stories with a particular kind of structure, readily recognisable to elementary school children and similar across cultures.' In this structure, a crisis strikes a settled world, heroic efforts are begun to solve it, terrible obstacles are surmounted and dreadful enemies are battled, until a new and blissful state is achieved. According to Professor Westen, the political left and the right each has a 'master narrative' that reflects this structure – a grand, over-arching plot that comes loaded with a set of core assumptions, that defines the identity of heroes and villains and promises a paradisiacal denouement.

A person who fears novelty might have an instinctive, emotional hunch that immigration is a bad thing. A charismatic politician who tells of the urgent necessity of halting the hordes, promises heroic attempts at controlling the borders, and predicts wonders to come if their opponents are conquered is confabulating on behalf of the listener. He is weaving a story in which the right-wing individual is on the side of heroes. He does so with passion and wit and drama and all these *amazing true facts*. How can that not be seductive?

In this way, each side tells a conflicting tale about how the world works. The two poles experience a different reality, recognise a different story with different heroes and villains, and join a different side. They become members of opposing cultures, aliens from warring worlds. Needless to say, when all this is happening, nobody is behaving especially rationally. As Professor Westen writes, 'The data from political science are crystal clear: people vote for the candidate who elicits the right feelings, not the candidate who presents the best arguments.'

This is why I want to meet Lord Monckton. His identity has a remarkable coherence; the stars of his beliefs seem to align in a perfect constellation of right-leaning thinking.

*

The 3rd Viscount Monckton of Brenchley has powerful hands and he lets you know all about them when he takes one of yours to shake it. He wears pinstripes and a large digital watch that looks like the kind of device a runner might wear to check his heart rate. His tie shows the elements of the periodic table and a wide golden ring clutches to his left little finger. The cartilage and bones in his nose push out from his skin in the shape of an anchor. His eyes peer from either side of the anchor's stock, and are not as bad as you might imagine from the newspapers: their startling fishlike bulbousness – his ocular proptosis, caused by Grave's disease – has lessened dramatically thanks, he says, to the top-secret cure he devised using his own 'completely bonkers' theory before concocting it 'on the library table, test tubes, and stuff bubbling away'. He believes his claimed breakthrough 'shows much promise in curing everything from HIV to malaria to multiple sclerosis.'

He leads me briskly through a corridor of the Oxford Union building, where he is to appear later in a debate. We head up the beautiful polished-wood staircase, looking for a quiet place to talk. He opens this door and that, each time bowing and apologising to the people inside whom we have startled. He races up another flight, suit-vent flapping like the wings of a skate, and finds an unoccupied room that is hung with rows of pen-and-ink portraits of high-collared gentlemen and lined with extravagant red, green and gold William Morris wallpaper.

We each pull out a leather-cushioned seat. He sits, bolt-straight before me, this liveryman of the Worshipful Company of Broderers, this Officer of the Order of St John of Jerusalem, this Knight of Honour and Devotion of the Sovereign Military Order of Malta, this former policy adviser to Margaret Thatcher, and I tell him that I am interested in heretics – those brave Davids who take the fight to the establishment Goliaths – and that I am really only here to listen to his story, about his battles and his heroes and his villains. 'Yes,' he says, smiling. 'Certainly.' He folds his hands in front of him on the table. 'I was born,' he begins, 'at the age of nought . . .'

Christopher Walter Monckton became the first son of Major General Gilbert Monckton, 2nd Viscount Monckton of Brenchley and Marianna, Dame of Malta on Valentine's Day, 1952.

'I came of exceptional parents,' he says. 'My father was the army's youngest general, my mother was the first woman High Sheriff of Kent since the fourteenth century and my father's father, the first Lord Monckton, had been the adviser to Edward VIII on his abdication, and had then served in Churchill's last cabinet and Eden's first. If we go back to my great-great-grandfather on my mother's side, he was the model on whom *Sanders of the River* was based – a wonderful pro-imperialist film about a district commissioner. They were the people who really had the power in the empire, as you know.'

Young Christopher's early years were a time of great happiness.

'My mother would use the whip,' he says. 'The horse whip. I was disciplined severely. Far more severely than was normal, even for that time. She nearly broke my finger once.'

'But you say you were happy?' I ask.

'It was indeed a very happy childhood. My parents gave me just the right amount of attention, which is not too much and not too little.'

From the whip of his mother he learned discipline, but from his father he learned a lesson of even greater value.

'I remember, at the age of two, sitting on his knee, and he had a book with the alphabet set out on little bows on the tails of kites. When I went to nursery school, at the age of three, I already knew the alphabet and could read. It was my father, not my mother, who had taught me that. It gave me an edge which I never lost. I realised there were advantages in being ahead. And I stayed ahead.'

Through discipline and toil he achieved success at prep school and at Harrow and then Cambridge University. But the post-war years were dark ones for Great Britain, for she was losing her empire.

'I felt infinite sadness. And nostalgia, of course. When I was at Harrow we had a wonderful school song which said, "From Harrow school to rise and rule". The education was very much that you are going to be the rulers of the world and the masters of the universe and, therefore, you need to know how to do it. But in order to do it, you had to understand the people who were going to be in your care. That's how it was – they weren't your servants. I mean, if you go back to the philosopher George Santayana, he said, "The world never had sweeter masters" and that's probably true, because we weren't really conscious of being masters. We weren't there to grind folk under our heel.'

Sadly, for the millions of recipients of Britain's gentle

colonial care, not everyone had the discernments that were bred into the schoolboy rulers of Harrow. 'We were taught this sensitivity which, unfortunately, turned out to be more or less wholly lacking in most of the political class. I could see, even from a very early age, that the empire – great though it had been – was over.'

The dismantling of our magnificent empire was, perhaps, the first victory for those who were soon to become Lord Monckton's lifetime enemies. It was an act of grand vandalism, wrought by the selfish and irresponsible left.

'Of course, it was all the consequence of the welfare state,' he explains. 'Britain was pretty bust after the Second World War. Then Labour got in on a "jam today, jam tomorrow, jam for ever" manifesto. Very typical Labour manifesto – very appealing to those who are not used to making their own way in the world. Somebody else will provide. So they got into office on this idea of a National Health Service, universal pensions, universal benefits, full employment.'

'Free stuff?' I say.

'Sweeties!' he nods. 'Bread and circuses! The problem was, we couldn't afford it and so we had to go to the United States to say, "Please can we have the money to pay for the welfare state and the health service?" They said to us, "If you want help, then you're going to have to bring the empire to an end." Which, of course, the Labour Party wanted to do anyway.'

It was in 1973, when he was reading classics at Cambridge University, that the richly educated young Lord decided that he would no longer indulge the kinds of people who were not used to making their own way in the world. The left were attempting to reform the exclusive Cambridge Union by changing it into an 'open' one that *anyone* could enter. 'It was going to be like any other students' union anywhere else,' he says. 'Beer and sandwiches and the occasional pop concert, as

I believe it is called. The traditions of what was still a civilised gentleman's club would've been swept away. All that history, nearly two hundred years of it, would've been gone. Debating would've been brought to an end. I thought, *Our ancestors went to some trouble to establish this place and foster the techniques of debating, which I have learnt, in the chamber, against the most difficult audience you could hope to face.* I didn't want it to be lost and I decided that, if nobody else would fight it, I would. I would disregard any consequences from my own Cambridge political career. I knew that one would never become President of the Union because, at the time, unless you subscribed to the' – he spits the word – 'so-called *consensus*, you couldn't.'

Lord Monckton went to work. He discovered that the Union was protected by the Literary and Scientific Institutions Act 1854, which said that any major change had to be the subject of a vote. He began a public campaign which saw life members returning from all over the world. 'On polling day there was a queue, almost as far as the railway station, which is a long way outside Cambridge.' The leftist insurgents lost the vote. The young Monckton was victorious.

On another occasion, the fellows of his college – 'all Marxists and atheists' – attempted to depose the chaplain. Lord Monckton launched another campaign. 'And they caved in.' That fight gave him a sudden and startling X-ray flash of the culture war that would define the politics of the latter half of the twentieth century. The left, he realised, were beginning to ally themselves with militant, atheistic scientists. 'They were increasingly using the language of science,' he says, describing a new, 'unholy departure from anything spiritual. I fought that, very successfully, just as I fought the Union thing. And what I learnt from those two episodes was that the lone wolf – provided he does not seek the approbation of his fellows and does not seek advancement or promotion to high office – can effect far more change for good than anyone who does hold high office, because he has not made the compromises necessary to get it.'

The history of this corrosive alliance between the left and atheist scientists had begun eleven years before Lord Monckton's Union campaign, when an American academic named Rachel Carson published her book *The Silent Spring*, which warned of the potential dangers of the pesticide DDT. It was to became totemic, a foundational text for the modern environmental movement that ultimately influenced policymakers who banned the use of the chemical around the world, even where it was being used to kill malarial mosquitoes.

'It was a stupid book,' says Lord Monckton. 'Carson was well intentioned, bless her little cotton socks, but stupid scientifically. A stupid book! The left had already decided that they were going to exploit science in a political cause, and they were totally unconcerned about whether the science was true or not. Even when they were putting this ban in place they realised that it would cause millions of children to die. In America they used to do massive sprays of DDT and the kids would run after the planes and play in the clouds. It didn't do them any harm. You can eat the stuff by the tablespoon.'

'So if they knew it was safe, and that banning it would kill millions of children, what was their motivation?' I ask.

He leans forward.

'Power. It showed who was boss. They would say, "We're here to save the planet," but they weren't at all. It was pure naked left-wing political power. They also wanted to whip up a cause which would bring in money from well-meaning rich people like Bill Gates, who knows absolutely fuck all about anything.'

Why, I wondered, do environmental groups today still want all this power and money?

'To shut down the economies of the West.'

Even in those days, when the two powers of the cold war were frighteningly evenly matched, the Soviet Union knew that they could not compete with capitalists. So they formulated a plan. To destroy the West and their systems of wealth, they realised that they had to attack our energy-making infrastructure. The KGB began secretly transporting influential British individuals to Moscow and Leningrad for training. Marxists infiltrated the new green groups, who were fomenting their own version of trouble. 'I've been told that the left, the KGB, realised that energy was the soft underbelly of the West,' says Lord Monckton. 'They used twin attacks via the working classes and the environment movement. They thought, "That's how we destroy the economies of the West." Not compete with – *destroy*. It's about nihilism, it's about destruction, tearing down what we're building because they can't compete with it and they're jealous of it. Jealousy is at the root of all socialism. Jealousy is at the root of all evil. Socialism *is* evil.'

And so, the Communist crosshairs fell upon Britain. We had links not only with the United States, but also with the Commonwealth and the European Union. If you brought down the United Kingdom, our ties with the rest of the world would stretch and pull as we tumbled into the void, wrenching damaging chunks from everyone else. We might even pull some of them in behind us. That was the grim plot that lay behind the miners' strike of the mid-1980s. It was a new front in the cold war, triggered by prominent Britons who had been covertly trained in Muscovite terrorist universities. The Communists hoped that the strikes would fatally damage our energy infrastructure and thereby threaten the 'most popular government in modern times' – that of the woman who, by then, was Lord Monckton's boss, Prime Minister Margaret Thatcher.

Lord Monckton's record in government, as recounted by Lord Monckton, speaks of a man of prescient counsel whose advice, if heeded, would have prevented the flowering of evil in many spheres. If the world had followed his advice during the AIDS crisis, to offer one example, millions of lives would have been saved. He described his views at length in an article for the *American Spectator*, published in January 1987:

> There is only one way to stop AIDS. That is to screen the entire population regularly and to quarantine all carriers of the disease for life . . . There are occasions when it is imperative to think the unthinkable and then to do the undoable. The AIDS epidemic is one such occasion . . . AIDS is more threatening than any plague which has previously afflicted mankind . . . Strict controls would be needed at all borders. Visitors would be required to take blood-tests at the port of entry and would be quarantined in the immigration building until the tests had proved negative . . . Although the idea of universal testing and isolation now sounds extravagant and preposterous, it will eventually happen.

Today, he insists that his article was 'very reasonable' and he has been unfairly quoted by people who fail to mention the paragraph where he says, 'of course the isolation does not need to be prison camps, or shoving them on an island somewhere. The simplest thing is, you just test everybody, tell them if they've got it, then they can isolate themselves. I'm a great believer in trusting people.' Which is all very mysterious because I read the entire piece only yesterday and, as I explain to Lord Monckton now, I don't remember reading *anything* like that. He mentions, rather vaguely, things that he 'went on to say in subsequent articles'. So, you know, I'm sure it's all fine, and the main point is if they had listened to Lord Monckton in the first place, then AIDS would have been 'practically stopped it in its tracks'.

Likewise, the global financial crisis. Lord Monckton saw it coming. Ultimately, he tells me, the economic terrors from which we are currently suffering are the result of the left's attempts at destroying capitalism, 'by making it terribly rich. They have learned that if you concentrate wealth in the hands of a few, they become resented then . . .'

'It is overthrown!' I gasp, barely believing what I am hearing. 'Of course!'

'Oh, yes,' he agrees. 'It's all part of the same picture.'

But, as everybody has been compelled to acknowledge, flaws in the level of banking regulation are also to blame for the crash. Indeed, Lord Monckton spent four years at No. 10, objecting to what one day would become the Financial Services Act, the legislation that would come to seed our economic downfall. 'But literally a month after I left Downing Street, the Civil Service pushed it through.'

'So that was deregulation?' I clarify.

He looks amazed.

'No, no, no. It was imposing, for the first time, the most staggering over-regulation in the City of London.'

I sit up.

'Hang on,' I said. 'I thought the banks began to behave badly because of a loosening of the rules – deregulation.'

'No, completely the opposite.'

'Really?'

'Oh, completely. I was there, you see. I said to Margaret, "For God's sake, don't go anywhere near this catastrophe." What happened was, people began to believe that because it was so heavily regulated, they could put their money into whatever financial instrument they chose and it would be safe.'

'So all that regulation gave everyone false confidence?'

'Absolutely. Entirely false sense of security. The result was that the banks then began messing around doing all these complicated credit-default swaps and you see what happened.'

Another crucial event that was taking place during Lord Monckton's time in government was the miners' strike. One of his recollections of those tense days begins with him sitting in his office in Downing Street as future cabinet minister Oliver Letwin came running in.

'Oh, it's terrible, it's terrible, where do we hide?' wailed Letwin. 'The miners are rioting in Parliament Square. It's so un-English!'

But Lord Monckton knew better. 'Don't be so silly!' he admonished the young Letwin. 'This is just what they do every Friday evening when the pubs tip out.'

Letwin, however, was frantic.

'They're coming this way!' he cried.

Lord Monckton glanced out of the window. Hmm, yes. There were thirty or forty of them by now, pressing against the rickety barriers. More still were arriving. But Lord M was not in the least perturbed.

'Oh, well,' he sighed, slipping on his overcoat. 'I'll just go and deal with that.'

And then he reached for his bowler hat. Letwin was agog. *A bowler hat?*

'They'll lynch you!'

'Of course they won't,' said Lord Monckton.

'What do you mean?'

'Look, why do I wear a hat in situations like this? It's the only way to make a polite gesture at a distance. This has been known to my ancestors since time immemorial. It ran the empire. If you wanted to indicate politeness to people who were charging you, you took your hat off to them and they stopped. It works every time. Just watch!'

Lord Monckton descended the steps of No. 10 and approached the angry miners, passing a pair of policemen who were nervously radioing for reinforcements. The revolting pitmen saw him. They began jeering. When Lord Monckton was halfway along Downing Street he suddenly stopped. He surveyed the horde. He took a breath. And he doffed.

Immediately, the jeering turned to cheering. Lord Monckton approached the men, promised to put their complaints in a note to Margaret Thatcher, and then offered them a pint. 'And you could have heard a pin drop,' he remembers, smiling. 'They were all docile and followed me across the road to the pub in double file. It was like a schoolmaster and his crocodile.'

Since the years of his heroic calming of Downing Street, the cold war might have ended, but the power-mad left, he tells me, remain a perilous threat.

'Once they had been motivated in these directions by the Communists, then these organisations took on a life of their own,' he says. 'They are essentially still following the KGB playbook without being aware that they're doing so. It's absolutely the same pattern. The main thing is power. That is the fundamental principle of leftism. It's about this absolute control over every detail, which is why the correct word for left is "totalitarianism".'

And today, the enemy – in the modern form of the European Union and the United Nations – appear to be winning.

'You don't know who they are. You can't really see them. But everybody in this *classe politique* is now beginning to argue for global governance.' He tells me that the UN held a meeting last May 'with all of its top people, to discuss ways of bringing the "nation state" to an end. It's code for bringing democracy to an end. That's actually at the top of the UN's agenda.' An early draft of the 2009 Copenhagen Treaty, he adds menacingly, 'describes that they're going to establish a global government'.

The Intergovernmental Panel on Climate Change, the environmental groups and many politicians sympathetic to the IPCC's views are part of this plan to institute what Lord Monckton has previously called 'a worldwide coup d'état by bureaucrats' who seek to 'impose a Communist world government on the world'.

And the people know it. Well, they don't *know* it, just know it. Not the details, the *facts*. They just have this hunch, you see. This intuition. This generalised emotion. Who knows where it comes from? When they hear Lord Monckton speak, they realise this *feeling* they have always had was true all along and, when they do, they react with such rapture, such *jubilation*.

'I began giving talks all over the place,' he tells me. 'Australia, America, Europe. Huge crowds would turn up and they would jump around – standing ovations practically every time. It was clear that there was a large feeling among ordinary people that something was going on in this climate story that they didn't like the smell of. They *knew* there was. They just couldn't quite work out what it was . . .'

*

When I spoke with Professor Jonathan Haidt, I was surprised to find him offering some advice that Lord Monckton might have approved of. 'Follow the sacredness,' he told me. 'Find out what people believe to be sacred, and when you look around there you will find rampant irrationality. The left have sacralised global warming. I am very certain, as a moral psychologist, that their discourse about it is not rational. They cannot be trusted to think straight about it. It's a classic moral crusade. And when a scientific community is all on one side, morally and politically, then its ability to be objective goes out the window. Unfortunately, this is the case with global warming. I believe that the scientists are correct, but we can't be *as* confident, because there are tribal dynamics going on.'

Professor Haidt believes that, as well as global warming, the left have 'sacralised victims and demonised capitalism' while the right have sacralised markets. 'They can't think straight about the ability of the markets to solve problems.' Perhaps comfortingly, he argues that the endless war between the political poles represents a relatively efficient model of governance. 'The most basic question that faces any society is change versus stick,' he asserts. 'Stay with what you have and know, or change and strike out into the future. And there is no correct answer – you have to have a balance of both.'

It was remarkable to observe how many of the battles of Lord Monckton were in the service of 'stick'. His emotional instincts were to conserve the world, to defend hierarchy and order and tradition. He is an archetypal Conservative.

But perhaps the most surprising thing that I discovered, as I was conducting my research into our political brains, is that allegiances are not defined by simple, calculating self-interest.

The studies that Professor Haidt has been involved with, and the data that he has been exposed to, have convinced him into a darker vision than the traditional one. We do not use free will in order to select beliefs and behaviours that will make the world 'a better place'. In *The Righteous Brain*, he writes that moral reasoning 'evolved not to help us find truth but to help us engage in arguments, persuasion and manipulation in the context of discussions with other people'.

In this alternative vision, the brain wants to make us into heroes in the eyes of those around us and also in our own. The stories we believe, and the demons that we imagine surround us, all tend to serve a crucial narrative – that we are exceptional, that we are morally holy, that we are on a meaningful journey, and that we are *right*.

And my encounter with Lord Monckton has also given me something extra – an unexpected method by which I believe we can spot faulty beliefs. Yesterday, the philosopher Dr James Garvey told me, 'Most people would say that something's true if it corresponds to the way the world is. This view goes back to Aristotle. But there are other people who prefer the coherence theory of truth, which says that if you have a completely coherent set of beliefs, that tends to be a true set of beliefs.'

Over the last few days, I have become convinced that the coherence theory could not be more wrong. If a person's set of beliefs all cohere, it means that they are telling themselves a highly successful story. It means that their confabulation is so rich and deep and all-enveloping that almost every living particle of nuance and doubt has been suffocated. Which says to me, their brains are working brilliantly, and their confabulated tale is not to be trusted.

*

I am walking through the courtyard of the Oxford Union, back towards the station, when I see a pair of young students laughing as they stride into the entrance. I get that thud, again. That feeling. *Avoid, dislike, unclean.* My left-brain interpreter seeks to explain, to justify. And I want to say, *spoiled*. I want to say, *privileged*. I want to say, *glad I never went to university*. But none of that would be true. What my emotions are really a response to is something that is utterly heretical to the story that I have always told of my life.

It is envy.

13

'Backwards and forwards
in the slime'

1 SEPTEMBER

Mid-afternoon
The assistant to Hitler's ambassador is a blonde and beautiful young American. I met her in the lobby of the grand Polonia Palace Hotel in central Warsaw, where she was ticking off arrivals for the week-long tour of Second World War sites that is being hosted by the ambassador himself, the notorious right-wing historian David Irving. Her name is Jaenelle Antas, and she has a measured and precise way of speaking that hints at artifice but is, I suspect, nonetheless indicative of a superior intelligence. I felt a sudden constriction of nerves when I saw her. She smiled and said, 'One or two of your fellow tour members are getting to know one another in the cocktail lounge. Perhaps you would care to join them?'

The room was draped about with glamorous Poles. There were bow-tied cocktail waiters, flavoured cashews served in white pots laid out on black napkins and, hanging from the ceiling, an enormous statement lampshade. I found the men up on stools, drinking lager at the bar – an American named

Mark and an Australian called Alex, both in their mid-to-late thirties. They chatted harmlessly about toy models ('I prefer dioramas. Planes, armour. German. Mostly 1:35.') as a waiter washed glasses at the other side of the bar. I bought drinks and relaxed a little, satisfied now that these men were smart enough not to say anything obviously offensive.

'Did you come straight from Australia?' I asked Alex.

'No, I've been having a bit of a holiday,' he said.

'Anywhere nice?'

'Dresden.'

'Right. Wow. Is that, wow. Dresden. And is Dresden nice?'

'Good, yes, good. Very pure,' he nodded, earnestly. 'I only saw two blacks and one Chinese.'

I had thought of this trip as an opportunity to test everything that I had learned so far on one of the twentieth century's most famous heretics. It would be interesting, I imagined. I had looked forward to it. But when I returned to my room, I realised what I actually had in front of me. Seven days, among these men. Seven days, being forced to suffer a gavage of fascism while giving the appearance of accepting every word. If there was some version of defecation or regurgitation or bloodletting that you could use to cleanse your mind of things that you have heard – of purging the thoughts of others from your neurons – then that is what I needed to do.

But there is no such thing. So I sat on my bed and I ate a mini-Toblerone.

Evening

I saw him at 7 p.m. in the lobby where our party were meeting. He was wearing loose corduroy trousers with a grey jumper and was carrying, in his right hand, a plastic Marks and Spencer's bag. His grey hair was brushed and parted, his flushed, bagged and obviously once-handsome face was set off with impressive eagle's-wing eyebrows. He glared emptily downwards, a couple of steps behind the fringe of the group, his gaze distant and forbidding and narrow. You could tell, even in his stillness, that he had a limp. One leg rested slightly too high, its corresponding arm lifting up and back a little, presumably to take some of the painful weight.

Irving's bad joint is a legacy of the thirteen months that he spent incarcerated in Vienna's Josefstadt prison. He was arrested on 11 November 2005 and convicted of 'glorifying and identifying with the German Nazi Party' on account of two lectures that he had given in 1989 in which he claimed that Nazi concentration camps contained no gas chambers and denied that six million Jews died in the Holocaust. During the trial, Irving pointed out that since making those speeches, he had changed his position. But even on its final day, as the then-sixty-seven-year-old was pleading for his freedom, he stubbornly insisted to the court that 'the figure of six million is just symbolic'. The prosecutor, Michael Klackl, called for his imprisonment, arguing that Irving was 'dangerous'. When his three-year sentence was passed down, the historian is said to have looked bewildered. The judge asked him, 'Do you understand your sentence, Mr Irving?'

'I'm not sure I do,' he replied.

In 1993 the American historian Professor Deborah Lipstadt wrote that David Irving is 'one of the most dangerous spokespersons for Holocaust denial' and accused him of distorting evidence, manipulating documents and misrepresenting data in order to suit his ideological beliefs. Irving sued her for libel. He represented himself, at one point accidentally calling the judge 'Mein Führer'. Things didn't go well.

The court's verdict was delivered on 11 April 2000. The

Honourable Mr Justice Gray said that 'Irving has misstated historical evidence; adopted positions which run counter to the weight of the evidence; given credence to unreliable evidence and disregarded or dismissed credible evidence.' He judged that Irving did this 'persistently and deliberately . . . for his own ideological reasons . . . and for the same reasons he has portrayed Hitler in an unwarrantedly favourable light, principally in relation to his attitude towards and responsibility for the treatment of the Jews.' He concluded that 'he is an active Holocaust denier; that he is anti-semitic and racist and that he associates with right-wing extremists who promote neo-Nazism.' He then ordered Irving to pay costs of nearly £2 million, plus £150,000 to Lipstadt's publisher.

Irving called the verdict 'indescribable' and 'perverse.'

I have been wondering about David Irving, and what we know about the effect of genes and emotions on belief, and the processes of confirmation bias and the 'makes sense stopping rule'. The court ruled that Irving was a conscious and deliberate liar. But aspects of his behaviour contradict this. In bringing his case against Professor Lipstadt (and a similar one against the *Observer*), he was inviting an overwhelming forensic and public examination of his work. If his distortions were conscious, it would be a kind of suicide. Why would he do this? If he was the kind of person who would dishonestly alter his beliefs just to suit his dastardly purposes, why did he persist in disputing the 'six million' figure even as he was beseeching a court for mercy?

Might a more credible psychological portrait tell of a man who is faithfully convinced of his view and who is using his powers of intellect – which other historians have acknowledged to be considerable – to unconsciously thump, squash, twist and banish any threatening contradictory evidence away, just as we all do?

There can be no doubt, of course, that Irving is wrong about an awful lot. My question is, does he *know* that he is wrong? Or have his emotional hunches led him astray, marooning him in a self-made universe of error that has been erected upon the foundations of a simple mistake? And that has been built up and up, by seven decades of research – thirty books, many thousands of interviews, millions of documents – with each new 'discovery' gifting the illusion more power and detail and reach?

Night

Before we left for the restaurant in the evening, Jaenelle gave us a motherly briefing during which Irving suddenly came alive. With a slightly dangerous look, he said, 'Can I interrupt?'

'I'm speaking,' Jaenelle said.

He looked affronted.

'You work for me!'

'No I don't,' she said, firmly. 'You're my client.'

He stepped back into his glowering repose, a fleeting taint of self-amusement evident about his lips.

We walked through the night, past vast Communist-built blocks that have been crowned with the neon hoardings of the conquering capitalists. My fellow holidaymakers are all men. As well as Alex and Mark there is a wealthy businessman who flew himself here in his own light aeroplane; a shorts-wearing university employee from America's wheat-belt with a huge rectangular bottom; a tall Australian call-centre operative with a German name; a genuine German who flew MiGs for the East German airforce; a lorry driver from Maidstone; and a man in his sixties with a sharp public-school accent who was born in colonial Kenya. All of them are immaculately ironed and tucked in. Three of them have moustaches.

We drifted into pairs as we walked, and I fell into conversation with Alex, the Australian who enjoyed the purity of Dresden. 'Where I live, we've got a lot of Lebanese,' he said.

'What's that like?' I asked.

'Well, they hate the Jews,' he said. 'But I still can't stomach them.'

As well as being an extravagant racist, it turned out that Alex is also a keen consumer of organic produce.

'Oh, I go organic, yeah – all the way. I'm not putting all that supermarket crap into my system,' he said. 'My sister's kids aren't vaccinated. They never get sick. Those vaccinations give you diseases in later life, you know. They've got mercury in them. That's the most toxic substance known to man.'

Behind us, the genuine German was becoming worried that the Polish restaurant would have no space for our party.

'We have no reservation?' he said. 'There are twelve of us!'

'I shouldn't worry,' said the posh Englishman. 'The Poles are used to being invaded.'

During the meal, Mark, the American ex-soldier, discussed Mexican immigration.

'They should be "ice cold" about it, as the Führer said,' he explained, gesticulating over his beer with his meaty hands. 'They should build a wall at the Mexican border, then take away the perks from the immigrants. No welfare, no health-care, no right to work. Then they'll start to self-deport. This is what everybody wants. They're just too scared to say it.'

*

At least in part, it was suspicious coherence that trapped Irving. Mr Justice Gray said, 'All Irving's historiographical "errors" converge, in the sense that they all tend to exonerate Hitler and to reflect Irving's partisanship for the Nazi leader. If indeed they were genuine errors or mistakes, one would not expect to find this consistency.'

This observation was also made by Richard Evans, the Professor of Modern History at Cambridge University who was hired by the defence to critically examine Irving's oeuvre. An edited version of his dossier was published in 2002, under the title *Telling Lies About Hitler*. In the book, Evans considers Irving's motives for bringing the case. He believed that ego played a part, writing that Irving 'was clearly incensed by a reference to him on page 180 of Lipstadt's book as "discredited"'. He also questioned the position of the defendant, saying, 'Whether or not Lipstadt was correct to claim that these people posed a serious threat to historical knowledge and memory was debatable.'

2 SEPTEMBER

Early afternoon
We stopped for a light lunch on our way to the concentration camp. I sat with Irving and Jaenelle, watching as the historian sprinkled salt on the table – an apparently superstitious ritual. 'He used to delight in finding pennies and saying, "See a penny pick it up, then all day you'll have good luck,"' Jaenelle said. 'He'd smile for a good ten seconds every time, then give them to me for safe keeping. It was some time before he realised that it was me, dropping the same penny over and over just to keep him in a good mood.'

'When I realised,' Irving mused gloomily, 'it was like the moment you discover that Father Christmas isn't real.'

Throughout the remainder of our journey to Lublin, I kept to myself, reading. At one point, I looked up to see the posh Englishman staring at me coldly.

As our silver minibus bumped down the access road that leads to the Majdanek concentration camp, I noticed two parked vehicles, whose occupants watched us pass – one a police car, the other not. A man in a polo shirt and wraparound sunglasses stood at an open door, holding a radio handset. Another had binoculars. Last year, when the media discovered that David Irving was hosting a recreational tour of Second World War sites, he was ambushed by journalists. The *Daily Mail* quoted a spokesman for the Polish embassy in London as saying, 'The secret service in Poland and in the UK are aware . . . The visit will be under strict observation.'

We made halting progress through the empty camp. Martin had a camera on a tripod that he kept carefully setting up before running out in front of the lens, as the electronic timer beeps rang out. He would then act nonchalant in the vicinity of David Irving until the photograph was taken. But Irving seemed to move out of shot, at the last possible moment, every single time. It was hard to know whether he was doing this on purpose.

'I wonder how fertile the land is with all the ashes they dumped here,' mused Mark idly as we walked towards the long, low wooden barracks.

Irving pointed to a hatch in the base of a guard's tower.

'That's the box office.'

We entered a building that had been converted into a museum. Two nuns in brown habits silently read a display.

'David?' asked Martin, eyes shining upwards, the eager schoolboy. 'What do you think of the swimming pool in Auschwitz?'

'I don't care,' he said.

Minutes later, Aldrich the German asked Irving a question about gas chambers.

'You've got gas chambers on the brain,' snapped Irving.

The historian browsed the exhibits alone, paying close attention to a period photograph of the Nazi headquarters in Warsaw. I approached him gingerly.

'Is that building still there, David?'

'I'm reading something,' he growled.

Mark shot me a sympathetic look. We walked together, into the safety of the shadow of an SS sentry booth. 'Don't take it personally,' he whispered. 'A couple of weeks ago, I sent him an SMS with some information that he'd requested and he shot back, "I haven't got time for this. I'm in the archives."'

Mark's impression of Irving was so accurate, and so unexpected, that I couldn't help but let out a snort of laughter. I stopped myself with my hand and glanced fearfully at the nuns.

We rejoined Irving. 'No more than fifty thousand people died here,' he announced to the group. 'A lot, but no more than was killed in a single bombing raid by British Bomber Command'. Behind him was a sign that read, in large English letters, 'Some 78,000 died in the camp'.

Further along the wall was a grainy photograph of Hitler saluting some guards. When he saw it, Irving snapped, 'Adolf Hitler never, in his whole career, visited a death camp. I am convinced that the decisions involved with the Holocaust were made on the periphery and then filtered up to the Führer's office who were by then too weak to say, "Stop this."'

We followed as he lurched out towards building number 42 – the fumigation plant, showers and gas chambers.

As soon as we entered the cold, concrete structure, the mood of the group changed. There was an uplift, a surge, a dangerous volt of activity. There were flashes of cameras and raised voices and people bunching in corners and pointing, running this way and that, tugging arms, *explain that, check this out* . . .

'This is a mock-up of a gas chamber,' announced Irving.

We were joined by a crowd of visitors. Dozens of them, young and female, many swollen-cheeked and teary. And yet, among our group, there was still that fever, still that flap and chatter and heat.

'You've got to be very sceptical about what you see in here,' Irving told the schoolgirls, interrupting their guide. 'The gas cylinders and pipes are quite clearly of recent provenance. This is an air-raid shelter. These are standard air-raid blast doors.'

Members of the girls' group exchanged glances of alarm.

'You're fighting a losing battle here,' said Martin.

'I don't care,' said Irving. He pointed at some metal canisters that were strapped to the wall. 'Those cylinders are carbon dioxide not carbon monoxide. A typical Polish botch job. There are handles on the inside of these doors. If this was a homicidal gas chamber, you wouldn't be going, "Excuse me, I'm just going to let myself out now."'

He barracked the guide again, this time in Russian. I could not stand it any more. I left discreetly and headed for a building that was kept in darkness as a memorial. Hiding myself in a corner I did something that I am uneasy about admitting, and that I still cannot explain. I stood in the shadows and I crossed myself and prayed.

Returning to building 42, I examined the doors. Yes, there was a rudimentary U-shaped handle on the inside, but it had no opening mechanism. And there were *bolts* on the outside, two of them, huge ones, each attached to clasps that would have locked the door closed over airtight seals. He saw the handle and he used it to angrily damn the manifest truth. He kept talking about it as we drove back to Warsaw. He saw the handle. What happened in his mind when he saw the bolts?

Night
There was a terrifying episode in the minibus. I have been secretly documenting the conversations around me by typing

279

them into my iPhone and by writing notes in the margins of my book. I was scribbling away surreptitiously when the posh Englishman turned to me and said, 'What's that you're reading?'

He held out his hand. I glanced down at the open page, on which I had recorded something I'd heard earlier. 'MARK, <u>V</u> RACIST JOKE, "WORLD'S FIVE SHORTEST BOOKS: JEWISH BUSINESS ETHICS, ITALIAN WAR HEROES, THE POLISH WHO'S WHO, NEGROES I'VE MET WHILST YACHTING, FRIENDS OF DAVID IRVING."' If he saw that, I would be exposed, right here and now, in front of them all. I flashed him the cover and made as if to continue reading.

His hand did not move.

'Let's have a look.'

Nobody spoke.

'Just let me finish this chapter,' I said.

'Come on, let's see.'

'Sure,' I said. 'Just let me finish this chapter.'

I dipped my head and stared at the page. When I was sure he had given up, I began using the nib of my pen to very slowly tear out the incriminating pages, which I pushed into the bottom of my bag.

Back at the hotel, I was walking through the lobby when I overheard Mark complaining to Jaenelle. 'The way he's acting, it's rude, the guys are getting pretty upset about it.'

'You're not telling me anything I don't already know,' said Jaenelle. 'He has no conception of good manners even in their most basic form.'

'Well, you can tell him I'm going to call the local faction of [anti-fascists] Antifa just to create some fun if he doesn't cheer the fuck up.'

'Why don't *you* tell him?' said Jaenelle, smiling.

'Umm, because he hates me?'

'Did he tell you that?'

'He doesn't have to,' said Mark sadly.

Even though he had a large tattoo of the insignia of the 1st SS Panzer Division Leibstandarte Adolf Hitler on his neck, I couldn't help but feel a bit sorry for Mark. He was being crushed, over and over again, by the disdain of his hero.

And my curiosity about Irving's relationship with Jaenelle was building. It seemed so odd and complex – defiant, affectionate, motherly and, at times, even flirty. Back in my room, I typed her name into an Internet search engine and found a 2009 article from the *Daily Mail*, which concerned a cache of Irving's emails that somehow happened to fall into their possession. The headline was 'Hitler historian David Irving and the beautiful blonde . . .' and the lead photograph was of Jaenelle in a red bathing costume. It said that she had become 'a neo-Nazi pin-up' after 'posting pictures of herself on Stormfront, an Internet discussion site for "pro-White activists" ', adding that, 'in an email to a friend, Irving reveals he has been asked about the "blonde bombshell" by a journalist and writes: "I emphasise . . . that there is nothing going on between us."'

On the website of an obscure publishing group, I found a long interview with her, in which she discussed her intellectual interests (Edmund Burke, Alexis de Tocqueville, Rousseau), her Black Metal preferences ('Nokturnal Mortum, Emperor, Deathspell Omega, just to name a few') and her love for her grandmother ('I would be happy if I could do at least half as much good as she has').

She also spoke about life with Irving.

'For a long time, David had only one pair of trousers which he had loved to death and I remember mending those on a regular basis. He still has them, but now he fixes them himself with staples because I told him they aren't worth mending any more and I won't do it. I've also done some rudimentary dental work on him.'

3 SEPTEMBER

Morning
Three months ago, before I paid my $2,500 fee (not including flights) for this trip, I requested interview time with Irving, for a project about people who have stood up to the orthodoxy. Irving replied, 'Jaenelle thinks I only like chatting with pretty girls, but that is a monstrous exaggeration; go ahead and book, and if I don't give you all the time you need, demand a refund. But I will, Will.'

But I had been becoming anxious. The other day, when I tried to arrange a sit-down, he appeared confused, as if he had no idea what I was talking about. Yesterday, when I broached it again, he seemed cross. Nevertheless, we agreed a time to meet and I was relieved to find him waiting for me in the hotel lobby in his usual outfit of corduroy trousers and polo shirt. As I sat down, he began to speak at length about the Lipstadt trial.

'They said, "Mr Irving is an anti-Semite, he's a racist, he's a pro-Nazi, he has an agenda, he consorts with Palestinians, he has Nazi associates". All these things were untrue.'

As he was talking, Aldrich walked past and politely bid us good morning.

'Good morning,' I said.

Irving failed to respond, apparently not noticing the German. As soon as I was able to wrench an opportunity between his words, I asked about his changing opinions regarding the Holocaust. Until 1988 he said that he 'believed that there had been something like a Holocaust. I believed that millions of people had been killed in factories of death. I believed in the gas chamber.' His denial came in 1989, and followed the publication of a flawed study by a man named Fred Leuchter, who had brick samples from Auschwitz-Birkenau and Majdanek tested for hydrogen cyanide and used the results to argue that only 'lice' were killed there.

Irving described Leuchter's report as 'the biggest calibre shell that has yet hit the battleship Auschwitz' and claimed that it 'totally exploded the legend'. In 1991 he reissued his most lauded book, *Hitler's War*, saying, 'You won't find the Holocaust mentioned in one line, not even in a footnote. Why should you? If something didn't happen, then you don't even dignify it with a footnote.' He had some advice for the Jewish people too, telling the *Jewish Chronicle* that they 'are very foolish not to abandon the gas chamber theory while they still have time'. The year after that, he was fined 3,000 marks in Germany for 'defaming the memory of the dead'. During the appeal, Irving declared, 'there were no gas chambers at Auschwitz. I will not change my opinion.' The judge multiplied his penalty by ten.

Then Irving's views appeared to waver. In 1994 he said that he was glad that he 'never adopted the narrow-minded approach that there was no Holocaust'. The following year he told an Australian radio host that 'four million' were killed in concentration camps, mostly of disease. In 1996 he admitted some Jews *were* systematically killed, but blamed Goebbels. Over the same period, he was banned from Germany and Australia, deported from Canada, spent a short period in a Munich prison and was dropped by his publishers in Britain and the US. In 1993 he complained that his 'life has come under a gradually mounting attack: I find myself the worldwide victim of mass demonstrations, violence, vituperation and persecution.'

How much of this wavering, I wondered, was caused by the

pressure that was being applied by his growing league of enemies?

'I have changed what I say because of the pressure of *evidence*, not because of the threats that have been applied to me,' he replied. 'I've come to my own conclusions. This makes me very unpopular with a lot of revisionists. Like the person who's walked past us just now, the German. He's unhappy about some of the things I said at Majdanek yesterday. He was saying, "The gas chambers! The gas chambers!" I said, "Forget about the gas chambers. There are other things to look at which are more interesting." I've not set out determined to be a nuisance to historians. I'm basically so lazy, I can't be bothered to falsify. To falsify is like lying.'

Behind us, a Polish family were talking loudly. It echoed sharply around the marble of the white-pillared lobby. Irving turned and bellowed at them: 'Jesus! Jesus! Jesus!' and muttered, 'That's what you call "trailer trash".'

Because of the focus of his legal trials, it is commonly assumed that Irving is a self-declared expert on the Holocaust. This is not true. In fact, his principal interest is Adolf Hitler, and the epicentre of his controversial view is that the Führer was a friend of the Jews who would have been horrified to know that millions were being killed in his name. Once, he had a long-standing offer of $1,000, never claimed, to anyone who could prove Hitler guilty of their extermination. It is hard to understand the emotional source of Irving's stubborn, passionate and decades-long defence of the Nazi leader. After all, he comes from a patriotic British military family. His brother, John, was an RAF officer, while his father was a naval commander who fought in the Battle of Jutland in the First World War, and had his ship, HMS *Edinburgh*, torpedoed by the Nazis in 1942. He survived the attack, and yet didn't return to the Irving home, in Ongar, Essex, instead moving to Wales. I wondered if Irving was affected by this abandonment. Perhaps his need to be an 'ambassador to Hitler' began as an unconscious rebellion against his dad. I began carefully, by asking how his father was viewed among members of the Irving family.

'My father was a hero figure,' he said. 'I've got a very nice photo of him in naval uniform on the table in our sitting room. I have a copy of it that you can use on your book. On my bedroom wall there is a photograph of him with the King.'

'It must have been devastating when he left,' I said.

'Stop trying to get me to say things,' he snapped.

'I'm not,' I said. 'I'm just interested in how you felt about him leaving.'

'I've got no memory of him having left. He just was never there.'

'So you didn't experience it as a loss?'

'We were a family without a father. It was just the way things were. I don't feel particularly deprived.'

Irving's earliest memory of heretical thought is during the war, when he was reading a magazine that contained a comic section called 'Ferrier's World Searchlight'.

'There was a picture of Hermann Göring with all his medals, Goebbels with his club foot, Hitler with his postman's hat and it was just generally making fun of them. If you're six or seven, you're looking at that, you're thinking, "But I've got no toys! It can't be that these cartoon figures are the ones causing all this nuisance."'

Behind us, the Polish family's child began screaming. Irving turned again and shouted, 'For fuck's sake!'

'So you didn't have toys?'

'I think they've got the message now . . . Nobody had toys. I remember finding a catalogue on the floor of our garage, from a toyshop called Gamages. So *that's* what toys look like.

Your little juvenile brain is so innocent and pure that you begin thinking. You say to yourself, "It's possible that I'm being sold a bill of goods by somebody here." And this little worm begins to grow in the back of your brain. You think, *When I'm older and have the means, I will investigate and find out.*'

As a boy, Irving went to public school in Brentwood where he was beaten repeatedly.

'Being beaten was a ritual, good God, yes,' he says. 'I don't understand how you can be a teacher without it.'

During his time there, he won an 'art appreciation' contest. It was 1955, and the seventeen-year-old was told that he could choose any book he wished as a prize. It would be handed to him at a special ceremony by the Deputy Prime Minister, Rab Butler. He chose *Mein Kampf.*

'Why did you ask for *Mein Kampf*?' I asked.

'To provoke,' he said. 'I've not read it, either then or since.'

After school, Irving attended Imperial College, London, where he became editor of the *Carnival Times*, one issue of which was said to contain a tribute to Hitler's Germany. Irving eventually left the role in the heat of scandal, describing himself to the *Daily Mail*, in comments he has since denied making, as 'a mild fascist'.

He also saw the fascist Sir Oswald Mosley speak at a rally and would go on to second him in a 1961 debate about Commonwealth immigration ('The Nottingham race disturbances were caused by coloured wide boys armed with knives,' he is reported to have said). When Irving lost his university scholarship by failing his pure maths exam, he suspected that he had been mis-marked by a corrupt Communist professor.

'When they failed me, I thought, "This cannot be right,"' he said. 'Obviously I had made myself unpopular with the university for my right-wing views – or *alleged* right-wing views. I found myself in 1959 without a degree, with no future.' He decided to try to follow his brother into the RAF. 'I passed all their tests, went to the recruiting centre at Holborn, and the guy there said, "Mr Irving, you have obtained the highest score in the last nineteen years." And then he failed me on medical grounds.' Suspecting, once more, that his political views were being used against him, he wrote to Krupp, the Nazi armaments manufacturer, with a request for work in their West German steel mill. When they turned him down, he secured a job with their rival Thyssen.

'Why Germany?' I asked.

Irving looked at me.

'This will be your last question,' he said. 'To learn the language. And I thought being a steelworker would be nice and tough.'

'Maybe I'm seeing patterns where there aren't any,' I said. 'But as a boy you were suspicious that you were being misled about Hitler. Then there was the *Mein Kampf* thing. Then the Hitler thing at university. Then the decision to go to Germany . . .'

'I don't think there's any particular sort of . . .'

'There seems to be a gravitation . . .'

'You begin to carve a rut, like a wheel running backwards and forwards in the slime. Eventually it becomes easier and easier to go in that direction. That's probably what happened.'

'Was there any interest in history at school?'

'History was the one O-level I failed. Now,' he said, pushing himself painfully to his feet, 'I've got to go and do some things.'

Evening

At noon, we left for Mragowo, a small town on the edge of a lake in what was once East Prussia, which was to be our base for the next few days. It was a long journey in a small

bus. They pored over maps as Mark said, 'I'm always interested in signs and roads and markers and boundaries.' He told
a story about his childhood au pair, whose family had been
sent to Kazakhstan from Russia by Stalin only for them to
move later to Germany. 'She told me, 'The Germans call us
Russian and the Russians call us German. I have no identity.
I have nothing.'' Mark's voice was desolate with pity as he
recounted this tale. It was as if it was the saddest thing that he
had ever heard.

I sat with Alex over lunch. 'You know the Queensland
floods?' he told me. 'Did you know that the Queensland government was negotiating with Thailand to buy weather-
controlling equipment just before it happened?'

'No!'

'Oh yeah. Have you seen the EU Parliament House? Have
a good look at it.' He leaned forward menacingly over his
chips. 'It's based on the Tower of Babel.'

On the journey's second leg, I asked the lorry driver from
Maidstone about his childhood. 'My dad beat the shit out of
me with his belt when I got done for shoplifting in Lewisham.'

'God, what a bastard,' I said.

'No!' he said, apparently surprised by my reaction. 'It was
the best thing he ever did.'

I asked how he came to his political beliefs.

'I saw a National Front party political broadcast,' he said.

'What did it say? Was it about jobs? Immigrants?'

He thought for a moment.

'I don't know,' he said, still slightly emotional after all these
years. 'Everything made sense. It *just fitted.*'

He told me he was worried about the possibility of spies
infiltrating the group. Apparently, Irving once accused *him* of
being a spy and made him account for his life all the way back
to school. Overhearing us, Mark said not to worry. 'Jaenelle has

a special piece of software she can check names against to ensure no journalists get in.'

As the bus turned into the hotel, the men who had been on last year's tour recalled bathing in the lake. Some began to tease Jaenelle, inviting her to join them for a 'skinny dip'. 'I'm not putting my hair in lake water!' she cooed. 'That's icky!'

Once we had checked in, I asked Irving when we could recommence our interview. 'I don't know,' he said tetchily, and stalked off down a gloomy corridor.

Night

I said to Jaenelle, 'I'm a bit worried that David might not give me any more time. We didn't cover much ground before.'

'I think he might be a little suspicious over your line of questioning,' she told me. 'I can try to have a word with him, but I should give you fair warning, there is only so much that I can do.'

We gathered in an upstairs conference room for a lecture. Irving told a story about his schooldays. 'I had a teacher who on the first day of term found the weakest, palest little pansy in the class and hit him hard across the face, and said, "If you get that for doing nothing, just imagine what you get if I catch you doing something wrong."' Everyone chuckled. 'Of course,' he added ruefully, 'you'd be imprisoned if you did that these days.'

As Irving's lecture rolled on, I realised that his knowledge of the war is truly staggering. Locations, dates, names, documents, *I've met him, I interviewed his wife, I've read his diaries.* At one point, he claimed to have read two million messages to German soldiers, each one delivering news of destroyed houses or dead family members. He uses his command of history like a shield, a baton and a very large hat, to defend and to intimidate and to impress.

Along the way, he mentioned that he had three unpublished books in note form – his memoirs, volume three of a work on Churchill and a biography of Himmler. 'I'm interested in personalities,' he told us. 'I want to find out how Himmler changed from pious schoolboy to mass murderer. I'm going with the Himmler book next. It stands the best chance of restoring my tattered reputation. It'll still upset a few people, though. I've still got a few puddles to stamp in. I'm always looking for puddles to stamp in.'

After he'd finished, the party fell into general chatter. One told a story about a talk he once gave during which he said that it was a 'well-known fact that eighty-three per cent of Jewish monuments are desecrated by Jews themselves. I completely made it up.'

4 SEPTEMBER

'You know that monument to fucking Stephen Lawrence?' the Maidstone lorry driver said to me, en route to the Himmler bunker. 'You know it was splashed with paint? My mate's a copper down in Eltham. He said it was the Afric-wog-niggers that did it. It's like the Zionists are behind eighty per cent of Jewish desecrations.'

After we had scrambled around the Himmler bunker for half an hour or so, we stopped off at another hidden network of old Nazi bases in the woods. Aldrich the German became uncommonly excited at the mud-caked display of found Nazi objects. He knelt in the dirt staring through the sights of a machine gun, before picking it up and demonstrating all the different ways it could be held, then leapt off in the direction of an enormous anti-aircraft weapon, desperately trying to explain, in his frayed English, how it worked. Even passing tourists were pulled into his berserk atmosphere.

'Speak English?' he demanded of one bemused couple.

'No.'

'Sprechen sie Deutsch?'

'No.'

He pointed anyway.

'Machine gun! Machine gun!'

I followed him through the maze of bunkers. He kept gripping his hands and shuddering with the thrill of it all.

'Amazing to think that Hitler was here,' I said.

'For me?' He mimed his forehead exploding. 'Just the power! The sheer power! The world will never see anything like it again. Just to walk in this place where such powerful people walked!' He thumped his chest. 'I am shaking.' He took a couple of paces, then began goose-stepping up and down, cursing himself for not going in a straight enough line.

When we were all back on the bus, there was a moment of silence. I heard Mark mutter from the back, 'Thank *God* Aldrich has gone back to normal.'

Earlier, when I asked Irving yet again about our interview, he brushed me off, saying. 'You keep bothering me about that.' I had another word with Jaenelle. 'I'm really worried he's going to shut me down,' I told her.

'He has done that before.'

When I reminded her that I had been offered a refund if I didn't get enough time, she promised, once again, that she would speak with him.

Back in my room, I telephoned my fiancée, Farrah. We are due to be married the day after I return from my Nazi holiday. The timing, I have to admit, has not gone down well.

'Are you safe?' she asked.

I decided not to mention the incident with the book.

'And do they know we're getting married?'

'Jaenelle has asked about it,' I said. 'She wanted to know why I proposed and I said, you know, it felt like the right time, and we want to have children and all that.'

'I wonder what they'd make of me,' said Farrah, who is of mixed English-Pakistani parentage.

'I could never introduce you to this lot,' I said. 'They spent about half an hour going on about "fucking mongrel people".'

'Mongrel people?' She giggled. 'Yeah, I'd take that.'

At dinner, Jaenelle sat down with a side-dish of salad heaped with raw chopped garlic and onion. 'It might stop me being gang-raped by the lake later,' she explained.

When we had finished our meal, she made an announcement to the group.

'You gentlemen might be interested to know that Will, here, is getting married because he doesn't want his children to be bastards.' She smiled and gave a gracious and approving nod. 'Do you have a photograph of your fiancée you can show us?'

Everyone was looking. Everyone was waiting.

'Uh,' I said. 'Ah. Not on me.'

Jaenelle gave me a quizzical look.

'That's odd,' she said. 'You don't carry a photograph of your fiancée?'

'Oh, you know,' I said. 'We've been together for years.'

And somehow the moment passed.

5 SEPTEMBER

Evening

While we waited for our guide at Hitler's bunker, I had a coffee with the posh Englishman. He told me, 'Do you know, Africans have no sense of past or future? They live entirely in the present. That is why, if they steal a flatscreen television, they won't think, "Will I get into trouble?" or, "Do I have room for this in my home?" They have no sense of compassion either. They'll think nothing of slashing a baby. Cutting a baby in half.'

We spent some time perusing a nearby display. Alex pointed at a German helmet. 'It's strange,' he mused. 'I remember asking for one of those for Christmas when I was ten. Even then I was sympathetic to the true German cause. It was intuition. I used to build models of German soldiers. My dad said, "But don't forget what they did." And even at that age I felt rebellion against it.'

Over the last few days I have learned that both of the quiet Australian's parents are German (he'll later decline to watch a screening of *Downfall*, as his father 'was there' and he finds it too upsetting); the university administrator has a German mother; Aldrich's German father fought in the war, and Mark, the American, has a German mother. It is hard not to speculate: are these men on an unconscious hero quest, seeking to defend the honour of their parents against history? Are they on a mission of love?

And if so, how do we explain David Irving? If what I have learned is correct, he is likely to sincerely believe that his beliefs are influenced only by superior data, while they actually spring from some irrational, emotional core – something, quite probably, from his childhood. But Irving's father was not sympathetic to Hitler. He *fought* the Nazis. His brothers, too, were straightforwardly patriotic. And Irving admired them all.

It doesn't make any sense.

Night
Jaenelle was delayed and when she finally arrived, she went to the buffet and helped herself to some chocolate cake, three

boiled potatoes and a ladle of stewed pork and gravy. It was all on the same plate, a precariously narrow corridor of clean china between the sweet and the savoury. Alex nodded approvingly at the arrangement. 'Good,' he said. 'Segregated.'

After dinner, we gathered in the basement bar area. Mark offered to buy me a beer and when I told him that I don't drink, he gave me an unnervingly steady look and said, 'I knew there was a reason that I didn't trust you.' I slunk away, unable to prevent visions of my being discovered, beaten-up and abandoned by twenty-first century Nazis, among the old East Prussian pines.

I was still fretting about Mark's comment when he persuaded the barman to lend him his laptop. Alex commandeered it excitedly. On YouTube, he found some footage from *Downfall* that had been comically re-subtitled to have Hitler raging about Ryanair. As we were laughing at the clip, a group of elderly German tourists settled on a next-door table. Mark, now drunk, seemed determined to get a reaction from them, shouting, 'We can't let anyone overhear us talking about our *juden hasse* [Jew hate].' Aldrich the German winced. 'It is very dangerous, you know.'

But Mark wasn't listening. He turned the laptop's volume to its maximum level and played 'The Horst Wessel Song', the Nazi Party anthem, over and over. He kept looking my way as he did this and I made sure to laugh along and nod my head and pretend to know the music. Then, he found Hermann Göring's 'total war' speech. He seemed familiar with all the words and kept glancing at me, checking my responses. I smiled and applauded loudly at the correct times. The elderly Germans talked among themselves, quietly, unsmilingly.

As soon as I found an opportunity, I slipped out of the garden door and walked through clouds of mosquitoes to the lake. The moon stared coldly over the black trees and the water moved softly on the shore, as if murmuring in sleep. I was startled to find somebody else there – Alex. To my surprise, he too was escaping Mark.

'I don't like that stuff,' he said. 'I mean, I might be old fashioned, but I think when you go to another country, you're an ambassador. I know some Aussies go overseas and act like pricks, but I'm not one of them. I don't want people thinking . . .' He loses his thread momentarily. 'Look, there's good and bad in every society,' he says. 'But you know how people like to put labels on you.'

And there was nothing I could think to say to that. Absolutely nothing at all.

6 SEPTEMBER

Evening

Over dinner, some of the tour members were openly hostile towards Irving. The quiet Australian asked Mark, 'How historically accurate is *Downfall*? Like, fifty per cent?'

'You'll have to ask the professor there,' Mark said, motioning across the room to Irving. His face scowled down into his uncanny impression. '"*I knew his wife, I've read his son's diary.*" I didn't ask you about his fucking son's diary, I asked you how accurate the film was.'

That evening, Mark and I took a walk along the lake. Last night, I had confided in him my worries about Irving not granting me any more time.

'We all put a major word in for you with Jaenelle this morning,' he told me. 'We told her you're getting a raw deal. David says he's interested in personalities and so are you – what's wrong with that? She said, "Well, David is suspicious of his questions." So I said, "Well, he's proved himself, you know?"'

'That's really kind,' I said. 'Thank you.'

And in that moment, I cannot deny it, I liked Mark a lot.

Night

I sat down with Jaenelle for an interview before our screening of *Downfall*. She told me that she first met Irving in August 2008, on a speaking engagement in the US. When I asked if there was 'an instant kinship' between the two of them, the idea of it seemed to destabilise her slightly.

'Er, he was, er, no, I don't know,' she said. 'I guess something about me interested him because he started emailing me several times a day.'

Irving invited her to London. Curious, she agreed. She now runs his online bookstore. Close proximity to the historian, she told me, is not easy. 'If someone frustrates him during the day and he gets in a bad mood, I'm the only one who's there for him to take it out on. And believe me, he does. He'll sulk for days at a time.'

I wondered if his touchiness might have anything to do with his childhood.

'I don't know, because David is the kind of person who tries to present things in his life as maybe being more positive than they actually are,' she said. 'I don't think he had any hard feelings for his father, though. And he looked up to his brother John like a father figure. He revered John until the day he died, which was recently. I've never seen him so upset about anything as when John died.'

'He doesn't seem to be a very happy man in general,' I said.

'Well, his happiness is his own choice. He goes out of his way to be miserable. That's just the kind of person he is.'

'I wonder if it's an anger thing,' I said. 'I'll have to ask him.'

She looked at me with a kind of speechless horror, as if I had just plucked out an eyeball.

'I would not ask him or even *suggest* that he's an angry person,' she said. 'He does sincerely believe that he's perfect in every way. I'm not even exaggerating about that.'

'Really?'

'Of course. Suggest that there's anything about him that needs changing – he won't even consider the possibility.'

'Wow.'

She shook her head, still apparently not quite believing what I had been planning.

'You'd get more than your head bitten off. He'd screw you up like a Polish slave.'

'He's a fascinating character.'

'Fascinating in small doses.'

'He seems keen on you.'

'He thinks he adores me and who am I to argue? But obviously he doesn't or he wouldn't blow his top at me every five minutes. Like, he has been known to scream at me because I didn't tie my hair back when he thought it should be tied back. I kid you not.'

'Does he think he's got a chance with you?'

'Yes. And even if he realises that maybe he doesn't, he definitely doesn't want to see that anybody else might. He gets awfully jealous. He has this image in his head that he is still a young, handsome, well-to-do fellow. And he has never been able to wrap his head around the idea that he is seventy-three years old, crippled and cantankerous.'

When I asked her for advice about what to do if I am granted a final interview, she told me that I should, under no circumstances, mention the incident from school, when he requested a copy of *Mein Kampf*.

'David is a prankster,' she explained. 'He also got in trouble for hoisting the hammer-and-sickle flag when he was at school, so it was not a political thing. It's whatever will get the biggest reaction. The further their jaws will drop the better job he thinks he's done. That's not to say that when he writes his books that that's the aim he's going for. But you would be setting yourself up for him stomping off if you asked how he got interested in Hitler. I would suggest you go over your questions and ask yourself, "Could this in any way possibly be construed by him as trying to get him to admit to being a neo-Nazi?"'

'This is really good advice,' I said.

'I'm doing all I can. The others are too. Did you know, they've all agreed to a pact to help you? They've been asking questions during the discussions that they think might be useful.'

Following my chat with Jaenelle, we all sat around a conference room table to watch *Downfall*. When we reached the part that we had seen the other night, re-subtitled to show Hitler raging about Ryanair, the room filled with the cough, spurt and snort of desperately suppressed sniggering. At the end, as we filed out, I asked Irving if there might be a suitable time to meet tomorrow. 'Oh Jesus, you keep going on about that,' he snapped. 'In the lobby, at eleven.'

Relieved, I joined the others. As they drank, Alex told me that when the active ingredient in marijuana is purified in a rice cooker, it becomes the cure for cancer. 'Big pharma', he explained, which is 'owned by the Jews', is behind the drug's prohibition. As he was talking, Jaenelle's voice cut through, bouncing accidentally on the top of the hubbub. She said his name, and then something like '. . . believes everything he reads on the Internet'. There was a horrible silence. Alex's eyes emptied. 'What did you say?' he demanded.

'Nothing,' said Jaenelle.

His face was bloodless. Utterly still.

'Repeat the last few words you said.'

'I was just . . .'

298

Mark broke the tension.

'Have you noticed how he's just got angrier and angrier since the trip's gone on?' he said. 'The headline will be, "'Ten Holocaust Deniers Killed by Conspiracy Theorist".'

And somehow the nervous laughter was just enough to lift Alex away from whatever it was that was about to happen.

*

Liar or deluded? Evil or mistaken? This is what I still don't understand.

Irving's insistence that Hitler was unaware of the Holocaust has, as its holiest artefact, the fact that no direct order from the Nazi leader has ever been found. But in her book *History on Trial*, Irving's libel defendant, Professor Lipstadt, wrote that historians 'do not, as Irving kept demanding, seek a "smoking gun", one document that will prove the existence of the gas chambers. They seek a nexus or convergence of evidence.' I am reminded of the observation that social psychologists Carol Tavris and Elliot Aronson make in *Mistakes Were Made*: 'Confirmation bias even sees to it that no evidence – the absence of evidence – is evidence for what we believe.'

An interview with Irving's brother Nicholas that was published in 2006 seems to add detail to the nature of the 'wheel' he describes running 'backwards and forwards in the slime'. David has denied all that Nicholas has said, of course, but his twin told the *Daily Telegraph* that, 'As children, he was always trying to drag me into his devilment.' He recalled an incident in which a German bomber destroyed a nearby house and the six-year-old David gave it a 'Heil Hitler' salute. '[But] there was nothing unpatriotic about David's views then,' he added. 'Like now, he liked to shock, to scandalise.'

During the Lipstadt trial, Irving issued a subpoena to Sir John Keegan, a noted historian who had declined an initial request to testify. 'Earlier experiences had persuaded me that nothing but trouble comes of taking sides over Irving,' Keegan wrote, in a subsequent account of his experience in the *Daily Telegraph*. 'I have written complimentary reviews of Irving's work as a military historian to find myself posted on the internet as a Nazi sympathiser.'

Many of Irving's enemies acknowledge his intelligence. They imply what I now know – that intelligence is no inoculation against bias. But researchers in the US have gone even further than this. They have found startling evidence that suggests that intelligence simply *does not work* in the service of truth. Psychologist David Perkins conducted a simple study in which he asked a range of participants to think of as many for-and-against reasons as they could for a number of sociopolitical issues. Naturally, people tended to come up with far more points that backed up their own opinions than ran counter to them – and the better educated people with the higher IQs came up with the most ways to conclude that their positions were correct. The surprise came when he discovered that their higher levels of intelligence only enabled them to think of arguments for why they might be right. Remarkably, the superior minds were *no better* at imagining why they might be wrong than those of weaker intelligence.

In his account of the Lipstadt trial, Sir John Keegan recounts a courtroom exchange in which he stated that Irving's view, that Hitler did not know about the Holocaust until 1943, 'defied reason, or common sense'. Irving challenged him, asking whether it would not be 'the most extraordinary historical revelation of the war' if it could be proved true? 'This was a very curious moment,' wrote Keegan. 'I suddenly recognised that Irving believed that Hitler's ignorance could be demonstrated.'

Some time in the early 1970s, David Irving had a remarkable idea. What if Hitler hadn't known about the Holocaust? What if he was actually a simple man, who was easily manipulated by others? And what if the industrial killing of the Jews was secretly organised by his immediate subordinates, who deliberately kept it from him? He recruited a German historian to find proof that he was mistaken. 'I'm hiring you because you're sceptical,' he told her. 'You're going to find the evidence to prove me wrong.'

Every argument that she produced was rejected by Irving. Some, he will admit, 'came close', such as the entry in Goebbels' diary from March 1942 which tells of deportations in which no more than 5 per cent of people survived.

'There's a whole page or two in his diary which describes this in very vivid terms, and said, "'The Führer too is in favour of a radical solution,'" Irving remembered. 'I said, "I'm sorry no. This is evidence against Goebbels. It shows that Goebbels *would like to believe* that Hitler was involved."'

In 1991 more diaries emerged, this time those of Adolf Eichmann, who had responsibility for the transportation of Jews to concentration camps. His journals report a conversation with Reinhard Heydrich. ' "I came from the Reichsführer [Himmler]," said Heydrich. "He has received orders from the Führer for the physical destruction of the Jews." ' Around the period in which Irving was considering this find, the writer Ron Rosenbaum interviewed him for his book *Explaining Hitler*. The author described finding Irving 'tormented' by this discovery. He told Rosenbaum, 'It rocked me back on my heels, frankly.' He admitted that he had thought, *Oops! How do you explain this one away?* and that he had to tell himself, 'Don't be knocked off your feet by this one.'

This is how he explained it away: even though Eichmann composed his memoirs before he was captured, Irving dismissed them as being concocted for use as evidence during an imagined future trial. 'I'm not saying Eichmann does it consciously,' he told me. 'But eventually he will begin saying to himself, "What would have been my only excuse in mitigation? That it was the Führer's orders."'

'You're using any excuse,' I said. 'Any way you can think around the problem of exonerating Hitler.'

'No. You have to be very precise. If Heidrich said that, why does it not exist in any document that followed? Why is there no paper trail?'

'Is it possible that you're being this forensic only with evidence that doesn't fit your thesis?'

'No, you're extra-careful because of this huge muck heap of world opinion that has been built up over the last sixty years. They've been piling more and more muck on top of it. It doesn't mean to say it's any righter. They're just quoting each other.'

I wondered if the Lipstadt trial had shaken his faith in his beliefs.

'They had a team of twenty historians,' he said. 'They spent twenty-nine months going through my thirty books and they found twelve errors. Half an error per book. Less than. Not bad going.'

It is a claim that Professor Lipstadt's defence team would surely be enraged to hear, and it is a stunning thing to observe: confirmation bias in action.

'So the trial actually *added* to your sense of self-esteem?' I asked.

He leaned back, smiling.

'And those twelve errors are *greatly* inflated.'

I moved on to further evidence that Hitler not only knew about the annihilation of the Jews, but predicted it. In a speech that he gave on 30 January 1939, Hitler said, 'Today I want to be a prophet once more: if the international finance Jewry inside and outside of Europe should succeed once more in plunging nations into another world war, the consequence will not be the Boleshevisation of the earth and thereby the victory of the Jewry, but the annihilation of the Jewish race in Europe.'

'Unfortunately you've got a problem with language,' said Irving. 'At no point does Hitler anywhere say, "We're going to liquidate the Jews."'

'He says "annihilate".'

'He uses a very common word in Germany, which is *"aus-rotten"*. Then he says it's a "prophetic warning for the Jews". That's a weird phrase.'

'But he's saying . . .'

Irving shook his head dismissively.

'You're not, you're not, you're not, *fine tuned.*'

I thought for a moment. I tried to tune myself up.

'It means he's looking into the future,' I said. 'Predicting.'

'Yes,' said Irving. 'That's right.'

'Predicting the annihilation of the Jews.'

'But you would say "warning" to the Jews. You wouldn't say "prophetic warning". The speech itself is six pages, single spaced. The actual reference to the Jews is three lines long. Only three lines in one column. Only that.'

They were three lines. They were in one column. And they prophesied the annihilation of the Jews.

'But the word he uses for annihilation is *"ausrotten"*,' he said. 'That's a word in German which *came to mean* liquidation.'

According to Irving, the meaning of *'ausrotten'* has changed since 1939. He knows this, because he has studied its use in a number of Hitler's speeches, and amassed several period dictionaries in preparation for the Lipstadt trial. Back then, he says, it meant 'extirpation', a word with a Latin origin whose literal definition was 'pulling the roots out'. Compared to today, its implication to Hitler's audience would have been mild. 'He was, at that time, using the word effectively to mean "emasculation".'

'And that also goes for the later speech when he said the annihilation had begun?'

'He never said that.'

I looked down at my notes.

'December the twelfth 1941, in a speech that recalled his prophecy of 1939, he said, "The world war is here. The annihilation of the Jewry must be a necessary consequence."'

'He's now saying the world war is going to lead to the destruction of the "Judentung", which is this vague concept of the Jewish entity.'

'For an outsider,' I said, 'it's hard to square that quote with the idea that Hitler somehow wasn't up for the annihilation of the Jews.'

'There's a great temptation here to extrapolate backwards from history and say, "Well, this happened, therefore he was saying it." I've been more selective.'

'It sounds to me like he's up for an annihilation.'

'That's because you're prejudiced by the history that has been propagated since the end of World War II. I can't do that. I've got to go back to the meaning of the words at the time. What you're doing is reading between the lines.'

'It's not between the line. It's on the line.'

'It depends how you translate the words.'

I found myself once more in the dilemma that is often faced when debating experts, no matter how controversial. Any argument can be closed down by an appeal to any evidence at all, as long as you are unfamiliar with it. Without immediate access to a 1939 English–German dictionary, I realised, there was nothing I could do.

I could, however, explore his more general feelings about the Jews. For a man who is so easily infuriated by accusations of anti-Semitism, he is remarkably anti-Semitic.

'The Jews like being talked about,' he told me. 'They're not happy if they're not being talked about. I always say if you want to be the bride at every wedding you run the risk of ending up being the corpse at every funeral. But I try to keep out of it.'

For Irving, many Jews share a common weakness, in which they cannot critically examine their actions. 'I can look at my own misfortune and say, "Well, I had it coming." But they will never look at their own misfortune and say, "Perhaps we as a people had it coming." They then say, "Well, we're hated because we're so financially successful." And I say, "Well, that's a racist remark that implies there is something in your genes that makes you good with money."'

'What do you think it is?'

He shrugged. 'Probably something different in their brains.'

For me, I told him, it is because humans are by nature tribal and the Jews' historical statelessness has probably made them unusually vulnerable to prejudice. To my astonishment, he nodded in agreement.

'It's in our microchip,' he said. 'We all have this glitch in our microchip. I could never fancy a black woman the way I fancy Jaenelle. It's my microchip.'

'So do you not accept, then, that psychological processes are behind anti-Semitism, rather than the Jews being especially "badly behaved"?'

'I think it's very likely,' he agreed. 'I try not to be anti-Semitic.' I grinned helplessly, convinced for one ridiculous moment that I might have made a breakthrough. 'But they don't make it easy for me.'

The great mystery, for me, is in the emotions that ferment

wordlessly beneath Irving's stubborn defence of Hitler. So many of the tour group had parents who had either served in the war or who saw it from Germany. Powerful adult beliefs rarely grow in rational, reasonable isolation. But Irving's was a patriotic family. He didn't rebel against his parents or siblings – he looked up to his father, idolised his RAF-serving elder brother. I began to wonder if I might have glimpsed a truth about the source of Irving's mission, however, when I challenged him on the moral relativity that he believes exists between the Nazis and the Allies.

'We wanted to stop the war,' I said. 'Whereas they wanted to take over Europe.'

'But it was no business of ours,' he snapped. 'We had no business getting involved with it. And because we did, we lost the empire, which was a huge force for civilisation around the world. What the empire was doing was worth everything and we should not have risked it. We were fighting somebody else's war because Churchill had been bribed by the Jews. He had been hired by them in 1936.'

'So it all comes back to the Jews?'

'In this case it does.'

'You would have preferred us to keep our empire . . .'

'I'm very proud of the empire.'

'. . . and for Hitler to have Europe?'

'I don't mind who has Europe.'

'You don't care.'

'I don't care. Why should I care? I'm not Jewish, I'm not a Communist, I'm not a faggot. Hitler had this *ambition*. He was going to build motorways everywhere. He was going to build great cities.'

'Don't you have any compassion for them? They were going to be slaughtered.'

'Well, that's what they were planning to do to us. Well,

maybe not the homosexuals, but the Communists certainly didn't have any good plans for us.'

'That's not my question,' I said. 'Don't you have any compassion for them?'

'Why should I? What kind of compassion?'

'You seem to have a worldview in which caring about people that aren't just like you is pointless.'

'We used to have a Communist Party in England—'

'I'm not saying we should all be Communists. The Communists were awful.'

'I know,' he said, mystified. 'I can't understand why you're sticking up for them.'

For the first time in the three hours that we had been speaking, Irving had lost his usual composure. Gone was the snippy, careful, lawyerly, narrow-eyed academic's pose. Suddenly, there it was: emotion. It made me wonder. Was *that* it? Perhaps he identified his family as one of *empire*. And he blames Churchill and the Jews for its loss. Could that be the wound that seeps beneath all of this?

I asked Irving if any of his relatives served the empire. He smiled proudly. 'Oh, yes. My uncles were with the Indian Army. One was a Bengal Lancer. They had a very good imperial life in India. And the other uncle was in Malaya and then on my mother's side of the family, her sister married Peter, who was on the same ship as my father. My uncle Peter was on the ship *Discovery*. They made several trips to the Antarctic on that. In fact, there are two islands, one named after my father and one after my Uncle Peter . . .'

This went on for some time.

Just before I stood to leave, I asked him a question of a different nature.

'Are you happy?'

'Very happy,' he replied.

'You don't strike me as a happy man,' I said. 'A lot of the people around you feel you are rude.'

'Well, let me explain,' he said. 'I've got an extremely painful right leg. Every day it fills my waking thoughts. It has crowded my horizon for the last four years. I find it very difficult indeed to be pleasant and jovial to people. I've been grumpy to you too and I'm sorry for that.'

And he surprised me, in that moment, did David Irving. He surprised me because he is one of life's devils. And when those who you demonise show a glimpse of vulnerability it can be shocking, because you were under the illusion that they weren't human.

EIGHT WEEKS LATER

Finally, it has arrived. From a second-hand book dealer in America – my Cassell's German–English dictionary. I can now know how listeners would have interpreted Hitler's 'prophecy' about the '*ausrotten*' of the Jews in 1939, because that is the year in which this dictionary was published. So what did the word imply back then? Emasculation? Or extermination?

Ausrott -en, *v.a.* extirpate, exterminate, root out.
Comp. **-ungs-krieg** *m* war of extermination.

14

'That one you just go, "Eeerrrr"'

He saw the handle, but he didn't see the bolts. He saw 'extir-pate', but he didn't see 'exterminate'. In the gas chamber and in the dictionary, David Irving appeared to suffer from an eerie and mysterious mode of cognitive blindness. He has been judged a liar, a historian who knowingly misleads. But to me, his behaviour suggests that he is genuinely and sincerely con-vinced of Hitler's innocence. That is where his thinking begins. And so any information that seems to dispute his thesis *cannot* be true. He sees it, but he *knows* his eyes are wrong. He reads it, but there *must* be an honest reason, some-where, to justify its dismissal. Instead of new unwelcome information, he trusts his feelings, just like the paralysed stroke victim who believed that she was in bed with an old man. Just like all of us.

It is as if no evidence could ever be good enough to per-suade Irving that the idea of his life has been a terrible mistake. That it is a mistake is proved by the facts, but that other sign is also loitering in the background, squinting ner-vously from one eye, hoping that nobody notices it. There is too much coherence; too much certainty. There has been a telling *ausrotten* of doubt.

Irving is proud of the empire and of his family who served

it. He shares this admiration with Hitler. And so the fight of his life becomes one of defending the man who recognised the achievements and moral eminence of his ancestors, of battling those whom he battled. He identifies with Hitler emotionally. He is his ambassador, and more.

Irving denies being anti-Semitic because that implies mistake and he, presumably, feels blameless. That is the illusion, and we all fall for it. We believe that we are not prejudiced, that we have arrived at our conclusions through a rational process of objective thought. Our biases disguise themselves as truth. We cannot see them, because the trick takes place behind our eyes. When he thinks of empire, he feels joy. When he thinks of Jews, he feels . . . well, *something else*. All the rest is confabulation.

This is, to be sure, a speculative and simplistic theory of the origins of one man's journey into forbidden beliefs. Even Irving himself does not have access to causes of the emotional impulses that unconsciously drive him. But in considering it, I believe we are closer to the truth than those who suggest that he is an evil and straightforwardly calculating liar.

Above all of this, though, what remains with me about my time with Irving are the moods and manners of the man. The ego, the stubbornness, the hunt for puddles to stamp in. 'The further their jaws will drop, the better job he thinks he's done,' Jaenelle told me, before hurriedly adding that that wasn't the aim of his work. But how can she know? How can any of us know? In that strange, chemical and alchemical moment when an unconscious decision is made about what to believe, how much is genetic, how much is rational, how much is concerned solely with reinforcing our dearly held models of the world? And how does personality collide with all of this? How does the character of the decider – all that complex emotionality, the calculation of possible outcomes, the current state of mind, the kaleidoscope of motives, the autobiographical hero-mission – pollute the process?

With these questions, we have struck rock. There is no answer. We cannot examine the neurons and synaptic patterns of David Irving and discover why or how he has made the decisions that he has. The mind remains, to a tantalising degree, a realm of secrets and wonder. Precisely how mysterious it is, though, is the matter of much dispute. It is, in fact, the schism that lies beneath a fight that has been taking place between two famous scientists for more than twenty years, now, and it is one that I have travelled to an upstairs room on the fringes of London's Hampstead Heath to hear all about – just as soon as I have had my psychic powers tested.

*

I sit in a wooden chair, facing a wall of books, on subjects such as the nature of time, Chinese medicine, cosmology, quantum theory and the philosophy of mind. Behind me, a large sash window looks out on to a huge and glorious tree, its branches and leaves a triumphal fountain of green and shimmering sunlight that fills the panes. It is a living portrait of nature and its energies and personality flood the room. On the sill beneath it sits a tray of sprouting fungi and a porcelain brain on a stem.

A man in his late sixties, wearing corduroy trousers, a loose shirt and black socks and sandals walks up behind me and passes me a blindfold, which I place over my eyes.

'I'm going to either stare at the back of your neck or look away at something else,' he says. 'There are twenty trials in all, and the beginning of each trial is indicated by a mechanical click. Thus.' *Click*. 'And after a few seconds you tell me whether you think I'm looking at you or not.'

'Okay,' I say. 'Great.'

'This works best if you just rely on feelings. The more you think about it, the less well you'll do.'

And so, we begin.

Click.

'Yes.'

Click.

'Yes.'

Click.

'No.'

It is surprisingly difficult not to think about your emotions. Despite the fact that I am getting no feedback on my success or failure, I quickly become convinced that I am getting it all wrong, and that starts me worrying, analysing even where there is nothing to analyse, gnashing on thin air.

When it is finally over I remove my blindfold and approach the scientist nervously. He has been marking me on a strip of white paper. And I can hardly *believe* the number of ticks.

'So, you got nine right,' he says.

Christ, I have it. I really do: the sense of being stared at.

'Wow,' I say.

'That's pretty close to chance,' says the scientist.

'Oh,' I say, my cheeks warming. 'Nine out of twenty. Oh, yes. Right. Of course.'

The man whose library this is has compiled the data from more than thirty thousand trials like this. The conclusion that it points to, if it is correct, proves that this mysterious 'sense of being stared at' is a genuine phenomenon, and that many or our fundamental theories of neuroscience are flawed. It shows that minds can extend out of the brain and communicate with other minds. It shows that extra-sensory perception (ESP) is real.

If it is correct.

*

It began, for Rupert Sheldrake, when he was five. He was at his grandmother's farm in the Nottinghamshire countryside, when he saw a row of fence posts that had sprouted branches and leaves. He was astonished. 'We made a fence and it came to life,' said his uncle Frank. Rupert stared at them, thinking, 'That's amazing!' The posts were made from willow – which is known to root easily – but for the boy this was a fantastic revelation; a vision of the power of nature.

Sheldrake grew up in a herbalist's shop near his grandparents' home. He was surrounded by pets and his father's brass microscopes were ranged in a laboratory next to his bedroom. They kept homing pigeons, whose mysterious abilities obsessed the boy. He loved science and studied at Cambridge University, where he won a double first in biochemistry, the university Botany Prize, a major scholarship and a general reputation for brilliance. Science, he was sure, held the answers to life. But, as he worked, he began to have terrible doubts. The young scholar found himself asking forbidden questions; ones that, since the dawn of modern thinking, have been thought of as heretical.

The world as we know it began in the eighteenth century. It was during the Enlightenment that radical thinkers began to use reason and evidence to take on the supernatural forces of religion. Since then, the sciences have been predicated on a truth that's still held in a kind of reverence. Everything – you, me and all the stars – is made from stuff. There is nothing else – no magic, no soul, no God, no afterlife. Human beings are machines, built by physics and chemistry. Reality itself is merely matter, held together by fields. This understanding – what is known as materialism – has built our civilisation. We have cities, computers, medicine and spacecraft because the idea of materialism works.

But as he killed animals and plants and ground them up

for study, Sheldrake began to wonder, 'Can we really discover all that we want by reducing everything down to ever smaller parts? Can life *really* be just a matter of molecular pulleys and gearwheels? Is materialism enough to explain the mysteries of reality?' Something, he believed, was missing from science – something that no amount of pulleys and gearwheels could surely generate. It was what his childhood love of nature had been surrounded by. *Life* was missing.

By the time he was twenty-eight, Sheldrake was a Cambridge don. For eight years, he had been developing a theory that sought to answer some of nature's most stubborn mysteries. How do pigeons home? How do spiders know how to spin webs without learning from other spiders? How do shoals of fish behave as one? What, he wondered, if there was some undiscovered force that every living thing tapped into? Something not material, exactly – more like a field that somehow carried information?

One evening, after dinner, Sheldrake was drinking port with Professor Albert Chibnall, an elderly but brilliant biochemist who had served in the Royal Flying Corps during the First World War, and who had taken a fatherly interest in him.

'This idea of yours is going to get you into trouble,' Chibnall warned him. 'You're perfectly positioned for a brilliant career. If you pursue this, you'll throw it all away. Take my advice. Wait until you retire.'

'But that's thirty-seven years away,' complained Sheldrake.

'It's dangerous,' said Chibnall. 'It'll ruin your career.'

Sheldrake ignored him and, in 1981, published his theory in a book, *A New Science of Life*.

One Saturday following its publication, Sheldrake was eating a breakfast of toast, marmalade and coffee. He had been pleased by his book's reception – the *Observer* had called it 'fascinating and far-reaching', the *Biologist* 'well-written, provocative and entertaining' and *New Scientist* had said it was 'an important scientific enquiry into the nature of biological and physical reality', elsewhere calling Sheldrake 'an excellent scientist; the proper, imaginative kind that in an earlier age discovered continents and mirrored the world in sonnets'. He was happily looking forward to the game of tennis he had planned for the morning when the post arrived, with the latest edition of the famous journal *Nature*. Sitting down, he gasped at the editorial's sensational headline: 'A Book for Burning?'

Good heavens! he thought. *What's this about? I've never seen anything like it.*

He read on. He felt winded. It was about *his* book. He had been denounced in one of the world's most prestigious academic journals. His idea had been called irrational; dangerous. He had become a heretic.

'So, you see – my idea did get me into trouble,' he tells me, having recounted his story. 'It did ruin my career. I was no longer able to get a job or a grant. Chibnall had been right.'

But there was more to come from Sheldrake. Grander theories and worse trouble. If it was true that these information fields existed, and that all living things tapped into them, then perhaps humans and animals could communicate non-verbally? Maybe telepathy could be real.

This is an outrageous postulation. It produces a violent species of contempt in many mainstream academics because it strikes at the very roots of science. The idea that the mind could function *outside* of the brain had been dispensed with hundreds of years ago, a cornerstone victory in the battle between reason and religion. The mind is *of* the brain and it is *in* the brain. If you accept that it might be able to function outside of it – that personalities might be able to exist beyond the boundaries of their physical selves – then what next? Ghosts? The afterlife? *God?*

'Materialists are afraid that as soon as you allow anything beyond the comfortable terrain of established science, you'll get religion and civilisation will crumble,' Sheldrake says with a dry smile. 'They think if you allow people to believe in telepathy you'll have the Pope flying in any minute. Compulsory Catholicism. They can't bear any questioning of science's basic dogmas.'

Materialists, of course, say that the mind is the product of nerve activity in the brain. This is the view that was summed up famously by a genius pioneer of the twentieth century, Nobel Prize-winner Francis Crick, who wrote that: '"You", your joys and your sorrows, your memories and your ambitions, your sense of personal identity and free will, are no more than the behaviour of a vast assembly of nerve cells and their associated molecules.'

'Crick was a fundamentalist,' says Sheldrake. 'He was desperate to have science confirm a materialist worldview and to expel mystery as much as possible.'

Sheldrake's explorations into telepathy in its various forms eventually led him to his trials of what he calls 'the sense of being stared at'. Using a variety of different protocols, he found that people answered correctly 55 per cent of the time. This may not seem dramatically significant, but he conducted so many trials that the odds of this score arising by chance became, he says, one in ten thousand billion billion. Proof, he believed, that the mind didn't rely wholly on the five senses. Proof that it extended outside the confines of the brain. Proof that materialism is wrong.

Next, he studied a psychic terrier from Ramsbottom. Jaytee would run to the porch window occasionally, when a cat walked past or a delivery man or who-knows-what-else. But he seemed to have a particular preponderance for being there when his owner Pam was coming home – even when she

316

arrived unexpectedly. It was almost as if Jaytee *knew*. So Sheldrake tested the dog. In over one hundred tests Sheldrake found that Jaytee spent an average of 4 per cent of his time at the window when Pam wasn't coming home and 55 per cent of his time there when she was. (If you're like me, you'll be wondering why these numbers don't add up to 100. The study was carried out in blocks of time, so that if, during a ten-minute period in which Pam wasn't coming home, the dog was at the window for 0.4 minutes, that's four per cent. If, during a ten-minute period when she *was* coming home, the dog was at the window for 5.5 minutes, that's 55 per cent.)

He published his studies in academic journals. He wrote books. He became a practising Christian. And the world didn't listen. Instead, things became worse for him. His dog studies were ridiculed in newspapers. He was treated with contempt by his colleagues in academia. In 2004 he took part in a debate with Professor of Biology Lewis Wolpert, who described telepathy research as 'pathological science' and remarked that 'an open mind is a very bad thing – everything falls out'. As Sheldrake described his studies, he claims Wolpert sat with his back to the projector screen, tapping his pencil, 'looking bored'. When Sheldrake was asked to speak at the 2006 Festival of Science, his presence was denounced by Oxford Professor of Physical Chemistry Peter Atkins, who said: 'there's absolutely no reason to suppose that telepathy is anything more than a charlatan's fantasy.' On a subsequent BBC Radio debate, Sheldrake asked Atkins if he had studied any of his work. Atkins said, 'No, but I would be very suspicious of it.' When Professor Richard Dawkins filmed Sheldrake for a segment in a documentary, the polemicist accused Sheldrake of being 'prepared to believe almost anything'. When asked if he'd actually read any of his evidence Sheldrake says that Dawkins replied, 'I don't want to discuss evidence.' (Dawkins denies this. In an email, sent to me via an intermediary, he called this claim 'outrageous and defamatory' and insisted that he had read 'several' of Sheldrake's papers.)

But perhaps the most damage has been caused by the tireless work of one man – a talented and famous speaker, author, lifelong conjuror, psychologist and adviser to the James Randi Educational Foundation. He is doggedly sceptical of all things paranormal. On national television he has successfully and amusingly debunked hauntings of castles and walkers on fire. His name is Professor Richard Wiseman.

'Wiseman tried to replicate your experiments with staring, and with Jaytee the dog,' I say to Sheldrake. 'He's convinced you're wrong.'

'Wiseman's a stage magician. A conjuror. A skilled deceiver,' he replies. 'He's a huge asset to the materialist movement. He's their hitman.'

The first paragraph of Wiseman's bestseller *Paranormality: Why We See What Isn't There* recounts what happened when he studied the psychic dog. 'As I gazed deep into the eyes of Jaytee, several thoughts passed through my mind. Was this cute little terrier really psychic? If not, how had he managed to make headlines across the world? At that precise moment, Jaytee gave a small cough, leaned forward and vomited on my shoes.'

'To understand materialists like Wiseman,' says Sheldrake, 'one has to realise that they totally believe these things are impossible. If someone comes up with positive evidence, either the experiment is flawed or I've cheated. Those are the only options on the menu: foolish or fraudulent. I've been through this argument with Skeptics again and again. They go through their various objections and I show them how I've accounted for them all. And then they say, "Oh, well, there must be some other flaw." I say, "Well, what is it?" and they say, "We haven't thought of it yet, but there must be one." The point is, you can't win. No evidence will ever be good enough. That's just one of the problems of doing research in this area. One has to deal with this level of arrogance and ignorance that purports to be objective, scientific and reasonable, but which is deeply unscientific and unreasonable.'

In 2006 Rupert Sheldrake was given a 'Pigasus' award by the James Randi Educational Foundation (JREF), for 'the scientist who said or did the silliest thing' during the previous year. 'This man's delusions increase as time goes by,' they said, on announcing the prize, 'and he comes up with sillier ideas every year.' Like all practitioners of what he calls 'woo woo', Randi points to Sheldrake's failure to apply for his 'Million Dollar Challenge' as evidence that he secretly knows that he is wrong. On his website, Randi writes, somewhat cryptically: 'Sheldrake is still clinging to some strange story he relates about a previous encounter with me, a tale that fails to make its point. He'll depend upon this to avoid becoming involved with any testing process related to the Million Dollar Challenge, of course. I find it not at all strange that these folks fear involvement with the JREF more than they fear Hell itself . . .!'

'Randi is a liar,' says Sheldrake. 'He's a man of very doubtful character indeed – a rude, aggressive, dogmatic Skeptic who knows nothing about science. He's taken seriously by people like Dawkins – they worship him – because they see themselves as engaged in a war against unreason and religion. And if you're in a war, you want to have thugs on your side.'

People such as Dawkins, Randi and Wiseman are suffering, says Sheldrake, from an acute sensitivity to doubt. 'Fundamentalists, whether religious, materialist or atheist, are people who need certainty,' he says. 'They're not prepared to live in a place with doubts. It's very similar to creationism. Some creationists will look at scientific evidence but only so that they can try and find some flaw. That's also true of the denialists about psychic phenomena.'

When I tell Sheldrake that I am going to be interviewing Richard Wiseman, I sense a moment of tension and then resignation. 'You'll probably find him very convincing,' he sighs.

*

It began, for Richard Wiseman, when he was eight. He was at his grandad's house in Luton when the old man asked him to write his name on a coin. With the wave of a handkerchief, the coin disappeared. Then his grandad produced a tobacco tin, whose lid was held fast with elastic bands. Inside that was another tin with more bands. Inside that, a cloth bag. And inside that, Richard's coin.

But the moment that truly ignited Richard's curiosity came weeks later, when his grandad revealed how the trick worked. Richard was aghast. How easy it was to fool the mind! How simple, to conjure the appearance of magic when, in fact, there was only illusion! For the boy, it was a fantastic revelation; a vision of the fallibility of humans.

Richard began studying tricks, digging through second-hand bookshops for guides to magic and debunking accounts of the silly mysteries believed by his classmates: spontaneous combustion, stigmata, the Bermuda Triangle. At the age of twelve, he had his own touring show. At university, he earned a PhD in the psychology of deception. When he heard about the work of 'parapsychologists' – actual *scientists* who studied subjects like telepathy – he became fascinated. In a universe that is constructed from simple matter, these things are impossible. So why do people persist in believing in them? How have they been fooled?

I meet Wiseman outside Foyle's bookshop on Charing Cross Road in central London, where he is appearing later as part of his *Paranormality* publicity tour. After he has baffled my demonstrably faulty brain with a coin trick in a nearby greasy spoon, I tell him that I want to write about his fights with Sheldrake, because they seem to represent a fascinating battle of ideas. He greets this suggestion with a contemptuous laugh.

'I've got a few problems with Rupert. If you look at the mainstream body of parapsychology, he's not very well represented. He's rarely even discussed. The reason is that there are often errors in his work.'

Wiseman tells me that a German academic named Stefan Schmidt conducted a meta-analysis of Sheldrake-inspired staring studies. And Sheldrake's work wasn't included. 'It's not even mentioned,' he says. 'And the reason for that is that it's just not good enough quality.'

The criticisms go on. To ensure that the person being stared at isn't somehow unconsciously 'learning' the right answer, you need a random mechanism to tell the starer when to look and when to look away. In some of his tests, Rupert used a coin toss. 'And that hasn't been an acceptable way of doing it since the 1930s. You only need a small bias in the coin to completely throw your data. Why wouldn't you just use any of the more sophisticated random number systems?'

He goes on to say that, even with the starer blindfolded and sitting behind a one-way mirror, there is no guarantee he couldn't somehow 'hear' when he was being stared at. When I respond with a doubtful face, Wiseman smiles. 'You've got better hearing than you realise. We know people hear below the conscious threshold.'

He then provides a study by academics at the University of Amsterdam who largely failed to replicate Sheldrake's tests. They think he might have got his 55 per cent score because people have a natural bias both towards saying 'yes' and changing their answer between 'yes' and 'no' – and, with bad randomisation, these alterations could affect the outcome.

Wiseman tried to replicate Sheldrake's staring tests with parapsychologist Marilyn Schlitz. On the first test, when Wiseman was the starer, they didn't get a positive result. But when Marilyn stared, they did. It happened on the second test, too. 'I never published that study because I'm not happy with it,' says Wiseman. 'We messed it up. But I can see proponents arguing that it was positive.'

'But you wouldn't agree with that?' I ask.

'No, but I wouldn't disagree with it either. That one, you just go, "Eeerrrr." '

Wiseman went on to conduct four tests on Jaytee the dog, at Sheldrake's invitation. His conclusions led to scathing newspaper headlines, such as 'Psychic dog is no more than a chancer' (*The Times*) and 'Psychic pets are exposed as a myth' (*Daily Telegraph*). All of this enraged Sheldrake. His first complaint was obvious – that he had carried out more than a hundred tests on Jaytee, while Wiseman had done just four, and yet the psychologist's claims were taken as superior. He also objected that Wiseman didn't even test his claim, that Jaytee was at the window *more* when Pam was on the way home. Rather, he tested to see if Jaytee's first visit of more than two minutes corresponded with the beginning of Pam's return. That was a different claim. And it didn't correspond. Well, it might have done on the final test, if Jaytee hadn't been sick.

Then there was a dramatic twist. Sheldrake requested Wiseman's data. When he analysed it, he found that they actually *confirmed* his claim. According to Wiseman's own figures, Jaytee was at the window 4 per cent of the time when Pam wasn't coming home and 78 per cent when she was. While Wiseman admits this is true, he attacks both this and the best of Sheldrake's evidence on the basis that Jaytee might have just been going to the window more frequently as time went on because he was missing his owner.

He explains that he tested his different claim because he had seen it on *The Paul McKenna Show*, because it was what Pam had told him and because his work took place at the beginning, before Sheldrake's claim existed.

'Our work was very, very early on,' he tells me.

'But I thought you came in *after* Sheldrake's work?' I say, slightly confused.

'No, at the same time as Rupert is doing his work,' he says.

'I thought he invited you in?'

'No. Rupert was doing it concurrently. So I don't know at what point he came up with this notion of plotting how long the dog is at the window for. It was not around when we were doing our work. It emerged after we had done it. And certainly our paper was published way before his.'

All of this is rather confusing. But it is important, because Sheldrake tells the story as if Wiseman was engaged in a kind of cynical, sceptical drive-by shooting. He says that he invited Wiseman to test Jaytee, only for Wiseman to come along and test a different claim, which was then used to slate him and his work – even though the data actually confirmed it. So I called Sheldrake and told him what Wiseman had said.

'I can't believe it,' he said. 'That is such a distortion.'

Sheldrake insists that his claim *was* there from the start, but Wiseman never asked him about it, instead seeking information from Pam (who, incidentally, wouldn't know how her dog was behaving because – obviously – she was out when he was doing it). He says that he began his work a year before *The Paul McKenna Show* reported on it. 'I arranged Wiseman's test and invited him to do it,' Sheldrake says. 'I even lent him my video camera.'

'He also said that his paper was published before yours,' I told him.

'Well, that's a simple fact,' says Sheldrake. 'And it's an

outrage that it was. When he told me he was going to publish it, I said, "Well, look, Richard, it means you're cutting in ahead of me. I'm not publishing my data because I haven't finished the studies yet. I'm doing a whole series of controls, I'm doing repeated tests." But he cut in. I'd done more than a hundred observations on this dog. He'd done four. Then I said to him, "Why haven't you referred to all the experiments I did in your paper?" He said, "I couldn't refer to them because they're unpublished." But I'd already shown him all the data. I mean, this is rather shocking. *Very* shocking. But the point is, in his own eyes, he's probably completely guiltless. It's a level of self-deception that I'm astonished by.'

Later I find a paper co-written by Wiseman in 'reply' to some of Sheldrake's criticisms. It confirms that Sheldrake 'kindly invited [Wiseman] to conduct his own investigations of Jaytee', and that they took place thirteen months after Sheldrake's experiments began.

I decide to look up the Schmidt meta-analysis that Wiseman talked about, which he said excluded Sheldrake's work because 'it's just not good enough quality'. I am surprised to find it concludes that there *is* a 'small but significant effect' of the sense of being stared at. But I am more surprised yet when Sheldrake tells me that he was excluded from it, not because his work was deemed sloppy, but because it is an analysis of experiments that separated starer from staree using CCTV – something that Sheldrake has never done. He addresses more of Wiseman's concerns, explaining that he has used three different kinds of randomisation – including one 'which I got a professor of statistics in Holland to supply and to check, so those are completely pukka' – and another that was *proposed by Wiseman himself* – and still his results were positive.

Meanwhile, the authors of the University of Amsterdam study that Wiseman sent me admit their criticisms only count when the staree was given feedback on how well he was doing. They concede that Sheldrake also carried out trials without feedback (as he did on me) and found smaller, but still significant effects. Sheldrake says that his different randomisation methods dispense with their other complaints. But then Wiseman sends more concerns. And Sheldrake counters them, adding a meta-analysis that confirms his view.

It goes on like this for some time.

So what is the ordinary human to do? What am *I* to do? When do I stop going back and forth between them? Is it even possible to find a truth to these matters? The answer, perhaps, is to step back. I ask Wiseman if he is one hundred per cent convinced that the claims of parapsychology – often shortened to 'psi' – are wrong.

'No,' he says. 'But I'm convinced enough.'

'Give it a percentage.'

'Ninety per cent.'

Wiseman's career as a celebrity Skeptic is predicated on there being no such thing as paranormal phenomena. He admits to never having had any 'interest in investigating if it's true because I've always thought it isn't'. So is it surprising that he is only '90 per cent' certain about this? Actually, it isn't. Many academics are prepared to admit that parapsychologists *have* proven psi phenomena by the standards usually demanded by science. Computer pioneer Alan Turing once said, 'How we should like to discredit [psi]! Unfortunately the statistical evidence, at least for telepathy, is overwhelming.' The *New Scientist* has reported that, 'For years, well-designed studies carried out by researchers at respected institutions have produced evidence for the reality of ESP. The results are often more impressive than the outcome of clinical drug trials because they show a more pronounced effect and have greater statistical significance. What's more, ESP experiments have been replicated and their results are as consistent as many medical trials – and even more so in some cases.' Celebrated physicist Freeman Dyson has said, 'paranormal phenomena are real but lie outside the limits of science.' As far back as 1951, pioneering neuroscientist Donald Hebb admitted that we have been 'offered enough evidence to have convinced us on almost any other issue', and admitted that his rejection of it 'is – in the literal sense – prejudice'. And far more recently, in 2008, a famously sceptical psychologist said, 'I agree that by the standards of any other area of science that [psi] is proven.' That was Professor Richard Wiseman.

They reject psi, despite the evidence for it, for the same reason that many scientists and Skeptics feel that they can dismiss Sheldrake's work without first having studied it. Because, what is more likely? That parapsychologists are mistaken or fraudulent? Or that a psychic terrier from Ramsbottom has proved that a foundational principle of science is wrong? A common materialist slogan, often attributed to Carl Sagan, says, 'Extraordinary claims require extraordinary evidence.' As Wiseman tells me, 'A lot of physics and psychology will be called into question the moment you accept psi. Therefore, it's reasonable to say that the weight of evidence for it must be much greater.'

I tell Wiseman that Sheldrake thinks science doesn't have to be overturned to accept his proposed new 'information field'. Rather, it would just need to expand, as it did when we discovered electricity, quantum theory and the electromagnetic field.

'But you could go the other way,' Wiseman replies, 'which is just assume there's no problem. That the mind is simply a by-product of the brain.'

But that is the thing. There *is* a problem. How is the conscious function of the 'mind' created? We look in the brain and see the hemispheres, the regions, the neurons, the glia, the synapses and all the highly complex feedback loops. We know that certain neural activity *correlates* with certain experiences – which areas of the brain are involved with seeing yellow, for example, or eating hummus. We have a good idea how we make decisions. We know that visual information is processed in around thirty different areas of the brain. But we don't even begin to see how all of that might come together – to coalesce into that incredible sensation of singularity – that feeling of 'I', of agency, that sits on top of the stew of emotions and urges and sensations and memories that we feel at any one moment. How do all these cells create private, subjective experience? Where do all these disparate brain regions unite in order to generate the illusion that you are the 'invisible actor at the centre of the world', the one who is seeing, hearing, smelling, remembering, talking and feeling sad or hopeful or brave?

And why? If our sole living purpose is the propagation of our selfish genes, then why shouldn't we just be zombies – unconscious decision-engines roaming the earth, maximising our chances of survival by making simple decisions, beating each other up and procreating as much as possible? Nobody knows. In fact, this is such a hard problem that it is actually known among philosophers and neuroscientists as 'the hard problem'.

A small number of academics believe that searching the brain for consciousness is akin to watching a television show and then hunting in its circuit boards for the presenters. For them, consciousness exists on an external field and our brains *interact* with it, a little like how the eye and our various visual processing areas interact with electrical impulses that are *out there* to create vision. That is why 'the hard problem' is proving to be so hard: because we have been looking in the wrong place.

If there is even a remote chance that this is true, then there is also a chance that Sheldrake and his fellow parapsychologists might be right. Because if such a crucial component of mind can be *out there*, then it theoretically might be able to interact with other minds that are also out there.

What is required is a referee. Someone who knows brains, is widely recognised as brilliant and yet has a foot in neither the Sheldrake nor the Wiseman camp. I decide to contact American neuroscientist Professor David Eagleman. Well known for his research into how the brain processes time, he has been profiled in the *New Yorker* and described as a 'genius' by the *Observer*; he calls himself a 'Possibilian', rejecting certainty in science as an 'absurd' position. But this is no anti-materialist. On the contrary, Eagleman is a disciple of Sheldrake's arch-materialist foe Francis Crick, and says that he spent all of his 'intellectual time' with him during his post-doctoral studies.

When I phone Eagleman, he is airport-bound, in the back of a New York taxi. After a quick preamble, and entirely without warning, I ask him this most dangerous of questions, the one on whose answer hangs our very concept of what a human being actually is. Is it possible that consciousness might exist outside the brain, perhaps as a kind of field?

There's a long, tantalising pause. 'Um . . . Ah . . .' Another silence. 'Here's what I think. I think it's . . . I think . . . I have to be very careful what I say. Okay. It's absolutely poss— er . . . let me back up a minute.'

'It's okay,' I say. 'I understand that this is a controversial area.'

'Yes,' he replies. 'Well, the idea of materialism is that we're nothing but pieces and parts. So if you put all those pieces and parts together, then you get consciousness. But we don't actually know that that's the right answer. We just assume it is.

And it's probably an okay strategy to burn up a generation doing that because you have to get all the way to the end of a problem to see if you get stuck or if there's a solution. But it is perfectly possible that materialism will not be a solution and that our science is too young to recognise something else that's going on. So I think it's appropriate to have some intellectual humility and scepticism about whether our current physics and biology are sufficient.'

'Wow,' I say. 'I really didn't think you were going to say that.'

'I wouldn't want to get quoted saying that I support Sheldrake's theories, because I'm not familiar with them,' he says. 'But I'm a supporter of people proposing wacky ideas because every single major advance started off as a wacky idea. We're at a very young period in our science right now. We need ideas. What doesn't make sense is to pretend that we know the answers and to act as if we're certain that materialism is going to bring us all the way home, because we have no guarantee of that.'

Of course, we must remember that Eagleman's admission doesn't mean that Sheldrake is right. Science still moves slowly, carefully and by a unique mode of bickering and begrudging nearly-consensus, as it should. And Sheldrake has his own coherence problem – his results tend to be far more significant than those of other parapsychologists, and they are not consistently replicated.

By the end of it all, though, I am reminded of the way that I felt about UFOs. Back then, no matter how powerful the arguments I heard, no matter how much I realised, rationally, that I should at least accept the possibility of alien space travel, I could not. My unconscious had made a decision. It would not be shifted. And once again, on the question of telepathy, it is broadcasting a great, dark lump of no. I am no less prejudiced than David Irving and the materialist Skeptics: no evidence could ever be good enough. My position is surely deeply unfair. But, still. There it is.

But I *am* less sure. A new grey space has been nudged between the black and the white. And it is invigorating to have some mystery back. It feels wonderful to have doubt.

And I have new doubts, too, that lie beyond the slender limits of telepathy. Sheldrake defended himself easily against many of Wiseman's attacks. It was the opposite experience from that which I had been led to expect.

So, what about this James Randi? Could Sheldrake's criticisms of him also be worth hearing? I have had a long-suppressed intuition, bulging and pleading to be noticed, that says there is something unsavoury about the so-called 'patron saint of the Skeptics'. Back at the anti-homeopathy gathering in Manchester, though, I had decided that my feelings on this matter were not to be trusted. They were emotional, not based on evidence, *irrational*. I accepted this in the spirit that I tend to accept most criticism; my scolders are right because *of course they are right*. The naughty boy, the thief, the failure, the terrified, obsessive lover. Wrongness is the story of my life.

But since then, I have learned that hunches can be the result of intelligent calculations. Often, they can be right. I begin to wonder about this 'strange story' about 'a previous encounter' with Sheldrake that Randi wrote of on his website. Could there actually be grounds for Sheldrake's calling this icon of reason 'a liar'? What happened between them? Could the silent warning song of my unconscious actually, for once, be true?

15

'A suitable place'

Everybody loves James Randi. He is a genius. He is an icon. He is truth's war dog and has been feasting on the feet of the deluded and the dishonest for longer than many of us have been alive. *Wired* magazine says that 'he knows more about the workings of science than half the PhDs in America'. Richard Dawkins has given him a 'Richard Dawkins award' and hosted sell-out thousand-dollar-a-head fundraising dinners for his educational foundation. Celebrity magicians Penn and Teller call him 'our inspiration, our hero, our mentor and our friend'. Professor Richard Wiseman credits his 1982 book *Flim Flam* as having a 'huge impact' on him, with its 'hardline approach' that assumed that 'none of it is true'. The former editor of *The Skeptic* magazine says, 'He has done more to promote scepticism worldwide than any living individual. And any dead individual as well.' The founding editor of the US edition has called him 'the pioneer of the skeptical movement'. The *New York Times* has described him as our 'most celebrated living debunker'. Isaac Asimov has said, 'His qualifications as a rational human being are unparalleled.' Sir John Maddox, the former editor of the world-prestigious science journal *Nature*, has said, 'I don't know what his IQ is, but I'm sure it's off the scale.'

And a man who claims to have met a psychic dog says that he is a liar.

It does not seem possible that Dr Rupert Sheldrake can be right. For one thing, Randi's boosters are known for their cautious and critical evidence-based thinking. When I was among the Skeptics in Manchester, I wondered how they felt about their own susceptibility to the biases that twist the perspectives of ordinary people. Michael Marshall, who helped organise the conference, told me that their natural inclination for questioning and analysis gave them an 'inoculation against dogma'. Skeptic celebrity Dr Steven Novella, a senior fellow at the James Randi Educational Foundation, said, 'The reason why scepticism is incompatible with dogma and ideology is, it's very anti-dogmatic and anti-ideological at its core.'

Hearing all that, it would seem abundantly unlikely that the man the Skeptics exalt as their 'patron saint' is a liar. But this is what Sheldrake claims. He says that Randi has a history of behaving in exactly the way that he so aggressively abhors in others – that he is a showman, who lies in service of his celebrity. The Skeptics do not accept this, Sheldrake says, because they are blinded by the biases from which they claim immunity.

I am not sure what to think. I mean, look at the facts – at that glistered register of acolytes: Dawkins, Wiseman, Novella, Maddox, the *New York Times*. The forces ranged against Sheldrake could hardly be more impressive. I cannot find a senior scientist or mainstream publication that has anything negative to say about Randi – or much positive about Sheldrake. There is a consensus here. And it is not singing the favours of the psychic dog man.

But what of my biases? My problem is, I *liked* Sheldrake. I did so for the same reason that I felt a warming attraction to Harvard's UFO professor, John Mack. They are fascinating minds, troublemakers, *heretics*. Their beliefs glitter and pulse and enchant. Wiseman was likeable and funny, yes, but he was the holder of the glitter-extinguisher. He was teacher. He was *Dad*.

I used to imagine that our biases and delusions existed on a layer above a solid and clear-sighted base. Beneath your mistakes, I thought, there is your human nature, which is rational and immovable and seeks only truth. If you came to suspect that you were in error, you could easily work your way back to sense. What I now know is that there *is* no solid base. The machine by which we experience the world is the thing that becomes distorted. And so it is impossible to watch ourselves falling into fallacy. We can be lost without knowing we are lost. And, usually, we are.

But if this is true for me, then surely it is true for everyone, no matter how publicly they declare themselves to be 'free' or 'rational' or 'critical' thinkers. Can anyone really be immune? What about Randi? I am suspicious of the coherence of his beliefs, which seem to be held with such a severe level of vehemence that no room is left for self-doubt. But even so, can Sheldrake possibly be correct? It would be testament, indeed, to humanity's powers of self-deception if the Skeptics, of all people, could be shown to have unquestioningly installed a liar as their leader. But it would be telling, too, if it turns out that Sheldrake is wrong. It would say much about the truth-finding power of consensus and the deceptive energies in Sheldrake's brain which have led him to unfairly malign a man who is a hero, and not an enemy, of science.

I start by reading and comparing the various life stories of Randall James Hamilton Zwinge that have been recounted in interviews that he has given to the media over the years. The stories that have been reported are astonishing.

James Randi was born an illegitimate 'genius or near

genius' on 7 August 1928. A child prodigy with an IQ of 168, he spent his leisure time pursuing personal projects, such as making photo-electric cells and doing chemistry experiments in his basement. By the age of eight he was arguing with other children about the existence of Santa Claus. By nine, he had invented a pop-up toaster. Canadian officials decided that he was too intelligent to benefit from school, so he was given a special pass that said he did not have to attend. Instead, he educated himself in the Toronto Public Library and the Royal Ontario Museum where, by the age of twelve, he had taught himself geography, history, astronomy, calculus, psychology, science, mathematics and ancient Egyptian hieroglyphics.

Randi was fifteen when he committed his first public debunking. He claims that his exposé of a ruse at a local Spiritualist church, the 'Assembly of Inspired Thought', led to his dramatic arrest. At seventeen he had a bicycle accident in which his back was broken. He spent thirteen months in a body-cast, using the time to teach himself the skills in magic and lock-breaking that would be essential to future work in conjuring and escapology. He confounded his doctors, who told him that he would never walk again (or, in a later account, walk *straight* again).

Still seventeen, he was back at school – Toronto's Oakwood Collegiate Institute – where he achieved 'mediocre' results, but only because he chose not to apply himself. He brought his first exam to a premature finish by writing beneath a question 'This is a premise I cannot support, signed Randall James Hamilton Zwinge' and walking out, refusing to take any more tests.

Still seventeen, he joined Peter March's Travelling Circus and began performing in a turban as a wizard named Prince Ibis. *Still* seventeen (he did a lot when he was seventeen), he took a job writing newspaper horoscopes as an 'experiment' in which he wanted see how easy it was to dupe the public with paranormal claims. That came to a dramatic end when he saw two office workers (or, in another account, two prostitutes) reading his column. When the office workers/prostitutes (or, in a third account, a waitress) told him that they took his astrological predictions seriously, he was so disgusted that he resigned, vowing never again to pose as having supernatural abilities. (In yet another contradictory account, this crucial, life-changing resignation came about when he was asked to use his telepathic powers to find a lost child.) 'I could not live with that kind of lie. So I went back to the rabbits and the handkerchiefs.'

Whether it was horoscope- or lost-child-related, Randi retired his psychic pretence when he was seventeen. At least that's what I thought, until I read an article in the *Toronto Evening Telegram* which reported that he first realised he had ESP aged nine and that he would habitually pick up the telephone before it rang because he 'sensed' that someone had dialled his number. In a follow-up article, he claimed: 'Certain perceptions have been given me and I have improved them by deep study of the science of mental telepathy and clairvoyance.' The headline was 'He Sees the Future'. It appeared in August 1950. Randi was twenty-two.

It was somewhere around this point that Randi became an escapologist. Interviews that he has given offer an almost unbelievable account of his daredevilry. He has freed himself from a straitjacket while hanging upside down over Japan, called his mother from a coffin in Halifax harbour, broken out of twenty-eight jail cells in Canada and the US (although sometimes he says it was twenty-two, 'all over the world'), sealed himself in an underwater casket for an hour and forty-four minutes, wrestled himself loose from a straitjacket as he hung by his heels above Broadway and from out of helicopters and from over the top of Niagara Falls and, in 1974, won a Guinness World Record for entombing himself unclothed in ice under medical surveillance for forty-three minutes and eight seconds.

He toured with Alice Cooper and got to know Salvador Dali. On a radio show in 1964, he first offered his cash prize – ten thousand dollars to anyone who could demonstrate a paranormal power under controlled conditions. His great fame as a debunker, though, began during a 1972 episode of *The Tonight Show*, on which he humiliated the celebrity spoon-bender Uri Geller by insisting that he couldn't touch the metal props before showtime, then watched as he spent an agonising twenty-two minutes with his super-powers mysteriously paralysed. That was to be the start of a feud that ultimately turned legal, at one point threatening to bankrupt Randi, who has said that a dying wish is to have his ashes thrown in Geller's eyes. Two years after *The Tonight Show*, Randi helped found the Committee for the Scientific Investigation of Claims of the Paranormal (CSICOP), the forerunner to today's James Randi Educational Foundation (JREF), a charitable organisation that seeks to protect people from 'the true danger of uncritical thinking'.

Since the 1960s, his challenge fund has grown to one million dollars and the celebrity and reputation of the man who has been declared 'one of America's most original and fearless thinkers' has swollen with it. And 'The Amazing Randi' is in little doubt as to the risks of his work. He has claimed to receive regular death threats, telling one journalist, 'I Xerox everything and send it to the FBI. If I die mysteriously they will know who to go to' and another, 'I don't answer the door unless I know who's there.' But it is worth it. For belief in the supernatural is heralding a new dark age. It can be even fatal. 'It's a very dangerous thing to believe in nonsense. You're giving away your money to the charlatans, you're giving away your emotional security, and sometimes your life.'

As for the JREF's cash prize, nobody has yet passed its preliminary stages. No formal test has ever been carried out. 'It's the simplest challenge in the world and nobody has even come close,' he has said. 'People continue to believe in this claptrap. The level of human gullibility simply amazes me. There are just millions and millions of suckers out there.'

*

He is a record-breaking, toaster-inventing, hieroglyphics-reading, jail-cell-escaping, helicopter-dangling, crook-baiting, doctor-defying, fear-baiting certified genius. No wonder they call him amazing.

Who knows what's behind the inconsistencies in his stories? But let's be charitable. James Randi is now in his eighties. He has been giving interviews for more than six decades. Journalists may make errors and memory may distort. Ages become confused. Narratives become simplified. But he does exhibit one particular self-deception on a rather grander scale: an apparent blindness to his own biases. It is common for Skeptics to claim that they are truly open-minded, even when their behaviour suggests that they are anything but. James Randi, though, takes this phenomenon to a fascinating new level. He even rejects the label 'debunker', insisting that 'I am an investigator. I don't go into things with the attitude that something is not so and that I am going to prove it to be not so. I am willing to be shown that something is true.'

And yet he is routinely merciless with proponents of what he calls 'woo woo'. He ridicules and insults them in public appearances and in blog posts. Those who criticise him often get called 'grubbies'. He gives annual 'Pigasus' awards to the offenders that he judges to be most egregious, explaining to reporters, 'We will give away the million dollars when pigs can fly.' It is incredible that Randi can sincerely hold these two violently opposing positions: trustworthy judge and vicious prosecutor. But that, I suppose, is the human brain.

Randi uses the JREF's challenge as a mode of evidence to indicate that scientists such as Sheldrake are deceiving people; that they don't *really* believe what they claim. 'Why isn't someone like Sheldrake coming after it?' he has asked. 'He stays away from it because, in my estimation, he knows full well that this business of being stared at and the dog that knows its owners are coming home will not pass any test. If it will pass the test I will give him the million dollars. I will give it to him in the middle of Piccadilly Circus, naked.'

Randi has also called the discipline of parapsychology 'a farce and a delusion' and has claimed that 'there is not a single example of a scientific discovery in the field of parapsychology that has been independently replicated. That makes parapsychology absolutely unique in the world of science.' It would be fair to say that these studies are not *consistently* replicated. It would be fair to say that their effect sizes are troublingly small. It might even be fair to say that the theories they test are unlikely to be real. But *this . . .*? Well, it doesn't read like the statement of a man who has a deep and even-handed interest in the subject. It doesn't speak of much 'original thinking', or of genius.

Sheldrake calls him 'a man of very doubtful character indeed'. He says he is a 'thug'. While Randi has, on one occasion, admitted a physical assault on a man who made unpleasant allegations against him ('One shot, to the chops. He went down, and was carried out. *Very* satisfying, I assure you') and threatened another, his aggression is otherwise verbal. 'I want people to consider my point of view,' he has said. 'If they wish to reject it they can crawl back into the traffic and get run over by the next lorry.' Back in the mid-1980s, when he represented CSICOP, he described himself to the *Los Angeles Times* as their 'hit man'. And even today, apparently genuine enquirers to the organisation of which he is president can be treated with a certain Randi-esque intolerance.

One such case involved Sean Connelly, who emailed Randi with a query about the form of 'negotiable bonds' that JREF, at the time, said their challenge money was held in. 'A bond is a certificate of debt,' he explained. 'It does me no good to have $1mil in bonds backed up by companies that can't float the bill.'

Randi responded: 'If that's your problem, I can't take the time to console you. Apply, or go away.' When Connelly politely persisted, Randi passed him to a JREF staff member. Connelly tried to clarify his point, 'If my reward is a bunch of worthless bonds, then it's pointless. Do you see my perspective?'

JREF replied, 'So far, you're just full of shit. That's *our* perspective.'

Unbeknown to Connelly, that JREF operative subsequently posted their exchange on the online forums. Except, in the new version, the words had been altered to, 'So far, sir, you're just full of baloney.' When a forum member defended Connelly, the JREF representative accused her of 'conveniently excluding some vital data'. On his initial contact, he claimed, 'a verification letter from Goldman Sachs was sent immediately to this potential applicant . . . [Connelly] received our respect and courtesy right up until he made it clear that said verification just wasn't good enough for him.'

But this, says Connelly, is not true.

An audiophile journalist also came away from dealings with Randi and the JREF feeling as though he had been treated dishonestly. Michael Fremer said that he could hear the difference between a pair of audio cables that cost thousands of dollars and a standard set. Agreeing that this was a valid claim for the challenge, Randi and Fremer began negotiating the test's parameters. There were three options, one of which involved Fremer testing $7,250 cables made by Pear Anjou, another the journalist's own cables, which cost $16,000. Randi preferred this option, adding, 'but I'll have to consult with my advisors'. Four days later, on a Friday afternoon, Pear Anjou decided that they were unwilling to provide their cables. No matter, thought Fremer. Randi had already expressed a preference for his using his own.

What happened the next day astonished him. That morning – a Saturday – Randi posted on his blog, 'this retreat by [Pear] effectively closes the current challenge, much to the relief of both Fremer and [Pear], of course. Actually, I must admit that this was a rather clever way of squirming out of the huge dilemma in which these two blowhards found themselves.'

Furious, Fremer demanded a retraction. He had not withdrawn from the challenge – the plan was to use his own cables. Publicly, Randi denied that this was ever an option. But privately, according to Fremer, Randi explained that he had been unable to check if his advisers were happy for him to use his own equipment, 'due to the interference of the weekend and to the fact that on Friday I was rushed to the local emergency hospital with what turned out to be a false alarm'. They decided that Fremer's cables could not be used as he might somehow 'tamper' with them. As they had also rejected the only remaining option on a technical point, the challenge was effectively off. But none of this stopped Randi persisting in his accusation that it was Framer who had backed out.

Another extraordinary tale comes from Professor George Vithoulkas of the International Academy of Classical Homeopathy in Athens. In 2003 Vithoulkas decided that he wanted to carry out a test into the efficacy of homeopathy that was first proposed by Skeptic Alec Gindis, and enter it for the Million Dollar Challenge. The two men made Randi a serious proposal: Gindis would sponsor the experiment, which would be arranged by Vithoulkas, and held in a hospital under the guidance of a team of independent scientists. It would involve at least three hundred participants for a minimum of one year.

Something this rigorous and expensive is no easy thing to organise. Randi agreed to waive the usual requirement for a preliminary test, and groups led by Vithoulkas and Gindis began work on the protocol. After months of effort, including lobbying of the Mayor of Athens, Vithoulkas managed to persuade a hospital to cooperate. But they had to act quickly: an election was coming up and the likely new mayor – a doctor – was known to be hostile to alternative medicine. Any delay and permission, surely, would be withdrawn. Then Randi fell ill. He required heart surgery, and would need six months to recover. In an email that he sent on 3 April, Randi insisted that the experiment would 'have to await my return to full function'.

As expected, the incoming mayor appointed a new, more sceptical hospital president and they were forced to start all over again. It took nearly two years, but on 14 May 2008, Vithoulkas's office emailed Randi to say that they believed new permission was likely to be granted and, if it was, 'we have to start the clinical trial immediately. If we will delay, then we will be accused of unfaithfulness and we will not have again the possibility to have a new permission.'

Randi responded on 26 May with a notarised letter, insisting that he would go ahead, but would not be rushed. At the end of July, Vithoulkas excitedly emailed 'great news', claiming that permission from the hospital had been granted. By now, appointees of Randi had travelled to Greece to visit Vithoulkas and the hospital. A team of ten medical doctors and a pharmacist had been recruited, funding had been raised, equipment loaned, participants hired, accommodation found. Vithoulkas estimated the cost of all this to be close to half a million euros. Final issues were discussed over a two-day meeting on the second and third of September.

Then a row broke out. Vithoulkas discovered that, back in March, Randi had written in his blog that 'A major test of homeopathy in Greece has met the expected fate, being abandoned by the homeopathy community.' Randi assured him that this was an error, and appended a correction. But then, in the forums, a JREF staffer noted that they 'have never received an application from Vithoulkas'. Panicking – and already mistakenly suspicious about the timing of Randi's 2006 heart surgery – Vithoulkas urgently sought reassurance from the Skeptic Alec Gindis: 'What is going on, Alec. For God's sake.'

The European Skeptics tried to ease Vithoulkas's fears. They told him that, as the preliminary steps had been waived, no application was necessary. But Vithoulkas, apparently not understanding, replied, 'We need urgently a confirmation from Mr Randi himself that there is such an application.'

And then Randi dramatically intervened.

The next day, on 17 October 2008, with the test finally approaching, Randi posted a blog entitled, 'George Vithoulkas Homeopathy Challenge – Starting Anew'. Randi abruptly withdrew his permission for the team to be waived the requirement for a preliminary test, meaning that they would now have to arrange *two* successful experiments. He also changed the agreed protocol, accused Professor Vithoulkas of arrogance and capriciousness and told him to submit a 'Million Dollar Challenge' application form, 'just as we require EVERYONE to do. Don't contact me personally on this matter. I'll not entertain any arguments or pleas.'

An apoplectic Professor Vithoulkas refused. Accusing Randi of bad faith, he formally withdrew from the project. One of the principal Skeptics involved told me, 'I clearly see that Vithoulkas was trying to find an excuse and quit the test.'

*

ESP experimenters, audiophiles and homeopaths. It is a weird gang. And it gets weirder still with the arrival of two parapsychologists who, in 1972, claimed that they had proved the existence of psychic forces by demonstrating that a man could change the output of a technical device called a magnetometer with the powers of his mind. These scientists, Russell Targ and Harold Puthoff, earned themselves a searing investigation in Randi's most famous and influential book, 1982's *Flim Flam*. In a chapter titled 'The Laurel and Hardy of Psi', Randi reported that the scientist who invented the magnetometer, Professor Arthur Hebard, was present at these tests and had concluded that the changes in the machine could have been created by all sorts of perfectly explicable processes. In the book, Hebard tells Randi that subsequent reports that these tests had been replicated were 'a lie'.

But a journalist named Scott Rogo has spoken with Professor Hebard more recently. Hebard, he said, disputed several of Randi's claims, and was 'very annoyed' by them. This, I realise, is salient turf. If it is true that Randi lied about Hebard in *Flim Flam*, then perhaps we can hand a definitive point to Sheldrake. Maybe Hebard will confirm the Skeptic's betrayal. After all, I think, if his views have been distorted to such an extent, he must *hate* Randi.

'I think Randi's marvellous,' Hebard tells me. 'I think very

343

highly of him indeed. And I certainly agree in every way that Targ and Puthoff didn't prove anything. I was amazed at how the experiment got out of control.'

'And you said that this idea that it had been replicated was a lie?'

'There was no repetition of the experiment at all,' he says.

'Well, that's that cleared up, then,' I say.

'I don't imagine myself using the word "lie", though. I've never used the word. I'm a scientist. But I don't believe that James Randi said that *I* said that's "a lie" either.'

In fact, he does. At one point, Randi has Hebard calling an account of the test 'outright lies from a sensationalist'. At another, Randi reports himself asking, 'You mean [the test] was misrepresented?' And Hebard replies, 'It's a lie. You can say it any way you want, but that's what I call a lie.'

'Well, I'm sorry that appears in Randi's words,' Hebard tells me. 'But I don't think I would have said that to anybody.'

Later, in the same chapter, Randi writes about Targ and Puthoff's experiments with his arch-enemy, the spoon-bender Uri Geller. The parapsychologists arranged for a film to be made of Geller somehow 'reading' the face of a die that had been sealed in a box. Randi said that this film was a 'highly deceptive' re-enactment, adding that in a 'masterpiece of evasion and license' they had 'appended to it – without his knowledge or permission – the name of Zev Pressman', a professional photographer. Pressman, says Randi, was not even present for these tests: 'he had gone home for the day . . . Pressman knew nothing about most of what happened under his name, and he disagreed with the part that he did know about.'

Zev Pressman has since passed away. But it is rumoured that much of this is untrue. Apparently, two signed statements by the photographer confirm this, and are in the possession of

Geller biographer, and perhaps the world's most famous hunter of poltergeists, Guy Lyon Playfair.

It is a dull July afternoon when I arrive at Playfair's grand high-ceilinged flat, just off the high street in London's Earl's Court. Playfair, now in his eighties, lets me into his shadowy lobby. By his telephone, he has taped a headline from an article: 'Unbelievable but True: Communication with the "Dead" and with Dwellers in Other Worlds via Computers and the Telephone Answering Machine'. Underneath, he has written in Biro: 'GO AHEAD'. Attached to the wall adjacent to his door is a yellowing newspaper poster from the *Enfield Gazette*: 'BRITAIN'S MOST HAUNTED HOUSE – amazing inside story'. It is a souvenir from the Enfield Poltergeist case that took place in 1977 and 1978, which Playfair investigated and wrote of in his classic *This House Is Haunted*.

I follow his slow passage into the lounge, where there is a PC, shelves filled with rocks and statues and old photographs of men with black beards and top hats and faraway eyes, books on psychic healing, twin telepathy and British birdsong and a Roland keyboard with a towel draped over it. A spoon, bent by Uri Geller, hovers in a plastic box that is screwed to the wall.

I sit for a while on a low sofa, while he rummages for his 'Randi file'.

'Are the Pressman statements in here?' I ask when he returns and lays a thick stack of documents on the coffee table in front of me. This is the evidence that Playfair has spent three decades gathering against Randi.

'Should be, yes.'

I sift through the sheets, which are faded and riven with fine crows-feet creases around the staples. There are copies of *FATE* magazine ('The World's Mysteries Explored'), manuscript pages from one of Playfair's books, *The Geller Effect*, and a typewritten sheet containing a blurry illustration and a caption: 'James Runty and his notorious DOGPLOP gang, shown here taking over a train'.

I sigh and pick up another tattered sheet.

'That is the clipping from 1974 when he got stuck in the safe in Toronto,' says Playfair proudly. 'It's very bad quality.'

I hold it close, and read what I can.

'RANDI – THE HOUDINI WHO DIDN'T. The Amazing Randi, magician by trade, almost died of embarrassment yesterday – not to mention a lack of oxygen – while bound and locked in *The Sun*'s office safe. The world-famous magician was pulled unconscious from the safe nine minutes and thirty five seconds after he entered it while horrified staffers looked on . . . Suddenly from inside, came the shout: 'Oh, oh . . . help me . . . get a drill . . . hurry it up . . .'

'You know,' says Playfair, 'he was a complete flop as a magician.'

'. . . Randi,' the article continues, 'looks more like a pleasant but absent-minded professor than the elite magician that he is.'

I say nothing, pushing the document back in the file. I just need to find the Pressman statements.

'That's an interesting case,' says Playfair, as I glance at the front page of another news-sheet. 'Possibly worth looking into . . .?'

The magazine is called *Saucer Smear*. It is the 'Official publication of the saucer & unexplained celestial events research society'. It advertises itself as, 'SHOCKINGLY CLOSE TO THE TRUTH!'

'Possibly,' I say, slipping it back in.

I get to the end of the file. There are no statements from Zev Pressman.

'It's not much, is it?' I say.

There is a silence.

'I'll give you an example of the kind of thing Randi gets up to,' he says. 'It was an interview with a Japanese magazine in 1989, claiming that Wilbur Franklin, the scientist who studied Uri, had killed himself by shooting himself in the head because Randi had exposed him for being a trickster. It was pure invention. Uri filed a lawsuit against him.'

'Didn't Randi say that he had been mistranslated, though?'

'I'm sure that's what he *said* . . .'

'Well, do you have the clipping?'

'I don't have the original because it never came out in English.'

I stand up to leave.

'Well, if the Pressman thing happens to turn up,' I say, 'will you post it?'

'You know,' says Playfair, 'Montague Keen kept a big file on Randi.'

'Did he?'

'Oh, yes,' he says. 'He had a huge falling out with him at a TV studio. I was there.'

'Really?'

'Oh, yes. Randi said something or other that was a lot of rubbish. It was pretty vicious.'

'What did he say?'

'I couldn't hear.'

'Oh.'

I watch for a while as he tries to recall what happened.

'No,' he says, glancing towards the window. 'I can't remember.'

'Do you think Montague Keen would remember? Do you think he'd let me see his Randi file?'

'Monty's dead.'

'Right.'

'But you could call his widow, Veronica. I'm sure she'd accommodate you.'

As soon as I get home, I call Veronica Keen.

'Randi!' she booms out in her Irish accent, the instant I mention his name. 'Oh, my God! Poor man. You don't dare disagree with Randi. We were in the TV studio, Monty and I, and Randi came towards me. I smiled at him and I said, "You're a fraud, aren't you, Mr Randi?" He went stark raving bananas. Oh, Jesus, it was fantastic.'

'How did Randi respond?'

'I can't remember. It will be in the file. But he wrote an article in which I was supposed to be huge and fat and all the rest of it. Monty said, "By the way, Randi will never ever . . .", I can't remember the exact words. It's all in the file. Someone has helped me tidy up and it's right up near the ceiling. I can't get up there.'

'Maybe I can come and have a look?'

'Did you know Monty has materialised? Several times. He actually materialised at a public seance. He walked down the whole length of the place and kissed me. People went bananas.'

'That sounds wonderful,' I say.

'Oh, I tell you, my life is so amazing. Oh, my God. Monty was the most amazing man. He is bringing too much information. He says that Jesus did exist but he was an Egyptian prince. The Joseph and Mary bit is – ' she pauses, lowers her voice – 'excuse me, but there's a word I've got used to using since Monty died . . . *bullshit*.'

'Veronica!'

'I know. My grandchildren are horrified.'

'Can I see you on Monday, then? For the Randi file?'

'I'll pick you up from the station,' she says.

'Well, I hope you have a good weekend.'

'Oh, it'll be lovely,' she says. 'I'm going to an ancient portal.'

'That'll be fun.'

'I've got a portal here anyway,' she adds, with an audible shrug.

'Where? In your house?'

'In the dining room.'

'Under the table?'

'No! It's the room.'

'Where does it take you?'

'It's a portal that links you to the other world.'

'Wow!'

'Ah, the things that happen in this life, my boy.'

That weekend, I track down Randi's account of his meeting with Veronica Keen. In his JREF newsletter of 15 August 2003, Randi described what happened after the filming of a British TV show, *The Ultimate Psychic Challenge*. 'This experience demonstrated for me once more just how angry, frantic, and hateful the believers in life-after-death can be,' he wrote, describing 'a direct affront, a rude insult, and an uncalled-for accusation from a very obese, unattractive woman coming from the studio audience, a person who had loudly shouted out abuse to me all during the taping. Passing me in the hall-way, she stabbed her finger at me, her face red and contorted with hatred. "Mr Randi, you're a fake and a fraud!" she screeched. I calmly said to her in my best Churchillian tone, "Madam, you are ugly, but I can reform."'

I also found a rebuttal from Veronica's deceased partner, Montague Keen ('a brilliant psychic researcher, journalist, agricultural administrator, magazine editor and farmer'). 'I am sure this is how Mr Randi would like to remember the episode,' Keen wrote. 'But I was alongside the lady at the time, and observed what went on . . . [she] smiled at Mr Randi and said quite politely but firmly, with no finger stabbing, and to his obvious astonishment, "Mr Randi, you're a fraud," whereupon he staggered back and stammered, "And you, you, you, you're ugly," to which the lady responded as he disappeared backwards through the double doors, "But at least I'm honest."'

That Monday, Veronica picks me up in her small red car from outside Totteridge and Whetstone tube station in north London. She is seventy-four and un-obese, with coiffed and dyed strawberry blonde hair, scarlet lipstick and a circular crystal on a gold chain around her neck.

'This is where John Mack died,' she says, idly, as she turns left on a suburban street on the way to her house. 'Knocked off his bike, poor man.'

I thought I must have mis-heard her.

'Who?'

'John Mack, you know. The Harvard professor.'

'*You knew John Mack?*'

'Oh, my God, yes. He was staying with us when he died. He always stayed with us when he was in London.'

I gaze though the rear window at the place where this great heretic came to the end of his own fantastic journey of belief, just as I am coming to the end of mine. I might have once thought this coincidence to be haunted with salience. But I don't. Not any more.

'Harvard tried to hound him out of his position,' I said.

'Well,' she says. 'It was the American government who were behind it.'

'Is that what John Mack said?'

'Yes.'

An emotional part of me, I realise, is still yearning to discover that Mack wasn't crazy.

'But he said that *after* he died?' I say, hopefully.

'No, no. When he was alive. He used to sit and talk to Monty and I. The pressure they put on him was huge. It was a cover-up. The American government didn't want it all exposed. He said to me, "I couldn't stop what I was doing. I had to do it."'

We park at a grassy verge in a pretty road and Veronica leads me into her lounge. It is a portrait of ordinariness, a still life of a perfectly happy elderly woman in middle-class Britain. There is a polite-sized television and family photographs and a coffee table and a box of pink tissues. There are net curtains and coasters and a shelf of VHS videos. There is a magazine that has slipped from the sofa arm onto the soft carpet. As I sit in the small dining area I ask what kind of information Monty usually imparts.

'Monty is one of a team of twelve on the other side,' she says, calling through from the kitchen, where she is unboxing a Mr Kipling strawberry sponge cake. 'They're working on a project.'

'Is John Mack one of the twelve?'

'John isn't. The only one I recognised was Einstein.'

'And what have they told you?'

She brings the plated cake through, and two mugs of tea.

'The whole thing is corrupt,' she tells me. 'All the music. Lady Gaga, will.i.am, Jay-Z. You get subliminal messages.'

'Will.i.am?' I say.

'Wake up!' she says. 'I said this to the young man next door and he said, "Oh, come on." Then, his friend was doing the security up at the O_2. The two of them ended up having a cup of coffee with the BBC engineers. And the boy next door was laughing saying, "My elderly neighbour says all this," and the BBC fella says, "Yeah, do you want to hear it?" And in the music was "kill, killing is good, kill, murder, carry knives, you'll feel big". Right through the music! It's going straight into the heads of the kids! And he came to me the next day and he said, "I owe you an apology." And I said, "What for?" And he said, "For what I've done."'

When we've finished our cake, Veronica leads me out of the portal and through to the cramped office that used to be Monty's domain. There are cases of cassette tapes, piles of books and a cluttered desk top with a strange pot next to a crumpled tissue. 'Those are Monty's ashes. He hates this place being so untidy. Do you see those bells on the cabinet? They were on top of the pyramids in Egypt.'

I start at a low shelf pulling out box file after box file. I have to find the Randi archive. As well as the Pressman documents, there could be all sorts of lost evidence in there, perhaps going back decades. Veronica watches me at work, from the doorway.

'Monty started telling us about Obama,' she says. 'He's a puppet of the Illuminati. And the Queen's got her case packed. She's ready to run.'

'Why?' I ask, pulling out another dusty box file.

'She's the head of the Illuminati. Remember when Diana died? Did that woman shed a tear? She stood there cold as ice.'

'With her lizard eyes,' I mutter, absentmindedly, as I check another.

'You've got it!' she says delightedly. 'They have a huge place in Colorado, you know. An underground place. It has every luxury money can buy and if you go within fifteen miles of it you're dead.'

Another file. Nothing. Another file. Nothing. Not a sign of Randi. Not a sign of Pressman. Not a sign, anywhere.

'Do you have any idea *at all* where this file might be?'

'Then suddenly the Queen and Obama were visiting Ireland. And Monty warned us – she was going back to the place where all the Irish kings and queens were crowned, to tap her left foot three times and reclaim it. But – ' she laughs triumphantly – 'a friend and I got there before her.'

'And what did you do?'

'We tapped first!' she says with a cackle. 'We reclaimed Ireland!'

'That's a valuable service you've provided,' I say, climbing gingerly on a wheely-chair to reach the top shelf.

'Oh, it's not the only thing we've done,' she adds, with a coquettish giggle.

An hour into the search, my patience is drying out.

'Well, I know they're here because Monty kept everything,' says Veronica.

I wipe my hands down my trousers and rub my eyes, which are itchy and tired.

'Well, could you contact him then?' I ask, thinly. 'Could you ask him where they are?'

Veronica looks away.

'It doesn't work like that. He speaks to me when he wants to.'

'But you've got a bloody *portal*,' I snap.

'The problem is, I'm *so* exhausted.'

Veronica yawns theatrically as I open another box to find a long correspondence with a famous parapsychologist from the University of Arizona – Professor Gary Schwartz.

'Oh, Schwartz,' she says dismissively, fingering her crystal. 'He had his run-ins with Randi. But watch out. Schwartz has an evil mind.'

'You're not saying that he's involved with the Illuminati, too?'

'He's a Jew and a scientist. Does that answer your question?'

And with that, I decide to go home.

*

I think I have decided to give up. These Pressman documents probably don't exist. The many decades' worth of amassed evidence from Guy Lyon Playfair – a friend of and believer in Uri Geller – was thin, sometimes lurid and often mean-spirited. And when you have Richard Dawkins on one side of an argument and Veronica Keen on the other, you . . . well . . . I don't even know how to finish that sentence.

It is not just Veronica Keen that has made me concerned about the kinds of people who criticise Randi. Some of the past applicants of the Million Dollar Challenge include a man named Colin who says he can cause a tone to sound by 'shooting energy out of his eyeballs', a 'human magnet' who can lift a fridge with his chest and a woman who can 'make people urinate themselves with the power of her mind'.

It is also impossible to ignore the fact that Sheldrake's motives for criticising Randi might be suspiciously emotional. He has, after all, been personally attacked by all of the worshipful satellites that exalt Randi. Read the list – they are all there. It was *Nature's* Sir John Maddox who wrote the editorial that asked if his was a 'book for burning'. Professor Wiseman, a JREF adviser, said that his work is 'messy' and debased by errors. Steven Novella has condemned his theory as 'made-up mystical BS that has no scientific basis'. Professor Dawkins has accused him of being 'prepared to believe almost anything' and dismissed his claims against him as 'outrageous and defamatory'.

Besides all of that, I have been feeling increasingly uneasy about this search. I keep hearing this voice, this accusing phantom, telling me that I am concocting a highly partial account. And I am! I have been looking for evidence that James Randi is a liar. The voice witheringly insists what I have discovered is no more than biographical memory slips and partial accounts from biased woo-woo proponents. It's just what you would expect of a fighting man who has been busy making enemies since before I was born.

And there is no doubt that Randi has acted heroically. Among his most brilliant and famous debunkings are those involving 'faith healers'. Wealthy televangelist Peter Popoff, for instance, was exposed after an investigation that took months. Randi ultimately forced him to publicly admit that he was fed information about the illnesses of audience members via an earpiece. Afterwards, Popoff went bankrupt. It is not for nothing that Professor Chris French, who as well as once editing *The Skeptic* magazine teaches anomalistic psychology at the University of London, says that Randi's material is 'pure gold' for his class and that 'the message is think for yourselves, question everything.' And we shouldn't forget, either, that Randi was once awarded a prestigious MacArthur 'genius grant' of $272,000.

But that, in turn, reminds me of how he told *The Times*, 'A bunch of Nobel Prize winners and other people I really respect have always said the work I do was important, but it was always private. Now it's official.' Then I remember how he told the *Washington Post* that UK scientists initially declared the 'Piltdown Man' fraud to be true because 'Britain always wanted to be the source of all life and culture, but they needed an early artefact that the public was willing to accept.' I recall how he once explained that drugs should be legalised because 'the principle of Survival of the Fittest would draconically prove itself,' as people who decided to use them 'would simply do so and die' and that 'any weeping and wailing over the Poor Little Kids who would perish' were 'crocodile tears, in my opinion'.

And the voice says, 'Those are all reasons why you are personally offended by him. They have nothing to do with his honesty.'

And a replying phantom says, 'This is true. But Randi has also said that his goal is to "Get people thinking. Have them ask questions. Don't believe me any more than you believe these people who make these claims. I'm making a claim too. It may or may not be true. Investigate it."'

And when I receive an unexpected package from Guy Lyon Playfair, I think, well, all right, then.

It is the Pressman documents, signed, photocopied and folded neatly. The photographer had written, 'Randi's book *Flim Flam* has me appearing to be critical of the manner in which the Uri Geller experiments were conducted. Nothing could be further from the truth.' He even disputes Randi's central allegation about his work. 'Each scene has been taken from film footage made during actual experiments; nothing has been restaged.'

Curious about the correspondence that I glimpsed at Veronica Keen's house, I decide to contact Professor Gary Schwartz, the parapsychologist who she told me was a member of the Illuminati. She may have been wrong about that, but she was certainly right that he had a tale to tell about Randi.

Schwartz – another unhappy recipient of a 'Pigasus award' – tells of an attempt made by Randi to acquire the raw data of his famous experiments involving psychics. He alleges that Randi wrote to an organisation associated with the University of Arizona, where he is based, and claimed that an expert committee would examine the work and, if it was shown to be sound, a one million dollar 'gift' would be awarded.

Curious officials passed the letter to Schwartz, who was immediately suspicious of the four names that Randi had listed as being members of his independent committee. 'I knew one of them personally,' Schwartz tells me. 'And I found it hard to believe that he would be involved. So I contacted him.' Schwartz's friend, a Dr Stanley Krippner, said he had not, in fact, agreed to serve with Randi. Schwartz informed the officials that Randi was dubiously misrepresenting his position. They declined his offer.

As usual, Randi took to the Internet to protest. He accused the university of protecting Schwartz and defended his Million Dollar Challenge as 'above reproach'.

But then a woman named Pam Blizzard reported Schwartz's version of what happened. Once again, Randi fought back in his blog. 'Either [Pam] is a blatant liar, or Schwartz has mis-represented the situation,' he wrote.' All four of those persons have agreed to be listed and to serve on the committee. Here's a challenge: If Pam Blizzard will identify this proposed person – who I notice is not named! – and provide the statement in which he said that if he had been contacted by me and asked to serve, he would have declined, I'll push a peanut across Times Square with my nose, naked. How can she pass up that offer? Pam, you're a liar. Unless, that is, Dr Schwartz – or someone claiming to be Schwartz – did make such a statement, in which case he is the guilty party. Inescapably, someone here is lying. It is not I. What's your response, Pam? Who is it, and where's the evidence? Derived from Tarot cards? Or just a plain old LIE?' /

It seems a simple matter to check. So I contact Dr Krippner and ask if he agreed to be on Randi's committee. His response came swiftly. 'No, I had not agreed.' Despite the fact that the accusation – and the naked peanut promise – remains on his blog as I write this, Krippner claims that Randi has since privately admitted his 'mistake'.

When Rupert Sheldrake sends me evidence of the apparently damning encounter that Randi had written about on his blog, I decide to stop searching. I have to. After all, I have requested a two-hour interview with the man himself, covering his life, his arguments and beliefs. It is now only days away.

*

After tangles with fortune tellers and modern-day witches, I have travelled far up the Yellow Brick Road (well, the yellow-pink pavement that leads from my hotel) to the South Point Hotel and Casino, in that Emerald City of the twenty-first century, Las Vegas. I am off to meet the wizard who hosts the annual 'The Amazing Meeting'. Or at least I will, just as soon as I collect my media pass. In front of me, in the queue, a woman is loudly discussing an argument that she recently had with her religious husband.

'And I told him, "Honey, I love you, but me and you are gonna have an education session."'

'What religion is your husband?' asked her associate.

'Woo,' she said. 'Straight up woo. And you know what he said to me? He said, "Where did all this *passion* come from?" And I said, "Truth. I mean, really."' She narrowed her eyes. 'Straight up truth.'

Around sixteen hundred people are gathered here for the planet's largest Skeptics' event. Over the next four days, all the superstars will be present – Randi, Dawkins, Wiseman, Novella, Penn and Teller – to speak, revel and enjoy workshops on everything from 'Problems in Paranormal Investigation' ('Skeptical investigators reveal the mistakes paranormal investigators make in their work') to 'Raising Skeptics' ('How can we inspire children to share our skeptical worldview without betraying our core values as free thinkers?'). There is a range of stylishly designed T-shirts, on one: 'TEAM RANDI'; another a pastiche of the wartime recruiting poster in which Randi is demanding, 'I Want You! For Science & Skepticism'; another a cartoon of Randi confronting Uri Geller and the psychic

Sylvia Browne with the simple word 'Debunk!' There are elasticated Randi beards, a stall selling 'Jewellery for Smart People' and another from which the Secular Student Alliance are raising funds, with a portentous warning from Richard Dawkins: 'The Secular Student Alliance is the future. Or it better had be, if there is to be a future worth having.' The JREF is asking for money too, with a leaflet on which words such as 'homeopathy, 'ghost hunters' and 'ear candles' crowd a plaintive cry of horror, 'WE'RE SURROUNDED!'.

Beneath us are the tourists and the gamblers who have somehow wandered as far as the South Point, and away from the heart of the world's most grotesque city. They are perched on stools, lost in a cosy stun of caffeine, donuts and dead repetition, of bleeps and flashes and calamitous odds. From what I can gather, these happily irrational souls seem rather perplexed by the pale army of angry brains that have gathered in their midst. As I was queuing for coffee earlier, I heard a barista confidently explain to a customer, 'Skeptics. They're like conspiracy theorists.'

Over the weeks that I have been researching him, I have somehow gained the impression that Randi has been old for most of the twentieth century. But when I do finally see him moving towards me down a corridor, it is a shock. He walks slowly, with a black stick and has that slightly caved-in look that the truly aged sometimes develop. When he sits beside me in the huge conference hall, which is empty bar one or two of his associates who remain present for the interview, I notice how soft and fragile his skin appears. He wears thick-soled black shoes, a suit of dark navy and a shirt of pale blue. On his lapel, there is a silver Pigasus badge. His beard, long but trimmed neatly, falls down his front like a hairy bib. It is a magnificent display of hominin peacockery. The eyes are the thing, though. They are sharp and smart and whip about the place, active, clever, canny.

'I was one of those unfortunate child prodigies,' he tells me. 'I say "unfortunate" because it was not a happy part of my young life. I didn't develop any sort of a peer group.'

I ask if, during the years that he attended school, there were any difficulties in the lessons.

'There were no difficulties,' he says. 'It was just I knew all the answers. I would sleep in the classroom. If they ever woke me up and asked me, I'd have the answer. It began to dawn on them that I was well ahead in just about everything. Geography, history, science, mathematics. I was already into differential integral calculus.'

'At *twelve*?'

'It wasn't difficult for me. It was a delight.'

He was a lonely youngster, he says, because as a pre-pubescent 'genius or near genius' he could only mix with people who were at university – and they 'were a little puzzled by the fact that I was that far ahead'.

In 1986 Randi's sister Angela told a Canadian reporter that, because 'the family couldn't really understand him', he was taken to Toronto General Hospital for psychological testing.

'I had all kinds of emotional problems,' he explains. 'I couldn't relate to adults and certainly, concerning my sexual mores and such, I didn't have any kids that I could discuss this with and my parents weren't very helpful in that respect.'

It was only recently, in 2010, that Randi publicly came out as gay. He was aware of his sexuality from an early age, he says, and growing up with this secret in the 1930s was 'very, very difficult. Impossible. My parents could never know about it.'

All of which makes me wonder about the nature of these

'emotional problems' that sent him to hospital. Did he feel a lot of anger?

'Yes,' he says. 'A typical amount of anger and dismay with people who didn't understand me and I couldn't go to them and tell them *why* they didn't understand me.' He says that he felt 'just generally grumpy about the whole thing', and 'anger towards society in general'.

All this contributed to a relationship with his parents that was, he says, 'very stormy. I didn't really speak to my father at all. We only spoke seriously twice in our lives. I remember both of them almost word for word.'

'What were they?'

'I don't recall one of them.'

'Can you tell me about the other one?'

'It was about sex, as a matter of fact. He had doubts about my sexuality. He tried to have a talk about it and I fluffed it all off and got out of it somehow. I don't remember the exact defence. But it was awkward,' he says with a nod. 'It was awkward.'

He claims that he didn't take any exams at school, and then a little later says that he did. (It is not the only time he seems to abruptly contradict himself. At one point he manages to do so within the same sentence: 'I didn't go to grade school at all, I went to the first few grades of grade school.') He recites the tale I have heard before, of his walking out of his English test in disgust at the question. Then he tells another, similar story, about a science exam that asked a question about Galileo. 'I knew that the person who had made up the examination was an idiot,' he says. 'I just snorted and walked out of the room.'

'And so you didn't go to university?'

'No, but I've lectured for the leading universities around the world.'

His schoolboy love of magic was, he says, partly motivated

361

by a desire to find a way out of isolation. 'I could succeed at this,' he explains. 'I didn't like hockey or baseball or any of those things, but this was a way that I could outdo the rest of my classmates.' Which strikes me later as a curious comment in the light of his insistence that he was already outdoing them, apparently on every subject that they were studying.

Our conversation soon arrives, inevitably, at Uri Geller. I ask about the lawsuit to which Guy Lyon Playfair referred. It came about, in part, because Randi was quoted in a Japanese magazine as having said that a scientist named Wilbur Franklin, who believed in Geller's psychic powers, shot himself when he realised that they weren't real. In fact, Franklin died of natural causes. But Randi denies ever saying this.

'No,' he says. 'The Japanese reporter spoke no English. He had a translator with him, an American, and that's not a very satisfactory way to do an interview.'

'So it was a translation mistake?'

'It was, essentially, a translation mistake.'

But there is a problem with this account. I have found a second interview from the same period, published in the *Toronto Star* in 1986, which quotes Randi as saying, 'One scientist, a metallurgist, wrote a paper backing Geller's claims that he could bend metal. The scientist shot himself after I showed him how the key bending trick was done.'

'Oh, no. No no no,' he says. 'A Canadian journalist *said* that I said this. There's a big difference.'

'So you didn't say it?'

'No,' he says, tetchily. He claims that what he actually said of Franklin's paper was 'that is what we call shooting yourself in the foot'.

He has offered this explanation in the past – but that time, it was for the Japanese quote.

'So it was just a coincidence that the same error happened in Toronto *and* Japan?' I say.

'Yes,' he replies. 'But it happened.'

It was another interview, years later, that triggered the Sheldrake-related 'story that doesn't go anywhere' that Randi has written of in his blog. In fact, the story *does* go somewhere, and it is a not a good place for the patron saint of the Skeptics.

It began when Sheldrake read an interview in *Dog World* magazine which mentioned his psychic dog tests and which quoted Randi: 'We at JREF have tested these claims. They fail.' When Sheldrake wrote to Randi, asking for details of these tests, he was twice ignored. It was only after he took his appeal to others at the JREF that Randi sent an email explaining that, regretfully, he couldn't supply the data, because it got washed away in a flood and that the dogs in question are now in Mexico and their owner was 'tragically killed last year in a dreadful accident'. Randi ended his note with a graceful touch. 'I over-stated my case for doubting the reality of dog ESP based on the small amount of data I obtained. It was rash and improper of me to do so. I apologise sincerely.'

But he subsequently went online and *attacked* Sheldrake. Of his own failure to provide the data, he wrote, 'A search of our site would have supplied [Sheldrake] with all the details he could possibly wish. Alternately, I could have supplied them, if only he had issued a request. That's what we do at the JREF.'

When I ask Randi about his dog tests, he is dismissive, 'That was a long time ago. What specific experiments are you referring to?'

'The ones you told *Dog World* you had done. In New York. The owner was killed, the dogs are in Mexico and you lost the files in a flood.'

'That was one of the hurricane floods,' he says nodding.

'So what prompted these tests?'

'I must admit to you that I don't recall having said that these tests were even done. But I'm willing to see the evidence for it.'

'I have these emails.'

'Oh.'

When I ask for a second time what prompted him to do these tests, his memory stages a sudden recovery. 'Curiosity,' he says. 'I'm an experimenter.' He remembers the name of the dog and its breed and that the experiment was 'very informal. I napped most of the time.'

When I press him about his treatment of Sheldrake, he insists that he didn't lie because when he made the offer to send the information, the data hadn't yet been lost. But he says that they were swept away in Hurricane Wilma, which happened in 2005 – four years *before* he stated that the data was available. And in the email, he tells Sheldrake a different story still – that the flood took place in 1998.

Nevertheless, we move on. I tell Randi about Hebard, the professor who was surprised to read in *Flim Flam* that he had called someone a 'liar'. 'Hebard told me he didn't say that,' I note.

'I don't know that he did, or not,' says Randi. 'That's the way I recall it.'

'What about Zev Pressman, the photographer who signed an affidavit saying that you lied about him?'

'This is stuff I really have to look into,' he says.

Fair enough. It was a long time ago. More recent, though, was the incident in which Randi falsely claimed that Dr Krippner had agreed to be on his committee, accused someone who accurately reflected the case of being a liar, and then offered to push a peanut naked across Times Square if he could be shown to be wrong.

'Well, that was perhaps a mistake of mine,' he admits.

'You called this woman a liar,' I say. 'But you were the one who was telling the lie.'

'I don't know,' he says. 'I'd have to look over the whole sequence.'

'Might you have been telling a lie?'

He turns a little on his seat.

'I'm not denying it,' he says. 'I'm not denying it.'

I move along to the 2005 audiophile incident, when Randi accused Michael Fremer of backing out of his cable challenge when the appearance, at least, was that the JREF had triggered the process's collapse by denying all available options. 'The JREF has not backed out,' he says. 'That is not the case at all.'

'What about the Greek homeopath?'

'Vithoulkas,' he nods.

Randi tells me that he approved the test's protocol in 2006 and then, before I can continue listing the events as I have been led to understand them, he says, 'Let me interrupt you. Vithoulkas has never made an application for the JREF prize. That is the first rule. He will not do that and he says he does-n't have to because he's too important.'

'That's not true,' I say. 'You agreed with his protocol, you waived the pilot study and you told him the test could go ahead.'

'But he didn't sign the document,' he says. 'They backed out when they would not fill out the form.'

'But you and your team had already agreed the protocol,' I say.

Suddenly, Randi is furious.

'We agreed with the protocol, yes!' he shouts. 'Okay! Now you sign the document and we'll go ahead with it. But he will *not sign the document*.'

'They were ready to go, and you wrote to them and said everything was starting from scratch.'

'I decided to tell them that until we received the application forms signed they were not applicants.'

'Why do you need a signature on a document after five years, just when everything was ready to go?'

'I need it! That's the rules! Vithoulkas says he's too important to do it.'

'That's not what he's saying.'

'Oh,' he says, sarcastically. 'That's not what he's *saying*.'

Of course, Vithoulkas and the team of European Skeptics spent half a decade trying to make this experiment happen. They lobbied politicians, negotiated terms and protocols, raised funds, recovered repeatedly after setbacks and fallings-out and bitter compromises. Then, just as it was about to happen, Randi insisted on a successful pilot study and changed the protocol. I ask Randi, 'Can't you see why he is furious?'

'Oh, I can see why he's furious.'

'So why did you change your mind at the last minute, just when they were ready to go?'

'He won't sign the fucking document! Will you get that through your skull? He wants out of it and that's the way he'll get out of it. When Vithoulkas signs the document we will go ahead with the test as agreed. End of discussion. I will not talk about it any more.'

I begin to feel as if I am ambushing Randi. Perhaps it is his age, but it almost feels as if I am committing some sort of violence upon him. He deserves some air. So I move on to an area which I believe that he will find easier to discuss, and presumably dismiss. I quote some of his comments that have concerned me, about his wish for drugs to be legalised so that users will kill themselves.

But, to my surprise, he does not dismiss them. Not even slightly.

'I think exactly the same thing about smoking,' he says

'They should be allowed to smoke themselves to death and die.'

'These are quite extreme views,' I say.

'I don't think so.'

'But it's social Darwinism.'

'The survival of the fittest, yes,' he says, approvingly. 'The strong survive.'

'But this is the foundation of fascism.'

'Oh yes, yes,' he says, perfectly satisfied. 'It could be inferred that way, yes. I think people should be allowed to do themselves in.'

'These are very right-wing views.'

'I don't look at them that way,' he says. 'I'm a believer in social Darwinism. Not in every case. I would do anything to stop a twelve-year-old kid from doing it. Sincerely. But in general, I think that Darwinism, survival of the fittest, should be allowed to act itself out. As long as it doesn't interfere with me and other sensible, rational people who could be affected by it. Innocent people, in other words. These are not innocent people. These are stupid people. And if they can't survive, they don't have the IQ, don't have the thinking power to be able to survive, it's unfortunate; I would hate to see it happen, but at the same time, it would clear the air. We would be free of a lot of the plagues that we presently suffer from. I think that people with mental aberrations who have family histories of inherited diseases and such, that something should be done seriously to educate them to prevent them from procreating. I think they should be gathered together in a suitable place and have it demonstrated for them what their procreation would mean for the human race. It would be very harmful. But I don't see any attempt to do that because everyone has the right to do stupid things. And I suppose they do,' he concedes. 'To a certain extent.'

As I sit, quietly stunned, in the nearly empty Las Vegas conference hall, I still feel as if we haven't quite exhausted the question that I first sought to answer. Is James Randi a liar? I begin gently, by telling him that my research has painted a picture of a clever man who is often right, but who has a certain element to his personality, which leads him to overstate.

'Oh, I agree,' he says.

'And sometimes lie. Get carried away.'

'Oh, I agree. No question of that. I don't know whether the lies are conscious lies all the time,' he says. 'But there can be untruths.'

*

During our conversation, I asked Randi if he has ever, in his life, changed his position on anything due to an examination of the evidence. After a long silence, he said, 'That's a good question. I have had a few surprises along the way that got my attention rather sharply.'

'What were these?' I asked.

He thought again, for some time.

'Oh, some magic trick that I decided on the modus operandi.'

'Just the way a magic trick was done?'

'Yeah.'

'So you've never been wrong about anything significant?'

'In regard to the Skeptical movement and my work . . .' There was another stretched and chewing pause. He conferred with his partner, to see if he had any ideas. 'No. Nothing occurs to me at the moment.'

I had thought that this alone condemned the great 'free-thinking' Skeptic. After all, how free can the mind be that has never travelled an inch? But, on reflection, I now believe that there is at least some indication that he is capable of heading

368

to unwelcome places when compelled to do so by the evidence. It is the brave admission of dishonesty that he gave this afternoon.

There are two narratives told of James Randi. In the heroic version, he is a fearless and genius free-thinker, a messiah of truth. The villain's tale speaks of a closed-minded bully and a liar. Which is correct? The answer, of course, is neither. Because they are stories, and stories are never true.

EPILOGUE

The Hero-Maker

I left Alice Springs in the early morning, dropped off the tarmac on the outskirts of town and drove north-west for six hours into the Australian Central Desert. Everywhere, it seemed, there was death. I saw skeletal kangaroos, the picked remains of starved calves, the upturned shells of cars, distant abandoned out-stations and, every now and then, a lonely white cross that had been planted in the dirt. The west Macdonnell Ranges behind me were once higher than the Himalayas, but eight hundred million years of weather have reduced them to low, crumbling bluffs. Dead animals, dead mountains, dead earth; from the bloodwood trees and the ghost gums to Mount Unapproachable and the Sandy Blight Road, the soul of this landscape is revealed in the way that it has been christened by its early white explorers. It is a place of murderous beauty: a wasteland of spiny shrubs, barren rivers and psychotic centigrades.

After six hours, I neared the remote community of Yuendumu. Alcohol is forbidden there and the town's limits were forewarned by a meteorite-shower of beer cans and broken stubby glass that had been thrown from car windows. A little over eight hundred men, women and children live in Yuendumu – it is mostly Warlpiri and Anmatyerr people who dwell in the forlorn government breeze-block houses. Its few dusty streets were scattered with abandoned cookers and snapped CDs and hounded by delinquent dogs that yelped and chased and fought. An atmosphere of dolorous stillness held the place. The violent jags of a shouting woman interrupted the silence every now and then. A derelict petrol pump rusted in the heat.

At the art centre, an old man with yellowish curly hair, oil-stained jeans and a pale stetson hat rattled open the wire gate. A pack of worshipful mongrels followed him in, fussing around his legs, shooting him meaningful glances. He settled on the concrete floor outside the building and I watched him use a narrow dowel rod to mark a large canvas with yellow dots of paint, apparently not bothered by the dogs that had begun making themselves comfortable, circling and lying on his work. The man was Shorty Jangala Robertson. A superstar.

Shorty's generation was born in the desert – the last nomads 'came in' as recently as 1984 – and so nobody knew his age, but he was thought to be in his nineties. Earlier, the manager of the art centre had told me his story. One day, Shorty was wandering unhappily around Yuendumu when she said to him, 'Shorty, come paint for me.' He told her, 'I'm hungry.' She replied, 'Well, I've got these nuts. If you come to the centre to paint tomorrow, I'll give you three hundred dollars.' The canvas that Shorty painted the next day currently hangs in the National Gallery of Victoria. He has since produced more than a thousand works. Each one sells, typically, for between eight and twenty thousand dollars.

I asked Shorty, via an interpreter, why he thinks his canvases are especially popular.

'He says he paints the water dreaming,' says the interpreter.

'But why do his paintings sell, while the paintings of others don't?' I asked. 'What is it that Shorty's doing that's unique?'

'He says it's water dreaming.'

'Yes,' I said. 'I know he paints the water dreaming. But what does he think white people like so much about the water dreaming?'

'He says it's because it's water dreaming.'

'Yes, but *why* does he paint water dreaming?'

By now, both Shorty and the interpreter had become visibly frustrated.

'Because it's *water dreaming, water dreaming.*'

It was only later that I understood. Aboriginal people don't see art in the same way that we do. They don't look at Shorty's work and judge it on its aesthetic quality but on something more fundamental. A painting is only as good as the story that it relates. As the manager told me, 'I've got lots of artists who paint a really good story but I can't *give* their paintings away and they don't understand.' For the Aboriginal people, story is everything. It is their history, it is their religion, it is their sense of identity and their register of ethical lore. It is how they have survived in these hostile lands for forty thousand years and more. It is their map of survival.

Every Aboriginal newborn is assigned a 'tjukurpa' – a story from the time of the world's creation which, in its details, will tell them everything they need to know about where to find food, medicine and water for hundreds of miles around. It will teach them about magic and spirits and detail an elaborate moral code. A tjukurpa is a cross between a Bible parable, a *Just So* story, a supermarket plan and a travel guide. It is a multi-dimensional map of life that speaks of time, space and meaning. Events in the story's plot – battles and birth-places and hide-outs – correspond to actual facets of the physical landscape, so you will know that you can find carrots, for instance, in the spot where the bush carrot beat the bush potato in a fight. Tjukurpas are incredibly complex. They are taught in stages, with each new level of detail being revealed by elders when an individual is considered ready. They are imparted in as many ways as possible: dance, song, body-painting, rock-carving and sand-drawings that cover a hectare. But they are highly secret. They are passed down strictly between members of the same 'skin group'. Men do not know the women's tjukurpas, and women do not know the men's. White people have only ever been told as much as the youngest Aboriginal children. The paintings that artists such as Shorty produce are highly codified and obscured, so that their tjukurpas remain hidden. But they are all based on these essential, ancient lessons.

It is said that the Australian Aboriginals belong to the oldest surviving culture on earth. It appears profoundly different from ours. But I have come to believe that, in one crucial sense, we are just like the Aboriginals. We share their means of negotiating reality. Our lives, to an almost unimaginable degree, depend on stories.

*

When you begin to look for stories – when you purposefully seek out that familiar, seductive pattern, the sly hook of the narrative – you realise that you are surrounded. On the news, in literature, film and song, in your memory, your sense of who you are and how you got there and in most of your conversation. *I did this, and it was terrifying.* Cause and effect plus emotion. It is the fundamental formula of your brain's understanding of the world. It is the fundamental formula of narrative.

Our compulsion for emotional narrative is why the BBC news chooses to report on 'Astro', the Australian horse that got stuck in some mud, and not the nameless thousands of humans who happened to die, the same day, in road accidents and of curable diseases and the effects of poverty. It is why $48,000 of US taxpayers' money was once spent on a twenty-five-day mission to rescue a small dog. It is why Saxon families revelled in the monster-slaying drama of *Beowulf* and why, twelve hundred years later, cinema-goers by the million queued to watch the monster-slaying drama of *Jaws*. It is why, in the seventeen years that followed the birth of silent cinema, more than *ten thousand* films were made in Hollywood alone. It is why we are addicted to celebrity magazines and to the grandest Russian literature. It is stories that lie at the root of vast world religions that hold genuine power over billions of faithful followers.

It is thought that humanity's earliest stories sought to explain the world. They were a primitive form of science, and indistinguishable from religion. At some stage we began to use those tales like the brain uses its models – to attempt to predict and to change the world. Rituals developed around them. We made sacrifices, sang songs and prayed to the gods to effect natural phenomena. The historian Mircea Eliade writes of the 'culture heroes' that were subsequently created to effect social phenomena. Western storytellers imagined legendary characters – Hercules, Aphrodite, King Arthur – whose ghostly archetypes appear in the myths of faraway cultures and in the blockbusters and bestsellers of today.

Sigmund Freud believed that we are emotionally satisfied by the hero's slaying of the monster because we are all secret Oedipuses, murdering our fathers to win the hand of our mothers. For the psychologist Otto Rank, the hero narrative unconsciously tracks our struggle out of childhood and into independence. For the mythologist Joseph Campbell it speaks to the formative adventures of early adulthood. These academics understood that fiction is the journalism of the unconscious, reporting back sensed truths from the silent realm of feelings.

Today's scientists have discovered that we experience the tales that we immerse ourselves in as if they are happening to us. We feel the heroes' feelings, fight their fights, love their lovers. This is possible because stories mimic the illusion of consciousness. The novel's narrator, the film camera's eye – they are points of singularity in which sound, sight, emotion, motive and mission are combined. As we surrender ourselves to the tale, we surrender our own minds to that of our hero. We become infected by the tales that we expose ourselves to.

Observing how fear spreads through a herd of antelope, Professor Bruce Wexler writes that 'contagion is at the heart of emotion.' It is significant, I believe, that contagion is also at the heart of stories. But to become contagious, a story requires surprise. According to Professor Daniel Kahneman, 'a capacity for surprise is an essential aspect of our mental life' and when we experience it, we feel 'a surge of conscious attention' as our minds seek new information to feed in to their re-creation of the world. And so it is with narrative.

Harvard Professor of Psychology Jerome Bruner writes, 'a story begins with some breach in the expected state of things.' In its most dramatic literary form, this narrative shock is Aristotle's 'peripeteia', a sudden reversal of circumstances. Peripeteia is the ultimate disruption – a life spun around without warning. What happened next? How did the hero struggle? Was resolution found? What valuable information can be harvested and fed into the neural models?

*

The brain constructs its models during childhood and adolescence, the period in which it is extraordinarily alive with creative activity. By the age of five, children have developed a sophisticated 'theory of mind' and are, therefore, 'story-ready'. During our formative years we absorb many thousands of tales of ever-increasing complexity of message. Professor of Psychology Keith Oatley has observed that learning to negotiate the social world requires weighing up 'myriad interacting instances of cause and effect. Just as computer simulations can help us get to grips with complex problems such as flying a plane so novels, stories and dramas can help us understand the complexities of social life.' We build our understanding of the emotional world through the myths and legends of our culture. We are all, in part, made of fairy tales.

*

But stories are not just cultural teachers. They can be motivators and agents for epochal change. Evolutionary psychologist David Sloan Wilson has compared their effect to an imaginary 'mutant gene' that appears in a primitive tribesman and serves to distort and magnify his dread and hatred of his enemy, thus pushing him to fight with superior violence. Marxist philosopher Georges Sorel believed that myths were essential for revolution. Writing in *Nature*, Professor Paul Bloom has observed that stories have helped shift the moral codes of nations: 'Harriet Beecher Stowe's 1852 novel *Uncle Tom's Cabin* helped to end slavery in the United States, and descriptions of animal suffering in Peter Singer's *Animal Liberation* and elsewhere have been powerful catalysts for the animal-rights movement.'

Stories change us first, and then they change the world.

*

The mind is addicted to story – *crisis, struggle, resolution* – because that is how it experiences life. We are in the world, and we are battling against foes in order to make better lives.

As our brains are bombarded with a superabundance of information, we are constantly searching for our plot among the chaos. Psychotics such as Rufus May are too sensitive to stories. They see salient details everywhere. But I sensed this tendency, too, in the people I have met who were not mentally ill. It seemed a common thing, to confabulate wild explanations of cause and effect that weren't really there. Veronica Keen and her Illuminati. Dr Valerie Sinason and her Satanists. Lord Monckton and his totalitarian United Nations. Hidden plots. Conspiracies that they were fighting, bravely.

All of it begins in the unconscious. We experience hunches about moral rights and wrongs; wordless desires and repulsions; powerful instincts that seem to come from nowhere. This constant throbbing of emotions can be unsettling. We sometimes feel things that we don't understand, or even want to feel. When we come across an explanation of the world that fits perfectly over the shape of our feelings – a tale that magically explains our hunches and tells us that it is all okay – it can seem of divine origin, as if we have experienced revealed truth.

When the racist lorry driver from Maidstone was a boy, he saw a party political broadcast by the National Front. 'Everything made sense,' he told me, shaking his head at the wonder of it all. 'It *just fitted*.' When I asked John Mackay how he knew that God was real, he explained, 'It's something in me.' When Lord Monckton's audience, with their right-wing brains, heard him talk of climate conspiracy, he realised that they always knew instinctively, 'that something was going on in this climate story that they didn't like the smell of. They just couldn't quite work out what it was . . .'

Stories work against truth. They operate with the machinery of prejudice and distortion. Their purpose is not fact but propaganda. The scientific method is the tool that humans have developed to break the dominion of the narrative. It has been designed specifically to dissolve anecdote, to strip out emotion and to leave only unpolluted data. It is a new kind of language, a modern sorcery, and it has gifted our species incredible powers. We can eradicate plagues, extend our lives by decades, build rockets and fly through space. But we can hardly be surprised if some feel an instinctive hostility towards it, for it is fundamentally inhuman.

*

I will never forget my own experience of the brain's incorrigible story-generating ability. Lying on Vered Kilstein's massage table, it took hardly a nudge for my mind to produce a vivid and emotional narrative of my life as a wartime widow. To recall its principal scenes, even now, is to slip into the drizzle of genuine melancholy. A part of me becomes that doleful woman. Vered spoke of clients who had reported similarly powerful experiences: the English knight who, after cavorting with his lover, was struck during a fight over his dishevelled appearance: a fantastic confabulation woven around a humdrum dodgy shoulder.

Consciousness is the first storyteller, and the greatest one of all. Its basis is the illusion that we are a coherent individual, in control of our beliefs and actions and operating freely at the centre of the world. Because we are driven to cause things to happen, and we witness their effects over time, we naturally experience our lives as a constantly flowing narrative. We have victories and failures, enemies and allies. We have hopes. We have goals. We have drama. Philosophers and neuroscientists ask why consciousness is necessary. Why go to the trouble of creating this sensation of singularity when we could just as easily pass on our genes as instinctively behaving zombies? Why have we adapted for this trait?

I believe that consciousness is the Hero-Maker. The mind reorders the world, turning the events of our days into a narrative of crisis, struggle, resolution, and casts us in the leading role. In this way, our lives gain motivation and meaning. We are coaxed into hope, into heroic acts, into braving impossible odds. We are made David against Goliath and, in this way, we become stronger and more successful. How many hero stories have I heard since that night in Gympie? How many people bravely fighting to change the world? John Mackay, giving up his career in an effort to disprove the Devil's propaganda and save unbelievers from hell. Swami Ramdev creating his paradisal world free of Western medicines. Ron Coleman campaigning to rescue the innocent from the brutish psychiatry industry. The Buddhist S. N. Goenka abandoning his business life to offer tens of thousands of people free mediation. James Randi braving death threats to prevent a coming 'dark age'. Vered Kilstein, who is 'one of the millions who are here to help people move to a new consciousness.'

The neural illusions that collude in the Hero-Maker are many. We believe that we are better looking than we are, more moral than we are, less susceptible to bias than we are, that our creations are worth more, that the 'spotlight' is always on us and that we are incapable of true evil. Our memories rescript our past in the service of our glory. And yet a witchbag of powerful forces works against us, silently guiding our behaviour: excessive obedience to authority; unconscious prejudices; genetic predispositions and situational and cultural pressures that can drive us to terrible acts. These forces are made invisible to us. To truly be a hero, we must believe that we are our own captains, and that we possess free will.

Through the Hero-Maker's lens, religions and ideologies are seen as parasite hero plots; prophets and political leaders become seductive storytellers. They provide ready-made con-

379

fabulations that have been generalised by use until they fit neatly onto the instincts of a certain kind of brain. Because they match up so well with an individual's unconscious moral hunches, they can appear to be more than true. They come from *out there* and can seem miraculous, sacred, even worth dying for. These parasite plots serve to make people happy because they validate their emotional instincts and then give them purpose – enemies to fight and the promise of a blissful denouement if their quest is successful. It is an illusion. It can be a profoundly dangerous one. And it can be a profoundly useful one.

*

Our lives are lived in two realms – the physical and the narrative. The model that our brain makes of the world of objects has to be accurate. If it wasn't, we would be bumping into walls and trying to eat chairs. But not so the invisible kingdom of feelings. That soft matrix of beliefs that we exist within – that ever-flowing narrative of loves and feuds and hopes and hatreds – can be a place of tremendous distortion. The story that is woven for us is concerned, primarily, with our hero status, and not objective truth. It is often wrong. The 'true' nature of reality can appear so clear and obvious that we frequently underestimate just how wrong it is possible to be. If others persist in seeing things differently, we conclude that they must be corrupt. It is what the Morgellons sufferers believe of the Centers for Disease Control. It is what James Randi thinks of Rupert Sheldrake. It is what the family of Carole Felstead believe of Dr Fleur Fisher. It is what David Irving thinks of his critics and what his critics think of David Irving.

We underestimate how perilous it can be, if we cling too hard to our hero delusion. An expert in the psychology of evil, Professor Roy Baumeister, has written that 'dangerous people from playground bullies to warmongering dictators, consist mainly of those who have highly favourable views about themselves. They strike out at others who question or dispute those favourable views.' Perhaps I saw this notion in its mildest form among the UFO-spotters who, when challenged, grumpily hardened their beliefs. And I saw it in a stronger form still in some of those whose dramatic personalities and intensely held positions have made them famous. Heretics are often betrayed by the spotless coherence of their plots. They tell the cleanest tales with the most perfect separations of good guy and bad. It is why they should not be trusted.

But the writer, too, tells a story. Like the mind, we pick out a plot through the superabundance of information that we gather on our chosen subject. What you have read in these pages is presented as if it is the whole truth, and yet it is just a narrow path that I have picked through a landscape of facts and incident. I spent seven full days travelling with David Irving and his acolytes. My interviews with the historian alone lasted for more than four hours, my transcript for the chapter is in excess of twenty-eight thousand words – nearly a quarter of the length of this book. I applied my own map of salience to all that evidence, elevating the moments that I believed most relevant and that told the story that I wanted to tell. If Irving was given identical materials, he would surely have crafted a different narrative. It would be just as true as the one that you have read, and it would be just as untrue.

*

If the covert modules of our minds conspire to make us feel like heroes, then this phenomenon has an evil twin, a dangerous corollary. The Demon-Maker.

To be a hero, we must have an enemy. Every David requires

a Goliath, and the tales in these pages team with those. John Mackay conjured himself a ferocious battle-scape of witchcraft and devils and necrophiliac priests. His ideological enemy Richard Dawkins insisted that Mackay's phantasmagorical beliefs are 'a serious threat to scientific reason'. The evolutionary biologist Nathan Lo was convinced that the creationists' suppressed motive was to make money.

On another side of the world, sufferers of unexplained itch confabulated complex stories about nanotechnology and government conspiracy. In a different country still, one highly regarded expert in schizophrenia called another 'a liar and a charlatan'. Lord Monckton blamed almost all the dreads that have befallen the West on the nihilistic, jealous, power-crazy left, insisting that the British empire fell because of the welfare state. David Irving, meanwhile, held an intrigue of scheming Jews responsible for the same event. Despite the fact that his version of wartime events has been almost universally rejected, Professor Deborah Lipstadt still worries that it somehow presents 'a clear and future danger' to historical knowledge. For the Skeptic Dr Steven Novella many practising homeopaths were 'psychopathic con artists', while for alternative medicine proponent Dana Ullman, Skeptics were often 'Big Pharma shills'.

We are betrayed by our maps of salience. They plot our narratives, identify our enemies and then coat them in distorting layer of loathing and dread. We feel that hunch – *withdraw* – and then conduct a *post factum* search for evidence that justifies it. We are motivated to fight our foes because we are emotional about them, but emotion is the territorial scent-mark of irrationality. We tell ourselves a story, we cast the monster and then become vulnerable to our own delusional narrative of heroism.

The Demon-Maker loves this kind of binary thinking. It

insists upon extremes: heroes and villains, black and white, in-tribes and out. This corrosive instinct is evident in the so-called 'culture wars'. For many Skeptics, evidence-based truth has been sacralised. It has caused them to become irrational in their judgements of the motives of those with whom they do not agree. They have also sacralised reason. When we spoke, James Randi was chilling in his expression of where pure logic can ultimately lead. Viewing the matter stripped of emotion, it might make sense to prevent people with 'mental aberrations' and 'histories of inherited diseases' from having children. But the idea is obviously repellent. Randi's belief demonstrates a truth that is sometimes forgotten by his followers: reason alone is not enough.

My encounter with the patron saint of the Skeptics was a crystallising moment. At the conference in Manchester, I struggled to work out what it was about the movement that made me uneasy. I believe that Randi's speech resolved the warning of my unconscious. *'These are not innocent people. These are stupid people.'* Skeptics can be reminiscent of creationists, who think that I will go to hell because I am not a Christian. They treat belief as a moral choice. If you do not choose as they do, you are condemned. And while beliefs can have moral consequences, which the law must appropriately punish, we should not judge others for thinking their thoughts, nor be censured ourselves for the form of our hearts.

Anyone who proudly declares themselves a 'free-thinker' betrays an ignorance of the motors of belief. We do not get to choose our most passionately held views, as if we are selecting melons in a supermarket. Gemma Hoefken is no more free to reject her conviction that homeopathy cured her cancer than I am to fall to my knees and flood myself with Jesus. And good. This monoculture we would have, if the hard rationalists had their way, would be a deathly thing. So bring on the psychics, bring on the alien abductees, bring on the two John Lennons – bring on a hundred of them. Christians or no, there will be tribalism. Televangelists or no, there will be scoundrels. It is not religion or fake mystics that create these problems, it is being human. Where there is illegality or racial hatred, call the police. Where there is psychosis, call Professor Richard Bentall. Where there is misinformation, bring learning. But where there is just ordinary madness, we should celebrate. Eccentricity is our gift to one another. It is the riches of our species. To be mistaken is not a sin. Wrongness is a human right.

*

The Hero-Maker tells us why intelligence is no forcefield and facts are no bullets. If you were to discuss the near-zero discount rate in the Stern Review with Lord Monckton, you would not be engaging in a simple matter of yes or no concerning an arcane point of science. Facts do not exist in isolation. They are like single pixels in a person's generated reality. Each fact is connected to other facts and those facts to networks of other facts still. When they are all knitted together, they take the form of an emotional and dramatic plot at the centre of which lives the individual. When a climate scientist argues with a denier, it is not a matter of data versus data, it is hero narrative versus hero narrative, David versus David, tjukurpa versus tjukurpa. It is a clash of worlds.

The Hero-Maker exposes this strange urge that so many humans have, to force their views aggressively on others. We must make them see things as we do. They must agree, *we will make them agree*. There is no word for it, as far as I know. 'Evangelism' doesn't do it: it fails to acknowledge its essential violence. We are neural imperialists, seeking to colonise the worlds of others, installing our own private culture of beliefs into their minds. I wonder if this response is triggered when we pick up the infuriating sense that an opponent believes that *they* are the hero, and not us. The provocation! The personal outrage! The underlying dread, the disturbance in reality. The restless urge to prove that their world, and not ours, is the illusion.

I used to believe that it was humanity's rational nature that built civilisation. Now I think it is our inherent desire to slay Goliath, to colonise the mental worlds of others, to *win*.

*

How many of us actually *are* heroes? Which of us have that treasured capacity? Do heroes of the kind found in literature, film and the imaginations of the masses even exist?

Over the course of twenty years, historian Laurence Rees has met hundreds of veterans from the Second World War: members of the SS, concentration-camp officers, rapists, mass-murderers, unreformed Nazi veterans. His films are justly decorated with awards.

A guiding question of his life's work seems to be, how do ordinary people become complicit in acts of evil? 'I've broadly come to this conclusion,' he told me. 'We massively underestimate the power of the culture that we are in to shape us. People say, "I wouldn't have done that." But they haven't been exposed to any of the things, culturally, that might have made them do it. And the warning I take is that the number of people in a group who will stand out against these cultural forces are much smaller than you think, and you're probably not one of them. In fact, I think you can probably tell if you are because you're pretty bolshie already. If you've got a good career, and you're pretty sociable and you're going up the hierarchy and all the rest of it, where are you going to get your sudden revolutionary spurt from?'

*

There are possible objections to the idea of the Hero-Maker, as well as questions to which I don't know the answer. The anthropologist Daniel Everett has studied the Pirahã, a hunter-gatherer tribe of around three hundred and fifty people in the Amazon, who seem to have no tradition of storytelling or myth. Their musical language is based on just eight consonants and three vowels. They are said to live as they speak: completely in the present.

But they do understand story. These distant and primitive people, who have been separated from the wider world for tens of thousands of years, lack a culture of art and who seem to be incapable of learning even basic counting, had no trouble enjoying a showing of Peter Jackson's 2005 film *King Kong*. Writing in the *New Yorker*, John Colapinto reported: 'The Pirahã shouted with delight, fear, laughter, and surprise – and when Kong himself arrived, smashing through the palm trees, pandemonium ensued. Small children, who had been sitting close to the screen, jumped up and scurried into their mothers' laps; the adults laughed and yelled at the screen.'

I worry, too, that the Hero-Maker is overly Western in its perspective. Do hero myths differ radically in various cultures and, if so, do these differences affect how individuals deal with conflict and struggle? A 2012 study, reported in *The Economist*, asked why levels of 'wisdom' in Japanese youngsters seemed to be so in advance of those of their American counterparts. Could the answer lie in the nature of the stories that they have been bathed in since birth?

In the closing stages of the writing of this book, I have experienced cold moments, in which I charge myself as being just as guilty of faulty reasoning as the most extreme people that I have met. Here I am: the atheist who concluded that religion is a 'parasite hero narrative'; the journalist suspicious of

James Randi who discovered him to be a liar; the novelist who found storytelling to be of vital importance to the advancement of humanity. Here I am: confirmation bias come alive.

I am also concerned that I have overstated my argument. In my haste to write my own coherent story, I have barely acknowledged the obvious truth that minds do sometimes change. People find faith and they lose it. Mystics become Skeptics. Politicians cross the floor. I wonder why this happens. Is it when the reality of what is actually happening in our lives overpowers the myth that we make of themselves? Are we simply pursuing ever more glorious hero missions?

*

If so, our missions can also fracture in a different way: one that has far more threatening consequences. Professor Bentall told me that 'depressed people have a huge gap between how they see themselves and how they would like to be – their ideal self.' Professor Lewis Wolpert writes, 'In the inner world of the depressive self, the self is perceived to be ineffective and inadequate, whereas the outside world is seen as presenting insuperable obstacles.'

The periods in my life when I have felt hopeless are the ones in which the narrative has collapsed. Goliath has grown too big and I have found it impossible to cast myself as the hero. The sense of non-specific wrongness that has always shrouded me is the product of a partially true, yet unhelpful plot. When I look back upon my early life I see myself at fault and in trouble, with parents, teachers, employers and lovers. My mind has seized upon these episodes to construct my autobiography. My map of salience has worked against me.

My wrongness is one story, but there are others. I look out at the Australian Central Desert and see a landscape of death while an Aboriginal sees water and shelter and food.

The Skeptic tells the story of Randi the hero; the psychic of Randi the devil. We all make these unconscious plot-decisions: what is relevant? What is salient? Which are the defining moments?

Why should I take it to be of such potent importance that my father believes in God? Or that a magazine journalist wants to bomb Tehran? Are these facts such a challenge to my hero illusion that I must alienate myself from friends and family? And why must I define myself chiefly as a man who used to steal and drink and be an unstable boyfriend?

*

Everything we know starts as electrical pulses, incoming from the senses. These pulses combine to construct a best-guess but distorted re-creation of reality.

Having learned this fact, and tracked some of its ramifications, I find myself creeping about my beliefs, timidly peeking over their rims, examining them for cracks and presenting them nervously. I have become wary of feeling too much passion, getting carried away and emotional. Does my knowledge of the Hero-Maker mean that I must forbid myself, for ever, from angrily fighting for a belief? If everyone was to do this, it would be disastrous. Progress would halt, civilisation would desiccate. I must conclude, then, that as dangerous as the illusion can be, it can also work for the good. And so the proper response is to accept my human nature, close my eyes, open my arms and fall back into it.

I will try to remember, though, that as right as I can sometimes feel, there is *always* the chance that I am wrong. And that happiness lies in humility: in forgiving others, and in forgiving myself.

We are creatures of illusion. We are made out of stories. From the heretics to the Skeptics, we are all lost in our own neural tjukurpas, our own secret worlds. We are just ordinary heroes fighting phantom Goliaths, doing our best in the service of truth when the only thing that we *really* know are the pulses.

Acknowledgements

I owe the largest debt of thanks to the great many people who have allowed me to interview them – especially to Professor Jonathan Haidt, whose account of confabulation in his amazing book *The Happiness Hypothesis* helped to inspire what was to become this one, and to Professor David Eagleman, whose *Incognito* was equally vital to my understanding of some of the principles that form the core of *The Heretics*.

I also owe thanks to the wonderful editors who commissioned the original work that comprises much of this book. In chapter order, they are: Judith Whelan, Christine Middap, Ceri David, Ross Jones, Charlotte Northedge & Merope Mills, Alex Bilmes and Ruaridh Nichol.

Thanks also to Ann Eve for the studies, Greg Taylor, Ed Yong, Andy Lewis for the extremely patient assistance and to my panel of brilliant brains for checking the manuscript: Dr Louise Arseneault, Dr Helen Fisher, Professor Sophie Scott, Professor Chris Frith, Professor Daryl Bem and Professor Chris French.

Finally, thanks to Charlie Campbell at Ed Victor Ltd. and to Paul Baggaley, Kris Doyle and all at Picador.

A note on my method

As a journalist, my knowledge is broad but shallow. It is the responsibility of the journalist to identify appropriate experts and to acknowledge significant disagreements in what those experts report, where significant disagreements exist. The majority of the science in this book involves the idea of the brain's modelling of the world, and the many psychological illusions that have been revealed by experimental psychologists. These ideas are well documented in a range of excellent books and periodicals – both academic and popular – which were my principal source for research. I supplemented this research with interviews with experts, generally on the professor level. Most of the concepts in this strand are relatively uncontroversial and broadly accepted.

In the areas where I explore more controversial science, I checked original studies where necessary and sought expert counsel where those studies threatened to be too complex for a lay journalist to appropriately understand. In the few incidents where interviewees made controversial claims about specific studies, I confirmed these claims either in the original papers, or with the authors of those papers.

Finally, when the first draft of *The Heretics* was completed, I recruited a team of academics with appropriate specialisms to read through the text. They offered notes and advice where I had erred.

This is an imperfect system, as it relies on many secondary sources. Moreover, I do not declare myself to be free of the biases that afflict any writer, and I'm certainly not immune to making mistakes. If any errors are noted, or if new findings supersede claims made in the text, I would be very grateful to receive notification via my website, willstorr.com, so that any future editions of *The Heretics* can be corrected and updated.

Naturally, this book contains only a fraction of a fraction of the relevant science. Other academics will, surely, disagree with those whom I quote in these pages. If any of it piques your interest, I urge you to dig deeper, where you will no doubt find science that is newer and in conflict with some of the work here.

Some names have been changed, all interviews are edited, the chronology of some episodes may have been altered in the interests of narrative coherence, ellipses are not used within hybrid quotes, which are used in the interests of concision. Several of these chapters have appeared previously, in a diffcrent forms, in periodicals.

Notes and references

1: 'It's like treason'

page

5 **offices in the US, Canada, New Zealand and the UK:**
http://www.creationresearch.net/team/contact.html.

6 **from august scientific bodies such as the Royal Society:**
Annabel Crabb, 'Darwin's evolutionary theory is a tottering
nonsense, built on too many suppositions', *Sydney Morning
Herald*, 7 May 2006.

6 **the British Centre for Science Education:**
http://www.bcseweb.org.uk/index.php/Main/JohnMackay.

6 **In 2006 the National Union of Teachers demanded new
legislation:** Jamie Doward, 'Creationist to tour UK
universities', *Observer*, 9 April 2006.

6 **which the National Secular Society described as:** Sarah
Cassidy, 'Creationist descends on Britain to take debate on
evolution into the classroom', *Independent*, 21 April 2006.

8 **Professor Richard Dawkins . . . once told the *Guardian*
newspaper:** John Crace, 'Six Day Wonder', *Guardian*, 2 May
2006.

15 **only for Mackay to be kicked out:** Michael McKenna,
'Biblical Battle of Creation Groups', *Australian*, 4 June 2007.

2: 'I don't know what's going on with these people . . .'

page

33 **UFO sightings by . . . airline pilots, military personnel and
police officers:** Peter Jennings, 'The UFO Phenomenon',
ABC News, 24 February 2005.

34 **over a hundred thousand billion potentially life-bearing
planets:** 'Billions Of Life-Bearing Planets Could Exist', Sky
News, 10 May 2012.

394

34 **Dr Michio Kaku . . . argues:** Peter Jennings, 'The UFO Phenomenon', ABC News, 24 February 2005.

34 **Mack initially assumed all abductees to be delusional:** PBS interview, http://www.pbs.org/wgbh/nova/aliens/johnmack.html.

34 **Working closely with more than two hundred individuals:** Angela Hind, 'Alien Thinking', BBC News, 8 June 2005.

34 **Mack quickly discounted the common 'sleep paralysis' theory:** 'Abduction, Alienation and Reason', BBC Radio 4, 8 June 2005.

34 **'These people, as far as I could tell, were of sound mind':** 'Abduction, Alienation and Reason', BBC Radio 4, 8 June 2005.

35 **he felt marginalised by the university:** 'The Aliens are always with us [Obituary]', Bryan Appleyard, *Sunday Times*, 3 October 2004.

Additional quotes re: Mack vs Harvard: 'Abduction, Alienation and Reason', BBC Radio 4, 8 June 2005.

3: 'The secret of the long life of the tortoise'

page

39 **the 'VIPs' . . . the lowly 'General Members':** http://www.pypt.org/35-membership.html.

41 **four cabinet ministers were sent to meet him:** 'When the Saints Go Marching In', *Newsweek*, 12 June 2011.

41 **one billion followers:** Bhupesh Bhandari, 'Meet Baba Ramdev, the swami who owns a Scottish Island', MSN News, 4 June 2011.

41 **two hundred and fifty million viewers:** http://www.swamiramdevyoga.org/about-us/swami-ramdevji.html.

41 **he had a reception with MPs at the House of Commons:** 'British House of Commons honours Yoga Guru Ramdev', One India News, 18 July 2007.

41 **tea with the Queen:** 'Swami Ramdev wins UK award', *Times of India*, 14 July 2006.

41 **addressed a United Nations conference:** 'Baba Ramdev to address UN meet in NY', *Mumbai Mirror*, 13 October 2009.

41 **'complete medication':** Interview with author.

41 **'like a miracle':** Interview with author.

45 **manufactures over a hundred and sixty herbal treatments:** 'Yogi cleared of animal parts row', BBC News, 8 March 2006.

45 **senior politician accused him of using human bones:** 'Guru accused of "human bone" drug', BBC News, 4 January 2006.

45 **the testicles of an otter:** T. K. Rajalakshmi, 'In the name of Ayurveda', *Frontline*, vol. 23, issue 02 (28 January–10 February 2006).

45 **twenty were arrested:** '20 supporters of Baba Ramdev arrested', *Times of India*, 6 January 2006.

45 **a sinister conspiracy of multinational pharmaceutical companies:** 'Yogi cleared of animal parts row', BBC News, 8 March 2006.

46 **claims that pranayama can cure AIDS:** 'Yoga can cure AIDS: Ramdev', *Times of India*, 20 December 2006.

46 **a statement Ramdev denied ever making:** 'I made no claims of curing AIDS: Ramdev', *Express India*, 22 December 2006.

46 **threatened with legal action by medical NGOs and . . . the Indian government:** Seema Kamdar, 'Baba Ramdev's website claims AIDS is curable', *DNA India*, 26 December 2006.

46 **have each paid more than £6,000:** http://www.pypt.org/35-membership.html.

48 **Coca-Cola will turn their skin dark:** Shivam Vij, 'The Stain that Just Won't Wash', *Tehelka*, 10 February 2007.

50 **a kind of greatest hits package of Ramdev's claims:** Acharya Balkrishna, *Yog: In Synergy with Medical Science*, Divya Prakashan, 2007.

NOTE: I read about many of the studies listed in this section, and in the chapters that follow, in books by those with appropriate expertise. Where academic studies are listed, it is for the convenience of interested parties. For details of my method please see above.

52 **'The Powerful Placebo':** Henry K. Beecher, 'The Powerful Placebo', *Journal of the American Medical Association*, 24 December 1955.

52 **although Beecher's interpretation of the data . . . highly careless:** For an excellent analysis of just how poor Beecher's interpretation of the data in his study was, see Dylan Evans, *Placebo*, HarperCollins, 2004, pp. 4–6.

52 **Valium . . . only actually works when the patient knows:** 'Why the placebo effect is rewriting the medical rulebook', *New Scientist*, 20 August 2008.

52 **Experts such as psychiatrist Patrick Lemoine:** Laura Spinney, 'Purveyors of mystery', *New Scientist*, 16 December 2006.

52 **75 per cent of the effect of . . . Prozac might be down to placebo:** Irving Kirsch and Guy Sapirstein, 'Listening to Prozac but hearing placebo: A meta-analysis of antidepressant medication', *Prevention & Treatment*, June 1998.

53 **Professor David Wootton . . . has written:** *Bad Medicine*, Oxford University Press, 2006, p. 68.

53 **Professor Fabrizio Benedetti, has gone so far as to state:** Steve Silberman, 'Placebos Are Getting More Effective. Drugmakers Are Desperate to Know Why', *Wired*, 17 September 2009.

53 **An individual's placebo response . . . expectation of what will happen:** Steve Silberman, 'Placebos Are Getting More Effective. Drugmakers Are Desperate to Know Why', *Wired*, 17 September 2009.

53 **brand-name headache pills:** A. Branthwaite and P. Cooper, 'Analgesic effects of branding in treatment of headaches', *British Medical Journal*, 16 May 1981.

53 **why zero per cent 'alcohol' can make you feel drunk:** Donald J. O'Boyle, Alice S. Binns and John J. Summer, 'On the efficacy of alcohol placebos in inducing feelings of intoxication', *Psychopharmacology* 15, nos. 1–2 (1994).

53 **why completely fake drugs can benefit the symptoms:** This

list is a compilation of all the sources noted in this section, as well as Dylan Evans, *Placebo*, HarperCollins, 2004, and Ben Goldacre, *Bad Science*, 4th Estate, 2008.

53 **athletes go faster:** Thomas Trojian and Christopher Beedie, 'Placebo Effect and Athletes', *Current Sports Medicine Reports*, July–August 2008.

53 **for longer:** C. J. Beedie, D. A. Coleman and A. J. Foad, 'Positive and negative placebo effects resulting from the deceptive administration of an ergogenic aid', *International Journal of Sport, Nutrition, Exercise and Metabolism*, 17 June 2007.

53 **with less pain:** F. Benedetti, A. Pollo and L. Colloca, 'Opioid-mediated placebo responses boost pain endurance and physical performance – is it doping in sport competitions?', *Journal of Neuroscience*, 31 October 2007.

53 **convince asthma sufferers they're better:** Michael E. Wechsler, M.D. et al., 'Active Albuterol or Placebo, Sham Acupuncture, or No Intervention in Asthma', *New England Journal of Medicine*, 14 July 2011.

53 **four sugar pills:** D. E. Moerman, 'Cultural variations in the placebo effect: ulcers, anxiety & blood pressure', *Medical Anthropology Quarterly*, 2000.

53 **sham injections work better:** A. J. de Craen, J. G. Tijssen, J. de Gans and J. Kleijnen, 'Placebo effect in the acute treatment of migraine: subcutaneous placebos are better than oral placebos', *Journal of Neurology*, March 2000.

53 **capsules work better:** M. Z. Hussain, 'Effect of shape of medication in treatment of anxiety states', *British Journal of Psychiatry* 120 (1972).

53 **big pills work better:** L. W. Buckalew and S. Ross, 'Relationship of perceptual characteristics to efficacy of placebos', *Psychol Rep.*, December 1981.

53 **complicated but useless electrical equipment:** A. G. Johnson, 'Surgery as Placebo', *Lancet*, 22 October 1994.

53 **electrodes in the brain:** Michele Lanotte, Leonardo Lopiano, Elena Torre, Bruno Bergamasco, Luana Colloca, Fabrizio Benedetti, 'Expectation enhances autonomic responses to

stimulation of the human subthalamic limbic region',
Brain, Behavior, and Immunity, November 2005.

53 **smelly brown paint:** G. H. Montgomery and I. Kirsch,
'Mechanisms of Placebo Pain Reduction: an Empirical
Investigation', *Psychological Science*, May 1996.

53 **the *unspoken thoughts* of your doctor:** R. H. Gracely et al.,
'Clinicians' Expectations Influence Placebo Analgesia',
Lancet, January 1985.

54 **when we know that our medication is pharmacologically
useless:** Ted J. Kaptchuk et al., 'Placebos without Deception:
A Randomized Controlled Trial in Irritable Bowel
Syndrome', *PLoS*, 22 December 2010.

54 **Professor Nicholas Humphrey . . . writes:** 'The Evolved Self-
Management System', *Edge*, 12 May 2011.

54 **Because it did:** Dylan Evans, *Placebo*, HarperCollins, 2004,
pp. 38–41, in particular his analysis of: S. Fisher and R. P.
Greenburg, 'How sound is the double blind design for
evaluating psychotropic drugs?', *Journal of Nervous and
Mental Disease*, 1993.

4: 'Two John Lennons'

page

57 **For a 1979 study that has been widely replicated:** H. Strupp,
S. Hadley, 'Specific versus non-specific factors in
psychotherapy', *Archives of General Psychiatry* [1979].

57 **despite the fact that different varieties of therapy:** M. L.
Smith and G. V. Glass, *The Benefits of Psychotherapy*, Johns
Hopkins University Press, 1980.

62 **Maarten Peters and his team at Maastricht University:**
M. J. V. Peters, R. Horselenberg, M. Jelicic and
H. Merckelbach, 'The false fame illusion in people
with memories about a previous life', *Consciousness and
Cognition*, March 2007.

63 **Psychologists at Harvard University led by Susan Clancy:**
Susan A. Clancy, Richard J. McNally, Roger K. Pitman,
Daniel L. Schacter and Mark F. Lenzenweger, 'Memory

Distortion in People Reporting Abduction by Aliens', *Journal of Abnormal Psychology* III (2002).

63 **Although this result wasn't replicated in an attempt by UK researchers:** Christopher C. French et al., 'Psychological aspects of the alien contact experience', *Cortex* 44 (2008), pp. 1387–95.

5: 'Solidified, intensified, gross sensations'

page

66 **plenty of sound evidence for the efficacy of meditation:** Michael Bond, 'Putting meditation to the test', *New Scientist*, 11 January 2011.

85 **the events that spiralled from a single phone call to a Kentucky branch of McDonald's:** Andrew Wolfson, 'A Hoax Most Cruel', *Courier Journal*, 9 October 2005. ABC Primetime Special, originally broadcast 10 November 2005.'Strip Search Case Closed?' ABC news website. 30 November 2006. Philip Zimbardo, *The Lucifer Effect*, Rider, 2007, pp. 279–81.

88 **In a 2012 paper, neuroscientist Professor Chris Frith:** Chris D. Frith, 'The role of metacognition in human social interactions', *Philosophical Transactions of The Royal Society, Biological Sciences*, p. 367.

88 **In 1951, Professor Stanley Milgram's boss, Dr Solomon Asch:** S. E. Asch, 'Studies of independence and conformity: A minority of one against a unanimous majority', *Psychological Monographs* 70 (1951).

89 **In 2005, Dr Gregory Berns, a psychiatrist and neuroscientist:** Gregory S. Berns, Jonathan Chappelow, Caroline F. Zink, Giuseppe Pagnoni, Megan E. Martin-Skurski and Jim Richards, 'Neurobiological correlates of social conformity and independence during mental rotation', *Biological Psychiatry* 58 (2005), pp. 245–53.

90 **In an interview with the *New York Times*:** Sandra Blakeslee, 'What Other People Say May Change What You See', *New York Times*, 28 June 2005.

6: 'The invisible actor at the centre of the world'

page

91 **six hundred million years ago:** Jonathan Haidt, *The Happiness Hypothesis*, Arrow, 2006, p. 15.

91 **first neurologically recognisable *Homo sapiens*, known as 'Mitochondrial Eve':** 'Colin Blakemore: how the human brain got bigger by accident and not through evolution', *Guardian*, 28 March 2010.

91 **prefrontal cortex, which enabled us to strategise, socialise and make lateral associations:** Michael S. Gazzaniga, *Human*, Harper Perennial, 2008, pp. 19–20.

91 **We left our sunny Eden in east Africa . . . evolutionary mystery took place:** J. Anderson Thompon Jnr, *Why We Believe in God(s)*, Pitchstone, 2011, pp. 34–7.

91 **a sudden explosion in creativity:** Michael S. Gazzaniga, *Human*, Harper Perennial, 2008, p. 215.

92 **Even today, we remain . . . more than two million:** J. Anderson Thompon Jnr, *Why We Believe in God(s)*, Pitchstone, 2011, pp. 34–7.

92 **two hundred and fifty thousand cells a minute:** David Brooks, *The Social Animal*, Short Books, 2011, p. 30.

92 **'an alien kind of computational material':** David Eagleman, *Incognito: The Secret Lives of the Brain*, Canongate, 2011, p. 1.

92 **capable of receiving millions of pieces of information at any given moment:** David Brooks, *The Social Animal*, Short Books, 2011, p. x, quoting *Strangers to Ourselves*, by Timothy D. Wilson of the University of Virginia.

93 **One cubic millimetre:** Email to author from Professor Chris Frith.

93 **It has eighty-six billion of these cells:** James Randerson, 'How many neurons make a human brain? Billions fewer than we thought', *Guardian*, 28 February 2012.

93 **each one is as complex as a city . . . a hundred trillion of them:** David Eagleman, *Incognito: The Secret Lives of the Brain*, Canongate, 2011, p. 1.

93 **a hundred and twenty metres per second:** Michael O'Shea, *The Brain*, Oxford University Press, 2005, p. 8.

93 According to the neuroscientist V. S. Ramachandran, 'The number of permutations': V. S. Ramachandran, *Phantoms in the Brain*, Harper Perennial, 1998, p. 8.

93 And yet, he continues, 'We know so little about it': V. S. Ramachandran, *Phantoms in the Brain*, Harper Perennial, 1998, p. 83.

93 Other mammals give birth to their young when their brains have developed: Jonathan Haidt, *The Happiness Hypothesis*, Arrow, 2006, p. 52.

93 babies create around 1.8 million synapses per second: David Brooks, *The Social Animal*, Short Books, 2011, p. 47.

93 Throughout childhood, the brain is extraordinarily alive: Bruce E. Wexler, *Brain and Culture*, MIT Press, 2008, p. 43.

94 In his book *Brain and Culture* Professor Bruce E. Wexler writes: Bruce E. Wexler, *Brain and Culture*, MIT Press, 2008, p. 5.

95 up to 90 per cent of what you are seeing right now: Richard Gregory, 'Brainy Mind', *British Medical Journal* 317 (1998), pp. 1693–5.

95 When writer Jeff Warren was trained to 'wake up': Jeff Warren, *Head Trip: Adventures on the Wheel of Consciousness*, Oneworld, 2007, p. 117.

96 The light is not out there: David Eagleman, *Incognito: The Secret Lives of the Brain*, Canongate, 2011, p. 40.

96 The music . . . rose petal has no colour: Richard Gregory, 'Brainy Mind', *British Medical Journal* 317, pp. 1693–5 (1998).

96 in the words of neuroscientist Professor Chris Frith: Chris Frith, *Making up the Mind*, Blackwell Publishing, 2007.

97 In a startling 1974 experiment that tested these principles: M. Solms and O. Turnbull, *The Brain and the Inner World*, Other Press, 2002, p. 154.

98 Scott Krepel, who was fitted with a cochlear implant: Interview with Ira Glass, via Marc Holmes (interpreter), *This American Life*, first broadcast on WBEZ Chicago 25 March 2010.

98 Estimates vary . . . we are all living half a second in the past: Jeff Warren, *Head Trip: Adventures on the Wheel of Consciousness*, Oneworld, 2007, p. 145.

98 **One-third of the human brain is devoted to its processing:** David Eagleman, *Incognito: The Secret Lives of the Brain*, Canongate, 2011, p. 23.

98 **Beyond ten degrees from this vivid centre:** Chris Frith, *Making up the Mind*, Blackwell Publishing, 2007, p. 41.

99 **happen up to five times per second:** Susan Blackmore, *Consciousness*, Oxford University Press, 2005, p. 57.

99 **neuroscientist David Eagleman in his book *Incognito*:** David Eagleman, *Incognito: The Secret Lives of the Brain*, Canongate, 2011, p. 1.

99 **in the back of each eye:** Michael O'Shea, *The Brain*, Oxford University Press, 2005 pp. 67, 68.

99 **in the visual area of the striate cortex V4:** Richard Gregory, 'Brainy Mind', *British Medical Journal* 317, pp. 1693–5 (1998).

100 **some birds and insects have four, five or even six colour receptors:** 'Inside Animal Minds', *New Scientist*, 20 August 2011, p. 34.

100 **According to Professor Eagleman, 'Our brain is . . .':** David Eagleman, *Incognito: The Secret Lives of the Brain*, Canongate, 2011, p. 54.

100 **less than a ten-trillionth of the spectrum is available to us:** David Eagleman, *Incognito: The Secret Lives of the Brain*, Canongate, 2011, p. 77.

100 **it is, he says, a 'map of signs about future possibilities':** Chris Frith, *Making up the Mind*, Blackwell Publishing, 2007, p. 41.

101 **quotes a figure of over eleven million:** Timothy D. Wilson, *Strangers to Ourselves*, Belknap Harvard, 2002, p.24.

101 **Professor John Gray has it at 'perhaps 14 million':** John Gray, *Straw Dogs*, Granta, 2002, p. 66.

101 **As V. S. Ramachandran writes, 'The brain must have some way . . .':** V. S. Ramachandran, *Phantoms in the Brain*, Harper Perennial, 1998, p. 134.

101 **the maximum number of points of information we are able to appreciate consciously:** David Brooks, *The Social Animal*, Short Books, 2011, p. x.

101 **'One option is to revise your story . . .' writes**

Ramachandran: V. S. Ramachandran, *Phantoms in the Brain*, Harper Perennial, 1998, p. 134.

101 cartoon characters, loved ones and historical characters: Todd E. Feinberg, *Altered Egos: How the Brain Creates the Self*, Oxford University Press, 2001, pp. 9–10.

102 Ten per cent of elderly people . . . similar processes: Chris Frith, *Making up the Mind*, Blackwell Publishing, 2007, p. 30.

102 Dr Clarence W. Olsen has spoken: Todd E. Feinberg, *Altered Egos: How the Brain Creates the Self*, Oxford University Press, 2001, pp. 28–9.

102 it takes between two and three weeks for their unpleasant situation: V. S. Ramachandran, *Phantoms in the Brain*, Harper Perennial, 1998, p. 150.

102 Academics at the University of Wisconsin: Daniel Levitin, 'The illusion of music', *New Scientist*, 23 February 2008.

103 V. S. Ramachandran has come across: V. S. Ramachandran, *Phantoms in the Brain*, Harper Perennial, 1998, pp. 40–2.

103 our world is 'not really . . . saints and sinners': Jonathan Haidt, *The Happiness Hypothesis*, Arrow, 2006, p. 15.

103 In New Guinea, the Gururumba men: Dylan Evans, *Emotion*, Oxford University Press, 2001, pp. 13, 14.

103 Many South Koreans are terrified of 'fan death': 'Newspapers fan belief in urban myth', *International Herald Tribune*, 10 January 2007.

104 contractors carrying out huge public works: Colin Nickerson, 'In Iceland, Spirits are in the Material World', *Boston Globe*, 25 December 1999.

104 They have a family member hold their shrinking part in place: David Brooks, *The Social Animal*, Short Books, 2011, p. 151.

104 we believe that alcohol is a disinhibitor: Kate Fox, *Watching the English*, Hodder, 2004, p. 261.

105 Studies by researchers in Switzerland: Dominique de Quervain, Urs Fischbacher, Valerie Treyer, Melanie Schellhammer, Colin Schnyder, Alfred Buck and Ernst Fehr

'The Neural Basis of Altruistic Punishment', *Science* 305, no. 5688, pp. 1254–8 (August, 2004).

105 **We have an additional, irresistible urge to divide the world:** Graham Lawton, 'The Grand Delusion', *New Scientist*, 14 May 2011.

105 **A study by three major US universities found:** 'Roots of Unconscious Prejudice Affect 90 to 95 percent of People', *Science Daily*, 30 September 1998.

105 **the only thing necessary to trigger tribal behaviour in humans:** J. Anderson Thompson Jnr, *Why We Believe in God(s)*, Pitchstone, 2011, p. 38.

105 **social psychologists Carol Tavris and Elliot Aronson describe:** Carol Tavris and Elliot Aronson, *Mistakes Were Made (But Not By Me)*, Pinter and Martin, 2007, p. 13.

106 **Psychologists know this as the 'makes sense stopping rule':** Jonathan Haidt, *The Happiness Hypothesis*, Arrow, 2006, p. 65.

106 **One of the neatest looked at unconscious sexism:** Graham Lawton, 'The Grand Delusion', *New Scientist*, 14 May 2011.

107 **Psychologist Deanna Kuhn found:** Michael Shermer, *Why People Believe Weird Things*, Souvenir Press, 2007, pp. 299, 300.

107 **One had people reading two arguments about the death penalty:** Thomas Gilovich, *How We Know What Isn't So*, Simon & Schuster, 1991, p. 54.

108 **In 2004, clinical psychologist Drew Westen:** Drew Westen, 'The Political Brain', *Public Affairs*, 2007, pp. x–xiv.

110 **participants trying to find a photograph of themselves:** Graham Lawton, 'The Grand Delusion', *New Scientist*, 14 May 2011.

110 **participants reading an essay about Rasputin:** David Eagleman, *Incognito: The Secret Lives of the Brain*, Canongate, 2011, pp. 62–3.

110 **A cognitive error we all share, known as the spotlight effect:** Graham Lawton, 'The Grand Delusion', *New Scientist*, 14 May 2011.

110 **Gamblers rewrite their memories:** Thomas Gilovich, *How We Know What Isn't So*, Simon & Schuster, 1991, p. 55.

111 **Athletes tend to put their victories down to training:** Thomas Gilovich, *How We Know What Isn't So*, Simon & Schuster, 1991, p. 55.

111 **74 per cent of drivers:** Graham Lawton, 'The Grand Delusion', *New Scientist*, 14 May 2011.

111 **94 per cent of university professors:** Thomas Gilovich, *How We Know What Isn't So*, Simon & Schuster, 1991, p. 77.

111 **When husbands and wives are asked to guess what percentage:** Jonathan Haidt, *The Happiness Hypothesis*, Arrow, 2006, p. 69.

111 **Half of all students in one survey predicted:** David Brooks, *The Social Animal*, Short Books, 2011, p. 214.

111 **having acted reasonably in the face of unfair provocation:** Roy Baumeister, *Evil: Inside Human Violence and Cruelty*, Barnes & Noble/W. H. Freeman, 1997, p. 43.

111 **The Nazis believed that they were on a mission of good:** Roy Baumeister, *Evil: Inside Human Violence and Cruelty*, Barnes & Noble/W. H. Freeman, 1997, p. 34.

111 **He writes, 'The perpetrators of evil . . .':** Roy Baumeister, *Evil: Inside Human Violence and Cruelty*, Barnes & Noble/ W. H. Freeman, 1997, p. 38.

111 **'many especially evil acts . . .':** Roy Baumeister, *Evil: Inside Human Violence and Cruelty*, Barnes & Noble/ W. H. Freeman, 1997, p. 29.

112 **We typically have a bias that tells us we are less susceptible to bias:** Emily Pronin, Daniel Y. Lin, Lee Ross, 'The Bias Blind Spot: Perceptions of Bias in Self Versus Others', *Personal and Social Psychology Bulletin*, March 2002.

7: 'Quack'
page
116 **four million pounds a year:** 'NHS money "wasted" on homeopathy', BBC News, 22 February 2010.

117 **billions in . . . the US:** 'The Use of Complementary and Alternative Medicine in the United States', National Center

for Complementary and Alternative Medicine, December 2008.

117 **Over fifteen thousand NHS prescriptions:** Martin Beckford, 'NHS spending on homeopathy prescriptions falls to £122,000', *Daily Telegraph*, 30 August 2011.

117 **score above 70 per cent:** 'NHS money "wasted"' on homeopathy', BBC News, 22 February 2010.

117 **Questions have been asked in Parliament:** http://www.publications.parliament.uk/pa/cm201011/ cmhansrd/cm100629/debtext/100629-0003.htm.

117 **the House of Commons Science and Technology Committee recommended:** 'NHS money "wasted" on homeopathy', BBC News, 22 February 2010.

117 **Even ex-Prime Minister Tony Blair has become involved:** 'Blair downplays creationism fears', BBC News, 2 November 2006.

117 **an eightfold drop in NHS prescriptions:** Martin Beckford, 'NHS spending on homeopathy prescriptions falls to £122,000', *Daily Telegraph*, 30 August 2011.

117 **just 0.001 per cent of the NHS's annual drug budget:** Martin Beckford, 'NHS spending on homeopathy prescriptions falls to £122,000', *Daily Telegraph*, 30 August 2011.

119 **which began in 1790:** (The birth of homeopathy is sometimes placed at 1792, but 1790 apparently represents the start of Hahnemann's experiments.) Simon Singh and Edzard Ernst, *Trick or Treatment*, Corgi, 2008, p. 119.

120 **one molecule . . . in your pill is one in a billion billion billion billion:** Simon Singh and Edzard Ernst, *Trick or Treatment*, Corgi, 2008, p. 124.

120 **a sphere of water that stretches from the earth to the sun:** Ben Goldacre, *Bad Science*, 4th Estate, 2008, p. 33.

122 **It is said that Vithoulkas dodged his judgement day:** 'George Vithoulkas Makes a Fool of Himself', *The Quackometer*, 24 February 2010.

122 **typically merciless statement that was published on Randi's personal blog:** James Randi, 'A Correction', Swift blog, 30 December 2008.

126 **Written by Dr Michael Shermer:** Michael Shermer, *Why People Believe Weird Things*, Souvenir Press, 2007, pp. 309–31.

132 **The American rationalist-celebrity Rebecca Watson:** Rebecca Watson interview, YouTube, uploaded 7 July 2008.

132 **This is why James Randi frequently rejects the title 'debunker':** 'The $18,000 question', *Straits Times*, 30 May 1991.

134 **the man Professor Chris French calls 'the patron saint of the Skeptics':** Interview, Chris French and James Randi, YouTube, April 2008, on behalf of *The Skeptic* magazine.

134 **Randi himself has said that 'any definitive tests . . . have been negative':** Interview [AP] *St. Petersburg Times* (Florida), 24 July 2007 and at JREF Staff page, http://www.randi.org/site/index.php/staff.html.

135 ***Nature*, published a study:** E. Davenas et al., 'Human basophil degranulation triggered by very dilute antiserum against IgE', *Nature* 333, June 1988.

136 **Benveniste was initially sceptical of homeopathy:** *Heretics of Science*, episode one, BBC2, 1994.

136 **his best researcher, Dr Elisabeth Davenas:** *Heretics of Science*, episode one, BBC2, 1994.

136 **the results were reportedly replicated by four laboratories:** Maddox, Stewart, Randi, '"High-dilution" experiments a delusion', *Nature*, 28 July 1988. (Description of *Nature* replication that follows is sourced from the BBC documentary, the *Nature* articles and *Trick or Treatment*, by Simon Singh and Edzard Ernst).

136 **Dr Elisabeth Davenas – a homeopathy proponent:** Simon Singh and Edzard Ernst, *Trick or Treatment*, Corgi, 2008, p. 151.

137 **When the result was revealed, some of Benveniste's scientists wept:** *Heretics of Science*, episode one, BBC2, 1994.

137 **Their report was published in *Nature* in July 1988:** Maddox, Stewart, Randi, '"High-dilution" experiments a delusion', *Nature*, 28 July 1988.

137 **Benveniste fought back:** 'Dr Jacques Benveniste replies',
     Nature, 28 July 1988.

137 **He described the investigation as a 'pantomime':** *Heretics of
     Science*, episode one, BBC2, 1994.

137 **Benveniste finished his grand defence:** 'Dr Jacques
     Benveniste replies', *Nature*, 28 July 1988.

138 **Two years later, he was fired:** *Heretics of Science*, episode one,
     BBC2, 1994.

138 **'Shang et al.':** Aijing Shang et al., 'Are the clinical effects
     of homoeopathy placebo effects? Comparative study of
     placebo-controlled trials of homoeopathy and allopathy',
     Lancet, 27 August 2005. (I made repeated attempts to
     approach Shang and members of his team for comment
     and assistance, but unfortunately they declined to help.)

142 **'One day,' he said, 'we are going to be able to get our drugs
     on the phone':** *Heretics of Science*, episode one, BBC2, 1994.

142 **'Today you can send a strand of your hair':** Interview with
     Andy Lewis, *The Quackometer*.

142 **'milk of the dolphin'. . . :** These are treatments
     recommended by Nancy Herrick in 'Animal Mind, Human
     Voices', noted on *Reviewed* by Edi Mottershead (accessed at:
     http://www.minimum.com/reviews/animal-mind.htm) and
     biography of Herrick on the website of the Hahnemann
     Clinic, Point Richmond:
     http://www.herrickmorrison.com/sitemap.html.

143 **The Cancer Act 1939:** Section 4: '(1) No person shall take
     any part in the publication of any advertisement –.
     (a) containing an offer to treat any person for cancer, or to
     prescribe any remedy therefore, or to give any advice in
     connection with the treatment thereof . . .'.

8: 'Some type of tiny wasps'

page

146 **Morgellons was named in 2002, by American mom Mary
     Leitao:** Brigid Schulte, 'Figments of the Imagination?',
     Washington Post, 20 January 2008.

146 **Using a microscope:** Chico Harlan, 'Mom fights for answers on what's wrong with her son', *Pittsburgh Post-Gazette*, 23 July 2006.

146 **blue, black and white fibres:** Elizabeth Devita-Raeburn, 'The Morgellons Mystery', *Psychology Today*, 1 March 2007.

146 **patients in 'every continent except Antarctica':** http://www.thecehf.org/morgellons-disease-bizarre-truth.html.

147 **Even folk singer Joni Mitchell has been affected:** Matt Diehl, 'It's a Joni Mitchell concert, sans Joni', *Los Angeles Times*, 22 April 2012.

147 **thousands of sufferers in the US have written to members of Congress:** Brigid Schulte, 'Figments of the Imagination?', *Washington Post*, 20 January 2008.

147 **In 2008, the CDC established a special task force:** 'CDC to Launch Study on Unexplained Illness', CDC Press Briefing Transcript, Moderator: Dave Daigle, 16 January 2008, 2:00 p.m. EST.

149 **academics such as Jeffrey Meffert:** Brigid Schulte, 'Figments of the Imagination?', *Washington Post*, 20 January 2008.

149 **Dr Mary Seeman, Emeritus Professor of Psychiatry:** Michael Mason, 'Is It Disease or Delusion? U.S. Takes on a Dilemma', *New York Times*, 24 October 2006.

149 **Dr Steven Novella of 'The Skeptic's Guide to the Universe' agrees:** 'Delusional Parasitosis', sciencebasedmedicine.org, 18 May 2011.

150 **In the spring of 2005, Randy Wymore:** Interview with author & Brigid Schulte, 'Figments of the Imagination?', *Washington Post*, 20 January 2008.

151 **the moment they discovered the job was related to Morgellons:** Randy Wymore, Presentation, fourth Annual Morgellons Conference in Austin, Texas, 2 April 2011.

159 **I find a 2008 paper on Morgellons:** Robert E. Accordino et al., 'Morgellons Disease?', *Dermatologic Therapy*, vol. 21, issue 1, pp. 8–12, January 2008.

160 **In 1987 a team of German researchers found:** Atul Gawande, 'The Itch', *New Yorker*, 30 June 2008.

167 **'No parasites or mycobacteria were detected,' it reports:**
M. L. Pearson, J. V. Selby, K. A. Katz, V. Cantrell, C. R.
Braden et al., 'Clinical, Epidemiologic, Histopathologic
and Molecular Features of an Unexplained Dermopathy',
PLoS ONE 7(1) (2012): e29908.
doi:10.1371/journal.pone.0029908.

167 **Commenting on the work, Steven Novella:** 'Morgellons,
Creating a New Disease', www.skepticblog.org, 6 February
2012.

9: 'Top Dog wants his name in'

page

180 **In his book *Doctoring the Mind*:** Richard Bentall, *Doctoring
the Mind*, Allen Lane, 2009, p. 131.

181 **A typical example is a 2004 paper:** P. Bebbington et al.,
'Psychosis, victimisation and childhood disadvantage:
Evidence from the second British National Survey of
Psychiatric Morbidity', *British Journal of Psychiatry* 185
(2004), pp. 220–6.

10: 'They're frightening people'

page

200 *Most recently (1991–1996) she has been the Head of Ethics
Science and Information for the British Medical Association*:
http://www.networkprivacy.gg/fleur.htm.

206 **accused of being 'fixated on finding satanic abuse':** Esther
Addley, 'I Could Not Stop Crying', *Guardian*, 21 October
2006.

206 **a cognitive-psychology student named Jim Coan:** Interview
with author.

212 **Dr Sinason's NHS-funded 'Clinic for Dissociative Studies':**
http://clinicds.com/3.html.

212 **Dr Sinason is well known in mental-health circles:**
http://valeriesinason.co.uk.

212 **an in-demand speaker . . . Department of Health:** Interview
with author.

212 **the Bulger killings:** Blake Morrison, 'Jon Venables is not yet beyond redemption', *Guardian*, 27 July 2010.

212 **Chris Langham:** James Hanning, 'Comic release: Is it time to forgive Chris Langham?', *Independent*, 6 December 2009.

212 **controversial condition known as multiple personality disorder or 'DID':** Amanda Mitchison, 'Kim Noble: The woman with 100 personalities', *Guardian*, 30 September 2011.

216 **paedophiles occasionally meddle with pagan rites and symbolism:** 'Kidwelly sex cult members face long jail sentences', BBC News Wales, 9 March 2011.

220 **'It turned out to be that, yes. The people didn't remember at first. They weren't aware.'** Dr Fisher has previously admitted to journalist Daniel Foggo that 'Carole had "no knowledge" of any ritual abuse when she first saw her.' Daniel Foggo, *Sunday Times*, 12 June 2011.

11: 'There was nothing there, but I knew it was a cockerel'

page

226 **in a paper published in the *Journal of Philosophical Studies*:** Lisa Bortolotti and Matteo Mameli, 'Self Deception, Delusion and the Boundaries of Folk Psychology', *Journal of Philosophical Studies*, vol. 20, pp. 203–21.

226 **Psychiatrist Robin Murray:** *The Life Scientific with Robin Murray*, BBC Radio Four, first broadcast 7 February 2012.

227 **According to Professor of Psychiatry Bruce Wexler:** Bruce E. Wexler, *Brain and Culture*, MIT Press, 2008, p. 9.

227 **Developmental biologist Professor Lewis Wolpert writes:** Lewis Wolpert, *Six Impossible Things Before Breakfast*, Faber, 2007, p. 36.

227 **Psychologist Jonathan Haidt has called effectance:** Jonathan Haidt, *The Happiness Hypothesis*, Arrow, 2006, p. 22.

227 **Professor Daniel Kahneman invites his readers:** Daniel Kahneman, *Thinking, Fast and Slow*, Penguin, 2011, p. 50.

228 **Professor Wolpert, meanwhile, writes of studies:** Lewis

Wolpert, *Six Impossible Things Before Breakfast*, Faber, 2007, p. 16.

228 **mode of language that is millions of years older:** Drew Westen, *The Political Brain*, Public Affairs, 2007, p. 57.

228 **every sight, every smell, every person, every idea, everything:** Michael S. Gazzaniga, *Human*, Harper Perennial, 2008, pp. 121, 124.

228 **Professor Michael Gazzaniga writes:** Michael S. Gazzaniga, *Human*, Harper Perennial, 2008, p. 124.

228 **incapable of making these decisions:** Michael S. Gazzaniga, *Human*, Harper Perennial, 2008, p. 120.

228 **hitting you with dread or desire:** David Brooks, *The Social Animal*, Short Books, 2011, p. 207.

229 **in the words of Professor David Eagleman:** David Eagleman, *Incognito: The Secret Lives of the Brain*, Canongate, 2011, p. 104.

229 **Professor Bruce Wexler writes:** Bruce E. Wexler, *Brain and Culture*, MIT Press, 2008, p. 125.

230 **he offers the example of young Native American men:** Bruce E. Wexler, *Brain and Culture*, MIT Press, 2008, p. 126.

230 **Eagleman, 'not at the centre of the action:** David Eagleman, *Incognito: The Secret Lives of the Brain*, Canongate, 2011, p. 9.

230 **Scientists at the Monell Centre, Philadelphia:** David Brooks, *The Social Animal*, Short Books, 2011, p. 16.

230 **When chickens are born in industrial hatcheries:** David Eagleman, *Incognito: The Secret Lives of the Brain*, Canongate, 2011, p. 57.

231 **Researcher Richard Horsey says:** Richard Horsey, 'The Art of Chicken Sexing', UCL Working Papers in Linguistics, 2002.

231 **a team led by Professor Antoine Bechara:** Antoine Bechara, Hanna Damasio, Daniel Tranel and Antonio R. Damasio, 'Deciding Advantageously Before Knowing the Advantageous Strategy', *Science* 275, no. 5304, pp. 1293–5 (February 1997).

233 **Professor Timothy Wilson writes in *Redirect*:** Timothy D. Wilson, *Redirect: The Surprising New Science of Psychological Change*, Allen Lane, 2011, p. 51.

233 their understanding that germs and food can cause sickness:
Lewis Wolpert, *Six Impossible Things Before Breakfast*, Faber,
2007, pp. 48–9.

234 In 1889 the German psychiatrist Albert Moll: Daniel M.
Wenger, *The Illusion of Conscious Will*, MIT Press, 2002,
p. 149.

234 Seventy-three years later, researchers at Columbia
University: Michael S. Gazzaniga, *Human*, Harper
Perennial, 2008, pp. 295, 296.

235 Why this is remains a mystery: Jonathan Haidt, *The
Happiness Hypothesis*, Arrow, 2006, p. 7.

235 (although some speculate . . . sources of light): Email to
author from Professor Chris Frith.

235 the left side is specialised for language: Jonathan Haidt,
The Happiness Hypothesis, Arrow, 2006, p. 7.

235 the right is effectively mute: Jonathan Haidt, *The Happiness
Hypothesis*, Arrow, 2006, p. 9.

236 he flashed a picture of a chicken claw: Michael S. Gazzaniga,
Human, Harper Perennial, 2008, p. 294.

237 Gazzaniga flashed the command 'Walk': Daniel Wegner,
The Illusion of Conscious Will, MIT Press, 2002, p. 182.

237 driven to constantly narrate our actions: Jonathan Haidt,
The Happiness Hypothesis, Arrow, 2006, p. 8.

237 Gazzaniga writes, 'Ah, lack of knowledge is of no
importance: Michael S. Gazzaniga, *Human*, Harper
Perennial, 2008, pp. 296, 297.

238 Opinions range from those of Professor David Eagleman:
David Eagleman, *Incognito: The Secret Lives of the Brain*,
Canongate, 2011, pp. 137, 148.

238 Professor of Psychology Daniel Wegner, who argues: This
summary of his position was confirmed as 'apt' in an email
from Professor Wegner.

238 'can at best be a small factor: David Eagleman, 'The Brain on
Trial', *The Atlantic*, July/August 2011.

239 A 1962 study by Professor Daniel Offer: Carol Tavris and
Elliot Aronson, *Mistakes Were Made (But Not By Me)*, Pinter
and Martin, 2007, p. 76.

240 **Social psychologists Carol Tavris and Elliot Aronson believe:** Carol Tavris and Elliot Aronson, *Mistakes Were Made (But Not By Me)*, Pinter and Martin, 2007, p. 76.

240 **One, for example, involves a man buying a chicken from a supermarket:** Jonathan Haidt, *The Righteous Mind*, Allen Lane, 2012, p. 3.

240 **After 1,620 harmless offence stories:** Jonathan Haidt, *The Righteous Mind*, Allen Lane, 2012, p. 24.

241 **"I know it's wrong, but I just can't think of a reason why":** Jonathan Haidt, *The Righteous Mind*, Allen Lane, 2012, p. 25.

241 **'moral reasoning is part of our lifelong struggle:** Jonathan Haidt, *The Righteous Mind*, Allen Lane, 2012, p. 50.

241 **Don't take people's moral arguments at face value:** Jonathan Haidt, *The Righteous Mind*, Allen Lane, 2012, p. xiv.

241 **We are selfish hypocrites:** Jonathan Haidt, *The Righteous Mind*, Allen Lane, 2012, p. xv.

241 **'myoclonic jerk':** Jeff Warren, *Head Trip: Adventures on the Wheel of Consciousness*, Oneworld, 2007, p. 31.

241 **As neuroscientist and sleep expert Dr Stephen LaBerge has said:** Jeff Warren, *Head Trip: Adventures on the Wheel of Consciousness*, Oneworld, 2007, p. 100.

241 **neuroscientist and philosopher Thomas Metzinger notes:** Thomas Metzinger, *The Ego Tunnel*, Basic Books, 2009, p. 138.

243 **Dopamine helps to tell us when our models need updating:** My understanding of this principle of dopamine was assisted by Professor Chris Frith.

243 **'It is so unsettling to think such thoughts:** Timothy D. Wilson, *Redirect: The Surprising New Science of Psychological Change*, Allen Lane, 2011, p. 52.

243 **Analysis of one hundred such papers:** Bob Holmes, Kurt Kleiner, Kate Douglas and Michael Bond, 'Reasons to be cheerful', *New Scientist*, 4 October 2003.

243 **Anthropologists at the University of Connecticut:** Matthew Hutson, 'In Defense of Superstition', *New York Times*, 6 April 2012.

244 He tells of an examination of a group of people: Timothy D.
Wilson, *Redirect: The Surprising New Science of Psychological
Change*, Allen Lane, 2011, p. 55.

244 Says Professor Wilson, 'Those who had learned: Timothy
D. Wilson, *Redirect: The Surprising New Science of
Psychological Change*, Allen Lane, 2011, p. 56.

12: 'I came of exceptional parents'

page

246 Christ Church? Was that it?: I subsequently discovered that
my father attended Exeter College.

248 Cognitive psychologist Professor Martin Conway: Charles
Fernyhough, 'Our Memories Tell Our Story', *Guardian*,
22 March 2010.

251 a popular speaker with America's Tea Party movement:
'Christopher, a Man of Many Talents'.
http://www.ukip.org/content/latest-news/1675-christopher-a-
man-of-many-talents.

251 He has labelled climate science the 'largest fraud of all time':
Leo Hickman, '"Chemical nonsense": Leading scientists
refute Lord Monckton's attack on climate science', *Guardian*,
21 September 2010.

251 believes that 'the Hitler Youth were left wing . . .
Nuremberg Rallies: Interview with Jacek Szkudlarek,
corbettreport.com, December 2009, YouTube.

251 he believes that 'very little' warming of the earth will take
place: 'Lord Monckton: Climate facts, not "consensus" ',
Daily Herald, 22 March 2010.

251 When the presentation . . . was heard by Professor John
Abraham: John Abraham, 'Monckton takes scientist to brink
of madness at climate change talk', *Guardian*, 3 June 2010.

251 Monckton responded by accusing Abraham: 'Monckton:
At Last, the Climate Extremists Try to Debate Us! (PJM
Exclusive)', PJmedia.com, 4 June 2010.

252 Our modern notion of 'left' and 'right' beliefs: John T. Jost,

"Elective Affinities": On the Psychological Bases of
Left–Right Differences', *Psychological Inquiry* 20 (2009),
pp. 129–41.

252 **clinical psychologist and political strategist Professor Drew
Westen:** Drew Westen, *The Political Brain*, Public Affairs,
2007, p. 82.

253 **In *The Righteous Mind*, Haidt writes that genes account for:**
Jonathan Haidt, *The Righteous Mind*, Allen Lane, 2012,
p. 278.

253 **An analysis of thirteen thousand Australians:** Jonathan
Haidt, *The Righteous Mind*, Allen Lane, 2012, pp. 277–9.

254 **In *The Political Brain*, Professor Westen writes:** Drew
Westen, *The Political Brain*, Public Affairs, 2007, p. 146.

254 **the political left and the right each has a 'master narrative':**
Drew Westen, *The Political Brain*, Public Affairs, 2007,
p. 158.

255 **'The data from political science are crystal clear':** Drew
Westen, *The Political Brain*, Public Affairs, 2007, p. 123.

255 **'shows much promise in curing everything from HIV to
malaria to multiple sclerosis.':** *The Lord Monckton Roadshow*,
ABC Television, Sunday 17 July 2011.

256 **this liveryman of the Worshipful Company of Broderers:**
Who's Who 2007, p. 1599.

262 **'There is only one way to stop AIDS':** 'AIDS: A British View',
American Spectator, January 1987, pp. 29–32.

266 **'a worldwide coup d'état by bureaucrats':** Interview with
Jacek Szkudlarek, corbettreport.com, December 2009,
YouTube.

266 **who seek to 'impose a Communist world government on the
world':** Speech to an event sponsored by the Minnesota Free
Market Institute, 14 October 2009.

267 **he writes that moral reasoning 'evolved not to help us find
truth:** Jonathan Haidt, *The Righteous Mind*, Allen Lane,
2012, p. 76.

13: 'Backwards and forwards in the slime'

page

270 **The assistant to Hitler's ambassador:** 'Mrs Jaenelle Antas worked for David Irving from August 2008 to December 2011.' According to David Irving's website: http://www.fpp.co.uk/docs/Irving/staff_Ja.html.

272 **Vienna's Josefstadt prison:** Ruth Elkins, 'Irving gets three years' jail in Austria for Holocaust denial', *Independent*, 21 February 2006.

272 **In 1993 the American historian Professor Deborah Lipstadt wrote:** The Hon. Mr Justice Gray, Judgment, Tuesday 11 April 2000, Court 36, Royal Courts of Justice.

272 **at one point accidentally calling the judge 'Mein Führer':** Christopher Hitchens, 'The Strange Case of David Irving', *Los Angeles Times*, 20 May 2001.

273 **'Irving has misstated historical evidence':** The Hon. Mr Justice Gray, Judgment, Tuesday 11 April 2000, Court 36, Royal Courts of Justice.

273 **Irving called the verdict 'indescribable' and 'perverse':** 'Unrepentant Irving blasts "perverse" judgment', *Guardian*, 11 April 2000.

273 **a similar one against the *Observer*:** 'David Irving v the Observer', *Observer*, 16 April 2000.

275 **'All Irving's historiographical "errors":** The Hon. Mr Justice Gray, Judgment, Tuesday 11 April 2000, Court 36, Royal Courts of Justice.

276 **Irving 'was clearly incensed:** Richard J. Evans, *Telling Lies About Hitler*, Verso, 2002, p. 12.

276 **'Whether or not Lipstadt was correct to claim:** Richard J. Evans, *Telling Lies About Hitler*, Verso, 2002, p. 8.

277 **The *Daily Mail* quoted a spokesman for the Polish embassy:** 'Controversial historian David Irving to tour Nazi death camps in Poland', *Daily Mail*, 8 September 2010.

281 **a 2009 article from the *Daily Mail*:** Jason Lewis, 'Hitler historian David Irving and the beautiful blonde on the rifle range', *Daily Mail*, 20 December 2009. Antas responds to

this piece on her blog, 'Make Lemonade', 4 April 2001.
http://www.alternativeright.com/main/blogs/exit-
strategies/make-lemonade/.

281 **'a neo-Nazi pin-up':** Jason Lewis, 'Hitler historian David Irving and the beautiful blonde on the rifle range', *Daily Mail*, 20 December 2009.

281 **On the website of an obscure publishing group:** Alex Kurtagic, 'Interview with Jaenelle Antas', 9 January 2011, Wermod and Wermod Publishing Group.

282 **he 'believed that there had been something like a Holocaust:** Speech, Calgary, Alberta, 29 September 1991, quoted in libel judgment.

282 **His denial came in 1989:** D. D. Guttenplan, *The Holocaust on Trial*, Granta, 2001, p. 53.

282 **flawed study by a man named Fred Leuchter:** Deborah E. Lipstadt, *History on Trial*, Harper Perennial, 2005, p. 35.

283 **'the biggest calibre shell that has yet hit the battleship Auschwitz':** Deborah E. Lipstadt, *History on Trial*, Harper Perennial, 2005, p. 83.

283 **In 1991 he reissued his most lauded book:** Deborah E. Lipstadt, *History on Trial*, Harper Perennial, 2005, p. 84.

283 **He had some advice for the Jewish people:** [Irving's website]: http://www.fpp.co.uk/docs/ADL/ADLQandA.html.

283 **he was fined 3,000 marks in Germany for 'defaming the memory:** Michael Shermer, *Why People Believe Weird Things*, Souvenir Press, 1997, p. 196.

283 **'never adopted the narrow-minded approach':** Michael Shermer, *Why People Believe Weird Things*, Souvenir Press, 1997, p. 195.

283 **The following year he told an Australian radio host:** Michael Shermer, *Why People Believe Weird Things*, Souvenir Press, 1997, p. 195.

283 **In 1996 he admitted some Jews *were* systematically killed:** Ron Rosenbaum, *Explaining Hitler*, Faber and Faber, 1998, p. 238.

283 **Over the same period, he was banned from Germany:**

[Irving's website]:
http://www.fpp.co.uk/Germany/docs/index.html.

283 **and Australia:** [Irving's website]:
http://www.fpp.co.uk/Australia/index.html.

283 **deported from Canada:** [Irving's website]:
http://www.fpp.co.uk/Canada/Legal/NiagFallsAdjudication.
html.

283 **spent a short period in a Munich prison:** Ron Rosenbaum,
Explaining Hitler, Faber and Faber, 1998, p. 224.

283 **dropped by his publishers in Britain and the US:** D. D.
Guttenplan, *The Holocaust on Trial,* Granta, 2001, pp. 54, 55.

283 **his 'life has come under a gradually mounting attack:**
Robert J. Van Pelt, *The Case for Auschwitz: Evidence from the
Irving Trial,* Indiana University Press, 2002, p. 56.

284 **he had a long-standing offer of $1,000:** Michael Shermer,
Why People Believe Weird Things, Souvenir Press, 1997,
p. 195.

284 **After all, he comes from a patriotic British military family:**
Miscellaneous biographical details from interview with
author.

284 **need to be an 'ambassador to Hitler':** Richard J. Evans,
Telling Lies About Hitler, Verso, 2002, p. 48.

286 **It was 1955, and the seventeen-year-old was told:** Interview
with author.

286 **one issue of which was said to contain a tribute to Hitler's
Germany:** Rosie Waterhouse, 'From Brentwood to
Berchtesgaden. Rosie Waterhouse traces the disturbing story
of the "revisionist" David Irving', *Independent,* 11 July 1992.

286 **to the *Daily Mail*, in comments he has since denied making:**
[Irving's website]
http://www.fpp.co.uk/docs/Irving/cesspit/mild/fascist.html.

286 **saw the fascist Sir Oswald Mosley speak at a rally:** D. D.
Guttenplan, *The Holocaust on Trial,* Granta, 2001, p. 42.

286 **'The Nottingham race disturbances were caused by coloured
wide boys:** University College Newspaper, 2 February 1961,
p. 1.

286 he suspected that he had been mis-marked: D. D.
     Guttenplan, *The Holocaust on Trial*, Granta, 2001, p. 41.
287 he wrote to Krupp, the Nazi armaments manufacturer:
     D.D. Guttenplan, *The Holocaust on Trial*, Granta, 2001, p. 42.
299 historians 'do not, as Irving kept demanding, seek a
     "smoking gun"**: Deborah E. Lipstadt, *History on Trial*,
     Harper Perennial, 2005, p. 133.
299 'Confirmation bias even sees to it that no evidence: Carol
     Tavris and Elliot Aronson, *Mistakes Were Made (But Not By
     Me)*, Pinter and Martin, 2007, p. 20.
299 An interview with Irving's brother Nicholas: Olga Craig,
     'David, what on earth would Mother think?', *Daily Telegraph*,
     26 February 2006.
300 'Earlier experiences had persuaded me': John Keegan, 'The
     trial of David Irving – and my part in his downfall', *Daily
     Telegraph*, 12 April 2000.
300 Psychologist David Perkins conducted a simple study:
     Jonathan Haidt, *The Righteous Mind*, Allen Lane, 2012,
     pp. 80, 81.
301 What if Hitler hadn't known about the Holocaust? Interview
     with author.
301 Around the period in which Irving was considering this find:
     Ron Rosenbaum, *Explaining Hitler*, Faber and Faber, 1998,
     p. 224.

14: 'That one you just go, "eeerrrr" '

page
312 compiled the data from more than thirty thousand trials like
     this: Actual number: 30,803.
312 mysterious 'sense of being stared at': Rupert Sheldrake,
     'The Sense of Being Stared At Part 1: Is it Real or Illusory?',
     Journal of Consciousness Studies 12, no. 6 (2005), p. 15.
313 Sheldrake grew up in a herbalist's shop: Biographical
     information from interview with author.
314 the *Observer* had called it 'fascinating and far-reaching':
     Rupert Sheldrake, *A New Science of Life*, Blond and

Briggs, 1981. [Reviews excerpted from Icon Books, 2009 edition.]

315 **'A Book for Burning?':** 'A book for burning?', *Nature* 293, 24 September 1981, pp. 245–6.

316 **Nobel Prize-winner Francis Crick, who wrote:** Francis Crick, *The Astonishing Hypothesis: The Scientific Search For The Soul*, Scribner, 1995.

316 **Sheldrake's explorations into telepathy:** Rupert Sheldrake, 'The "Sense of Being Stared At" Confirmed by Simple Experiments', *Biology Forum* 92 (1999), pp. 53–76.

316 **one in ten thousand billion billion:** Rupert Sheldrake, 'The Sense of Being Stared At Part 1: Is it Real or Illusory?', *Journal of Consciousness Studies* 12, no. 6 (2005), p. 15.

316 **Next, he studied a psychic terrier from Ramsbottom:** Rupert Sheldrake and Pamela Smart, 'A Dog That Seems To Know When His Owner is Coming Home: Videotaped Experiments and Observations', *Journal of Scientific Exploration* 14 (2000), pp. 233–55.

317 **Lewis Wolpert, who described telepathy research as 'pathological science':** The RSA Telepathy Debate, Royal Society of Arts, London, 15 January 2004.

317 **tapping his pencil, 'looking bored':** Philip Stevens, 'Rupert Sheldrake and the wider scientific community', dissertation, London Centre for the History of Science, Medicine and Technology 2008/09.

317 **asked to speak at the 2006 Festival of Science, his presence was denounced:** Mark Henderson, 'Theories of telepathy and afterlife cause uproar at top science forum', *The Times*, 6 September 2006.

317 **'No, but I would be very suspicious of it':** BBC Radio Five Live debate, 6 September 2006.

318 **The first paragraph of Wiseman's bestseller:** Richard Wiseman, *Paranormality: Why We See What Isn't There*, Macmillan, 2011.

319 **In 2006 Rupert Sheldrake was given a 'Pigasus' award:** The 11th Annual Pigasus Awards, awarded 1 April 2007, http://www.randi.org/pigasus/index.html.

319 **Randi writes, somewhat cryptically:** James Randi's Swift
blog, 8 September 2006, www.randi.org/jr/2006-09/
09806guess.html.

320 **It began, for Richard Wiseman, when he was eight:**
Biographical information from interview with author and
from Richard Wiseman, *Paranormality: Why We See What
Isn't There*, Macmillan, 2011.

321 **a German academic named Stefan Schmidt:** Stefan Schmidt
et al., 'Distant intentionality and the feeling of being stared
at: Two meta-analyses', *British Journal of Psychology* 95
(2004), pp. 235–47.

321 **a study by academics at the University of Amsterdam:** Eva
Lobach and Dick J. Bierman, 'Who's Calling At This Hour?
Local Sidereal Time And Telephone Telepathy', University of
Amsterdam, Parapsychological Association Convention
2004.

322 **to replicate Sheldrake's staring tests with parapsychologist
Marilyn Schlitz:** R. Wiseman and M. Schlitz, 'Experimenter
effects and the remote detection of staring', *Journal of
Parapsychology* 61 (1997), pp. 199–207.

322 **Wiseman went on to conduct four tests on Jaytee the dog:**
R. Wiseman, M. Smith, and J. Milton, 'Can animals detect
when their owners are returning home? An experimental
test of the "psychic pet" phenomenon', *British Journal of
Psychology* 89 (1998), pp. 453–62.

322 **'Psychic dog is no more than a chancer':** *The Times*,
21 August 1998.

322 **'Psychic pets are exposed as a myth':** *Daily Telegraph*,
22 August 1998.

322 **While Wiseman admits this is true:** 'Collaboration Between
Skeptics and Paranormal Researchers', *Skeptiko*, 17 April
2007.

324 **Later I find a paper co-written by Wiseman:** Richard
Wiseman, Matthew Smith and Julie Milton, 'The "Psychic
Pet" Phenomenon: A reply to Rupert Sheldrake', accessed
on Wiseman's website: http://www.richardwiseman.com/
resources/psychicdogreply.pdf.

324 **another that was *proposed by Wiseman himself*:** Rupert
Sheldrake, 'The Sense of Being Stared At Part 1: Is it Real
or Illusory?', *Journal of Consciousness Studies* 12, no. 6 (2005),
p. 24.

324 **the authors of the University of Amsterdam study . . . admit:**
From the above study: 'These simulations show that the
effects found in staring studies involving feedback to the
staree might explain the difference between the effects
reported by Sheldrake and the absence of those effects in
ours. However, as we noted above, Sheldrake has since
reported quite a number of studies that do not provide
feedback to the staree, and these show somewhat smaller,
but still large effects (Sheldrake, 2001b), unlike our three
studies, so it leaves our question in part still unanswered.'.

325 **But then Wiseman sends more concerns. And Sheldrake
counters them:** For those interested, I'll note a brief
summary of these concerns and Sheldrake's responses:.

   Wiseman's concerns about the dog trials:. The first series
of thirty dog trials wasn't randomised, therefore the dog
might know from Pam's routine or dress or reactions of
other people.

   Sheldrake's response: The first series did have Pam
returning at a wide variety of times. Jaytee had already been
observed to wait at the window when Pam was on the way
home at different times of day when she was returning in a
non-routine manner. These data were documented in the
part of the paper that described preliminary investigations.
[http://www.sheldrake.org/Articles&Papers/papers/animals/
pdf/dogknows.pdf] The distribution of return times is shown
in Fig. 1 and the details of each journey, including the
distances are given in Table 1, and show that Jaytee
anticipated Pam's return on 85 out of 100 occasions,
irrespective of the time of day and mode of transport.

   Says Sheldrake, 'We had documented his behaviour, and
done some experiments on random return times and modes
of transport in considerable detail before we began our

filmed tests. We already knew from these observations that this was not a matter of routine, and that Jaytee's responses could not be explained in terms of hearing familiar vehicles. The 30 filmed tests took further this series of observations under real-life conditions. Only by disregarding all the details can Wiseman suggest that these could be explained in terms of routine anticipations of Pam's patterns of behaviour.'

Another concern about the dog trials: The second series of trials was randomised. But in these, the dog might simply be going to the window more and more over time (and therefore is there most when Pam returns).

The way to assess this is to compare short, medium and long trials. There are not enough of them in the random series to do this. Sheldrake does do this with the non-random homecomings, but that isn't of any use because they might have cues regarding when Pam might return (see above).

Sheldrake's response:. The complaint that Jaytee might have been simply going to the window more and more over time had been controlled for.

Sheldrake: 'The reason we did the control trials when Pam was not coming home was precisely to address the question that Wiseman raises as to whether Jaytee went to the door more and more the longer Pam was out. We had already shown he did not do that in the 30 trials, comparing long, medium and short, and there is no suggestion he was doing that in the randomised trials. But the control data show clearly that there was no such pattern. Wiseman simply ignores these data. You can see these in Fig. 5 of this paper: http://www.sheldrake.org/Articles&Papers/papers/animals/pdf/dog_video.pdf.'

325 **adding a meta-analysis that confirms his view:** Dean Radin, 'The Sense of Being Stared At: A Preliminary Meta-Analysis', *Journal of Consciousness Studies* 12, no.6 (2005), pp. 95–100.

325 **Computer pioneer Alan Turing once said:** John Horgan, 'Brilliant Scientists are Open-Minded about Paranormal Stuff, So Why Not You?', *Scientific American*, 20 July 2012.

325 *New Scientist* **has reported:** Robert Matthews, 'Opposites Detract', *New Scientist*, 13 March 2004.

326 **Celebrated physicist Freeman Dyson has said:** John Horgan, 'Brilliant Scientists are Open-Minded about Paranormal Stuff, So Why Not You?', *Scientific American*, 20 July 2012.

325 **As far back as 1951, pioneering neuroscientist Donald Hebb admitted:** Montague Ullman, *The Comprehensive Textbook of Psychiatry*, Vol. 3, 3rd edition, Chapter 56, Section 15, pp. 3235–45, 1980. [Accessed: http://siivola.org/monte/papers_grouped/copyrighted/ parapsychology_&_psi/Parapsychology.htm].

326 **in 2008, a famously sceptical psychologist:** Danny Penman, 'Could there be proof to the theory that we're ALL psychic?', *Daily Mail*, 28 January 2008 [In its original form, this quote specifically refers to remote viewing. Elsewhere, Wiseman confirms this as 'a slight misquote because I was using the term in more of a general sense of ESP. That is, I was not talking about remote viewing per se, but rather Ganzfeld, etc. as well.': {http://www.skeptiko.com/rupert-sheldrake-and-richard-wiseman-clash/}].

15: 'A suitable place'

331 *Wired* **magazine says that 'he knows more:** Rob Beschizza, '10 Tips For Dealing With James Randi: Claim Your Million Today!', *Wired*, 26 October 2007.

331 **Richard Dawkins has given him a 'Richard Dawkins award':** About James Randi: Detailed biography on JREF website: http://www.randi.org/site/index.php/component/content/ article/58.html.

331 **hosted sell-out thousand-dollar-a-head fundraising dinners:** Sheilla Jones, *Globe and Mail* (Canada), 10 July 2010.

331 **Celebrity magicians Penn and Teller call him:** '"I don't

know"— and that's no act', Penn Jillette, *Los Angeles Times*, 3 July 2008.

331 **Wiseman credits his 1982 book *Flim Flam*:** 'Richard Wiseman on Debunking the Paranormal', *The Browser*, 2 April 2012.

331 **The former editor of *The Skeptic* magazine says:** Interview with author (quote is from Professor Chris French).

331 **The founding editor of the US edition has called him:** Patricia Cohen, 'Poof! You're a Skeptic: The Amazing Randi's Vanishing Humbug', *New York Times*, 17 February 2001.

331 **The *New York Times* has described him as:** Michael Sokolove, 'The Debunker', *New York Times*, 25 December 2005.

331 **Isaac Asimov has said:** Interview with Scot Morris, *Omni* Magazine, April 1980, p. 78.

331 **Sir John Maddox, the former editor of the . . . science journal *Nature*:** 'The $18,000 question', *Straits Times*, 30 May 1991.

332 **the man the Skeptics exalt as their 'patron saint':** Interview, Chris French and James Randi, YouTube, April 2008, on behalf of *The Skeptic* magazine.

333 **James Randi was born an illegitimate:** Trailer for documentary, 'An Honest Liar', viewed at: http://www.skepticmoney.com/an-honest-liar-the-story-of-the-amazing-james-randi/.

333 **'genius or near genius':** Interview with author.

334 **A child prodigy:** Interview, Chris French and James Randi, YouTube, April 2008, on behalf of *The Skeptic* magazine.

334 **IQ of 168:** Jeanne Malmgren, 'The "quack" hunter', *St Petersburg Times* (Florida), 14 April 1998.

334 **making photo-electric cells:** Paul Vallely, 'Now he sees it . . .', *The Times*, 5 February 1987.

334 **chemistry experiments in his basement:** Chris Beck, 'On the Couch', *The Age*, 26 June 1993.

334 **By the age of eight he was arguing with other children:**

Patricia Orwen, 'The Amazing Randi', *Toronto Star*, 23 August 1986.

334 **invented a pop-up toaster:** Patricia Orwen, 'The Amazing Randi', *Toronto Star*, 23 August 1986.

334 **too intelligent to benefit from school . . . educated himself:** Interview, Chris French and James Randi, YouTube, April 2008, on behalf of *The Skeptic* magazine.

334 **geography, history . . . mathematics:** Interview, Chris French and James Randi, YouTube, April 2008, on behalf of *The Skeptic* magazine.

334 **calculus:** Jeanne Malmgren, 'The "quack" hunter', *St Petersburg Times* (Florida), 14 April 1998.

334 **astronomy . . . psychology . . . hieroglyphics:** Paul Vallely, 'Now he sees it . . .', *The Times*, 5 February 1987.

334 **fifteen when he committed his first public debunking:** Chris Dafoe, 'Magician spearheads war against supernatural claims', *Globe and Mail* (Canada), 29 May 1987.

334 **At seventeen . . . never walk again:** Patricia Orwen, 'The Amazing Randi', *Toronto Star*, 23 August 1986.

334 **(or, in a later account, walk *straight* again):** Interview with author.

334 **achieved 'mediocre' results:** Interview, Chris French and James Randi, YouTube, April 2008, on behalf of *The Skeptic* magazine.

334 **'This is a premise I cannot support:** Interview, Chris French and James Randi, YouTube, April 2008, on behalf of *The Skeptic* magazine.

334 **'signed Randall James Hamilton Zwinge':** Interview with author.

334 **refusing to take any more tests:** Interview, Chris French and James Randi, YouTube, April 2008, on behalf of *The Skeptic* magazine.

334 **Still seventeen, he joined Peter March's Travelling Circus:** Patricia Cohen, 'Poof! You're a Skeptic: The Amazing Randi's Vanishing Humbug', *New York Times*, 17 February 2001.

334 **he took a job writing newspaper horoscopes:** James Randi, *Flim Flam*, Prometheus, 1982, p. 62.

335 **saw two office workers:** James Randi, *Flim Flam*,
Prometheus, 1982, p. 61.

335 **or . . . two prostitutes:** Interview.

335 **or . . . a waitress:** Daniel B. Caton, 'Life Is Really Not In The
Stars . . .' *Charlotte Observer* (North Carolina), 26 September
2006.

335 **'I could not live with that kind of lie:** Interview with Scot
Morris, *Omni* Magazine, April 1980, p. 77.

335 **habitually pick up the telephone before it rang:** Wessley
Hicks, 'Snoops on Minds', *Toronto Evening Telegram*,
14 August 1950 (reprinted in James Randi, *The Magic of
Uri Geller*, Ballantine Books, 1985, p. 304).

335 **'Certain perceptions have been given me:** Wessley Hicks,
'He Sees the Future', *Toronto Evening Telegram*, 28 August
1950 (reprinted in James Randi, *The Magic of Uri Geller*,
Ballantine Books, 1985, p. 305).

335 **Japan . . . Halifax harbour:** Virginia Corner, 'Debunking
myths is magician's game', *Toronto Star*, 15 June 1987.

335 **twenty-eight jail cells in Canada and the US:** Patricia Orwen,
'The Amazing Randi', *Toronto Star*, 23 August 1986.

335 **sometimes he says it was twenty-two, 'all over the world':**
Interview, Chris French and James Randi, YouTube, April
2008, on behalf of *The Skeptic* magazine.

335 **underwater casket . . . above Broadway:** Patricia Orwen,
'The Amazing Randi', *Toronto Star*, 23 August 1986.

335 **out of helicopters:** Michael J. Ybarra, 'The Psychic and the
Skeptic', *Los Angeles Times*, 13 September 1991.

336 **top of Niagara Falls:** Interview, Chris French and James
Randi, YouTube, April 2008, on behalf of *The Skeptic*
magazine.

336 **won a Guinness World Record:** Claim confirmed to author
by Guinness World Record Organization.

336 **toured with Alice Cooper:** Interview, Chris French and
James Randi, YouTube, April 2008, on behalf of *The Skeptic*
magazine.

336 **got to know Salvador Dali:** Chris Beck, 'On The Couch', *The
Age*, 26 June 1993.

336 **radio show in 1964:** James Randi, *Flim Flam*, Prometheus, 1982, p. 252.

336 **humiliated the celebrity spoon-bender Uri Geller:** *St Petersburg Times* (Florida), 24 July 2007.

336 **'the true danger of uncritical thinking':** James Randi Million Dollar Challenge FAQ. JREF.org.

336 **'one of America's most original and fearless thinkers':** Patricia Cohen, 'Poof! You're a Skeptic: The Amazing Randi's Vanishing Humbug', *New York Times*, 17 February 2001.

336 **'I Xerox everything and send it to the FBI:** Paul Vallely, 'Now he sees it . . .', *The Times*, 5 February 1987.

336 **'I don't answer the door:** Sven Nordenstam, 'Mystics can pocket a million – when pigs can fly', Reuters News, 3 December 2004.

336 **a new dark age:** Patricia Cohen, 'Poof! You're a Skeptic: The Amazing Randi's Vanishing Humbug', *New York Times*, 17 February 2001.

336 **'It's a very dangerous thing to believe in nonsense':** Sven Nordenstam, 'Mystics can pocket a million – when pigs can fly', Reuters News, 3 December 2004.

337 **'It's the simplest challenge in the world':** Bryan Johnson, 'Claptrap or an unknown world?', *Globe and Mail* (Canada), 13 April 1985.

337 **'I am an investigator:** 'The $18,000 question', *Straits Times*, 30 May 1991.

337 **often get called 'grubbies':** James Randi, 'A Champion Grubby Speaks Out', Swift blog, 22 April 2009.

338 **'We will give away the million dollars when pigs can fly.':** Sven Nordenstam, 'Mystics can pocket a million – when pigs can fly', Reuters News, 3 December 2004.

338 **'Why isn't someone like Sheldrake coming after it?':** Interview, Skeptiko podcast, 1 April 2008.

338 **'a farce and a delusion':** James Randi, *Flim Flam*, Prometheus, 1982, p. 326.

338 **scientific discovery in the field of parapsychology:** JREF

430

Challenge FAQ http://www.randi.org/site/index.php/
1m-challenge/challenge-faq.html [Quote comes from
'Randi's Personal FAQ' subsection].

338 'a man of very doubtful character indeed': Rupert Sheldrake,
interview with author.

338 'One shot, to the chops: James Randi, 'A Champion Grubby
Speaks Out', Swift blog, 22 April 2009.

338 'I want people to consider my point of view,': 'On The
Couch', *The Age*, 26 June 1993.

339 'hit man': Kay Bartlett, '$272,000 Stipend to "The Amazing
Randi" Magician-Debunker Conjures Up "Genius Grant"',
Los Angeles Times, 14 September 1986.

339 **Sean Connelly, who emailed Randi:** 31 January 2005, 12:40.

339 **Randi responded:** 31 January 2005, 17:11.

339 'Do you see my perspective?': 2 February 2005, 20:46.

339 'you're just full of shit': 3 February 2005, 17:25 [Email from
'Kramer'].

339 **in the new version:** Posted by 'Kramer', 4 February 2005,
10:15.

339 **a verification letter from Goldman Sachs:** Posted by
'Kramer', 8 February 2005, 14:21.

339 **an audiophile journalist:** I discussed this issue directly with
Michael Fremer, via email, and also used his account at The
Swift Boating of Audiophiles, Michael Fremer,
Stereophile.com 17 February 2008, and Charlie White, 'Pear
Cable Chickens Out of $1,000,000 Challenge, We Search
For Answers', *Gizmodo Australia*, 26 October 2007.

340 'but I'll have to consult with my advisors': Email, 15 October
2007, 19:53.

340 'this retreat by [Pear] effectively closes: James Randi, 'Blake
Withdraws from PEAR Cable Challenge', Latest JREF News,
20 October 2007, 10:42.

340 'due to the interference of the weekend: James Randi,
'The Latest on PEAR Challenge Refusal', Latest JREF News,
22 October 2007, 11:17.

340 **he might somehow 'tamper' with them:** Charlie White, 'Pear

Cable Chickens Out of $1,000,000 Challenge, We Search
For Answers', *Gizmodo Australia*, 26 October 2007.

340 **none of this stopped Randi persisting in his accusation:**
James Randi, 'Yet Another Snag in Cable Challenge',
22 October 2007, plus email exchange, Michael Fremer and
James Randi, 16 January 2008.

340 **Another extraordinary tale comes from Professor George
Vithoulkas:** My account of this long, complex and fraught
process was reconstructed from Randi's various blog
postings as well as direct communication with George
Vithoulkas, Maria Chorianopoulou, Althea Katz and Gabor
Hrasko.

343 **Randi reported that the scientist who invented the
magnetometer:** James Randi, *Flim Flam*, Prometheus, 1982,
p. 132.

343 **reports that these tests had been replicated were 'a lie':**
James Randi, *Flim Flam*, Prometheus, 1982, p. 133.

343 **But a journalist named Scott Rogo:** Michael Prescott, 'Flim-
Flam Flummery', http://michaelprescott.freeservers.com/
FlimFlam.htm.

344 **'outright lies from a sensationalist':** James Randi, *Flim Flam*,
Prometheus, 1982, p. 135.

344 **You can say it any way you want, but that's what I call a lie.':**
James Randi, *Flim Flam*, Prometheus, 1982, p. 133.

344 **'masterpiece of evasion and license . . . Zev Pressman':**
James Randi, *Flim Flam*, Prometheus, 1982, pp. 144–5.

349 **Randi's account of his meeting with Veronica Keen:** James
Randi, Swift blog, 15 August 2003.

349 **I also found a rebuttal:** Accessed at:
http://www.victorzammit.com/articles/montaguereplies.html.

354 **Some of the past applicants of the Million Dollar Challenge:**
Compiled from the 'Previous Applicants' section on the
JREF website.

354 **'made-up mystical BS:** The Skeptic's Guide to the Universe
podcast, 339, 14 January 2012.

355 **Wealthy televangelist Peter Popoff . . . Professor Chris**

French: Interview, Chris French and James Randi, YouTube, April 2008, on behalf of *The Skeptic* magazine.

355 **Randi was once awarded a prestigious MacArthur 'genius grant':** Charles Storch, 'The Geniuses; Where are they now – and how did they spend their money? Revisiting 25 years of the MacArthur Foundation's celebrated "genius" grants', *Chicago Tribune*, 14 September 2006.

355 **'A bunch of Nobel Prize winners:** Paul Vallely, 'Now he sees it . . .', *The Times*, 5 February 1987.

355 **'Britain always wanted to be the source of all life and culture:** Guy Gugliotta, 'Dusting Off the Remains of a Hoax', *Washington Post*, 3 November 2003.

355 **'the principle of Survival of the Fittest would draconically prove itself':** James Randi, 'Following Up . . .', Swift blog, 28 April 2009.

356 **'Get people thinking. Have them ask questions:** Interview with Professor Chris French for *The Skeptic* magazine, April 2008.

357 **As usual, Randi took to the Internet to protest:** James Randi, Swift blog, 8 April 2005.

357 **Or just a plain old LIE?':** James Randi, Swift blog, 11 May 2001.

360 **'the family couldn't really understand him':** Patricia Orwen, 'The Amazing Randi', *Toronto Star*, 23 August 1986.

360 **recently, in 2010, that Randi publicly came out as gay:** James Randi, 'How To Say It?', Swift blog, 21 March 2010 12:37.

362 **I have found a second interview from the same period:** Patricia Orwen, 'The Amazing Randi', *Toronto Star*, 23 August 1986.

363 **'We at JREF have tested these claims. They fail.':** *Dog World*, January 2000.

363 **Randi sent an email explaining that, regretfully, he couldn't supply the data:** Email, 6 February 2000.

363 **But he subsequently went online and *attacked* Sheldrake:** Brandon K. Thorp, 'The Sheldrake Kerfluffle', Swift blog, 2 December 2009 [which quoted Randi, 'earlier this afternoon'].

Epilogue: The Hero Maker

[Many of the statements and quotes in this chapter are restatements from earlier in the text. References to these points can be found in their appropriate places.]

373 **in most of your conversation:** Michael S. Gazzaniga, *Human*, Harper Perennial, 2008, p. 96.

373 **'Astro', the Australian horse:** 'Sinking horse pulled from mudflats in Australia', BBC News, 29 February 2012.

374 **$48,000 of US taxpayers' money was once spent:** Dan Ariely, *The Upside of Irrationality*, HarperCollins, 2010, p. 249.

374 **the birth of silent cinema:** David Denby, 'The Artists', *New Yorker*, 27 February 2012.

374 **humanity's earliest stories sought to explain the world:** Robert A. Segal, *Myth*, Oxford University Press, 2004, p. 13.

374 **Rituals developed around them:** Robert A. Segal, *Myth*, Oxford University Press, 2004, p. 61.

374 **The historian Mircea Eliade writes:** Robert A. Segal, *Myth*, Oxford University Press, 2004, p. 55.

374 **Sigmund Freud believed:** Robert A. Segal, *Myth*, Oxford University Press, 2004, p. 93.

374 **the psychologist Otto Rank:** Robert A. Segal, *Myth*, Oxford University Press, 2004, p. 94.

374 **the mythologist Joseph Campbell:** Robert A. Segal, *Myth*, Oxford University Press, 2004, p. 106.

375 **we experience the tales that we immerse ourselves in:** Annie Murphy Paul, 'Your Brain on Fiction', *New York Times*, 17 March 2012.

375 **We feel the heroes' feelings:** 'Losing Yourself' in a Fictional Character Can Affect Your Real Life', *Science Daily*, 7 May 2012.

375 **'contagion is at the heart of emotion':** Bruce E. Wexler, *Brain and Culture*, MIT Press, 2008, p. 34.

375 **'a capacity for surprise is an essential aspect:** Daniel Kahneman, *Thinking, Fast and Slow*, Penguin, 2011, p. 71.

375 **'a surge of conscious attention':** Daniel Kahneman, *Thinking, Fast and Slow*, Penguin, 2011, p. 24.

375 **'a story begins with some breach:** Jerome Bruner, *Making*

Stories: Law, Literature, Life, Harvard University Press, 2002, p. 31.

376 **By the age of five:** Jeremy Hsu, 'The Secrets of Storytelling: Why We Love a Good Yarn', *Scientific American Mind*, 18 September 2008.

376 **Professor of Psychology Keith Oatley has observed:** Jeremy Hsu, 'The Secrets of Storytelling: Why We Love a Good Yarn', *Scientific American Mind*, 18 September 2008.

376 **Evolutionary psychologist David Sloan Wilson has compared:** Mark Pagel, *Wired For Culture*, Allen Lane, 2012, p. 150.

376 **Marxist philosopher Georges Sorel believed:** Robert A. Segal, *Myth*, Oxford University Press, 2004, p. 128.

376 **Professor Paul Bloom has observed:** Paul Bloom, 'How do morals change?', *Nature* 464, 25 March 2010, p. 490.

380 **'dangerous people, from playground bullies to warmongering dictators:** Roy Baumeister, *Evil: Inside Human Violence and Cruelty*, Barnes & Noble/ W. H. Freeman, 1997, p. 135.

381 **my transcript for the chapter is in excess of twenty-eight thousand words:** The exact number is 28,321. I rounded it down for neatness.

382 **'a clear and future danger':** Deborah E. Lipstadt, *History on Trial*, Harper Perennial, 2005, p. 25.

386 **anthropologist Daniel Everett has studied the Pirahã:** John Colapinto, 'The Interpreter', *New Yorker*, 16 April 2007; Rafaela von Bredow, 'Brazil's Pirahã Tribe Living without Numbers or Time', *Der Spiegel*, 3 May 2006.

386 **A 2012 study, reported in *The Economist*:** 'Older and wiser?', *The Economist*, 7 August 2012.

387 **'In the inner world of the depressive self:** Lewis Wolpert, *Six Impossible Things Before Breakfast*, Faber, 2007, p. 107.

Index

culturally unique 103
and decision-making 228, 229, 232
see also anger; happiness
energy
clean 31
generation 261
Enfield Gazette (newspaper) 345
Enfield Poltergeist case 345
Enlightenment 313
envy 265
epinephrine 234–5
Epley, Nicholas 110
escapology 335–6, 346
Escher, Sandra 177–8
ESP *see* extra-sensory perception
Ethics Committee of the Federal
        Australian Medical Association
        50
European Union (EU) 265
European Union Parliament House
        288
Evans, Dylan 103
Evans, Richard 276
Eve 6, 14
Eve, Mitochondrial 91
Everett, Daniel 386
evidence, denial of 317–19, 321–6
evil
problem of 3
psychology of 85–8, 90, 129,
        379–81, 385
'supremely good' motivations for
        111
evolution 91–2
arguments against 3–8, 12–17, 33
arguments for 23–4, 124–5
experimental psychology 109, 125, 177,
        392
extra-sensory perception (ESP) 312,
        325–6, 343, 363
alien 30

sense of 'being stared at' 311–12,
        316, 321–2, 324–5

facts
and belief 250
inefficacy of 32–3
fairies 104
faith, as journey 27, 165
false memories 200–1, 205–12, 214–16,
        218, 220–3
false memory syndrome 193
familiar, the, attraction to 227
'fan death' 103–4
FATE magazine 345
fear 250, 253, 254
Feinberg, Todd E. 102
Felstead, Anthony 199, 203
Felstead, David 197–9, 203, 218
Felstead, Joan 199, 203, 205
Felstead, Joseph 198–200, 204, 205
Felstead, Kevin 199, 203
Felstead, Richard 197–9, 203, 218–19,
        223
Felstead family 202–6, 211, 218–19,
        223, 380
Festinger, Leon 106, 232–3
Financial Service Act 263
first impressions 232
First World War 284
Fisher, Fleur 200, 202–3, 204–6, 211,
        218–20, 223, 380
Flim Flam (Randi, 1982) 331, 343, 356,
        364
Flood, biblical 17
fMRI *see* Functional Magnetic
        Resonance Imaging
foetal development 92
fossil record 12–13, 15–17, 23–4, 124–5
Fourth Annual Morgellons Conference,
        Austin, Texas 150, 151–9
Fox, Kate 104

441

443

445

448